KT-406-840

KA 0275953 5

WITHDRAWN FROM THE LIBRARY

UNIVERSITY OF WINCHESTER

ABOUT THE BOOK

Arts Under Pressure analyses the relevant forces behind decision making in cultural matters worldwide – specifically in the field of the arts – under the influence of economic globalisation. The book contains hundreds of examples of cultural practices drawn from all fields of the arts and from all parts of the world, linked together by solid critical theory. The arts can be seen as an arena where emotional incompatibilities, social conflicts, and questions of status between people collide more intensely than they would in ordinary communication. Add to this the huge economic interests at stake in the cultural field and we find ourselves in highly charged territory. This is certainly the case now that economic globalisation is causing substantial changes in the structure of many cultural institutions.

The book focuses on the cycle of creation, production, distribution, promotion, reception and influence. It asks the key questions: who has the power to decide what reaches audiences, in what quantities, with what contents, and surrounded by what kinds of ambiances? Refuting the 'natural' existence of mass culture, Arts Under Pressure argues that what does exist are artistic creations that are produced, distributed and promoted on a mass scale. This mass scale undermines the public attention to diversity that – from a democratic perspective – any society desperately needs.

Smiers argues that countries must take culture out of the grip of WTO and sign a new International Convention on Cultural Diversity. This would give them the full right to take all necessary measures to reduce significantly the market domination of cultural industries and to formulate their own cultural policies. The neoliberal world order is incapable of protecting the fragile blossoming of artistic diversity at all level.

Smiers concludes by setting out a completely new vision of copyright. The abolition of copyright, he suggests, would be advantageous to artists, third world countries and the public domain. In the digital domain we can see that the spontaneous meltdown of copyright is already happening.

ABOUT THE AUTHOR

Joost Smiers is Professor of Political Science of the Arts at the Utrecht School of the Arts, the Netherlands, and formerly Visiting Professor, Department of World Arts and Cultures, UCLA, Los Angeles. He is a board member of the European Research Institute for Comparative Cultural Policy and the Arts (ERICArts).

He has written, lectured and researched extensively in the area of decision making in cultural matters worldwide, and on new visions of creative and intellectual property, copyright and the public domain.

ARTS UNDER PRESSURE
Promoting Cultural Diversity in the Age of Globalization

Joost Smiers

Hivos

THE HAGUE

Zed Books

LONDON · NEW YORK

KING ALFRED'S COLLEGE
WINCHESTER

Arts under Pressure: Promoting Cultural Diversity in the Age of Globalization was first published by Zed Books Ltd, 7 Cynthia Street, London N1 9JF, UK and Room 400, 175 Fifth Avenue, New York, NY 10010, USA in 2003.

www.zedbooks.demon.co.uk

Copyright © Joost Smiers, 2003

The right of Joost Smiers to be identified as the author of this work has been asserted by him in accordance with the Copyright, Designs and Patents Act, 1988. Nevertheless, the author discusses in this book the untenability of the present copyright system.

Cover designed by Andrew Corbett
Set in Monotype Fournier and Univers Black by Ewan Smith, London
Printed and bound in Malta

Distributed in the USA exclusively by Palgrave, a division of St Martin's Press, LLC, 175 Fifth Avenue, New York, NY 10010

A catalogue record for this book is available from the British Library

ISBN 1 84277 262 7 cased
ISBN 1 84277 263 5 limp

The Hivos Culture Fund has generously supported the distribution of this book to libraries in Africa, Asia and Latin America. The Fund, initiated by Hivos in 1995, supports independent and innovative initiatives of artists and cultural organizations in developing countries. It believes that cultural diversity and cultural exchange on a basis of equality among different communities around the world is of vital importance, and that commercially driven infringements of creative and artistic property rights especially affect artists working on the periphery of the world market system.

Hivos, Raamweg 16, 2596 HL, The Hague, The Netherlands
tel.: + 31 (0)70 376 55 00; fax: + 31 (0)70 362 46 00
e-mail: hivos@hivos.nl; internet: www.hivos.nl

Contents

Introduction

This is a book about the arts. In it I ask what local artistic life remains in the era of economic globalization, and why this is a question that needs to be discussed. Music, theatre, dance, design, television, films, stories, poetry, songs, paintings, sculptures and photographs are essential forms of communication in every society. The arts can inform us about our deepest feelings; they can give us pleasure; they can accompany us in times of sadness; they can entertain us; they are often used to entice or persuade us in one way or another. In some societies, various forms of artistic expression have been banned, considered to be offensive or dangerous. In more and more societies people are confronted with visual images or subjected to background music almost every moment of the day.

The arts have never been marginal. And today they are less so than ever. Advertisements use artistic creations. Films, video and music are all big business, as is the book industry. Some parts of the visual arts world are as precarious as the stock market, with huge sums of money changing hands. The Internet is becoming an effective transmitter of a great variety of artistic creations. Meanwhile, hundreds of thousands of artists are trying to make a more or less modest living from their work, and only a few make considerably more than that.

What have these observations to do with economic globalization and world-wide free trade? Or to put it the other way round: why are the arts important in any society, and why should they be connected with a particular society rather than reflecting the influence of cultural and economic forces operating at the global level? The answer is: democracy. A characteristic of democracy is that many different voices can be heard and many different opinions expressed. The public domain in any democratic society is the mental and physical space in which the exchange of ideas and an open debate about all sorts of questions can take place without interference from state agents, who may have their own agenda, or from commercial forces whose only purpose is to sell as much as they can.

The arts are crucial to democratic debate and to the process of responding, emotionally and otherwise, to the multitude of questions that life raises. For this to happen, a wide diversity of forms of expression and channels of communication is needed. Along with other factors, people's opinions are formed by the books they read, the music they hear, the films they watch and the images they see

– not always at a rational level. The arts, which in this book include all forms of entertainment and design, touch our often hidden emotions and drives, our perceptions of ourselves, our hopes and our desires.

It can happen that artistic creations coming from different parts of the world have an impact on specific groups of people within a particular society at a certain moment in history. Nevertheless, it is important that a substantial part of artistic communication reflects, without being nostalgic, what is going on in any given community, including those formed through the Internet or linking people in various countries and regions. It would be a loss if none of the sentiments expressed in the arts was any longer related to the conflicts, the desire for conviviality, the way people enjoy themselves, the specific kinds of humour and aesthetic preferences that are to be found in a *particular* society.

Moreover, it is important that within any society a *diversity* of forms of artistic expression is created and distributed by a diversity of producers and distributors. People are different; and what is more human than hoping to find forms of theatre, music, visual arts, literature or film that express adequately one's own confusions, feelings of delight or aesthetic tastes?

If it is vital to democracy that the arts are created and presented in a way that relates, at least to some extent, to individual societies, one may wonder what the effects of economic globalization are. All things considered, respect for local endeavours is not a priority in the system of worldwide free trade. Does this mean that in many societies artistic life becomes 'delocalized'? Does it become harder for artists to get their work distributed to a significant extent in their own surroundings? Does it mean that throughout the world most public attention will be focused on a limited number of artistic products and their creators that are promoted everywhere? Does it mean that taste will be homogenized worldwide? Or would it be more accurate to speak about 'delocalization' taking place everywhere?

These are the kinds of issues I shall address in this book, not forgetting that all over the world many, many artists continue to create and perform exciting works of art.

In the first chapter we will see that the arts are pre-eminently a field in which emotional incompatibilities, social conflicts and questions of status collide in a more concentrated way than happens in everyday communication. Add to this the considerable economic interests that always penetrate the cultural field and we find ourselves in an area of human life that is highly charged. This is even more the case now that economic globalization is radically changing the structure of many institutions and activities in the cultural field.

Most people watching television, listening to music, reading a book, enjoying a movie or buying a painting are unaware of who owns the means of production, distribution and promotion of these works of art, these vehicles of entertainment or illumination, depending on how we view them. Why should they be? Nevertheless, as discussed in Chapter 2, the question of ownership of the means of cultural production, distribution and promotion is the core issue in a worldwide battle; the fight is about who can reach the largest audiences, rather than catering to the taste of a small group of aficionados.

In Chapter 3 I argue that artists, in rich and poor countries alike, should be remunerated fairly for their work. Many people still maintain that copyright is one of the most important sources of an artist's income, evidence to the contrary notwithstanding. In fact, copyright – which on the European continent is usually called authors' rights – is becoming one of the most important commercial products of the twenty-first century. This phenomenon makes it unlikely that the copyright system is any longer protecting the interests of the majority of musicians, composers, actors, dancers, writers, designers, visual artists and filmmakers. The public domain is dwindling, anyway, with the ongoing privatization of the creative and intellectual commons. To turn this tide, I propose in Chapter 6 the complete abolition of copyright, which would, according to my analysis, be to the advantage of artists, the public domain and Third World countries.

In Chapter 4 I consider the role of the arts in social life, on a local and a global level. At the end of the twentieth century, there were movements that claimed there was no such thing as society. The assertion was that we are all self-determining individuals and global citizens, unhindered by social convention or contextualization. At the beginning of the twenty-first century we have come to realize that this is only partly true, and for most people it is not true at all. We know, too, that it is not desirable to be completely divorced from our immediate social surroundings. After experiencing the delocalization that neoliberalism has offered us, we know better than ever that the world is too big and too complex for us to be able to orient ourselves within it and find something like a safe haven. In this chapter I first present examples of the vast domain of cultural production that is happening worldwide, and then analyse the cultural delocalization – rather than homogenization – that is also taking place.

Chapter 5 looks at the fact that there is no major constraint on *what* can be consumed: all social relations, activities and objects can in principle be exchanged as commodities. In today's world, where the cultural conglomerates are able to spread their ideas of what culture should be, the crucial question is: whose stories are being told? By whom? How are they manufactured, disseminated and received? Works of art are becoming more and more the vehicles of commercial messages and have the task of creating the ambience in which the production of desire can take place. Often this context is full of violence. Every artistic creation conveys an atmosphere, a content, a reflection on a way of life, an idea of pleasure. The question we should not avoid is: does this influence me, you, us, them? Probably the biggest influence is the absence from the dominant discourse and consumer culture of a whole raft of issues. If we think of values such as respect, equality, sobriety, wisdom, conviviality, morality, human solidarity, community, sustainability, or the conviction that inflicting pain or celebrating violence should be avoided, we find that all these, and many others, are actually non-issues for the world of corporate culture.

In Chapter 6 we shall look at the *New York Times*'s comment (March 1998) on Bertelsmann's purchase of Random House, namely that this was just business as usual in the publishing world:

> The trouble is simply how familiar this sale feels. It provokes only a sigh, which suggests how much we have come to take for granted the steady convergence of all media under ever widening corporate umbrellas. But in that convergence ... something is lost – call it the broadly dispersed ownership of media outlets, call it even a productive democratic inefficiency in the marketing of information. The road away from conglomeration will be a hard one to find.

Since then, the *New York Times* has not made it a priority to find a road away from conglomeration in the cultural field. This part of the book will fill this gap and also propose several solutions to the problems analysed in the previous chapters.

From this short description, it should be clear that this is not a book about individual artforms or a comparative study of the arts in different regions of the world. It is a study by a political scientist of the ways in which the arts are being handled worldwide.

I encountered major methodological obstacles while planning and researching this book, and many questions had to be answered. First, I had to decide whether to do the research alone or with others. In the absence of a team of scholars drawn from all corners of the world, I felt it was better to work on my own. It would be impossible, too, to travel throughout the world, doing research on the spot; this was not practical for financial reasons but, in any event, how much could I hope to learn about changes being caused by economic globalization when staying for just a short period in a country or region that I didn't know well or even at all? So, I was largely dependent on secondary sources. Several daily newspapers, such as *Le Monde* and the *International Herald Tribune*, as well as monthlies and other journals, contributed greatly to my understanding of day-to-day developments and changes that have not yet been described in studies of any length or detail.

I am grateful to many librarians in various institutes specializing in regional studies and in the fields of arts and culture. However, not all the books I hoped to find were there; perhaps they have not yet been written. Working circumstances for many scholars in non-Western countries are hard, and they do not always have the opportunity to do the research they would like to on the social, economic and cultural conditions of the arts in their parts of the world, or they may not have been able to find a publisher operating within the international market. Many studies have never been translated. If readers take this as a plea for huge funds for translation and publication, they do so correctly. I shall come back to this need in Chapter 6.

This book is concerned with freedom *and* protection. For many people it might seem obvious that artists – and artistic production, distribution and reception – deserve freedom. However, in this time of global neoliberalism, it seems to be less self-evident that we should actively care for the artist as a creator or performer. A rich and diversified cultural climate is something that needs protection. So we have to keep our balance as we walk the tightrope between freedom and protection. Anyone who loves the circus knows this requires great skill, but the result is beautiful.

The author would like to thank the following people for their encouragement during the research and development of this book: Kiki Amsberg, Barbara Clarke, Cees Hamelink, Dragan Klaic, Jaap Klazema, Ole Reitov, Merieke van Schijndel and Giep Hagoort, my colleague in the Research Group Arts and Economics at the Utrecht School of the Arts.

ONE
The Arts and the World

THE ARTS: AN ARENA OF STRUGGLE

We tend to cherish the notion that the arts provide us with the best moments in our lives – moments that are harmonious, pleasurable, entertaining, or that offer unique occasions for reflection. This may be true, and it's worth hoping for, but it is not the whole story. The arts are pre-eminently a field where emotional incompatibilities, social conflicts and questions of status collide in a more concentrated way than happens in daily communication. Add to this the considerable economic interests that always penetrate the cultural field and we find ourselves in an area of human life that is highly charged. There are, for instance, people who are irritated by background music; there are people who feel that for the last seventy years most architecture has had little to offer aesthetically; there are people who object to advertising that uses images of seductive women. There are also people who become aggressive when forms of artistic expression clash with their deepest convictions, or who feel that they have been urged – explicitly or implicitly – to commit acts of violence.

What represents beauty and joy for one person may be objectionable to another. Seldom do people agree about what is valuable in theatre, film, dance, music, the visual arts, design, photography or literature. The arts can provoke complaints, intolerance, aggression; it is not unusual for certain works of art to be banned in particular societies or at least considered extremely suspect; artists have been killed because of their work; often there is a lack of economic support for certain forms of art while others get funding in abundance for production and distribution; artistic creations may be praised to the skies or meet with deafening public silence. And often it seems that this support or lack of support is unrelated to any degree of quality, or lack of quality, that one may imagine.

Most acting in contemporary Hollywood movies, I would say, is amateurish and the music is often boring, but that does not seem to matter as long as people enjoy the film. 'In recent years, Taiwan has witnessed an unprecedented number of young popular singers. These highly commodified performers are young, good looking, stylish, and usually possess little or no talent at all,' Leo Ching (1996:

177–8) observes. In Zimbabwe, there is a flourishing market in stone sculptures that at first were mainly produced for tourists. Because they were made in series, their prestige among Zimbabweans themselves was low. But now local people are getting to like them and are buying them and appreciating them as works of art. The passage of time has led to a reappraisal (Rozenberg 1994: 16).

Thus, quality, or the importance granted to a work of art, is a relative concept. Within each distinguishable area of artistic production there exist enormous differences in quality, and the people who feel attached to certain genres believe they know why some works within these are better than others. However, in the broader social context it is mostly criteria other than quality that are decisive for why some works of art gain a prominent place in society and others seem to be of no importance at all. It is not so easy to get a grip on these criteria in general terms, because they differ from one society to another and from one period of time to another.

There are such differences in social appreciation because the arts engage our deepest emotions. Music, theatrical performances, soap operas, images of different kinds, films, novels and poems are structures of feelings. They embody our beliefs and our sentiments, giving structure to these (see Edelman 1995: 1–9). They provide us with a way of orientating ourselves in domains that are not part of the rational or logical components of our lives. It is, therefore, a mistake to think that the arts contribute exclusively to the beautiful, pleasurable, innocent or morally respectable aspects of our existence. On the *personal* level, they feed our open and secret aspirations in the various spheres of life we like to be part of, which may contain many different elements ranging from the sleazy to the mystical.

The arts are also part of a *social* struggle about which expressions of pleasure, aggression, desire, tenderness, power, cynicism or fear may be shared with others and thought desirable and which may meet with disapproval. What is considered as beautiful, entertaining, amusing or exciting will depend on the specific social context. Which is more beneficial from a cultural perspective: the immediate gratification that the artistic experience is expected to deliver, or the long, slow process of learning what is valuable in the arts and what gives life a more profound dimension? What kinds of references to actual political or social situations can artists make, and which are they well advised to avoid? Lionel Tiger reminds us that 'there is a fierce endemic contest in many communities about who gets pleasure, which pleasure, when, with whom, and with what cost or tax' (Tiger 1992: 6).

It is not without cause that the arts have been called 'symbolic battlegrounds' (Shohat and Stam 1994: 183). Nor is it self-evident that the many different art-forms, and opinions about the arts and what artists should or shouldn't do, can co-exist harmoniously. There are many examples of struggle, with different consequences, that can be cited. I give some of these below.

On 10 November 1995 the Nigerian government executed the writer Ken Saro-Wiwa along with eight other Ogoni leaders who had protested against pollution and exploitation in their part of the country, for which they held Shell responsible (Klein 2000: 383–4; Larson 2001: 140). The Taliban in Afghanistan destroyed traditional music instruments, as did the dictator Idi Amin in Uganda (Gründ 1995: 10). Also in Afghanistan, the Taliban's interpretation of Shari'a law led to the denunciation of all 'non-religious' forms of cultural expression that include human actions – this included entertainment, music and dance – as un-Islamic and sinful. As a result, the expressive arts were banned.[1]

Translators, distributors and publishers of Salman Rushdie's *The Satanic Verses* all over the world have been threatened and in some cases killed. The singer Lounès Matoub, famous throughout the Arab world, was murdered in June 1998. He came from the Kabylia region of Algeria, whose people feel oppressed by the central government. He was well known for his struggle in defence of the Berber language, which is all but banned in Kabylia, and against Muslim fundamentalism.[2]

These are just a few examples that show how cruel the 'symbolic battle-grounds' can be.

In the West we are so obsessed with freedom of speech that we are not prepared to understand how this freedom may appear to other people to lead to fundamental disrespect for what is most sacred to them. As long as this principle of freedom without any restraints remains unchallenged, a dialogue on how to bridge the gap between cultures will be difficult. Let us look at the example of the Brooklyn Museum of Art in New York, which in the autumn of 1999 put on an exhibition featuring a portrait of the Virgin Mary in which her breasts are decorated with pieces of what has delicately been described as elephant dung. This is a work by the British Nigerian artist Chris Ofili, who 'discovered' the use of elephant dung during a British Council-funded trip to Zimbabwe (see Stallabrass 1999: 107–17). Was his use of it in this painting disrespectful to Catholics and their beliefs? New York's mayor Rudolfo Giuliani thought so and threatened to withdraw the city's subsidy from the museum. Or was his contempt for this work of art a bid for popular support in his contest with Hillary Clinton for a seat in the American Senate? A debate on the relationship between artistic freedom, on the one hand, and respect for the fundamental values of specific sections of society, on the other, would have made more sense than playing the censorship card. In a civilized society, is there anything wrong with respecting other people's deeply felt beliefs or customs, even if it means artists restraining themselves somewhat?

Our Creative Diversity, the Report of Unesco's and the United Nations' World Commission on Culture and Development, problematizes this issue by opposing individual and collective cultural freedom: 'Most freedoms refer to the individual – freedom to speak one's mind, to go where one wishes, to worship one's gods, to write what one likes. Cultural freedom, in contrast, is a collective freedom. It refers to the right of a group of people to follow or to adopt a way of life of their choice' (Pérez de Cuéllar 1996: 25). In the Western world the dominant belief has been that individual freedom is the only real form of freedom, and everybody must accept this. The fact that there can be, and are, more worthwhile forms of freedom, which may have contradictory consequences and effects, seems scarcely to exist in the Western mind.

An interesting case in this context came to court in Beirut. One of the Arab world's best-loved singer-songwriters, Marcel Khalife, had set to music a poem, 'Oh, Father, It is I, Youssef', which ends with a verse from the Qu'ran. The chief magistrate of Beirut, a Sunni, indicted Marcel Khalife on charges of committing a crime against the country's dominant religion, Islam. The grand mufti, Muhammad Kabanech, explained why this had happened:

> When you include a musical instrument to accompany the Koran, you go beyond the respect due to the word of God on earth. There are rules which must be respected. This issue has nothing to do with freedom. An artist can use the words written by people as he wishes, but he doesn't have the right to use the word of God.[3]

The judge, however, rejected all charges: 'The defendant has sung the sacred Koran verses solemnly. Thus, he did not violate the sacredness of the Koran, neither did he encourage others to do so.'[4]

There are many other social conflicts and contradictions, not all influenced by religious sentiments, that find their flash point in the arts. Chris Waterman describes, for example, how in Yoruba society in Nigeria the captain of a jùjú music band controls biographical information concerning each important guest at a given celebration in order to enlarge his income.

> The captain uses this information to generate formulaic texts, which form the basis for solo and call-and-response singing. The major themes of jùjú song texts are prayer (àdúrà), money (owò), honor (olá), individual destiny (orí), jealousy (ìlara), competition (idíje), and, most prominently, the praising (yìn) of well-known celebrants and abusing (bú) of their enemies (òtá) and rivals (abánidjíje).

Thus, the music and the texts add fuel to the fire of already existing social and personal tensions.

An individual sitting at a table or dancing in front of the band hears the singer call his name (*dárúko*) and the names of his parents, spouse(s) and offspring. As he and his kin are metaphorically linked to the lofty silk-cotton tree (*àràbà*), the elephant (*àjànàkú*), or a mighty rock on a mountain (*òkè àpáta pìtì*), while his enemies are denigrated with references to the miserly tortoise (*ahun*) and the treacherous bush rat (*òkété*), he feels pride in his accomplishments, confidence in his personal destiny (*orí*), and safety in the company of supporters and clients. (Waterman 1990: 186)

In 1997, Hindu 'fanatics' in India destroyed some nude paintings of the goddesses Saraswati and Durga by the painter Maqdool Fida Husain, who happens to be a Muslim. Immediately there was intense debate about their reasons for doing so. Was it the nudity in the painting or the Islamic background of the artist that offended them? One view expressed at the time was that the artist did indeed offend Hindus, although Saraswati, the goddess of art and science, had for centuries been depicted as naked. However, according to one fellow artist, a Mrs Shambhavi, the conflict arose from the changing perceptions of nakedness in contemporary society, and had nothing to do with the confrontation between Hindus and Muslims. She tells the story of visiting the famous temple of Khajuraho, which is full of erotic statues. A busload of Indian tourists arrived, apparently well-to-do people wearing Western clothes and equipped with video-cameras. It was clear that they felt embarrassed by the statues, and reacted by giggling. On the same occasion a woman from a nearby village arrived, placed some flowers near the statues, took her blessings and left. For this woman it was all about sacredness, and this was the way goddesses are. But the 'modern' people from the city had a completely different frame of reference concerning sexuality, eroticism, delight and titillation, and this confused them.[5]

In July 2001, the conductor Daniel Barenboim, himself a Jew, caused an uproar in Jerusalem by conducting a German orchestra in a performance of music by Richard Wagner, Hitler's favourite composer. The incident came at the end of the concert, when Barenboim turned to the audience and offered the piece as an encore. 'If you don't want it we'll go quietly,' he said. Some people accused him of being a fascist and shouted, 'This is a disgrace and a deception!', calling it 'concentration camp music'. After these people had stalked out, banging the doors behind them, most of the audience stayed on and gave the orchestra a standing ovation for its performance of selections from *Tristan und Isolde*. Civic and festival officials roundly condemned the conductor's action, and he also came in for criticism from Prime Minister Ariel Sharon, who said that there were many people in Israel for whom this issue was very hard, and that it was perhaps still too early to perform Wagner there. Jerusalem's mayor,

Ehud Olmert, commented: 'What Daniel Barenboim did was brazen, arrogant, uncivilized and insensitive.'[6]

A completely different conflict on the battleground of the arts involves the differing attitudes of the American and French film industries, which became clearer than ever at the 52nd Cannes Film Festival in May 1999. The French newspaper *Le Monde* (25 May 1999) was happy with the exceptional number of very good films, which showed 'the liveliness of cinematographic art on a world scale'. In the winning films there were some extremely gifted actors, including some amateurs. In most of the movies the family and its disintegration as well as the loss of old certainties played a central role, expressed aesthetically in ways that were characteristic of film-making in Europe and quite different from the American style. Delight all over the place. Not so in the American press.

In the *International Herald Tribune* (8 June 1999), Joan Dupont rejected the choice of festival winners: 'It was a vote for the artless (or seemingly artless) over art (or seemingly art) cinema, a manifesto in lavish praise of low-budget, no-nonsense cinema-vérité as if it were the noblest genre.' *Variety* critic Todd McCarthy was angry too. Why had those films been so praised by the critics, he wondered. They were miles away from the lives of ordinary people, there was no story in any of them that would keep an audience breathless for two hours or more, and the ideas behind them were intellectually esoteric.

The winner of the Golden Palm at Cannes in 1999 was *Rosetta*, directed by Luc and Jean-Pierre Dardenne from Belgium. The film is about the miseries of social exclusion and so impressed the Belgian audience that the government en-acted a new measure to stimulate job creation for the unemployed; it was called 'the *Rosetta* plan'.[7] Whereas the American critics expressed their disdain for the film, the Belgian audience knew very well why this movie was an important aesthetic and social event.

The problem is that for European films such as this, there are very few dis-tribution channels within European countries despite what *Le Monde* called the 'liveliness of cinematographic art on a world scale' evident in 1999 in Cannes. In Europe, as in most places in the world, the majority of people have no choice but to watch movies made in the USA according to the recipe described, for instance, by Strauss Zelnick when he was president and chief executive of Twentieth Century-Fox: 'Our formula is: One, all movies need to be story driven; two, higher budget movies can be star driven and story driven; three, never make a movie that is neither story driven nor star driven, or an expensive story-driven movie that is not also star driven' (Ohmann 1996: 19).

In what sense does a list of the twentieth century's 100 best books in Eng-lish represent a battleground on the symbolic matter of words, written words, literature? The American organization Modern Library took the initiative to compile a list – an idea that sounds interesting and, one would expect, neutral. However, the selection committee was made up of nine white men and one white woman, with an average age of 68.7. These people produced a list with only nine books by women, three by black people and only four published since 1975. Modern Library is a daughter organization of Random House, a publisher in the Bertelsmann group. Fifty-nine of the 100 books came from publishers in the Bertelsmann group. The 'top 100' all of a sudden turns out to be a tool in an economic battle.

There is also a fundamental problem with such lists, and the concepts of greatness, excellence and quality on which they are based. Katha Pollitt argued in *The Nation* (24–31 August 1998): 'They sound terrific, abstract; who, after all, champions mediocrity? Once you get down to cases, they prove so flexible – What stories matter most and to whom? What is universal, what particular? What makes a prose style pleasurable? How important is pleasure, anyway? – that they leave you in much the same straits as if you didn't have these concepts.'

Ashoke Chatterjee, adviser to India's National Institute of Design, witnessed a conflict, if not of cultures, then at least of value systems in design in his country and in many other Third World countries as well. He bemoans

> glossy images pouring in from richer countries. The common denominator is one of affluence and obsolescence, the catering to inconsistent whims which spell high profit. The vigour with which this new understanding of design is insinuating itself into the consciousness of the elite mocks every modest step that designers have taken over the past two decades. The concept of real need is sought to be replaced with the image of design as the five-star life-style. (Whiteley 1993: 4)

All these are issues about who has the power to speak for themselves in the form of texts, images, films or music, who will be heard, who lacks this power, and who can prevent troubling questions being raised. Edward Said says, for instance, in relation to colonialism:

> cultural forms like the novel or the opera do not cause people to go out and imperialize – Carlyle did not drive Rhodes directly, and he certainly cannot be 'blamed' for the problems in today's southern Africa – but it is genuinely troubling to see how little Britain's great humanistic ideas, institutions, and monuments ... stand in the way of the accelerating imperial process. We are entitled to ask how this body of humanistic ideas co-existed so comfortably with imperialism. (Said 1993: 81–2)

We may add to his amazement the question of why in European countries, which colonized all corners of the African continent, there are no major exhibitions (apart from a new musuem concerned with slavery, in Bristol, UK) devoted to the centuries of atrocities (Nederveen Pieterse 1997). Likewise, John Holt (1996) considers that 'The apparent problem of Western encounters with "Islamic Art" is heightened by the lack of Western understanding of contemporary Islamic history and thought. This absence of a clear context within which to place the work of both "traditional" and "modern" "Islamic Artists" leads, inevitably, to a stereotype, or more, an indifference to the arts of the Asian sub-Continent.'

'The capacity to represent, portray, characterize, and depict is not easily available to just any member of just any society,' Edward Said (1993: 79–80) points out; certainly not on a world scale. So we may also understand why there is such a deafening silence in the Western world about the massive destruction of the extremely rich cultural heritage of Iraq as a result of the bombing during the Gulf War and since.

Obviously, not all artistic creations and performances cause conflicts day after day. We may feel irritated, but why make a fuss about it? If power relations, in the arts as in other matters, are the way they are, why keep on saying that it is not justifiable for certain forms of artistic communication to receive attention and funding, for instance, while others are suppressed or neglected? Basically, controversies within the symbolic battlefields (the arts) are latent and only sometimes explode, and it is surprising that so many people, all passionate about different forms of art and entertainment, can live together peacefully in a given society and not disturb each other's enjoyment too much!

Basically, too, it is power relations that determine why some works of art, entertainment or fashion, have a higher status than others. Apinan Poshyananda (1992) gives the example of the role played by banks and corporations in Thailand in respect of the arts. They have

> the ability to shift both the degree of commercial value and the degree of aesthetic value which are in direct correspondence. By establishing their own collections of modern Thai art, these economic and financial institutions have the power to approve or endorse good art and to discriminate against what they consider bad art. In this way, the corporate patrons and their selecting committees can dictate the aesthetic and financial climate of the art scene in Thailand.

This brings us to the question of the complex relationship between art, commodity and taste. The acquisition of modern art has become a status symbol for the privileged in Thailand; for the rich and famous, it demonstrates their principles of value and quality in a society that strives to emulate the capitalism of the West.

But, as art works have become increasingly commodified – as buyers from the commercial sector have entered the scene – many Thai artists have adapted their style according to the trend and demand in the art market. Clearly, banks and corporations have replaced the religious sector as leading art patrons ... [Artists find it] necessary to compromise – to create 'safe' art belonging to the mainstream, which generally does not include erotic, social protest, political, anti-religious, or anti-government themes or any experimental works such as conceptual art and installation. By creating 'high art' for the easy consumption of the *nouveau riche* and consumer culture, numerous Thai artists are forced through the motion of self-censorship to be part of the norm. (Poshyananda 1992: 174–5)

Apinan Poshyananda underlines the fact that the creation, production, performance, distribution and promotion of the arts depend most of all on the efforts of those who want to see, read or hear particular works themselves, or to gain profit or status from them, and are therefore prepared to do their utmost to help bring them to life and into the public arena.

This phenomenon operates mainly through infrastructures and selection mechanisms, the control of which makes it easy to decide who is hired or commissioned. After all, the arts and artists go where the power is. It may be that some artists express in their work feelings or codes that forecast the future or that indicate symbolically that the present is no longer viable, and in this sense it may happen that they are agents of ideological change. Nevertheless, artists are not capable themselves of changing the economic structures that feed them. When economic, social and political changes are happening in particular societies, at particular moments in history, the control of the infrastructures and selection mechanisms for the arts are likely to change as well, and these structures will be replaced if deemed necessary by the new groups in power. Of course, as we may expect, these processes can cause a great deal of friction.

This observation includes a warning as well. In Chapter 6, my analysis leads me to propose a number of infrastructural changes for the artistic domains in contemporary societies all over the world. However, we cannot expect that such changes and turnarounds of selection mechanisms can be realized independently of changes in economic and social relations, particularly in the neoliberal and corporate-driven power relations that currently prevail, nor independently of the social, economic, ecological and labour movements that are trying to transform dominant worldwide power structures.

SPECIFIC FORMS OF COMMUNICATION

The tensions, conflicts and contradictions surrounding the arts show that films, books, television, images, theatre, music and dance are not the innocent adornments of life that we might imagine. This observation is the more important because the arts constitute a broad field of social activities that penetrate almost all aspects of our daily life. Try to imagine, for instance, a day without music or images.

It would be a mistake to limit the arts to mean what in the Western world has been considered 'high culture'. We should keep in mind that the arts are a broad field of social activities but have special characteristics. In the arts, *specific forms of communication* take place. The arts are not a neutral field. What is deemed by some to be of high aesthetic merit is of no appeal to others (see Eagleton 1990: 28). What was once considered disgusting may, some years later, under the influence of particular experiences, receive a more positive value judgement – and it may be the same person whose perceptions have changed. There are always social, cultural, historical, economic or personal circumstances that influence notions and definitions of 'high' or 'low' culture, or what is more or less important or interesting (Frith 1996: 94–5). This has always been the case, and will continue to be so.

This observation is not the expression of a seasoned relativism. I agree with John Gray's judgement that 'Homer's *Iliad* is a greater achievement than the screenplay of *Silence of the Lambs*', and I can imagine with him that the Zen temple at Ryoanji is superior to a drive-in church (Gray 1998: 124). It is up to me to convince others that there is a value in recognizing these differences if I happen to think, for example, that a particular work of art is a spiritual resource for a community.

Second, the arts are also a *specific* field of communication because what they communicate is usually more dense, more focused, possibly funnier, or more reflective, than we are used to in our normal daily contacts.

Third, it is also clear that the arts, as *specific forms of human communication*, often take place in specific *places* that tell us that something special is happening, for instance a theatre, a gallery, a magic circle in a city square where a clown performs her act, or a television screen. However, we can cycle and sing at the same time; take part in a meeting and draw; make love and recite a poem; or walk in the street with just a little bit of dance in the movement of the body. The shouting of drunken people may sound as if they are about to break into song.[8] A book is only partly a literary creation or the outcome of a design process; there is a considerable economic aspect represented in it, too, and the environmental consequences of printing so many millions of books are becoming a matter of increasing concern. All advertising tells us that we should be buying, but the packaging of the message consists largely of artistic creations such as music, poetic texts or concentrated images.

It may happen that a work of art – *a specific form of human communication* – exists as a rather separate social phenomenon, such as a concert or a film; however, more often than not, the arts are part of other social activities or interests.

Mike Featherstone, for instance, analyses the aestheticization of everyday life. He observes the collapse of some of the boundaries between art and everyday life and the erosion of the special protected status of art as an enclaved commodity, which goes hand in hand with 'the migration of art into industrial design, advertising, and associated symbolic and image production industries' (Featherstone 1991: 25). However, we should not imagine that this is a new phenomenon: the churches and the courts have always integrated the arts into their activities, and mostly not without purpose. Aesthetic production today has largely been integrated into commodity production generally, which is the result, according to Fredric Jameson, of a 'frantic economic urgency of producing fresh waves of ever novel-seeming goods (from clothing to airplanes), at ever greater rates of turnover' (Jameson 1992: 4–5).

The arts – those specific forms of human communication – mould our mental framework, our emotional texture, our language, our tonal and visual landscape, our understanding of past and present, our feelings about other people, our sensibility. The arts are important producers of our ideology. By ideology, Stuart Hall means 'the mental framework – the languages, the concepts, categories, imagery of thought, and the systems of representation – which different classes and social groups deploy in order to make sense of, define, figure out and render intelligible the way society works' (Morley and Chen 1996: 26–7). Speaking about the movie industry as big business, French film director and producer Marin Karmitz reminds us: 'Behind the industrial aspect, there is also an ideological one. Sound and pictures have always been used for propaganda, and the real battle at the moment is over who is going to be allowed to control the world's images, and so sell a certain lifestyle, a certain culture, certain products and certain ideas' (in Barber 1996: 82).

People often speak of 'culture' when they are mainly referring to the arts. In Western societies the dominant thinking has long been that only one culture – their own – was of real value, and that the arts were the highest representation of this culture. People in the West have now come to know that there are many cultures, in the broad anthropological sense, within which completely different forms of art play many distinct roles. This means that what has been considered valuable in the broad field of the arts is a matter of personal and social judgement. However, any judgements about culture are also undoubtedly the result of social power struggles, including who has the means to steer, more or less effectively, the value judgements of many sections of a particular population or society.

To gain a better understanding, it is important to include in our personal and social appreciation or dislike of certain artistic presentations and events – film, dance, music, theatre, novels, video art, television or whatever – an analysis of the cultural processes that influence the production, distribution and reception of these artforms. It makes sense to link analytically the specific forms of communication that the arts represent with their surrounding cultures. 'For every text, a context,' Salman Rushdie concluded, and he clarified this with an example. In the Thatcher period there were several British Indian films that glorified the British colonial past – a process he calls 'Raj revisionism' – evident, for example, in Richard Attenborough's *Gandhi*. There are brilliant actors in films such as this, but we should not forget that these movies were 'the artistic counterpart of the rise of conservative ideologies in modern Britain'. From this perspective it does not matter that the film-makers may, ideologically, have been working quite 'innocently' (Rushdie 1992: 92).

Artists who see themselves as making choices independently, and even for the good of humankind, and who consider their success related to their talent, may be fooling themselves. As Janet Wolff argues: 'In the production of art, social institutions affect, amongst other things, *who* becomes an artist, *how* they become an artist, how they are able to *practise* their art, and how they can ensure that their work is produced, performed, and *made available* to a public.' She adds to this a down-to-earth conclusion: 'Furthermore, judgments and evaluations of works and schools of art, determining their subsequent place in literary and art history, are not simply individual and "purely aesthetic" decisions, but socially enabled and socially constructed events' (Wolff 1989: 40). In this context an example given by Roger Wallis and Krister Malm is instructive. Hotels in warm and poor countries, where 'tourists can do things they would never do at home', offer major sources of employment for musicians. This ambience may, for instance, spur a Tunisian folk musician performing at a hotel 'to show how he can balance five beers and three Cokes on his head whilst blowing his *ʒoukra* (shawm), [rather] than demonstrate how the music functions' (Wallis and Malm 1984: 62).

To give another example of shifting power relations influencing the arts: in former times construction workers were often highly esteemed craftsmen, and many were artists in their own right. They can be compared with musicians who play or sing a composition written by someone else. Construction workers carried out the architectural plan, but the quality of the house or church they built depended among other things on their capacity to give form to the aesthetic plan as beautifully as possible. For most construction workers nowadays this is no longer the case. Their craft, and their own contribution to carrying out the architectural plan – the aesthetic composition of the building – are no longer desired or valued. Similarly, this is increasingly the case for musicians, too, who are in the business of recording background music, rather mechanically, for hour after hour. There may come a time when their work is taken over by computers, and then they'll be out of a job!

A TRIANGLE AND A HI-TECH ARCHIPELAGO

This book discusses the impact of economic globalization on artistic cultures worldwide. Until now I have discussed some aspects of artistic cultures. What about economic globalization? If globalization means that the world is a seamless unity in which everyone participates equally in the economy, obviously it has not taken place. Masao Miyoshi remarks: 'We do not live in an integrated economy, nor are we likely to do in the foreseeable future. Similarly, if globalization means merely that parts of the world are interconnected, then there is nothing new about this so-called globalization: it began centuries ago, as Columbus sailed across the Atlantic, if not earlier' (Miyoshi 1998: 248). Let us try to imagine, for example, cities such as Calcutta, Singapore or Rio de Janeiro at the beginning of the twentieth century. These were crowded places, where many cultures from different parts of the world made life 'colourful' and where one could see the results of unequal global power relations openly on the streets. What we now call globalization was already a reality, usually an unpleasant one, for many people a century ago (Morley and Chen 1996: 328–9; Savigliano 1995).

Masao Miyoshi focuses more precisely on the present form of globalization. 'The only novelty is the degree of expansion in the trade and transfer of capital, labour, production, consumption, information, and technology, which might be enormous enough to amount to a qualitative change' (Miyoshi 1998: 248). A couple of definitions may help. Anthony Giddens sees the present form of globalization as 'the intensification of worldwide social relations which link distant localities in such a way that local happenings are shaped by events occurring miles away and vice versa' (Burnett 1996: 4). Colin Hines describes it as 'the ever-increasing integration of national economies into the global economy through trade and investment rules and privatization, aided by technological advances' (Hines 2000: 4).

It is true that events, decisions and interventions emanating from one part of the world can have major consequences for individuals and communities in other parts (Petrella 1994a: 46). In former times a more or less logical relationship existed between the source of decisions and the place where the consequences of those decisions were felt. This linear relation no longer exists in the same way. In colonial times the ties between the 'mother country' and the colony formed the greater part of global relations. Now, however, lines of influence extend almost everywhere on earth. The apexes are, literally, the satellites, which beam information of all sorts to different spots all over the planet, including entertainment and other artistic forms.

The character and dimensions of this spread of communication all over the globe – call it globalization – are, however, not easy to determine. It is fair to say that flows of influence and transport lines do not go absolutely everywhere. In the field of trade and commerce, to give one example, it is unlikely that markets are essentially global. 'Globalization is not really global. Transnational business activities are concentrated in the industrial world and in scattered enclaves throughout the underdeveloped world' (Barnet and Cavanagh 1994: 427). Not all enterprises can easily make 'random walks' to all places on earth. The number of basically transnational enterprises is limited in the cultural field, too. The majority of intra-regional trade is between the three big powers, the United States, Europe and Japan. Only 15 per cent of the world's population lives in this *triangle*. On the other hand, it is a reality that no single country can extract itself from the pressure and influence of multinationals and the international financial markets (Went 1996: 42–3).

The concept of globalization should be relativized even more, according to Saskia Sassen. She emphasizes that a limited number of mega-cities are playing strategic roles in the world economy. Despite all the dreams about a 'virtual' world, in which real places would no longer be important, economic activities are more than ever clustered physically in particular places. She gives the examples of New York, Tokyo and London:

> Beyond their long history as centres for international trade and banking, these cities now function in four new ways: first, as highly concentrated command points in the organization of the world economy; second, as key locations for finance and for specialized service forms, which have replaced manufacturing as the leading economic sectors; third, as sites for production, including the production of innovations, in these leading industries; and fourth, as markets for the products and innovations produced. (Sassen 1991: 3–4)

These cities have undergone massive and *parallel* changes in their economic base, spatial organization and social structure.

In these mega-cities artistic workers play important roles, as writers or designers, as providers of entertainment or producers of luxury products. The large Western cities of today also concentrate diversity; their spaces are inscribed with the dominant corporate culture but also with a multiplicity of other cultures and identities. Saskia Sassen observes:

> For instance, through immigration a proliferation of originally highly localized cultures now have become presences in many large cities, cities whose elites think of themselves as cosmopolitan, as transcending any locality. Members of these 'localized' cultures can in fact come from places with great cultural diversity and be as cosmopolitan as elites. An immense array of cultures from around the world, each rooted in a particular country, town, or village, now are reterritorialized in

a few single places, places such as New York, Los Angeles, Paris, London, and most recently Tokyo. (Sassen 1998: xxxi)

Riccardo Petrella estimates that there are thirty mega-cities worldwide: 'Instead of national states which try to find their place in a new global power equilibrium, a *high-tech archipelago* of rich, hyper-developed city regions rises up from a sea of poverty.'[9] Inside these big cities, according to Sassen: 'Disparities, as seen and as lived, between the urban glamour zone and the urban war zone have become enormous. The extreme visibility of the difference is likely to contribute to further brutalization of the conflict: the indifference and greed of the new elites versus the hopelessness and rage of the poor' (Sassen 1998: xxxiii). This disparity, which was, and is, 'normal' in cities such Calcutta, Singapore and Rio de Janeiro, has become an intrinsic element of many big Western cities as well.

We may wonder whether it is even right to speak of globalization. Jan Nederveen Pieterse's analysis is that 'globalization begins in and emanates from Europe and the West. In effect it is a theory of Westernization by another name ... With this agenda, it should be called Westernization and not globalization' (Nederveen Pieterse 1994: 163). Nevertheless, since the word 'globalization' has become the order of the day, it has become impossible to avoid it.

Meanwhile, it has become clear that within the present form of globalization the economic aspect is particularly important. Economic historian Richard DuBoff argues that 'capitalism has always been an international system, but *globalization* now implies an internationalizing of financial and economic flows that is far more integrated and puts new constraints on domestic policy options' (Schiller 1999: xiv). Therefore it makes sense to speak about economic globalization, which we see happening nowadays.

Globalization, though, has also been given a structure. In 1994, the World Trade Organization (WTO) was established as the successor to the General Agreement on Tariffs and Trade (GATT). Nearly every country in the world is a member of the WTO; China joined in 2001. The WTO has in fact a dual purpose, which makes it difficult to discuss it adequately. Its first purpose is to draft multilateral rules concerning international trade, and to make these rules binding; this was not the case with GATT. There is no real major disagreement about this aim in general; how it works out concretely is another matter, as will be discussed below. Transparency in conditions for trade and uniformity of norms for commerce can avoid trade wars.

The second purpose, however, is the source of the growing number of conflicts surrounding the WTO and economic globalization alike. The rules, which have been conceived, accepted and practised during the last decade, are based on neoliberal principles, which Riccardo Petrella summarizes as 'the six commandments of the new table of law'. The first commandment is that we should go global. Respect for what is important from a local perspective, and what deserves protection, is out of order. The second is that all proven production methods should yield to the new technologies, backed by a blind belief in digitalization. The third is that the human condition should be considered as a game in which there are only winners and losers. Everyone is always in competition with everyone else. The fourth is that countries should liberalize their markets; no protection of what is considered valuable is allowed. The fifth commandment is that all regulation should be put aside. The state as guardian of a diversity of interests and of long-term needs is redundant. The sixth commandment is that everything in the public domain should be privatized. Private property delivers a better mechanism for the acquisition of happiness and fortune than any public intervention can offer.[10]

These 'six commandments of the new table of law' provide the basic philosophy for the WTO, which aims to reduce trade barriers, prevent increases in tariffs and promote multilateral negotiations on lower tariffs. The central principles of WTO rules are summed up by Colin Hines. First, liberalization or 'market access': 'this is the goal of gradually reducing most forms of protection and fixing or "binding" these reduced levels'. Second, reciprocity: 'the negotiating process whereby each country makes successive tariff reduction offers until a schedule of mutually agreed reductions is reached'. Third, non-discrimination: 'this concept, implying equality between WTO members, takes three forms: first, WTO rules apply equally to imports and exports; second, trade concessions granted to any country must be extended equally to all other WTO members – the "Most Favoured Nation" (MFN) principle; third, no tariff, tax or other measure should discriminate between domestic and foreign suppliers – the "National Treatment" (NT) principle'. The fourth WTO principle, as summarized by Colin Hines, is transparency: 'any form of protection a signatory chooses to use within the framework of WTO rules should be clearly and firmly stated, should be consistent and ideally should take the form of visible tariffs'. In fact, the laws of every member state must conform to WTO rules (Hines 2000: 15–16).

The World Trade Organization has a dispute resolution court that arbitrates on matters of international commerce. However, this is basically a *private justice system* as it has the authority to override local and national legislation if there is a violation of the terms of the agreement, and hence it can discipline sovereign states (Sassen 1998: 98). The WTO dispute resolution court is composed of three unelected pro-trade officials who meet in secret; there is no media or citizen participation; no unsolicited submissions of evidence are accepted; decisions are binding and enforceable (with fines and trade sanctions); appeal is virtually impossible (Starr 2000: 19). The judges may simultaneously pursue private business careers. Ralph Nader calls the WTO highly anti-democratic, including its privatized judicial system. It is 'a system of international governance with powerful legislative, executive and judicial authority over member nations' (*The Nation*, 10 October 1994).

When the WTO was instituted, national governments had imposed on them, according to Richard Barnet and John Cavanagh, 'the obligation to sacrifice local and state laws that protect consumers, the environment, and a variety of other local interests. Free trade of this sort sets global standards in health, safety working conditions, and environmental protection based on the lowest common denominator' (Barnet and Cavanagh 1994: 351). Through the neoliberal economic globalization that became confirmed in WTO rules and standards, small businesses in almost every locality now face competition from powerful multinational corporations. Amory Starr argues that these conglomerates 'use huge advertising budgets to homogenize preferences (in the guise of "choice"), cut prices based on their socially costly comparative advantage, eliminate inconvenient regulations and protectionist policies of all kinds, and now have the very definition of competition legally defined in their interests' (Starr 2000: 10).

In the Third World, 'globalization is devastating as it empowers corporations to drive local businesses out and to move production operations constantly, leaving behind economic devastation. Deregulation, privatization and investment liberalization hand the economy over to multinational corporations' (Starr 2000: ix). These processes have been accompanied by the so-called IMF and World Bank *structural adjustment programmes* that were supposed to discipline profligate governments, but paradoxically made the developing countries even more open to foreign capital inflows from northern financial centres. For while tight fiscal and monetary policies were imposed on the state, foreign exchange controls were lifted and capital account liberalization was promoted with the objective of freeing the market from the straitjacket of state regulation. Walden Bello comments that 'the upshot was a dramatically reduced role for the state as a mediator between the domestic private sector and foreign capital' (Bello et al. 2000: 8).

After the mass demonstrations that took place during the G8 meeting in Genoa in July 2001, William Pfaff commented in the *International Herald Tribune* (26 July 2001) that the sovereign merit of deregulation and expanded trade is taken for granted, occupying the same status of self-evident truth that the benevolence and progressive character of colonialism did in the 1920s and 1930s: 'There is a resemblance between globalization and colonialism. Both are motivated by the wish to export to the colonial/globalized market; to make use of its work force, where wages are less than those in the home country; and to exploit the colonized country's resources, material as well as human.' Of course, there are justifications. 'We are told today that globalism means progress, education, prosperity and economic modernization. This is only half the story. Yes, it brings investment and industrial technology – but also social and political disruption, destruction of cultural infrastructure and ruin for internationally uncompetitive local industries and agriculture.' I will return to the question of the destruction of cultural infrastructure in Chapter 4.

We know that at least one billion global citizens – that is, one in five or six – live in extreme poverty, with insufficient shelter, food and basic amenities (Sardar 1998: 18–19). Unhampered Western exports of cheap food destroy local farmers' livelihoods in Third World countries instead of empowering their agricultural activities; yet support for Third World agriculture is absolutely vital, not only to feed the hungry poor but also the fast-growing world population, since in a couple of decades the world will need three times more food than is available today.[11]

The dominant tendency, however, as we have seen, is for global markets to be as open as possible, not subject to any regulations. We should therefore pay particular attention when two prominent advocates of neoliberal globalization – Klaus Schwab, founder and president of the annual World Economic Forum in Davos, and Claude Smadja, managing director of the Forum – observe that globalization has entered a critical phase. In 1996, in an article in the *International Herald Tribune* (1 February), they observed that a mounting backlash against the effects of globalization, especially in the industrial democracies, was already threatening to have a disruptive impact on economic activity and social stability in many countries. Their analysis comprised four elements.

First, the 'lightning speed at which capital moves across borders, the acceleration of technological changes, the rapid evolution of management and marketing requirements increase the pressure for structural and conceptual readjustment to a breaking point. This is multiplying the human and social costs of the globalization process to a level that tests the social fabric of the democracies in an unprecedented way.'

Second, they acknowledge that the globalization process is in essence a redistribution of economic power at the world level. This can be seen very clearly in income distribution across the world. The Dutch politician Jan Pronk has since summarized this trend, pointing out that in 1960 the richest 20 per cent of the world population had an income that was thirty times as high as that of the poorest 20 per cent. By 1997 it was eighty times as high (Pronk 2000). Ignacio Ramonet, chief editor of *Le Monde Diplomatique*, presented figures in January 1999 that were equally shocking. The 225 wealthiest people in the world had a combined fortune of more than US$1,000 billion. This was the same amount of money as the yearly income of the poorest 2.5 billion people in the world. There were individuals who were richer than states; and the fortune of the fifteen richest people in the world exceeded the gross national income of all countries in Africa south of the Sahara. The 1999 *Human Development Report* also mentioned that more than eighty countries still had 'per capita incomes lower than they were a decade or more ago' (*Human Development Report* 1999: 2–3).

The cultural conglomerate created out of the merger between Viacom and CBS in September 1999, according to Ignacio Ramonet, had a yearly turnover of $20 billion. This is far more than the gross national product (GNP) of countries such as Tunisia, Equador or Sri Lanka. Sherif Hetata noted in 1998 that the countries that formed the G7, with their 800 million inhabitants, controlled more technological, economic, informatics and military power than the rest of the approximately 4.3 billion people living in Asia, Africa, Eastern Europe and Latin America. 'Five hundred multinational corporations account for 80 per cent of world trade and 75 per cent of investments. Half of the multinational corporations are based in the United States, Germany, Japan, and Switzerland. The OECD (Organization for Economic Cooperation and Development) group of rich countries contributes 80 percent of world production' (Hetata 1998: 274). According to Augustín Papie, a former member of the North–South Commission, the 'invisible transfers' from the South to the North amounted in 1996 to $200 billion a year (Went 1996: 42–3). In view of such statistics, it is not surprising that Klaus Schwab and Claude Smadja fear that any 'change of this magnitude in the global balance of power is bound to have a profound destabilizing effect'.

Third, according to Schwab and Smadja:

> [it] becomes apparent that the head-on mega-competition that is part and parcel of globalization leads to winner-take-all situations; those who come out on top win big, and the losers lose even bigger. The gap between those able to ride the wave of globalization, especially because they are knowledge- and communication-oriented, and those left behind is getting wider at the national, corporate, and individual levels.

Jeremy Brecher and Tim Costello call it a 'race to the bottom'. In *Global Village or Global Pillage* they argue:

> All over the world, people are being pitted against each other to see who will offer global corporations the lowest labour, social, and environmental costs. Their jobs are being moved to places with inferior wages, lower business taxes, and more freedom to pollute. Their employers are using the threat of 'foreign competition' to hold down wages, salaries, taxes, and environmental protections and to replace high-quality jobs with temporary, part-time, insecure, and low-quality jobs. Their government officials are justifying cuts in education, health, and other services as necessary to reduce business taxes in order to keep or attract jobs ...

If you fear that the growing freedom of corporations to move jobs around the world threatens you and what you value, you are probably right. (Brecher and Costello 1994: 3)

This brings Schwab and Smadja to the fourth, and concluding, element in their analysis: that there is popular scepticism about the win–win effect of the global economy. It is 'becoming harder in the industrial democracies to ask the public to go through the pains and uncertainties for the sake of benefits yet to come'. There is also the phenomenon that globalization tends to delink the fate of the corporation from the fate of its employees. It is 'now routine to have corporations announce new profit increases along with a new wave of layoffs'.

After this short discussion of economic globalization and the WTO, Chapter 2 looks at the impact of economic globalization on artistic life worldwide. The effects of the WTO and neoliberal globalized norms rule out any local protection of domestic service industries, inhibit the development of indigenous service industries, and diminish local control over key service industries. Cees Hamelink concludes that once we realize that among such domestic service industries are the mass media, telecommunication services, advertising, marketing and tourism,

> it becomes clear that the application of these norms reduces local cultural autonomy. Local cultural markets are monopolized by transnational corporations that leave little space for local cultural providers. Liberalizing world trade to the extent that smaller and less resource-rich countries open their services markets to outsiders, stimulates the development of consumerist lifestyles and erodes the competitive capacity of people's own cultural industries. (Hamelink 1994a: 100)

Such cultural issues, placed in a global perspective, are the themes discussed in the rest of this book.

NOTES

1. Bruce Kpeke, 'Researching Performing Arts in Badakshan', *ISIM Newsletter*, 5, 2000.

2. *Le Monde*, 28 and 29 June 1998.

3. 'Lyric from the Koran is Off-key in Lebanon. Arab World Star Faces Trial for Blasphemy', *International Herald Tribune*, 30 November 1999.

4. 'Libanese zanger beledigde islam niet', *NRC Handelsblad*, 15 December 1999; see also Smyth (2000: 169–73).

5. 'Miss India. Het dubbelhartig zelfbewustzijn van hindoevrouwen', *NRC Handelsblad*, 25 January 1997.

6. 'Wagner Draws an Unproar in Israel', *International Herald Tribune*, 9 July 2001.

7. Jean-Pierre Stroobants, 'La Belgique s'arme d'un "plan Rosetta" pour combattre le chômage des jeunes', *Le Monde*, 11 January 2000.

8. Simon Frith (1996: 100) observes: 'Music is an ordered pattern of sounds in the midst of a vast range of more or less disorderly aurality. Music is marked out as different from noise; as our sense of noise changes, so does our sense of music.'

9. Riccardo Petrella, 'De wereld valt uiteen door technologische apartheid', *De Volkskrant*, 7 September 1992.

10. Riccardo Petrella, 'Litanies de Sainte Compétitivité', *Le Monde Diplomatique*, February 1994.

11. Jean-Luc Vidal, 'Laissez les paysans du tiers-monde protéger leur marché', *Le Monde*, 27 July 2001.

TWO
The Power to Decide

THE EFFECTS OF SHEER SIZE

Economic globalization and digitalization provide the new conditions for most artistic production and distribution worldwide, specifically in the fields of music, film, books, photography and design, but more and more for the visual arts as well. Massive changes have been taking place. Some examples may illustrate this.

The figures may differ slightly, but there is no doubt that 80 to 90 per cent of music recordings all over the world – a market worth $40 billion – have been distributed by a handful of transnational cultural conglomerates, or their subsidiaries (Throsby 1998: 195–6). Not in India, nor yet in China, but nearly everywhere else, most of the films shown originate in Hollywood. There is a good chance that any book, journal or magazine bought anywhere has been brought on to the market by a publishing house owned by one of the major publishing conglomerates. Among these transnational companies, active in nearly all fields within the arts, we find the names of AOL/Time Warner, Vivendi-Universal, Sony, BMG, EMI, Disney, News Corporation, Viacom. These companies own distribution outlets themselves or are linked with them through joint ventures, cross-ownership, co-productions or pre-sales contracts. This means that, on a substantial scale, cultural production and distribution are vertically integrated.

In contrast to the chauvinistic enthusiasm in some circles in France that a French cultural corporation, Vivendi, had bought Seagram/Universal and became Vivendi-Universal – one of the five big cultural conglomerates – Pierre Musso's reaction was negative: 'When the merger becomes a success, the unavoidable consequence is that the French public authorities can no longer withstand the demands of the North American industry, which has been a constant element of French cultural policy since the '20s, because otherwise the European "champion" Vivendi-Universal will be hindered in its conquering of Hollywood.' The demands were always for a market that the Americans could enter freely, not for the protection of French audiovisual products. Pierre Musso envisages a failure of the Vivendi-Universal merger as horrific for the European, and specifically the French, audiovisual situation: 'Then, there is no other choice than complete submission to the dream factory of Hollywood, which can feed unhampered the multitude of European channels of distribution of all audiovisual material. In any case, America will be the winner.'[1]

Why exactly do these firms feel the need to be so large, even when people know that in many instances the promised synergies never materialize?[2] Robert McChesney suggests: 'It is when the effects of sheer size, conglomeration, and globalization are combined that a sense of the profit potential emerges. When Disney produces a film, for example, it can also guarantee the film showings on pay cable television and commercial network television' (McChesney 1998: 14). What follows is the posters, the T-shirts, the hats and the badges, and the whole range of other products sustaining the constructed 'desirable lifestyle'.

Films are no longer just films but, according to Thomas Schatz,

> 'franchises', blockbuster-scale hits which can be systematically reproduced in a range of media forms. The ideal movie today is not only a box-office smash but a two-hour promotion for a multimedia product line, designed with the structure of both the parent company and the diversified media marketplace in mind. From *Jaws* to *Jurassic Park*, the New Hollywood has been driven by multipurpose entertainment machines which breed movie sequels and TV series, music videos and sound track albums, video games and theme park rides, graphic novels and comic books, and an endless array of licensed tie-ins and brand-name consumer products. (Schatz 1997: 73–4)

What we see happening is the confluence of entertainment, information and advertising (Schatz 1997: 101). What is also happening is that in selling commercial time to advertisers to sell products, broadcasters are *also* selling a product: their audiences. In effect, the broadcaster's product – the audience – is transformed into a segmented market. The various divisions of the audience market 'can be sold to advertisers either separately or cumulatively as target markets' (Andersen 1995: 5).

Not so long ago, editors used to decide what books would be published. This has changed radically in large companies where power has shifted to so-called publishing committees, in which the financial and marketing staff play pivotal roles. Profit margins for book publishing used to be around 2 per cent. The demand now is for 15 per cent. The costs of salaries – for instance, the head of McGraw-Hill earns $1.5 million a year – expense accounts and showy offices have risen accordingly. Sales conferences at Random House can cost a million dollars each, twice a year. The consequence is that small print-runs are out of the question and predictable losses on some books considered culturally important – the risks publishers took in former times because they loved books – will no longer be covered by the profits from other books. Each book is now calculated separately, and must also throw in a contribution to overheads – sometimes over $100,000 – to justify its place on the list (Schiffrin 1999).

There are more examples of changed cultural entrepreneurship. For instance, the average cost of films, including their marketing, has doubled in the last five years to $50.4 million, but people are no longer amazed by the price tags: $225 million for *Titanic*, $200 million for *Waterworld*, $200 million for *Speed 2, Cruise Control*, for which the actress Sandra Bullock received a fee of $12.5 million for running around in a life-jacket on the ship; which is $4.5 million less than the writer Stephen King received as an advance on a not-yet written book; which is more than Hillary Clinton was paid, $6 million, as an advance for her memoirs of life as the First Lady; which is $4 million less than her husband received for his memoirs. The cornerstone of these sweet deals in the entertainment industry is the contract, a 25- to 100-page legal document prepared by high-priced lawyers designed to do one thing and one thing alone: protect the company at all costs. One word in a 100–page agreement can mean the difference between financial security and bankruptcy (Brabec and Brabec 1994: 68, 366–7)

Billboard magazine has argued that the takeovers in the field of music threaten the development of new artists and emerging musical styles, but this is true for all cultural conglomerates. Most of the acquisitions of independent labels placed major conglomerates deeply in debt, discouraging them from taking creative risks on unknown artists or music. The major labels are now preoccupied with launching blockbuster hit albums by established stars to increase short-term profits rather than developing new artists (Banks 1996: 149).

In the music business a decisive role is played by the so-called international staff who are responsible for the international repertoire and the international market. The majority of people involved in acquiring artists are white males with a college-rock background (Negus 1992: 57). In collaboration with senior business affairs executives they draw up a 'global' priority list of fifteen to twenty artists who will be judged according to economic criteria, based on the international staff's understanding of the international market.

Keith Negus calls the process 're-imagining the world for "global marketing"'. Assessments about the world of music are often based on a taken-for-granted reservoir of knowledge and a set of cultural assumptions espoused by the international staff.

This includes aesthetic judgements about the instruments, tempos, rhythms, voices and melodies that are able to 'travel well'. It incorporates semiotic judgements about the type of images that are more suitable for an 'international audience'. It includes political judgements about areas of the world considered to be 'unstable' or where certain types of music are banned for moral or religious reasons.

It includes economic judgements about the number of potential consumers who can be reached, and assessments about parts of the world where the corporation may have difficulty collecting revenue. It includes marketing judgements about the arrangements for the distribution of recordings (the availability of radio, retail outlets, television broadcasting) and the 'penetration' of the technologies of musical reproduction (tape machines and CD players). Finally, it includes pragmatic judgements about the popularity of various sound carrier formats (cassettes, mini disks or compact disks) and the existence of copyright law that will ensure that recordings broadcast by the media, played in public and circulated for purchase will generate rights revenue that will accrue to the corporation. (Negus 1999: 156)

Once chosen, an artist will be promoted in a systematic way. Employees in the regional offices of a music conglomerate are given clear targets, something they often find frustrating because they prefer to work with their own artists than with prioritized American or British mega-stars. Nevertheless, the major record companies have raised the minimum standards for 'successful' sales of albums from 100,000 copies to more than a million (Banks 1996: 147–8). So, for the regional managers, there is no escape.

In order to reach the desired number of viewers, buyers or listeners, substantial investments in marketing are required. It is like a war. Promotion staff are described as being in the 'front line' and involved in 'targeting' specific individuals and radio stations. On the promotion 'battlefield', the recording industry is concerned with developing global personalities who can communicate across multiple media and who represent Anglo-American ideas and cultural biases (Negus 1992: 1, 101; Wallis et al. 1999: 25–6).

The break-even point on recordings is high – 250,000 CDs for a major company – reflecting the high-risk nature of the industry and the fierce competition that keep tensions high. In the 1980s barely one record out of five sold enough copies to recoup its recording costs (Burnett 1996: 91); at the turn of the century, Conrad Mewton stated: 'the music industry writes off \$5 billion in unrecoverable investments each year because 95% of debut albums fail ... Artists come and go very quickly in today's volatile and unstable climate. There is absolutely no guarantee that, just because your first album has been successful, the second will equal or better its success' (Mewton 2001: 73).

At the same time, the music conglomerates must try to conquer their audience on, for instance, radio, where there has been an enormous increase in hours of programme output but only a small increase in the time people spend listening. Take the example of Sweden: in 1980 there were approximately 70,000 hours of programme output; by 1990 this had risen to 400,000, an increase of nearly 400 per cent. However, the time people spent listening to the radio increased in the same decade from 115 to 134 minutes per day, which is around 16 per cent (Malm and Wallis 1992: 13).

An increase in hours of radio output does not necessarily lead to a greater variety of programming, as the example of France shows. By the late 1990s, around 1,000 albums were produced annually, with a choice of more than 10,000 tracks. However, in more than one-third of the radio programmes no more than 100 different tracks were broadcast (Pichevin 1997: 73).

Some countries in Latin America, Southeast Asia and Eastern Europe have markets that promise enough growth for them not to have to depend on the international repertoire; they are allowed by the big conglomerates and their subsidiaries to produce and promote regional artists as well (Mediacult 2000: 121–2). However, the category 'domestic repertoire' in the statistics of the IFPI (the International Federation of Phonographic Industry) often refers to an imitation of musical programming taken from the international repertoire, or it indicates only that the music has been produced in that region (p. 17).

It may happen that forms of music such as calypso, salsa, reggae, rai, jùjú or highlife become internationalized through a process of re-ethnicization or hybridization. The local flavour is there, but basic musical structures, aesthetics and ambience reflect the international repertoire. This market segment has been called 'world music', or sometimes ethno-music, ethno-pop, ethno-rock or worldbeat (Mediacult 2000: 162).

One of the problems for rap music, for instance, is that the guidelines for the international repertoire are not easily applicable. Another problem is that rap has no 'catalogue value'. Keith Negus points out:

> Rap tracks are routinely compared to conventional songs and it is asserted that they cannot be 'covered' – re-recorded, re-sung, re-performed by other artists. Hence, rap tracks are judged to have a short catalogue shelf life, in terms of their ability to bring in ongoing copyright revenue from their re-use. In addition, the revenue that rap can generate during any assumed 'shelf life' is considered to be less than other types of music. (Negus 1999: 93–4)

Gangsta rap stands a chance, however, because lyrics about guns and women sell.[3]

In film, black artists are less welcome than should be the case, admits Strauss Zelnick, at the time president and chief executive of Twentieth Century-Fox.

> Movies starring black people often don't work overseas ... we have a unique ethnic population in this country. Other parts of the world are more homogeneous in their racial populations. People in Japan do not tend to go to see a movie with black stars unless it is an action movie. Our black subculture, which is reflected

in most of our movies, makes little sense to the rest of the world. Also, we tend to make a lot of comedies where the humour comes from ethnic issues that mean nothing overseas. (Ohmann 1996: 22)

Zelnick is probably overstating the case in saying that black subculture is represented in most Hollywood movies, not to speak of the hundreds of other cultures in the USA; at the same time it is more appropriate to speak not about subcultures but about real live cultures.

The studios have to remember as well, according to Strauss Zelnick, that airlines don't like bad language, sex or violence. 'Hotel/motel pay-per-view is different because it is essentially a softcore porn business. When you go to a hotel room and you see ten movies on Spectradyne, you'll see two softcore porn movies and eight current theatrical movies. People watch the softcore porn movies. The current movies are basically just for show' (Ohmann 1996: 25).

Without doubt there are big interests at stake in the worldwide game of conquering markets. After all, every year consumers around the world buy $300 billion-worth of movie tickets, compact discs, videotapes, video and computer games, books, magazines and other entertainment products (Burnett 1996: 10). In 1997 the *International Herald Tribune* even spoke of 'the $1 trillion global film and television business'.[4] Industry experts estimate that the new video game *The Matrix* cost as much as $20 million. The game, laced with an hour of new *Matrix* film scenes and megabytes of cinematic tricks, represents the closest collaboration so far between the converging orbits of movie-making and game production in an entertainment universe that is finding new profits, partnerships and possibilities in ever more sophisticated digital technologies. Developers of video games have been quick 'to capitalize on securing licenses to movies, gambling millions of dollars on whether movie premises and characters can make top-selling games'.[5]

Often the interests of the transnational cultural conglomerates are interwoven, as can be seen in the example of the triangle of forces that surrounds radio and television. The *corporations* that own the channels have basically one purpose – to sell audiences that are as big, or targeted, as possible to *advertisers* – and by so doing to increase their advertising revenues. In order to attract those audiences they need to have *programmes* that enough people like to watch or hear. The interest of these channels, then, is to have attractive programmes for a set budget. Where the programmes come from or which genre they represent are less important than the ratio of price to ratings. The interest of the advertisers is to place their ads in programmes with the highest viewing figures, or at least next to a programme that attracts large numbers of viewers or listeners. They too have no interest in issues such as diversity or responsibility for standards of quality and ethics. The interest of the producers of programmes is to have as many outlets as possible for their entertainment products, whatever these may be, and to gain the competitive edge over the few other remaining cultural conglomerates.

Economic globalization opened the door for mergers and made the resulting companies globally operating entities. This changed the character of what is produced and distributed, under what conditions, and with which economic and cultural consequences. The next question is: who pulls the strings in this nervously operating cultural merry-go-round?

THE QUESTION OF OWNERSHIP

Most people are unaware of who owns the means of production, distribution and promotion of works of art, and vehicles of entertainment and edification. Nevertheless, the question of ownership of the means of cultural production, distribution and promotion is the core issue in a worldwide battle to reach the largest possible audiences. Benjamin Barber notes that 'a free and democratic society depends on competition of ideas and heterogeneity of outlets' (Barber 1996: 123).

The company that has the capacity to manufacture its cultural products in large quantities and continuously, that is able to distribute them effectively to many parts of the world, that is in a position to persuade huge numbers of people that what is on offer is something they want to see, buy or listen to, that has the know-how to transform all those single products into a tasty soup of not-to-be-missed experiences, that is capable of upgrading its international operations to a privileged position by expanding horizontally and tapping emerging markets worldwide, that is capable of forging vertical alliances at all levels and in all branches of the cultural market, and that can attract the investment money to undertake all those activities – *this cultural conglomerate has power.*

It is not just the power to decide at the end of the process when the transaction is signed and the deal completed who will continue to be a client, a viewer or a listener; but power that extends to all the moments before this. It is the power to select a few artists and reject the rest; and to give those who are selected massive distribution and promotion. These key decisions limit and, more often than not, effectively create, the field of cultural options that many people experience as the only ones. Isn't it a fact that you only want what you think you can get? (Burnett 1996: 82). In order to want something else, you need a well-developed imagination and a conviction that cultural life can offer more than what is currently and seemingly unavoidably on offer on a mass scale. The content of mass-produced and mass-distributed products, however, does not generally stimulate the imagination or encourage such a conviction.

More and more, the decisive question thus becomes: who has access to the communication channels of the planet, both digital ones and, for a long time to come, material? Who has access to the emotions of large numbers of people and to their purses? The question of evaluating the content, ethical standards and quality of what the cultural industries offer is secondary to the major issue of oligopolistic control. Corporations exercise this to steer creativity, select artists, set up the means of seduction, prepare a favourable reception, and manufacture a range of experiences around the prioritized singer, writer, dancer, director, designer and his or her products and the broad range of gadgets more and more inextricably surrounding their work.

Oligopolistic access on the part of a limited number of cultural conglomerates to all these stages in the process from creative idea to cultural consumption is what we are witnessing today. We live in *The Age of Access*, to borrow the title of Jeremy Rifkin's book, published – not surprisingly – in the year 2000. This nearly monopolistic access severely limits the amount of democracy that exists at the level of access. According to Benjamin Barber: 'with a few global conglomerates controlling what is created, who distributes it, where it is shown, and how it is subsequently licensed for further use, the very idea of a genuinely competitive market in ideas or images disappears' (Barber 1996: 89).

Not only does the healthily varied market disappear – I shall come back to this issue later in the chapter – but corporatization of the market of ideas, images, texts and sentiments has also caused a shift to the political right. Corporate owners push their favoured interests, and in the decision-making process are less tolerant of anything that places a question mark against existing society and its rulings. A profound and critical debate on urgent social questions does not contribute to making maximum profit, so it does not happen; nor does the art that has serious consideration at its core. In any case it would not attract advertisers, who more and more actively control the surroundings in which their messages appear, and who urge media owners to get rid of anything that interferes with the message of their advertisements.

The way in which this happens becomes clear from a case in Brazil, where Robert Marinho's conglomerate Globo controls the media landscape. Nilanjana Gupta describes Globo's *telenovelas* (Latin American soaps), as

> one of the most effective vehicles of articulating social problems or representing pressing issues. For instance, a programme on a drought-stricken area brought many of Brazil's environmental problems into focus. But these programmes stop short of advocating truly radical measures. Marinho has been accused of person-ally ordering censorship of scenes depicting the disputes between landowners and peasants in Brazil. While TV Globo has united an economically, culturally and socially diverse country through its popular programming, it has simultaneously

transmitted and imposed the cultural, political and social values of the ruling elite of which Marinho is an extremely powerful member. (Gupta 1998: 6–7)

These chains of conservative and right-wing-oriented decisions by the cultural conglomerates have negative implications for the exercise of political democracy, Robert McChesney observes. The trend 'encourages a weak political culture that makes depoliticization, apathy and selfishness rational choices for the citizenry, and it permits the business and commercial interests ... to have inordinate influence over media content' (McChesney 1997: 6–7). And the consequence of the unification of the economically, culturally and socially diverse country that Brazil was, and still is, is that many forms of human expression, representing the wide variety of cultures found in Brazil, such as Afro-Brazilian traditions, Indian rituals and legends, north-eastern costumes, German, Italian and Japanese customs, the southern gaucho heritage, and so on, are seldom (if ever) portrayed in *telenovelas*. Omar Souki Oliveira concludes that 'the domain of the genre is restricted to the needs of those who can buy; therefore, it emphasizes lifestyles that suit the industrial mode of production, and denies space to autonomous cultural manifestations ... In most Brazilian soaps, the American lifestyle portrayed by Hollywood productions reappears with a "brazilianized" face' (Oliveira 1993: 128–9).

This is the Third World copy of Western values, norms and patterns of behaviour, with local flavour added. Because of the mass scale on which the cultural conglomerates such as Globo operate, their choices have by definition a widespread effect.

The real war, then, in which the cultural industries are winning more and more battles, is over *the control of distribution channels worldwide*. Try to imagine how many people must watch a film which costs $200 million for the investors to earn back their money tenfold. This can happen only when there is as straight a line as possible from production to distribution to the channels that tell people that, once again, there is something on offer they cannot afford to miss.

Every weekend four new Hollywood productions go into circulation in American cinemas. During the summer and around Christmas this number rises dramatically. 'If a movie isn't a success right away, theatres yank it away for a new film that might attract more ticket buyers,' David Lieberman observes. 'If a film is a flop, then it's usually dead. It probably will also flop on videocassette' (Lieberman 1997: 138). Either a film is a blockbuster or not. *Jurassic Park: The Lost World* brought in $100 million in its first six days. Moviegoers in the USA spent an estimated $7.7 billion at the box-office in the year 2000.[6]

Whereas in the United States eight distribution companies control 90 per cent of the film market, in Europe there are between 600 and 700 companies all trying to give their films fair distribution. Compared to the high level of film production, this fragmented distribution system is inadequate. It becomes more and more necessary to have a vertically integrated relationship with a chain of cinemas, which the European offices of the big American studios have and all the hundreds of European distributors lack (Farchy 1999: 49–50). In Chapter 6 I propose a completely different and more efficient distribution system for films throughout the region in which they are made.

The need to revise the present film distribution situation is becoming even more pressing with the explosive growth in the number of multiplexes all over Europe, which have several advantages for the cultural industries. They ensure that production and distribution are more adequately vertically integrated. People are less likely to go to the cinema to see a specific film; they go to the multiplex and there make the choice of which movie they will see. Critics, who formerly helped viewers to develop themselves as a critical audience, something we might think desirable, become superfluous in this process; the multiplex is the guide, offering more screens than ever for the huge numbers of blockbusters with which the public is bombarded. Films can subsequently be transferred quite easily to an appropriate-sized hall and milked for further profits.

As multiplexes have spread across Europe in the past decade, the number of moviegoers has soared, to 895 million in 1999 from 757 million just five years earlier. The number of screens rose to 27,466 from 23,108 in 1994. At the same time, the number of American movies in the biggest markets, Britain and Germany, climbed to more than 80 per cent from less than 70 per cent in 1997.[7] Even in France the share of American films is rising. Of the 155 million movie tickets bought in 1999, 68 per cent were for films from the USA – thanks to the multiplexes; 27 per cent were for French films; and, somehow or other, films made elsewhere managed to attract 5 per cent of the visitors.[8]

The consequences? One example. Dutch film critic Peter van Bueren complains that in the Netherlands thirty-two screens were reserved for the feeble sequel to *The Blair Witch Project*. For the Flemish film *Everybody Famous* (*Iedereen beroemd*) only one small cinema was available. This film is a superb and hilarious expression of the dreams parents cherish about their children's potential to become famous. The film couldn't have been made anywhere else but in the Dutch-speaking part of Belgium; the beautiful language, the humour, the social setting it contains are all aspects of a movie that has a rich texture and knows how far to exaggerate. Peter van Bueren remarks: 'The way cinema bosses make their economic policy is their affair. But this policy is a disaster for film culture in the Netherlands. The cinema bosses keep their halls closed to non-American films, which do not attract a big enough public, because the public cannot know any more that those other films exist at all.'[9]

Apparently, the Hollywood studios regret that China is not yet an open market for their films. The *International Herald Tribune* (22 November 1995) reported that Hollywood executives are itching to get into China: 'China's film industry looks like an untapped gold mine, overdue for an invasion by Hollywood producers. Five billion movie tickets are expected to be sold this year, about four times the number sold in the United States.' The figure was 21 billion in 1982, and fell again in 1999 to only 800 million tickets. In fact, Chinese film-making and distribution nearly collapsed at the beginning of the twenty-first century. Like many questions discussed in this book, film in China is a highly dialectical subject. Film professionals in the People's Republic fear that the agreement between China and the United States about China joining the WTO may open the floodgates for Western cultural industries to enter mainland China. On the other hand, this threat has helped influence Chinese film studios to modernize and merge with each other; and the American company Kodak and Golden Harvest from Hong Kong are building multiplexes, which will also provide some opportunity for Chinese films to be screened.[10]

The Midnight Special is a diversely stocked and welcoming bookshop on Third Street in Santa Monica, California, which holds regular debates and readings by authors. After reading in the *Los Angeles Times* in February 1993 that through mergers a duopoly in the field of book distribution had come into existence in the United States, I discussed the news with one of the shop's employees. He was shocked because the two distributors – Ingram and Baker & Taylor – were certain to give a better service to the two big book chains in the USA: Barnes & Noble and Borders. This means that independent bookstores, vital for freedom of communication and diversity of opinion, are once again disadvantaged. In 1999 independent bookshops in the United States accounted for only 17 per cent of book sales.[11]

The giant publishers pay the two bookstore chains for window placement of their bestsellers. The independent stores do not get such a 'subsidy'. Neither can they profit from the practice of returns. Marc Crispin Miller describes this practice, also ecologically disastrous: 'The superstores have generally ordered tons more books than they ever could sell – and then paid for those they've sold by sending back the ones they haven't. This titanic ripoff has distorted the whole trade.'[12]

Another weapon in the fight for an oligopolistic position was the low prices that lured customers to the national chains from independent stores and bumped up bestsellers' sales by making them much cheaper than other titles. By the end of the year 2000 this discount era in the bookstores virtually came to an end. 'Barnes & Noble Inc. and Borders Group Inc. have quietly raised their prices. So have the online stores Amazon.com, Barnesandnoble.com and Borders.com just after discounts of as much as 50 per cent on best-selling titles intensified the price wars. As a result, consumers everywhere are paying more for books.'[13] The chains have made their decision, based on rising costs and slowing growth rates. The price increases, combined with the shipping costs, makes buying books online even more expensive than offline. The *International Herald Tribune* commented: 'But independent bookstores, bloodied by 15 years of struggling to compete against the chains' discounts, are breathing a sign of relief.'[14] Or those that didn't die in the meantime are!

We may conclude that cultural entrepreneurship is narrowing its scope to concentrate on only one question: which gold mine is still to tap? This is one effect of the economic globalization.

CULTURAL PACKAGE, POLITICAL FREIGHT, ECONOMIC WEIGHT

The capital that feeds the cultural conglomerates is becoming more and more international and much information and entertainment material is now owned by non-American companies. Nevertheless, it is important to remember, as Robert Burnett points out, that most of these cultural products are 'still created by Americans, for the simple reason that Los Angeles remains the film, music and television production capital of the global entertainment industry' (Burnett 1996: 10). Brinsley Samaroo, a government minister in Trinidad in the 1980s, once said: 'If you go to St. Vincent or Grenada you get about eight American stations. The effect is absolutely disastrous on those nations. It is really unfortunate that a nation that is least able to provide moral guidance to the world has, because of its enhanced technology, taken over that role. It's like a drunk person driving a car' (Malm and Wallis 1992: 77–8).

Without being anti-American, it is clear that this situation raises several problems. One objection to American culture, as it represents itself worldwide, is that it stays on the surface instead of fathoming the deeper emotions of the soul and transcending the immediate here and now, according to Rob Kroes (1992: 39). It is an empire with a minimum of moral substance, to use Irving Kristol's expression.[15] The American system too easily picks 'exotic' elements from abroad and incorporates them without due respect (Jameson 1998: 63). What irritates people is that the USA thinks it has a mission.

Disney considers itself a spiritual guide for everybody, and pretends to work for timeless values and the triumph of the human spirit (Eudes 1989: 262). Companies such as MTV create expectations and illusions that are not within the reach of the majority of people throughout the world (Malm and Wallis 1992:

44–5; Tenbruck 1990: 205). An important aspect of the American way of life is its destructiveness, carelessness and consumerism, encouraged by an endless barrage of images and sounds (Jameson 1998: 64).

Of course, there are many Americans who are not happy with the image and reality of their own society; and there are many other countries that are also not modest in their pretensions. Why, though, have American pretensions become so dominant (apart from the fact that the country is big, wealthy and the only remaining superpower)? Yves Eudes speaks about the combination of *cultural package* and *political freight*, and I suggest that *economic weight* should be added to this duo (Eudes 1982: 121). The title of his book on the first decade of the Cold War is *La Conquête des esprits: l'appareil d'exportation culturelle américain* (*The Conquest of Minds: The American Cultural Exports Machine*).

Such a junction of culture, politics and economics is not revolutionary in itself. In all countries, works of art – and nowadays entertainment, too – have always served as carriers for social and political messages and interests. The difference lies in the rational and systematic ways in which US government and cultural enterprises have fine-tuned economic interests, foreign policy concerns and cultural content; and they continue to do so, as we will see, for instance, in Chapter 6 where I discuss the WTO and negotiations on culture. Jesús Martín-Barbero's analysis is that the US-based media universalize a lifestyle, but this style is a 'Westernized universal culture which is basically an economic force invading and controlling other markets of the world' (Martín-Barbero 1993a: 142).

Notwithstanding the official rhetoric that the market is self-regulating and independent of the state, there is close collaboration between the US state and US enterprises, which enhances all manifestations of US power. This combined and cumulative effort can be observed throughout the history of the USA (Ellwood 1994: 9). John Gray comments:

> American government has never observed a rule of non-interference in economic life. The foundations of American prosperity were laid behind the walls of high tariffs. Federal and state government were active in building railways and highways. The West was opened with an arsenal of government subsidies. Outside the economic sphere, American government was more invasive of personal liberty in the pursuit of virtue than that of any other modern Western country. No other modern Western state, for example, has attempted the enforcement of Prohibition. To represent the United States as a country with a history of minimum government requires considerable imagination. (Gray 1998: 104–5)

A successful example of this combined and cumulative effort of US state and US enterprises, in which a political aim and economic weight were supported by a cultural package, is an episode that took place after the Second World War. The

American troops who landed in Europe also facilitated the transfer of Hollywood executives in whose interest it was to (re)conquer the European film market and to have an additional outlet for their cinematographic wares. The political aim of this flooding of the European market with American movies was to present European audiences with a filmic counterweight to what the fascists and Nazis had shown them, and to keep them away from communist and other leftist tendencies by seducing them with Hollywood films promoting the American way of life.

The Hollywood studios therefore got permission from the American authorities to operate abroad as a cartel, the Motion Picture Export Association, and they functioned in various ways that were strictly forbidden at home. Blind bidding, block-booking, cross-collateralizing (bunching profits and losses to reduce risks), the outright dumping of films, the purchase of foreign studios in order to shelter profits – all these practices were now permitted. One of the conditions for European countries' receiving Marshall aid was the obligation to buy certain quantities of American films and to give the Motion Picture Export Association the permission to change European currency into dollars, a transfer of hard currency that the European countries obviously did not like. Additional to these measures was the installation of the International Media Guaranty Program, which guaranteed remittances from US cultural exports to Europe.

This diversified set of regulations could only be realized by the global presence of US military power in the postwar period, which necessitated highly organized and extremely efficient communication and transport systems. The technological advance the USA had built up came from the vast research and development efforts directed and underwritten by the Pentagon. If we wonder why American films are so dominant in Europe, here is one of their starting points (Twitchell 1992: 145–6; Swann 1994: 182; Schiller 1989a: 34–5, and 1992: 5).

This did not stop after the end of the Cold War. After the fall of the Berlin Wall the Media Committee of the Hungarian Parliament, for example, was set to pass a statute in 1995 bearing the imprint of European guidelines requiring that private channels give at least 20 per cent of airtime to Hungarian-made programmes and a total of at least 51 per cent to European productions. Initially, those rules covered cable as well. Not for long. Lobbyists from Warner, MTV, CNN and other US cable interests, along with Jack Valenti, president of the Motion Picture Association of America, launched an aggressive campaign to repeal the quotas. The US Commerce Department, according to several MPs involved in the negotiations at the time, made clear its support for the companies' position. Mark Schapiro concluded: 'For new members, the admission ticket into the OECD and its capitalist markets is free trade in all products, including entertainment ... By the time the new media law was enacted, restrictions against cross-ownership of production and delivery systems were also removed.'[16]

Around the turn of the century the trade in audiovisual services between the European Union and the USA was running at a deficit of more than $6 billion, while British exports to the United States had reached $550 million, and those of the other member states of the European Union only $156 million.[17]

In an article in the *Washington Post*, Mikhail Gorbachev, the last president of the former Soviet Union, asked some serious questions about uneven power relations in the world:

> For while America's role is acknowledged throughout the world, her claim to hegemony, not to say domination, is not similarly recognized. For this reason, I hope, Mr. Bush, as the new American president, that you will give up any illusion that the 21st century can, or even should, be the 'American Century'. Globalization is a given – but 'American globalization' would be a mistake. In fact, it would be something devoid of meaning and even dangerous.

The headline of his article was unambiguous: 'Mr. Bush, the World Doesn't Want to be American.'[18]

In Chapter 6 I make some proposals for a better cultural balance in the world, and will also discuss the concept of globalization in the fields of the arts, culture and entertainment, because there is not just one form of globalization!

SECOND-TIER CORPORATIONS

Besides the handful of huge transnational cultural conglomerates, in some larger countries there are cultural industries that dominate the national and sometimes regional market, and that also export to a considerable number of other countries, usually in the same language area. Several of these second-tier corporations around the global media market have extensive ties and joint ventures with the largest transnational corporations, as well as with Wall Street investment banks. The roster of second-tier media firms from North America includes Dow Jones, Gannett, Knight-Ridder, Hearst and Advance Publications, and among those from Europe are the Kirch Group, Havas, Hachette, Prisa, Canal Plus, Pearson, Reuters and Reed Elsevier.[19] There is also Berlusconi's Mediaset and the Dutch corporation Endemol, which invented *Big Brother*.

Two giant second-tier cultural corporations can be found in Latin America: Globo (Brazil), and Televisa (Mexico). Both have practically monopolistic control over their national markets, as well as enormous political power in the selection and even removal of national leaders (Fox 1994: 4). Televisa controls around 95 per cent of its home market. One of the characteristics of its huge production of *telenovelas*, television films and shows is that it is fast and dirty. Speed and quantity overrule quality.[20] By contrast, Globo is known for its high-standard and high-quality *telenovelas* (*Padråo de qualidade Globo*), which find mass audiences in more than a hundred countries. In 1999 the conglomerate ranked fourteenth in the Global 50 list of the world's top media and entertainment companies compiled by *Variety*, and generated $4.9 billion in revenues.[21]

With around 800 films a year, India is by far the world's biggest producer of films. In 1997 foreign ticket sales were only $90 million; however, in 1999 they amounted to $350 million, and it was estimated that this figure would rise to $3.4 billion by 2005.[22] Meanwhile, the Indian government has decided to make earnings from the sale of entertainment abroad tax-free. The biggest-budget films cost about $5 million. The markets are the Arab countries and the Indian diaspora of more than 25 million people in Southeast Asia, East Africa, the United States and Europe. M. Madhava Prasad considers that the Hindi film is conceived as an assemblage of prefabricated parts, including the story, the dance, the song, the comedy scene and the lighting, in the film text as a whole. This is completely different from the Hollywood film, where the story 'is the point of departure of the production process and its transformation into a narrative film is the final goal of that process' (Prasad 2000: 43). India's most popular releases are love stories and films centred around large, extended families. India's family values may be more familiar to people in some parts of the world than the dysfunctional families often featured in American films.[23]

Less harmonious in the Indian film world is Bollywood itself. Since the Indian market was liberalized in 1991, the mafia has started to penetrate the always unstable world of film finance, with its excellent opportunities for laundering money made on the black market. In India the production and distribution of films are not so much in the hands of cultural corporations as controlled by a limited group of single producers and distributors. They, along with actors and directors, have become prey to – and sometimes perpetrators of – murder, extortion, blackmail, kidnapping and other forms of extreme violence. The different mafias are doing big business at any price. Several film producers have left Bombay hoping to find safe havens in fast modernizing cities in Bangalore and Madras in the south of India.[24]

Things Japanese have become immensely popular throughout East Asia, especially among young people, many of whom adore Japanese music, movies, television, animation, fashion and food, a fact that made an *International Herald Tribune* journalist visiting this part of the world wax lyrical. He observed that in South Korea Japanese-style cafés and teahouses are rapidly replacing American fast-food restaurants and European-style coffee houses; Japanese rock and jazz bands are more popular than their Korean counterparts; and many soap operas and television dramas are direct copies of Japanese programmes. In Hong Kong, newsstands cannot stock enough copies of Japanese comic books and fashion magazines. Japanese TV dramas have huge followings. In China, Singapore, Indonesia, the Philippines and Thailand, bootleg copies of recorded Japanese music and movies, and merchandise such as 'Hello Kitty' dolls are popular. The number of Asians studying Japanese has increased by 29 per cent in the past five years.[25] Among Japan's gifts to the world we may count karaoke (Lent 1995: 4).

The production of strip cartoons, which can be as thick as a telephone directory, magazines and other popular books is one the biggest industries in Japan. The largest cultural businesses are Gakken, Kôdansha, Shôgakkan and Shûeisha (Sakai 1987: 235). Karel van Wolveren notes that this mammoth industry takes care that Japanese people get their bread and circuses (Wolveren 1991: 293). Here too the mafia has penetrated. For instance, for years the Toei studios have had close relations with the Yamaguchi criminal syndicate and have produced hundreds of films in which the traditional 'morality' of gangsters has been glorified, as well as films with clear nationalistic tendencies dealing with the time of the Second World War and the postwar period.

The most successful record producer in Japanese history is Tetsuya Komura, who 'haunted Roppongi clubs to see what young women – his target audience – considered cool in fashion, hairstyles, make-up, and music; scoured data from karaoke on-line services to find out what tunes they liked to sing' (Schilling 1997: 101). Based on this knowledge he uses samples from thousands of rhythms and melodies to create his hits. Having conquered Japan, Komura made a deal with Rupert Murdoch's News Corporation to establish a joint venture called tk news for scouting, developing and promoting new Asian artists.

PRODUCTION AND DISTRIBUTION ON A MASS SCALE

Besides their far-reaching power to make all the decisions, the huge cultural industries leave other traces in the cultural landscape. One is the simple fact of their massive scale. The huge investments they make have to be earned back as quickly as possible. This means that as many people as possible should read, watch, listen to and use their cultural wares, notwithstanding the fact that they also serve some niche markets – though these, in fact, are never very small, and local parameters are taken into consideration in order to make these markets profitable. My main grievance, however, is with the mass scale on which cultural wares are produced and disseminated.

Having established this, it does not necessarily follow that cultural products produced, distributed and promoted on a mass scale are, for instance, bad, morally degrading or banal. At the same time, we cannot exclude from the picture the fact that the drive to conquer mass markets tends to lead to the lowest common denominator. I shall come back to this issue in Chapter 5. It is important to remember that the mass-scale domination of different cultural markets by definition limits the number of other attractions available. It becomes more difficult for people to find real alternatives.

Besides, it could be claimed that those alternatives do not cater to the taste of the majority of the population. An example may contradict this. Thirty or forty years ago, all over Europe, there were audiences for European films. The work of Bergman, Fellini and many others was distributed and seen widely in this part of the world. Nowadays it is seldom that a film made in Europe travels through Europe, and even distribution in the country in which it was made is far from simple. Are these contemporary films more 'difficult' than the films made thirty or forty years ago? It is unlikely. More plausible is the fact that the films made by the cultural conglomerates are so heavily promoted and widely distributed that they seem to be the only ones on offer.

In substantial parts of the world market there is no longer any place for films from smaller producers and distributors who lack the ability to keep on shouting that they too are offering something attractive. From a democratic perspective it is a considerable loss when there are no longer many decision-makers involved in artistic processes. The oligopolistic cultural conglomerates occupy the space that would otherwise be available for many different kinds of artistic work, produced, distributed and promoted by a rich variety of cultural entrepreneurs.

The mass character of the cultural conglomerates also means that their wares are produced and disseminated for consumers who remain outside the creative process. Nilanjana Gupta discusses the term 'mass', as in 'mass media'. She contends it has been used 'to designate the consumers for whom the culture is provided from a limited number of centres of cultural production, not the producers, who are few in number' (Gupta 1998: 36–7). This may seem to contradict, for instance, Camille Paglia's claim that the public votes for and influences culture through ratings and dollars's (Paglia 1992: ix). However, it is more acurate to say that ratings and dollars are the only remaining ways for people to express something about their likes and dislikes.

Basically, for most people in the world, cultural products originating from the big industries are made far away from their societies, and their fears, joys and inclinations. The ingredients for the 'right' receptive atmosphere are prepared elsewhere too. However, we may raise the question: do we need to have only cultural home-cooking? Of course not. What we need is many different cultural elements that contribute in one way or another towards building societies, for better or worse. They may work harmoniously or cause friction. They may flow over from 'distant' societies and cultures and add something special to what is going on in another society or they may make it more dull. Who knows?

In any case, 'mass culture' is a double-edged concept. Do we mean culture that originates from the masses of the people? Or are we referring to culture that is produced, distributed and promoted on a mass scale? The latter automatically leads to mass audiences who time and time again buy a ticket, record, poster or book. In Chapter 6 I argue that from a democratic perspective we should get rid of the oligopolistic control of the means of cultural production, distribution and promotion. However, we also know that many people love the products of these industries – and they are made to be loved – and see no problem in these ownership relations. So who cares?

The term 'mass culture', therefore, is not very helpful because it suggests a culture that originates from the mass of the people. Understandably, the industry promotes this connotation. Of course, it is true that in its products elements can be found that have a long history in, for instance, folk tales, or where reference is made to current events and desires. Similarly, this happens, and happened, in the cultural creations that have sometimes been called 'high' culture.

Some theories find an explanation in history for the observed reality that the masses are fascinated by liminal excess, as Mike Featherstone has put it. 'The popular tradition of carnivals, fairs and festivals provided symbolic inversions and transgressions of the official "civilized" culture and favoured excitement, uncontrolled emotions and the direct and vulgar grotesque bodily pleasures of fattening food, intoxicating drink and sexual promiscuity' (Featherstone 1991: 22ff.). Perhaps less publicly visible, but those phenomena were, and are, also not uncommon in the richer strata of Western society. The difference between the present and the past may be that these excesses are now taking place at least every weekend whereas, even a fairly short time ago, they occurred perhaps only once or twice a year.

We can agree with the observation that different cultures influence each other. However, it is one step too far to conclude that mass-produced, -distributed and -promoted culture is therefore the culture of the masses of the people. William Leach describes, in *Land of Desire. Merchants, Power, and the Rise of a New American Culture*, the construction of consumer capitalism in the United States in the nineteenth century. He discusses the claim made by economists that capitalist markets cannot perform unless they respond well to the 'real' needs and desires of consumers – or at least have their consent – in the entertainment field, as in other areas. The truth is, rather, he suggests,

[that] the culture of consumer capitalism may have been among the most nonconsensual public cultures ever created, and it was nonconsensual for two reasons. First, it was not produced by 'the people' but by commercial groups in cooperation with elites comfortable with and committed to making profits and to accumulating capital on an ever-ascending scale. Second, it was nonconsensual

because, in its mere day-to-day conduct (but not in any conspiratorial way), it raised to the fore only one vision of the good life and pushed out all others. In this way, it diminished American public life, denying the American people access to insight into other ways of organizing and conceiving life, insight that might have endowed their consent to the dominant culture (if such consent were to be given at all) with real democracy. (Leach 1993: xv)

Until now I have spoken mainly about the cultural products that come through the pipelines of the cultural conglomerates. We may wonder, however, whether decision-making processes in the broad field of the visual arts are as easily recognizable.

VISUAL ARTS MARKETS: AS NERVOUS AS THE STOCK MARKET

In the spheres of films, books and music we see more and more mergers, resulting in a concentration of power in the hands of fewer and fewer corporations. In the broadly defined domain of the visual arts market relations are different, at least at first glance. There are, for instance, many more than just five companies making about 80 per cent of the decisions relating to the creation and distribution of paintings, statutes, photos, design products, multimedia works and suchlike. The first impression is that there are quite a lot of decision-makers, and that the market is complex and open to all. According to estimates of the European Commission and Unesco, there are several hundred thousand visual artists living in Europe. The number for Europe as a whole and the United States may be a million.[26] Worldwide, the figure may be several millions.

Specifically in the fields of design and photography, some artists are employed but most are independent workers with no access to billions of buyers. The supply of contemporary art is almost limitless, and the whole notion of how to assess artistic value is full of uncertainties. In the various processes involved in the visual arts market, curators, brokers, collectors, gallery owners, state and regional authorities, consultants and many different kinds of managers all have their say. Works can be commissioned, or may be sold, for instance, in street markets, furniture shops, tourist spots or 'highly respected' galleries.

However, the multiplicity of works of art is not reflected in the outlets available; few artists sell well on the 'open' market or through the restricted range of galleries of contemporary art to be found in the Western world. In this sense one may compare the situation in the visual arts with music, literature, film and other, mixed-media artforms, where the number of artists is overwhelmingly large but where only a few will receive any public attention.

Raymonde Moulin describes the terrible dilemmas that face visual arts students who feel drawn to the artistic profession. They are encouraged into the illusion that originality is what counts, that their personal 'signature' is important, because this represents market value, while the reality is that hardly any of them will make it on to the market. 'Emphasis has been put on the originality of action, idea and charisma. The signature of the artist defines an effort or an object as artistic, and cements their irreplaceable character in a monopolistic and structured market' (Moulin 1992: 364).

The number of aspiring artists has been greatly increased by the despecialization of the visual arts métier, the absence of barriers for those trying to enter the artistic field, the prestige that goes with the artistic profession, and by the universally shared ideology of creativity. 'But the mechanisms dominating international artistic life, which emerge out of interactions of the artistic field and the market, allow only a small number of artists to filter through to lucrative careers, in order to preserve the scarcity and the price of art.' According to Raymonde Moulin, therefore, the visual arts market is monopolistic, and structured by the mechanisms dominating international artistic life. How do these filtering processes actually happen? In any case, research indicates that a tiny proportion of artists in all parts of the visual arts domain are receiving substantially more attention than all the others, and this division is becoming ever more skewed. On the other hand, there is not one recognizable international division or marketing department of a big conglomerate that does this extraordinary process of filtering in a market that turns over something like $17 billion worldwide.[27]

In the 1930s, Walter Benjamin thought that works of art would lose their aura because of the fast-developing processes of mechanical reproduction happening at that time (Benjamin 1963). Perhaps the opposite has proved to be true. Through the reproduction techniques now widely available some artists have become well known, even famous; and this contributes to the fact that their works, old and new alike, are making fabulous prices on the market. The aura has not diminished; on the contrary, it has increased in a market where the prices are volatile. As one gallery owner put it: 'Is there any intrinsic value? No. It's all fantasy. Prices can go to, for example, $40 million, or much more, and so what? Why not higher? Any amount of money can be justified' (Bolton 1998: 27). However, most artists don't make a penny from their work.

Economic globalization has increased this concentration on a few star artists.

The art market has been transformed by American and transnational capitalism. The age of junk bonds has also been the age of fame and fortune for artists living and dead. Wall Street has not been the only site of profiteering – the art capitals of the world have also witnessed unprecedented speculation. This traffic in art mirrors the fervent trading of the stock exchange; investment indexes for art continue to climb; contemporary works of art are discussed like real estate investments; gallery owners trade artists and make deals in the style of corporate raiders. (Bolton 1998: 24)

In the field of photography and many other kinds of images a dramatic development is taking place, which is also characteristic of today's economic globalization. The company Corbis, owned by Bill Gates, already controls 76 million images worldwide. Although only 2 million photographs have been digitally scanned for online access, the company is digitizing all of its current production, about 500 photographs a day. Corbis had a revenue of $150 million last year. 'This puts it well behind Getty Images Inc., a publicly traded company based in Seattle and controlled by Mark Getty, grandson of the oil magnate J. Paul Getty. With archives of 75 million images, the company earned last year $480 million.' But Corbis's expansion is closing the gap, according to the *International Herald Tribune*, which is monitoring the market.[28] Corbis and Getty are currently buying the rights to every image that may have or obtain a market value.

One of the important playing fields for transactions in the fine arts is that of the auction houses; Christie's and Sotheby's together boast 90 per cent of sales in the $4-billion-a-year auction world.[29] An example may make clear how economic globalization has changed the world of the auction houses. At the end of the 1990s, all Christie's jewellery departments worldwide started to work as a team. Together they consider which market can raise the best price for a particular item. In the case of a briolette the choice was Hong Kong. What happened? The briolette was estimated to be worth between $1.2 million and $1.5 million, but it zoomed to more than $2 million, paid by a private Hong Kong buyer against a Taiwanese private contender who, in turn, had defeated another Hong Kong buyer. Had the sale been in Geneva, Christie's would not have been able to communicate their enthusiasm to their Far Eastern clients who would probably not have travelled just to attend the sale. The 'one-team' method had won that day, the *International Herald Tribune* commented. 'In the auction arena at least, globalization is working at full blast.'[30]

Meanwhile, the two chiefs of Christie's and Sotheby's have admitted having had secret conversations and meetings in apartments, restaurants and limousines to discuss fixing the commissions paid by thousands of customers, dividing up rich clients and taking a host of other steps to stifle competition and pump up profits. At the same time, a third auction house has for some years been a major force, namely Phillips, which until 2002 was owned by one of the richest people in France, Bernard Arnault. He was in bitter competition with his rival, another extremely wealthy Frenchman, François Pinault, the owner of Christie's. Bernard Arnault is also the owner of the fashion, design, perfume, champagne and cognac group LVMH. François Pinault owns, among other enterprises, the chain of department stores Pinault Printemps Redoute. In 2002 Bernard Arnault withdrew from the competition, which had cost him too much money.[31]

In the commercial world to which the visual arts and design become linked, banks and galleries play major roles. Galleries used to get their purchases financed by banks, which until the mid-1990s provided loans without restraint. The galleries would then sell the works of art at the auction houses, which resulted, according to *Le Monde*, in a vicious circle. This situation has changed. The banks have cooled down, and the big money is coming from elsewhere. *Le Monde* suggests that this 'elsewhere' is, for instance, black-market drugs money whose source is in Columbia.[32] Even photography runs the risk of becoming the object of speculation, Michel Guerrin, writing in *Le Monde*, observes. In this field many of the players are young collectors who have made big money in the information sector and have a certain familiarity with images. His judgement is that the high prices fetched do not reflect the quality of the photos; mostly, what sell best are the most spectacular and immediately eye-catching images.[33]

We have seen that the auction houses constitute one key group of decision-makers in the process of filtering works of art and sending prices skyrocketing. Others are the collectors, the galleries, the corporations that buy art and the curators. The big collectors, who own several hundred works, build up important positions on the market while being discoverers, promoters, commissioners, buyers and sellers. In the art world, they represent power – as people who frequent artists' studios, as museum board members or trustees, or as patrons of major exhibitions. In Raymonde Moulin's assessment, their combined position as economic and cultural actors gives them the chance to intervene in all dimensions that concern the value of artists and their works, even ahead of, for instance, museum directors (Moulin 1992: 51–3).

Some art collectors are well known, such as Charles Saatchi (Stallabrass 1999: passim), or the Italian John-Christophe Pigozzi, who is said to have the largest collection of contemporary African art in the world (Oguibe and Enwezor 1999: 115). But there are also fabulous collections of paintings – in Japan, for instance, and Mexico – in the hands of unknown collectors who evade tax or who have bought works through the black market, with money made from the drugs trade. Thus, quite a few famous paintings have disappeared without trace after being bought at auction.

Richard Bolton remarks that 'establishing a value for a work of art helps to create control over the work, influencing how the work will function and who will see and own it'. From this position of control, he continues, 'the market can be manipulated deliberately. Important collectors can change the status of the work of artists merely by shuffling their collections' (Bolton 1998: 27–8). He describes how, in the highly speculative art market of the 1980s, the nature of collecting changed. 'Traditionally, collectors had behaved, well, like collectors, keeping a work for a generation or more. Today's collector often places the work back on the market as soon as profit is glimpsed. Paintings at times never leave the warehouse.' Some investors don't even pick up the pictures after the auction. 'In this atmosphere, twentieth-century art – even the work of emergent artists – has become a target for speculative acquisition' (p. 26).

The artist is the first to know his or her own work but the gallery owner knows what to do with this knowledge and has for the time being a monopoly on this information. The gallery owner can stock works for a while, hoping that prices may rise, or can create favourable conditions for speedy sales through recourse to a particular artist's 'aura' or by taking advantage of a current craze, or by suggesting that speculative purchases will soon multiply in value (Moulin 1992: 46). All of this is a normal part of the game. However, in an economically globalizing world, a few leading galleries are becoming even more inventive in their sales tactics.

For instance, a leading gallery – as Leo Castelli was for many years – is able to build up, at the international level, an important network of galleries, each operating within its own particular market. The leading gallery heads an informal coalition of traders, something like a closed shop, with the purpose of promoting an artistic movement or a certain artist (Moulin 1992 48–51; Klein 1993: 159, 226). Raymonde Moulin concedes that at any moment in an artistic struggle 'many different choices can be made'. However, because of their position in the market, the leading galleries contribute substantially to the process of deciding which artistic trends are dominant. Thus, choices are mediated 'through the conflicts between the major cultural and economic players who control the *input*, to use the language of economists' (Moulin 1992: 47). This is an example of a point made in the first chapter: that the arts are both a symbolic and an economic battlefield.

In this battlefield the big corporations, too, are major players. The arts have played an important role in marketing strategies since the beginning of the twentieth century, as Richard Bolton reminds us, and as William Leach (1993) has also described extensively. Artistic advances were incorporated into commodity design and advertising techniques. 'Such contributions to *style* were a vital part of the rationalization of production and consumption' (Bolton 1998: 29). Over the last few decades the artist has begun to serve as a member of the research and development team of consumer culture, as a leisure specialist, as an aesthetic technician picturing and prodding the sensual expectations of would-be consumers. Richard Bolton points out that advertisers use works of art in their marketing strategies: 'The public sees the artist as a powerful outsider, and the mythology of artistic withdrawal creates an illusion of nonconformity that will sell the product. Artists have thus become prime candidates to endorse any number of commodities: the advertisement portrays art as the natural companion of mink coats, makeup, and real estate' (p. 36).

However, companies also collect art on a bigger scale than ever before. It is estimated that over 60 per cent of all Fortune 500 corporations do this. Most company-owned collections are composed of contemporary work, which is less expensive and easier to obtain than other art, and these collections are also investments and expected to appreciate in value. Apinan Poshyananda describes how this process started in Thailand at the beginning of the 1990s:

> Corporate patronage began to make its presence felt as the Thai Investment and Securities Co. Ltd, the Bangkok Bank, the Thai Farmers Bank, the Bank of Thailand and several companies staged art contests and sponsored art exhibitions. Businessmen began to purchase and commission art works. Mainstream art became associated with bank art because of the rapid fame that could be achieved by winners of these competitions. For many artists this meant stardom rather than starvation. They did not care if their products were criticized as stagnant and repetitive as long as they had a market. (Poshyananda 1992: 99)

There are a number of reasons why companies collect works of art. The American Business Committee for the Arts (BCA) offers the answer that it 'increases sales, attracts employees, enhances relations with employees, broadens public awareness of business, and in some instances, increases property values' (Bolton 1998: 29). Corporations also like to sponsor exhibitions, specifically concerning issues and ideas that complement their activities. Thus, Mobil contributed to an exhibition of Maori art when it was opening a new plant in New Zealand. It also decided to fund the Islamic galleries at the Metropolitan Museum in New York, as well as the exhibit *Unity in Islamic Art*; the corporation calls this 'affinity-of-purpose marketing'. United Technologies, among other things a well-known weapons manufacturer, concentrates on sponsoring the arts in Europe, Australia and other places where there are strong disarmament movements (p. 31).

In Argentina, Jorge Glusberg is the owner of one of the largest lighting companies, which gives him the resources to finance the activities of several artists, united in the *Grupo de los 13*, and the extremely influential Centro de Arte y de Comunicación (CAYC) in Buenos Aires. During the dictatorship period he had excellent relations with the military government. His exhibitions abroad were officially promoted while, at the same time, many artists were being tortured, killed or forced to leave the country as refugees. Néstor García Canclini remarks that Jorge Glusberg is a master when it comes to feeling which way the wind is blowing politically. In December 1993, one week after the collapse of military rule, he organized the *Sessions for Democracy* in the CAYC and in other Buenos Aires galleries (Mosquera 1995: 43–5).

One of the ideas in the background when corporations choose to do something concerning the arts is that the arts are associated with freedom. William Blount, of the BCA, made this link more explicit in a speech entitled 'The Arts and Business: Partners in Freedom'. Art and commerce each require as much freedom as possible to survive, according to him. There used to be artists who saw communism and socialism as the wave of the future. There were also businessmen who saw government as an ally of business and commerce. 'Time and experience have changed both perceptions. Are we, businessmen, instruments of the federal government? No, not willingly. We fight against it. So do the artists.' Thus, he concludes: 'We depend on an environment of freedom to flourish and prosper' (Bolton 1998: 30).

In the first chapter I expressed doubt about whether the arts should be concerned only with freedom, or free expression, and this is a question I return to throughout the book. Equally, it is an illusion that the arts are, or should be, mainly associated with comfort, or with making life more comfortable. In this connection, Richard Bolton is worried about the involvement of corporations with the arts. One of his main arguments is that a public realm has been brought under corporate control. 'Conservatism has extensively restructured cultural production. The corporation that performs as a good citizen doesn't really donate its capital, it *invests* it, developing a corporate culture and extending business's reach into all walks of life' (Bolton 1998: 28). This is one of the themes of Chapter 5.

The ways in which economic globalization is changing the general culture that surrounds the arts have a specific influence on the profession of curator and on the character of exhibitions. Until recently, curators functioned as arbiters of taste and quality, and in this sense they were educators. Reesa Greenberg notes that the authority of this arbiter role 'derives from an absolute – ultimately ideological – set of criteria grounded in the restrictive parameters of the canon of Western (i.e. First World) Modernism/Post-Modernism'. She describes the way in which, for instance, the task of art curators consisted of judging the quality of one picture against another, or of one artist versus another, according to the conventions of rupture and formal experimentation established by the European and North American avant-garde movements. 'The results, as we know, often resembled a league championship of winners and losers.' Of particular interest is her argument that winning or losing has become more and more dependent on a configuration of subtleties that are difficult to explain. 'More than art critics or gallery dealers, curators establish the meaning and status of contemporary art through its acquisition, exhibition and interpretation' (Greenberg 1996: 22–3; see also Moulin 2000: 22–3).

With the proliferation of exhibitions and art collections around the world, the art curator's role as arbiter has been gradually replaced by that of cultural mediator, for which Reesa Greenberg prefers to use the term 'broker'. We might also say that the curator functions these days as a pressure cooker of conflicting interests. Let's try to imagine the various interests that present themselves at the door of contemporary modern art museums. Leading galleries and art dealers want to see the work they represent shown extensively, since this may enhance the status and monetary value of the work. Collectors and corporations may get into the limelight through exhibitions in the major museums, which is not a bad thing for them economically. As everyone knows, the idea of a single canon is unfashionable. So, artists from all over the world should be exhibited; but who will be selected? In making their choices, curators – as brokers – have to take account of the views of specialists of various kinds, galleries and collectors and, in many European countries, public authorities, who all have vested interests. A further question, raised for instance by Hans Belting, is whether art from other cultures has been represented in ways that make sense when shown in Western institutions and hence are transplanted into Western cultures (in Scheps et al. 2000: 325).

'Curatorial function is, thus, inherently restricted by the larger or more powerful groups and constituencies,' Reesa Greenberg concludes. 'To pretend that any type of alternative field of action exists outside the web of market or institutionally dominated interests is fallacy.' It seems fair to say that most of these groups and constituencies are Western-oriented and work according to the basic principles noted above. There may be many artists, but few are selected.

Another major change has been described by Robert Hewison who noted that in the nineteenth century museums were seen as sources of education and improvement, whereas now they are treated as financial institutions that must pay their way (Webster 1995: 117). The Museum of Modern Art (Moma) in New York attracted 1.9 million visitors in 1999 and had a target of 2.5 million. The financial capital of the museum is $420 million.[34] In this context it is worth reintroducing the concept of the canon. After all, such huge public exposure is bound to involve standard-building. The Guggenheim museum is doing the same by establishing annexes, in Las Vegas, Bilbao and Berlin, among other cities. The architectural tour de force in Bilbao helps to give its mediocre collection more fame than it deserves (Hoffmann 1999).

Frank Webster observes that there is, of course, a grey area between making exhibitions accessible and trivializing artistic and cultural works.

> Many commentators, however, believe that the boundaries have been crossed, and here they point to the paradox of a boom in commercial museums alongside ongoing crises in state-supported institutions ... [Furthermore,] the paradox is resolved when these ventures are seen as expressions of the *leisure industry*, 'museums' which offer easily-digested and unchallenging *nostalgia* in a Disney style of elaborate sound effects, eye-catching scenery, quick changes of attractions, video games, animatronic dinosaurs, re-created smells and symbols, and above all 'participation' for the paying customers who are urged to 'enjoy' and have 'fun'. (Webster 1995: 120)

Let's be clear: there are hundreds of thousands of artists who work outside the circuits described here. I will speak about these in Chapter 4, which deals with local artistic cultures. But they are not the ones producing the artistic creations that have gained public notoriety. This does not mean that the work of the few 'chosen' artists, the price of which is soaring, is worthless – aesthetically or otherwise. Of course not; maybe it is, maybe it isn't. The matter is irrelevant when compared with the fact that in the world of the visual arts and design there are mechanisms working to create rarity – in this case of fame and reputation – through which enormous economic value and status can be obtained.

In the visual arts these mechanisms are not to be found in single institutions, unlike in the realms of film, literature and music where cultural conglomerates hold sway. It is more the principle of the stock market that dominates the world of the visual arts. There are several powerful parties involved in establishing values. They watch each other carefully, from minute to minute. In this nervous process, certain stocks are all of a sudden 'overvalued' or 'undervalued', or all stocks suddenly start falling or rising. Based on – what? Guesses, fear, optimism; in any case, fragmented information. Cultural prestige and economic values become intermingled. Important collectors, corporations, leading galleries, respected curators, banks, auction houses, black-market money-dealers and sometimes artists too are participants in the game, which is all about fame and money. Anyone who follows aesthetic debates only may miss the fact that aesthetic preferences are, in large part, the outcome of underlying power structures and selection mechanisms.

AFTER THE MAGNETIC TELEGRAPH

The internet and digitalization have started to penetrate all fields of artistic creation, production, distribution, promotion and reception. In Chapter 4 we will see artists using those tools while freeing themselves from the pressure of the oligopolistic structures that have been discussed above. Here, first, I will explore the myths surrounding the new communication technologies. After that, we must face the reality that the cultural conglomerates operating worldwide have taken over large chunks of the new technologies which, up until 1995, had promised a new era of democracy and freedom in human communication.

Several apparently absurd questions must be raised in connection with the new communication media. Reading *Walden* by Henry David Thoreau one may feel challenged, for instance, to reflect on why there is such a hullabaloo about the information superhighway. He comments: 'We are in great haste to construct a magnetic telegraph from Maine to Texas; but Maine and Texas, it may be, have nothing important to communicate' (Postman 1987: 66). His scepticism about the need for 'great haste' could be applied to the internet and digitalization.

Riccardo Petrella touches upon another problem that likewise has bizarre dimensions. He calls it obscene to construct 'superhighways of information' costing billions of dollars while 1.4 billion people have no fresh water to drink. His advice is first to construct water pipelines everywhere in the world. Afterwards, he says, it would be wise to create an information network of small roads, countryside tracks and squares where people can meet each other.[35] The statements of Thoreau and Petrella help us realize that the value of the new communication media is not self-evident.

Another question that should be addressed is whether we live in the kind of societies that should be named 'information societies'. James Billington, the librarian of the American Library of Congress, feels there is good reason to relativize this issue as well. He calls it significant that we speak about the Information Age, not about the Knowledge Age. To reach the stage of knowledge more is needed than roaming around endless quantities of information. 'Raw data can be turned into information, which then, through much added effort and value, can rise to the level of knowledge, which is the foundation for wisdom.' According to Billington, this wisdom does not come into being enough. 'Our society is basically motion without memory.'[36]

Nor is the concept of 'network societies' a very helpful description. What else were the colonial powers if not network societies, for instance? How otherwise did they maintain their domination over distant territories? Apparently, the character of the media, which are pouring out information worldwide, is less important than who dominates those media and what kind of information is distributed.

The concept of 'virtuality' has often been used to characterize the new communication media. However, we may wonder how virtual those digital media are, knowing that they consist of very material satellites, cables, disks and computers, which are physically programmed or controlled, mostly by high earners, and are embedded in the framework of actually existing enterprises. Virtual reality is also not the right concept to indicate the billions of dollars that have been invested in the information superhighway, all the gadgetry associated with it, not to mention human resources.

Recognizing the myths surrounding the new communication media, we must also acknowledge that vast changes are taking place, influenced by the new communication technologies; changes in the character of global capitalism as well as in the circumstances of production and distribution for artists, which is one of the issues this book is concerned with. Manuel Castells points out that the different forms of communication are integrated in an interactive network, producing Super-Text and Meta-Language, 'that, for the first time in history, integrates into the same system the written, oral, and audiovisual modalities of human communication'. This changes fundamentally the character of the communication. 'Because culture is mediated and enacted through communication, cultures themselves, that is our historically produced systems of beliefs and codes, become fundamentally transformed, and will be more so over time, by the new technological system' (Castells 1996: 328).

Manuel Castells is concerned about the context in which these innovative technological developments are taking place. He observes that a renovated and more brutal capitalism is now evident that promotes flexibility, gives management considerably more power than workers, puts pressure on everybody by competition, and forgets about non-profitable parts of the world. Today's capitalism is essentially different from its predecessors and is based on the convergence of information, productive innovation and technology. 'Both culture and technology depend on the ability of knowledge and information to act upon knowledge and information, in a recurrent network of globally connected exchanges' (Castells 1998: 338–9).

According to Castells, power still governs societies but it 'is diffused in global networks of wealth, information and images which circulate and transmute in a system of variable geometry and dematerialized geography' (Castells 1997: 359). However, isn't it time to put a question mark against all this? Castells suggests that when power is 'diffused' in a 'dematerialized geography', it can no longer be located. I would say that he is right, that information and capital now move at lightning speed through the world, and are difficult to trace, but it has always been difficult to investigate where power resides. Nevertheless, it should be possible to control and regulate these streams of information and entertainment quite effectively; Robert Went observes that the new technologies make it even easier, for instance, to trace financial transactions and to register them (Went 1996: 57). Whether this is done or not depends on the political will.

Then we arrive at the controversy over whether the digital field enlarges space for creativity, freedom and democracy or whether it is mainly the playing field of commerce and military affairs. Andrew Shapiro wonders why in progressive circles there is such scepticism about the potential of the new communication media. He claims that, already, the diversity of cyberspace is a bracing alternative to the conformity of the media. 'Artists are showing their work in virtual galleries. Musicians are uploading their compositions for others to hear. As bandwidth expands and technologies improve, internet *auteurs* might even go head-to-head with the Disneys of the world – creating a wide-open market for cheap video distribution.'[37] The new communication media offer excellent tools for the improvement of intercultural and intracultural communication. The digital domain also stimulates more progressive thought. Rigid structures of thinking may obtain greater openness and flexibility by the use of digital procedures.

Edward Herman and Robert W. McChesney claim that the internet combines several possibilities that did not exist before.

> The relevant media analogy for the internet, then, is not that of broadcasting with its limited number of channels, but, rather, that of magazine or book publishing. Assuming no explicit state censorship, anyone can produce a publication, but the right to do so means little without distribution, resources and publicity. At the same time, it is important to note that the Internet permits people who want it global access to the entirety of the 'marginal' online websites. This is a radical difference from the magazine or book publishing analogy. (Herman and McChesney 1997: 124–5)

In view of these expanded opportunities, the authors express the hope that the internet will remain a vital tool for political organizing; and I would like to add to this, for a broad range of diverse artistic creations, which may find many different digital outlets. Herman and McChesney maintain their enthusiasm for the internet, 'even if its dominant trajectory is as a commercially driven entertainment vehicle'.

They are right, indeed, to make this reservation. The hundreds of billions of dollars already invested in all aspects of the digital domain and the foreseen expenditure are so enormous (Schiller 1999: 60) that one must fear there will be limited (cyber)space left for the enhancement of, for instance, democratic communication, which is not commercial or fun-oriented. The late 1980s and early 1990s were breakthrough years in the revolution of technology, as Jerry Mander describes:

> Brand new compatibilities among global-scale technologies such as satellites, lasers, television, high-speed computation, advanced high-speed travel, instantaneous resource transfer, and others 'popped' communications capabilities into a global dimension. This made it possible, and inevitable, for corporate powers to rapidly accelerate their expansion beyond national boundaries. In fact, corporate form and

technological form *coevolved* in a symbiotic relationship; the corporations pushed the technologies that, in turn, made it possible for the corporations to become *primary* international players, beyond the control of the sovereign states that had spawned them. It was the technology that made it possible for central corporate management in one locale to have instantaneous contact with and control of its hundreds of distant parts throughout the world. (Mander 1993: 14)

Consequently, the actual development of new communication technologies has placed many obstacles on the road to worthwhile local democratic life, including in the fields of the arts and culture.

By 1990, the technology was in place to map all the world's land and sea resources from space. And the new merger of computer, laser, and satellite technologies combined the possibility to produce instantaneous worldwide corporate communication, capital transfer and resource control. Meanwhile, the globalization of television transmission via satellite and the ubiquitousness of advertising enabled Western industrial corporations to spread commodity culture and Western material values everywhere, even to nondeveloped countries that had no roads. This led in turn to rapid global homogenization of cultures within a Western economic paradigm ... The notions of *local economy* and *local control* became anomalous and increasingly impossible. (Mander 1993: 15)

What matters, therefore – and I repeat the point already raised in this chapter – is who controls the multiple lines of communication.[38] Who is able to catch the eye of the person searching the Net? Advertisers, for instance, are prepared to pay the owners of webportals thousands of dollars for one search word. American Online has exclusive contracts with advertisers amounting to hundreds of millions of dollars a year (Hamelink 1999: 150–1). The relatively short economic crisis at the beginning of the twenty-first century may have cut back those prices somewhat, but not for ever.

Around 1995 the internet shifted from being a participatory medium that served the interests of the public to a medium through which corporations deliver consumer-oriented information. Robert McChesney expresses regret:

Perhaps the most striking change in the late 1990s is how quickly the euphoria of those who saw the Internet as providing a qualitatively different and egalitarian type of journalism, politics, media and culture has faded. The indications are that the substantive content of this commercial media in the Internet, or any subsequent digital communication system, will look much like what currently exists. Indeed, advertisers and commercialism arguably have more influence over Internet content than anywhere else. Advertisers and media firms both aspire to make the Internet look more and more like commercial television, as that is a proven winner commercially. (McChesney 1997: 33–4)

At the end of the 1990s, the WTO agreed to open basic telecommunications markets within some seventy countries, accounting for 94 per cent of world telecommunications markets – around $600 billion in overall annual revenue – and just half of the world's population (Schiller 1999: 47).

The 1996 United States Telecommunication Act has consolidated the commercializing tendencies by allowing a single enterprise to possess many radio and television stations at the same time as being active in all imaginable, or even not-yet-imaginable, media. This concentration of ownership is contrary to the democratic need for diversity, particularly in decision-making in the fields of knowledge, information and creativity. During the debates on the Telecommunication Act this question was hardly raised in the news, while the V-chip – designed to exclude violence from the living room – was mentioned 1,391 times in the first six months of 1996. 'It comes as no surprise that the culture trust devotes little energy to analysing itself,' Todd Gitlin (1997: 10) concluded. 'I have never seen anything like the Telecommunications Bill,' Robert McChesney quotes a career lobbyist as saying. 'The silence of public debate is deafening. A bill with such astonishing impact on all of us is not even being discussed' (McChesney 1997: 43).

Patricia Aufderheide thinks that 'our middle-range communications future will probably be one of a rather small number of huge, complex corporations, wielding international clout, and making alliances of convenience with each other. Think of it as chaos theory meets oligopoly. This makes a powerful case for the continued role of regulation in maintaining and managing competition' (Aufderheide 1997: 160–1). However, for reasons of competition other countries may follow the example of the United States in giving unlimited power to monopolistic communication enterprises.

A striking example of the internet changing from public domain to a space representing private interests can be seen in the challenge made by Edwin Artzt, the chief executive of Procter & Gamble, to the American Association of Advertising Agencies in 1994 when he declared: '[We have] to grab technology in our teeth again and make it work for us.' How can this be done? 'We can use interactive technology to engage consumers in our commercials. We can provide direct consumer response. If a consumer wants to know which Cover Girl nail polish matches the lipstick she saw in our commercial, we can tell her on the spot' (Schiller 1999: 116–17). Brand-building has been considered most effective when consumerism and entertainment have been experienced at one and the same time (Baran 1998: 132; Herman and McChesney 1997: 124–5; Klein 2000; McChesney 1997: 33–4).

Artists contribute substantially to these commercially-oriented processes, precisely by the creativity and craftsmanship they can deliver. After all, they are the experts and the producers of the cultural ambiences, codes and images that make it so difficult to understand what processes are going on in our world. They produce 'infotainment', the news packaged as a show. They create the conditions in which people feel 'non-stop' well-being and pleasure. As actors they perform the thousands of murders that are presented as fun and which children see from a very early age. They design, for instance, the annual report of Nike, which does not tell us that 'the entire Indonesian operation that employs 30,000 women costs Nike less than when it pays Michael Jordan for his endorsement of the brand, some $20 million' (Miyoshi 1998: 257). And artists create the interfaces, contents and surroundings of the digital domain, for business and entertainment.

Advanced branding consists of nudging the host culture into the background and making the brand the star, as Naomi Klein has described. She reminds us that

> many artists, media personalities, film directors and sports stars have been racing to meet the corporations halfway in the branding game. Michael Jordan, Puff Daddy, Martha Stewart, Austin Powers, Brandy and *Star Wars* now mirror the corporate structure of corporations like Nike and the Gap, and they are just as captivated by the prospect of developing and leveraging their own branding potential as the product-based manufacturers. So what was once a process of selling culture to a sponsor for a price has been supplanted by the logic of 'co-branding' – a fluid partnership between celebrity people and celebrity brands. (Klein 2000: 30)

Where big interests are at stake, the terminology of war has been used as the normal way of expressing that competition is fierce, in the digital domain as elsewhere. Listen, for instance, to journalist Elisabeth Bumiller reporting on the battle going on between Amazon.com and Barnesandnoble.com:

> Here is a great war story. On one side is Amazon.com Inc., the giant on-line bookseller (market value: $5.5 billion), led by its 35-year-old Seattle-based founder, Jeffrey Bezos. On the other side is Barnesandnoble.com Inc., the small but aggressive No. 2 with the brand name and a very rich partner (Bertelsmann AG), led by our subject today, Jonathan Bulkeley. Mr Bulkeley, 38, who started America Online's British operation, was hired last month in an attempt to make Mr Bezos as miserable as possible.

Her report from the 'war front' continues thus: 'Thomas Middelhoff, the Bertelsmann chief executive who hired him – and invested $300 million for a 50 per cent stake in Barnesandnoble.com – said Monday that Mr Bulkeley "was the answer to Jeff Bezos". Mr Bulkeley: "We're motivated. We've got a killer team."'[39]

In global neoliberal hands digital domains and the internet have become nervous playing grounds. Let's go back, for example, to 1994. In that year leaders of the big European communication industries presented a report to their governments and to the European Commission that said that in the digital field there was only one choice: be a winner in the information society or lose heavily. Anyone who does not dictate the course of events will be confronted with a disastrous decline in investments and reduction in employment.[40]

Try to imagine industrial leaders from rich Europe preaching doom and disaster when the battle around the internet is lost. Try to imagine what the situation will be for countries very much poorer than those in the European Union, confronted with this heavy competition for dominance over the information superhighway. Manuel Castells calls the resulting inequality 'alarming' (Castells 1996: 34). Effective entry to the new communication technologies has apparently been reserved only for a small minority of the world's population. This also means that these media are scarcely available, if at all, to artists from non-Western countries.

Around the turn of the century, not only did Nasdaq, the stock market for the digital world, lose significantly after the bubble profits of a couple of years before; the whole digital building collapsed. For instance, Pop.com, a site from Steven Spielberg's DreamWorks, Image Entertainment, and Paul Allen, co-founder of Microsoft, closed their doors in September 2000, after an entire year without a trace of a film. Walt Disney decided to shut down its Go.com internet enterprise, which cost between $500 and $750 million.[41] The alliance between Silicon Valley and Hollywood had ended in a great misunderstanding, the French newspaper *Le Monde* concluded.[42]

Through large-scale mergers cultural conglomerates are established that seem to be taking over the internet, but they try to keep afloat in troubled water, which is not virtual at all! In such uncertain times, when the stakes are extremely high, cultural conglomerates think they have one powerful tool that keeps them going. This is copyright. As Conrad Mewton put it, for instance, concerning music: 'Owning copyright has always been the surest way of making money in the music industry, and content is ever more valuable in the online marketplace' (Mewton 2001: 75). But for how long will this remain the case? And why do artists imagine they have a shared interest with the cultural industries in defending the concept and practice of copyright? These questions will be discussed in the next chapter. The conclusion of the analysis may be that it is perhaps time to get rid of the idea and the reality of copyright. It may be that the abolition of copyright would benefit artists, Third World countries and the public domain alike. This an issue to be addressed in the Chapter 6.

NOTES

1. Pierre Musso, 'Vivendi-Universal: l'Amérique gagnante', *Le Monde*, 8 December 2000.

2. 'Big Media Firms, Puny Results. For Investors and Consumers the Benefits are Still Hard to See', *International Herald Tribune*, 16–17 December 2000.

3. Marc Crispin Miller, 'Who Controls the Music?', *The Nation*, 25 August–1 September 1997.

4. 'Tailoring Film and TV for the World', *International Herald Tribune*, 2 October 1997.

5. 'The Matrix, Where Films and Games Meet', *International Herald Tribune*, 21 February 2003.

6. 'Record Year at the Box Office, but No Sensations', *International Herald Tribune*, 6–7 January 2001.

7. 'Movie Screens Multiply Across Western Europe', *International Herald Tribune*, 28 January 2000.

8. 'L'exceptionelle part de marché des films américains', *Le Monde*, 27 December 2000.

9. 'Pathé wil enkel geloven in films uit Amerika', *De Volkskrant*, 2 November 2000.

10. 'Le cinéma chinois étouffée entre Hollywood et la bureaucratie. En Chine, la production cinématographique est en chute libre et le public se tourne massivement vers les films américains', *Le Monde*, 5 September 2001.

11. 'André Schiffin contre la censure du marché', *Le Monde*, 7 May 1999. See also: Crispin Miller (1997: 119); Marc Crispin Miller, 'The Crushing Power of Big Publishing', *The Nation*, 17 March 1997; David Sarasohn, 'Powell's Bookstore Has a Mission in Social Responsibility and Fighting Censorship', *The Nation*, 17 March 1997. Powell's bookstore is in Portland, Oregan.

12. Crispin Miller, 'The Crushing Power of Big Publishing'.

13. 'Book Price War Ends as Big Discounts Fade. Net Retailers Capitulate and Pursue Profit', *International Herald Tribune*, 10 October 2000.

14. Ibid.

15. Irving Kristol, 'The Emerging American Imperium', *Wall Street Journal*, 18 August 1997.

16. Mark Schapiro, 'When Communism Crashed, HBO Wrote the Rules', *The Nation*, 29 November 1999.

17. 'Les Etats-Unis renforcent leur domination sur l'audiovisuel européen', *Le Monde*, 7 September 2000.

18. Mikhail Gorbachev, 'Mr. Bush, the World Doesn't Want to be American', *International Herald Tribune*, 30–31 December–1 January 2001.

19. Robert McChesney, 'The New Global Media. It's a Small World of Big Conglomerates', *The Nation*, 29 November 1999.

20. 'L'empire mexicain de Televisa', *Le Monde*, 21–22 July 1996.

21. Bill Hinchberger, 'Brazil's Media Powerhouse Seeks New Life in Latin America', *The Nation*, 29 November 1999.

22. 'Hollywood in Bombay', *De Volkskrant*, 13 December 2000.

23. 'Indian Movies Speak to a Global Audience' and 'Financing Films on a Personal Basis', *International Herald Tribune*, 20 October 2000.

24. 'Blaffers in Bollywood', *NRC Handelsblad*, 27 June 1998.

25. 'Japanese Culture Sweeps East Asia. Music and Fashion Captivate Youth', *International Herald Tribune*, 7 December 1999.

26. Artprice.com, July 2000.

27. Ibid.

28. 'When Art, Business and Digital Rights Collide. Corbis and Photographers Try to Hash Out a Contract', *International Herald Tribune*, 29 January 2001.

29. 'Breakthrough in Art-Auction Probe', *International Herald Tribune*, 9 October 2000.

30. 'Christie's Global Policy Pays. One-Team Approach Brings Gems to Buyers', *International Herald Tribune*, 21–22 August 1999.

31. 'Is LVMH Rethinking Its Strategy?', *International Herald Tribune*, 21 February 2002.

32. 'Voyage à New York chez les deux colosses du marché de l'art', *Le Monde*, 23 November 1999.

33. 'La photographie au risque de la spéculation', *Le Monde*, 20 November 1999.

34. 'Achter de schermen van het Moma', *NRC Handelsblad*, 22 December 2000.

35. Interview by Joost Smiers, May 1995.

36. 'Is the Information Age Making Us Any Wiser?', *International Herald Tribune*, 16 March 1999.

37. Andrew L. Shapiro, 'New Voices in Cyberspace', *The Nation*, 8 June 1998.

38. See, among others: Bagdikian, 'Lords of the Global Village', *The Nation*, 12 June 1989; Barber (1996); Daly et al. (1994); Hamelink (1994b); Jameson and Miyoshi (1998); McChesney (1997); McChesney et al. (1998); McPhail (1981); Petrella (1994); Ramonet (1997); Schiller (1976, 1989a). See also, 'Who Controls TV?', *The Nation*, 8 June 1998.

39. Elisabeth Bumiller, 'Buying Books On-Line Just Got Interesting', *International Herald Tribune*, 9 December 1998.

40. 'L'Europe et la société de l'information planétaire. Recommandation au Conseil Européen', Brussels, 26 May 1994.

41. 'Small World of Disney Gets Smaller', *International Herald Tribune*, 31 January 2001.

42. 'Le cinéma et Internet, ou l'échec de "Sillywood"', *Le Monde*, 24–25 December 2000.

THREE
Doubtful Originality

It would be good to see artists, in rich and poor countries alike, being remunerated fairly for their work. Many people still believe that copyright is one of the most important sources of an artist's income. In fact, copyright, which on the European continent is usually called authors' rights, is becoming one of the most valuable commercial products of the twenty-first century. This makes it unlikely that the system still actually protects the interests of the majority of musicians, composers, actors, dancers, writers, designers, visual artists and film-makers. The public domain is shrinking anyway, with the ongoing privatization of the creative and intellectual commons.

There are urgent reasons for trying to find other ways to ensure that artists can make a living from their work and that their creations and performances really get the respect they deserve. And we must realize once again that we hinder the social and cultural development of our societies when we continue to neglect the public domain of knowledge and creativity.

The information and cultural conglomerates embrace the whole world with waves and cables. Besides conveying business data, news and contracts, these superhighways serve as carriers of entertainment, which is partly a trade product in itself though most of the time it also acts as the stimulus for buying and consuming other products. Entertainment, or what we like to call the arts, has moved from the sidelines of society right into the middle of the so-called new economy. This is one of the reasons we are again seeing a rush of mergers in the cultural field, such as the one between AOL and Time Warner.

It does not make much sense to have oligopolistic control of nearly all the information pipelines of the world if you don't also own the 'content' to be delivered by the new technologies. Therefore, as Janine Jacquet says, content is king. Content holds value because many thousands of hours of music and miles of images and texts are needed to fill the pipelines. The best way to acquire rights on huge quantities of entertainment and other artistic materials is by merging. 'Synergy' is the rationale for media conglomerates snatching up as much copyrighted material as they can: 'Today's mergers aren't just about grabbing more of the market share by buying yet another record label or movie studio or book imprint. They're also about acquiring the rights to music, movies and books. It's an investment in intellectual capital, i.e. creative expression, the twenty-first century's most valuable commodity.'[1]

The consequence of these mergers is that in the near future just a handful of cultural conglomerates will 'own' most artistic creations from the past and the present. Anyone who has the intellectual property rights to artistic material wants to see it used, exhibited, performed, recorded and distributed as much as possible, through all available channels and in entertainment-related items such as computer games, gadgets, video jukeboxes and interactive media of all kinds.

> Entertainment corporations are increasingly attempting to gain the maximum revenue possible from exploiting the ownership of copyright; using the mass communications media available to place recordings across multiple sites, and lobbying for the licensing of ever more public spaces where music is being used (such as shops, clubs, restaurants, pubs, and hairdressing salons) and supporting the deployment of copyright inspectors to enforce these policies and prosecute outlets engaging in the unlicensed use of music. (Negus 1999: 13)

What happens is that we are pushed more or less into a closed circle. Most of the artistic creations from the past and the present are becoming the property of a limited number of cultural conglomerates, which try to present us, in one way or another, at any moment of the day, with the cultural content they own. TRIPs, the intellectual property treaty of the World Trade Organization, enables this intellectual land grab of buying copyrights to take place without restrictions or borders. *Our Creative Diversity*, the report of Unesco's and the United Nations' World Commission on Culture and Development, suggests that TRIPs 'has caused a subtle reorientation of copyright away from the author towards a trade-oriented perspective' (Pérez de Cuéllar 1996: 244).

The once sympathetic concept of copyright is turning into a means of control of the intellectual and creative commons by a very limited number of cultural industries. This is not just an abuse that can easily be repaired. The monopolistic control of copyright is a widespread practice. The Canadian anthropologist and copyright scholar Rosemary Coombe observes that 'in consumer cultures, most pictures, texts, motifs, labels, logos, trade names, designs, tunes, and even some colours and scents are governed, if not controlled, by regimes of intellectual property' (Coombe 1998: 6). Copyright has become a trade issue, Jessica Litman states: 'Copyright today is less about incentives or compensation than it is about control' (Litman 2001: 80).

The consequences of this monopolistic control are terrifying. The few remaining huge cultural industries pump through their channels only the artistic fare and entertainment to which they own the rights. They do this in a manner and on a scale that is commercially attractive to them, taking melodies and images from all over the world and adapting them for Western ears and eyes. Owning copyright gives them the opportunity to promote just a few 'stars', to invest heavily in them and to earn further fortunes from the gadgetry they create to surround these stars. Because investments and risks are high and the cultural industries seek multiple returns on their investments, marketing involves an aggressive targeting of every citizen in the world, as a result of which other cultural options are pushed off many people's mental map. The cultural industries own the means of production as well as the distribution channels of the cultural fare. This vertical integration is a further reason for alarm. The situation has become even more critical with the introduction of the American Digital Millennium Copyright Act. Actually, 'all appearance of works in computers – at home, on networks, at work, in the library – needs to be effected in conformance with, and with attention to, copyright rules', Jessica Litman explains. 'That's new. Until now, copyright has regulated multiplication and distribution of works, but it hasn't regulated consumption' (Litman 2001: 28).

The concentration on only a few 'stars' has the logical consequence that, worldwide, less attention is paid to a diversity of artistic expressions which, from a democratic perspective, we are desperately in need of, as discussed in Chapter 2. Stardom is a monolithic system that leaves no room even for the possibility that cultural diversity is a richness that should be cherished. The artist who is not famous – and in the present system most artists cannot be – has a hard time finding an audience. The kind of curiosity that seeks out new or obscure and unfamiliar artistic endeavours has found it hard to resist the dominant ideology, which claims that happiness comes from buying the latest gadgets associated with 'your' favourite star.

Whether we like it or not, the system of copyright, one of the purposes of which has been to provide a fair reward for artists, is rapidly being removed from artistic creation itself and being brought into the realm of big business. What we see too is the build-up of complete legal control over every artistic creation. The cultural conglomerates buy rights all over the place, surround them with extremely detailed property regulations, and hire highly specialized lawyers to defend their interests. The consequence is that every artist who has created or performed something has to take care that his or her work is not taken away by a cultural industry. So, as soon as they have created a piece of work, artists are obliged to ensure it is given the demonstrable status of an artistic work under the copyright regime.

The chance of a dispute arising over this property title is greater than ever. Therefore, even an 'average' artist, who is not famous, is more and more often obliged to hire lawyers to defend her or his case, something which obviously he or she cannot afford to do on the same scale as the industries. This tendency to seek legal recourse means that the intellectual and creative commons is less secure than may be desirable because the cultural world is becoming a place of private property rights and the domain of lawyers.

A striking example of this recourse to law is the artist Daniel Buren's claim on copyright for the fountains he designed for the monumental Place des Terreaux in Lyon.[2] He insists that everybody who takes a picture of the square should pay him copyright. But hasn't he already been paid for the design of the fountains? Probably generously! He has made a contribution to the square, to the cultural heritage of centuries, no more and no less. What has gone wrong in our society that artists like Daniel Buren have the nerve to claim rights to the whole square? In April 2001 a French court ruled that the challenged picture postcards show not only Daniel Buren's fountains but a square in which his fountains happen to be. Buren lost the case, and the concept of copyright has not been extended even further, in this case at least, in France.[3]

HUNT THE PIRATES?

There are several reasons for assuming that the system of copyright is near its end. We must think, for instance, of the piracy taking place at the industrial level and the piracy that 'democratizes' the use of music and other artistic materials through home-copying. The latter has become easier and cheaper since the introduction of MP3, Napster, Freenet, Gnutella and other systems, through which music from all over the world becomes available to every house with a computer.

Let's first discuss piracy at the industrial level. It is by owning copyright that the cultural industries make their fortune. However, we live in a world in which free enterprise is seen as highly desirable and control of commercial traffic and capital flows is negligible. This makes it understandable that piracy of all those copyrighted and profit-making works is tempting. Anyone trying to follow the debates on intellectual rights must get the impression that there is only one real issue that is spoiling a booming and socially and culturally useful business! This is piracy, which accounts for a turnover that actually exceeds $200 billion a year.[4]

Consequently, a war against piracy has started, on different levels, in the material and in the digital world as well. First, the USA has tried to get the European countries, mainly those in the European Union, on its side. This has not been too difficult because European film and television production industries share the same interests as American corporations. 'Furthermore, the fusion of European and US finance capital within the media sector puts European and US filmed entertainment companies directly into alliance, giving West European media capitalists a clear stake in an effective international intellectual property regime as well as in "legitimate" home-video markets.' A concentrated effort has been launched, according to Ronald Bettig, amounting to 'a combination of active pursuit of copyright protection by copyright owners, stricter laws and penalties against piracy, and more effective enforcement of these laws' (Bettig 1996: 216). There are three levels in the war against piracy: information, monitoring and sanctions.

Bonnie Richardson, spokesperson for the Motion Picture Association of America (MPAA), is delighted with the initiative of the United States Information Agency (USIA): 'The USIA has a number of programmes that are helpful in getting out the message about the need for protection of intellectual property. They sponsor the dialogues with countries that are looking at reviewing their intellectual property laws, giving the MPAA the chance to participate in the dialogue and get our views known.' In an interview in 1994 she cited the example of Russia, where breach of copyright is epidemic: 'The United States is trying to assist Russia. We as an industry have participated in a seminar, for instance, to help educate Russian prosecutors and law enforcement officials on how to identify pirated products.' In March 2001, the mayor of Moscow decided to close the Gorbouchka market, not far from the city centre, where every weekend 1,200 stalls offered all that can be imagined in the field of music production, video and information. It has been estimated that 5 million videocassettes and 3 million CDs were being sold every month.[5] A decision is one thing, Russian reality another. Moreover, people simply don't have the money to buy things at official prices.

When fighting piracy, the next stage is to know whether, where and by whom piracy takes place. 'US embassies are now routinely used to monitor the infringement of US trademarks – whether it is Marlboro in Algeria or Mickey Mouse in China' (Boyle 1996: 122). Inside the United States the FBI is active in this field, as Bruce Sterling suggests in his novel *The Hacker Crackdown*. He describes how someone illicitly copies a small piece of Apple's proprietary software: 'Apple called the FBI. The Bureau takes an interest in high-profile intellectual-property theft cases, industrial espionage, and theft of trade secrets. These were likely the right people to call' (Sterling 1992: 233). The FBI's and CIA's increased focus on piracy and industrial theft may be one of the reasons why they have not been spying on terrorists.

Outside the USA different kinds of spies are at work. 'Richard O'Neill, a former Green Beret who received a Silver Star and six Bronze Stars in the Vietnam War, now hunts video pirates in Korea on behalf of the Motion Picture Export

Association of America.' The Korean government, eager to increase its exports to the United States, permits this private American police operation (posing as a market survey) on its territory. O'Neill has also extended its operation to Thailand (Barnet and Cavanagh 1994: 142–3).

The purpose is, of course, to stop piracy. A whole range of other means must serve this purpose as well. The soft approach is the one used by several multi-nationals such as Disney, Paramount and Time Warner. Special software has been developed for them with which they search the internet. If an infringement is discovered they send a request to remove the copied material from the Net. Mostly this seems to be effective. If not, the infringer will be sued. The main interest is to fight large-scale infringements. They reason that minor cases will always continue to occur (Westenbrink 1996: 88).

There are also tougher approaches to fighting piracy. Countries may expect trade sanctions. James Boyle explains: 'The "Super 301 Regulations" of the United States Trade Act of 1988 establishes a "watch list" and a "priority watch list" for nations whose lack of intellectual property safeguards represents a signifi-cant trade barrier to US business' (Boyle 1996: 122). To avoid such trade sanc-tions countries must organize the repression internally. Richard Barnet and John Cavanagh give the example of Singapore, a small republic of malls and assembly plants, which is totally dependent on exports: 'Its authoritarian government has gone out of its way to cooperate with music giants by enacting a draconian copy-right law that provides for five-year jail sentences and $50,000 fines for possession of pirated tapes with intent to sell. Teenagers can earn up to $150 by acting as in-formants for the police' (Barnet and Cavanagh 1994: 142). In April 1998 alone, US authorities announced trade sanctions against Honduras for 'overt and unaccept-able' piracy of US videos and TV signals, prompted by complaints from recording and movie industry trade groups (Schiller 1999: 77–8). The obligation to hunt pirates will also cost most Third World countries more than they can afford.

A comparable measure of severe sanctions, affecting Trinidad, has been described by Krister Malm and Roger Wallis:

> Throughout the 1980s, music piracy was rife in Trinidad. The audio cassette market, even for calypso music, was dominated by street-corner pirates. Such cassettes often provided entertainment in taxis as well as in so-called maxi-taxis (minibuses) that constitute the better part of the Trinidad public transport system. Thus they also functioned as a form of promotion of the music and artists featured/pirated. In 1986, lobbying by the Copyright Organization of Trinidad and Tobago (COTT, formed in 1985) led the government to introduce fairly severe legal sanctions for cassette piracy. These include prison sentences of up to six months for the first offence and up to two years for any subsequent

offence. As a result, the most obvious forms of street-corner music piracy of calypso music have been wiped out. Cassette piracy has been limited to foreign music. Exceptions occur in the carnival season when local calypso and soca hits are likely to appear on 'top hit' sampler tapes featuring 'diverse artists'. (Malm and Wallis 1992: 67–8)

It is interesting to note that the sanctions seem to work better for local music than for foreign products.

Besides information, monitoring and sanctions there are other ways to try to prevent piracy. According to Ronald Bettig:

The filmed entertainment industry has also resorted to market strategies to capture Middle Eastern home-video markets for 'legitimate' distributors. These efforts include offering a video product with a superior visual image to that of pirated products, supplying a dubbed audio track on the prerecorded videocassette or Arabic subtitling, and releasing prerecorded videocassettes closer to the date of initial release in the United States. The same combination of government pressure and market-based strategies are being used throughout Asia to combat piracy. (Bettig 1996: 213)

Interviewed in April 1998, Atsen Ahua, director of Synergies African Ventures, described a market approach to preventing piracy that comes from local music producers in Ghana and Nigeria:

They have organized a network of middlemen and retailers by which thousands of cassettes find their way rather quickly to buyers all over the country. This makes it more difficult for pirates to break into this market structure. In some cases they nevertheless have done, so they got the chance to operate within the framework of the network. The market is big enough to give them also a place under the sun. If they refuse to collaborate some violence may be necessary to bring them back to order because mafia tendencies should be suppressed immediately. We tell them: 'If you copy Rambo, do it, not our products, but come in business with us. Otherwise you kill us.'

According to Atsen Ahua, in a country such as Kenya, by contrast, it is more difficult to introduce such a system because the entrepreneurial impulse is lacking: 'People are more attuned to being employed. Now this is beginning to be changed.' The system in Ghana also has another form of protection against piracy. On the cassettes a numbered revenue band has been glued on, as on cigarette packs, and this seems to limit piracy (Bender 1994: 486).

All those actions notwithstanding, piracy will continue to happen as long as it is easy to copy material. This is more and more the case; with digital technologies

KING ALFRED'S COLLEGE LIBRARY

the thousandth copy is as good as the first. Thus, the industry's strategy to bring high-quality cassettes quickly on to the market is losing its effectiveness. This issue will become even more important in the future with the further development of laser disks and other new communication technologies. Richard Barnet and John Cavanagh observe with some amusement: 'stars now count on being seen and heard somewhere around the world many times a day. But the bigger the hit, the more likely it is that its creators and owners will have to share the profits with pirates. While intellectuals and politicians in poor countries denounced the "cultural imperialism" of the global media giants, underground entrepreneurs did something about it' (Barnet and Cavanagh 1994: 141). Dave Laing claims, interestingly, that 'piracy's most important effect is not the damage it does to the income of transnational companies and their recording artists, but the way in which it encourages the spread of international music and discourages the full development of national recordings in many countries' (Burnett 1996: 88–9).

Undeniably, a sharp contradiction exists between the producers of software and hardware. It is in the interests of hardware producers to sell machines that can copy easily. And this is exactly what film, music and book producers hate. The risk that the day after it goes on the market their software will be copied many times over, and even be of good quality, makes them hesitate to put their wares on pay-per-view, for example. What we see, therefore, are internal contradictions inside huge corporations that produce both software and hardware. These sections are actually in competition with each other while having different interests. This is one of the weak points of the synergies arguments and practices of the big mergers in the field of communication enterprises in the recent past. 'All sorts of new wrinkles in hardware development could eventually render the compromise between the producers of sound equipment and the producers of music obsolete. Electronics-hardware companies have picked up three of the six record majors and several of the most successful independent record labels. This means that future fights over entertainment technology will increasingly take place inside megacorporations rather than between them' (Barnet and Cavanagh 1994: 145).

Let's have a look at the results of these attempts to hunt the pirates. Sales of pirate CDs in the United Kingdom, for example, soared by a third in the year 2000, with the black market then estimated to be worth £20 million. Worldwide sales of pirate CDs rose by a quarter in the year 2000, accounting for one in three sales. The underground business is now thought to be worth £3 billion. A report published by the International Federation of Phonographic Industries described how organized crime in Italy, Eastern Europe, Russia and Asia is slowly bringing the music business to its knees. Global sales of legally recorded music fell for the first time in 2000, while gangs have developed techniques for producing good-quality pirate CDs for less than a euro or a dollar, massively undercutting the industry. The *Guardian* reports that 'police believe there is evidence to suggest that big crime syndicates are turning to music piracy as a lucrative, less risky alternative to drugs'.[6]

China's well-oiled copyright-piracy 'machine' is running smoothly despite government promises to shut it down. The disks are mocking reminders of the difficulties China had in carrying out trade agreements even as it was joining the World Trade Organization. The *International Herald Tribune* reported: 'Some people contend the government has been reluctant to crack down on the pirates because the steady stream of cheap US movies has helped keep alive the state-owned factories producing disk players by the millions.' At the time there were 300,000 legitimate copies of *Titanic*.

> But pirates sold 20 million to 25 million copies of the film. Even with less popular films, the pirates outsell legitimate distributors about 35 to one. Pirates have films on the streets in China as soon as two days after their debut in the US theatres, while legitimate distributors must wait nine months or more for video release. But even if a factory is found and closed down, the equipment is sometimes simply moved, and production starts up again.[7]

There is, therefore, no reason to imagine that the 'struggle' against such mass-scale piracy can be won, certainly not when many chairmen of Chinese regions have major interests in this business. In Hong Kong, police seized $90 million-worth of illicit compact disks (Schiller 1999: 77–8). But did it help? The statistics given above suggest this is unlikely.

Even the invention of very sophisticated safety measures against copying does not seem to be the solution. The Recording Industry Association of America (RIAA) created the Secure Digital Music Initiative (SDMI), whose task is to find ways to hinder copying. The group settled on a concept called 'digital water-marking'. This system hides a digital data stream inside a piece of music without affecting the quality of the sound. The interesting question then becomes: how can you beat a watermarking system? The answer is: by somehow identifying and removing every trace of the digital watermark without affecting the quality of the music. If this can be done, the SDMI security system is useless. At the end of 2000, SDMI sent out samples with four different kinds of watermarks, and challenged scholars and hackers to break them open. A team lead by scientist Edward Felten at Princeton University rose to the challenge and removed the watermark from all four samples. Actually, they did it not as a big research project, but during their spare time![8]

This made the industry nervous. So nervous that RIAA threatened Edward Felten with legal action if his research group presented a paper at an academic conference in April 2001 describing how it is possible to circumvent an industry music protection system. The research field in which they are working is known as steganography, or the science of hiding information from public view. Matthew Oppenheim, head of RIAA's litigation office, who is also secretary of the Secure Digital Music Initiative, defends the industry's legal action thus: 'There is a line that can get crossed, and if you go further than academic pursuit needs to go, you've crossed the line and it's bad for our entire community, not just the artists and content holders, it's everyone who loves art and it's also bad for the scientific community.'[9]

A problem for Edward Felten is that the 1998 US Digital Millennium Act makes it a crime to manufacture or 'offer to the public' a way to gain unauthorized access to any copyright-protected work that has been secured by a technique like data encryption.[10] This Act is not the only one to protect cultural conglomerates operating in the digital domain. In December 1997, President Clinton signed into law the No Electronic Theft Act, which made it a criminal offence to possess or distribute multiple copies of online copyrighted material, for profit or *otherwise*. With strong support from the publishing, movie and music industries and from the Clinton administration, during mid-1998 the US Congress worked to pass legislation that would expand copyright protections to online content, while extending the term of corporate copyright protection to ninety-five years from first publication. Dan Schiller notes: 'defenders of democratic information access worried that the bills conferred well-nigh absolute power over digital information to copyright owners. Even customary "fair use" of copyrighted materials by librarians, students, and educators could be deemed illegal' (Schiller 1999: 78). So, acquiring the tools needed for education and the development of artistic processes may turn into 'theft'.

MP3, NAPSTER, FREENET ...

The struggle against home copying seems to be at a dead end since the invention of Napster. First there was MP3 for downloading music without permission. This took a lot of time and did not always deliver a high quality. In 1999 a nineteen-year-old high-school kid invented a program he called Napster, which costs nothing and which makes it possible to share music files on the MP3 format with other web-surfers. Currently, all the computers with Napster on their hard drive together form something like a virtual juke-box on a world scale. In a couple of seconds anyone can find almost any piece of music he or she wants to hear. Napster acts as a conduit, allowing users across the globe to access each other's private collections.

Of course the record industry and the RIAA tried to get Napster and comparable systems banned through court rulings, which is also the ardent wish of all the other cultural conglomerates dealing in images, film, texts and other data. Yves Eudes commented: 'Without any doubt, we will witness the emergence of a powerful system of references and sharing of digital products of different kinds, which develops behind the scenes of the Web, uncontrolled. Even when the original site of Napster is forced to close, the spirit is out of the bottle.'[11] Not long after Eudes wrote this, Napster indeed was closed.

And so it happened. Napster has since been refined by stronger and more decentralized programs including Gnutella, Freenet, Kazaa and Morpheus. These programs not only facilitate the sharing of even bigger quantities of music, but also of videos, films, software programs, games and complete databases, which until now could be transferred only by very powerful computers. The basic principle is 'peer-to-peer' computing, allowing users to download free software and gain direct access to files on others' computers. At present, every connected computer within such systems controls its own music catalogue. The separate catalogues are connected with each other by contacting at least two other computers in the network, which are connected in their turn with two more computers. When someone gives the command to search, for instance, for a piece of music, then his or her computer looks into the catalogue of the next computer, and so on, until the desired item has been found. Furthermore, the film industry finds itself threatened by the development of DIVX, which makes it possible to compress a DVD and put it on the internet. The visual and auditory quality is comparable to that of VHS.[12]

Meanwhile, an American judge has said that Napster infringes the copyright of the record companies. Immediately after, Napster Inc., which attracted a staggering 38 million users in its first eighteen months of existence by wresting control of music distribution from the major record labels, said it would join forces with the media giant Bertelsmann AG to develop a fee-based service. At the same time, Bertelsmann's music division is still suing Napster in the context of RIAA's lawsuit! The *International Herald Tribune* commented:

> for Bertelsmann, the deal means access to the most passionate group of music lovers on the Internet. For Napster, it means a chance to make money on a service that has so far been as unprofitable as it has been enormously popular. Bertelsmann will lend Napster an undisclosed sum to develop tracking technology that would enable labels and artists to be compensated for the music using Napster's service.

The heading of the article is 'Will Napster's Bargain Turn Off Loyal Users?' This was a good question indeed, as Napster prepared for an existence as one of the many fee-based digital music services that compete fiercely with each other. Coming back to the question of whether Napster's bargain will turn off loyal users, the answer is yes. Figures released in July 2001 showed an explosive growth in less centralized services welcoming millions of Napster refugees.[13]

Yet another aspect of the continuing digitalization process makes it less likely that the present copyright system can be maintained. The computer and the Web provide artists with a unique opportunity to experiment using material from all corners of the artistic landscape, past and present. The observation could be made that there's a need for critics who are competent to judge what is worthwhile and what is arrant nonsense in these new fields of artistic activity.

Another way of looking at it is that these artists are doing nothing different from what Bach, Shakespeare and thousands of other artists in all different cultures did before them. In all cultures it has always been quite normal to incorporate ideas and 'quotations' from the works of predecessors. Only the system of copyright hampered this self-evident process of ongoing creation. This freezes the ongoing creation and pretends there is culturally an end-point, i.e. a specific artistic work that has been made at a specific moment in history and that should not be changed any more. Infringement on this static situation is what we call plagiarism. Artists who 'borrow' from other work do not feel that they are doing anything wrong. The concept of plagiarism is disappearing from the consciousness of many artists, even more quickly than it appeared some centuries ago in Western culture.

THE CONCEPT OF ORIGINALITY

So much for the *practice* of artistic digitalization, which is more and more in conflict with the existing system of copyright. On the phenomenon of plagiarism the philosopher Jacques Soulillou makes an interesting comment:

> The reason it is difficult to provide proof of plagiarism in the field of art and literature is that it is not enough only to show that B has been inspired by A without quoting his or her sources, but you also have to prove that A has not been inspired by someone else ... [If] it could be proved that A has been inspired by and, as it were, has plagiarised from an 'X' who is situated earlier chronologically, A's case disintegrates. (Soulillou 1999: 17)

His analysis reminds us that the system of copyright is not only less and less tenable, it has also been grounded in a concept that is less self-evident than it might appear. Is it possible to imagine a poem without all the poems that preceded it? Our modern culture easily lets us forget that the author or performer uses many different sources – language, images, sounds, rhythms, colours, movements – that are part of our common heritage. It is impossible to claim absolute originality. This is probably why both the TRIPs agreement and national laws do not define what an invention is (Correa 2000: 51). Nevertheless, this lack of definition does not seem to prevent patents from being awarded on a huge scale (Shulman 1999), which actually provide monopolistic power over and exploitation rights on those so-called inventions. As Jessica Litman says, it is also rather amazing that 'copyright protection has never required a government examination for originality, creativity or merit' (Litman 2001: 79).

Roland Barthes has already explained in *The Death of the Author* that, in what he called 'ethnographic societies',

> the responsibility for a narrative is never assumed by a person, but by a mediator, shaman or relator whose 'performance' – the mastery of the narrative code – may possibly be admired but never his 'genius'. The author is a modern figure, a product of our society insofar as, emerging from the Middle Ages with English empiricism, French rationalism and the personal faith of the Reformation, it discovered the prestige of the individual, or, as it is more nobly put, the 'human person'. (Newton 1988: 155)[14]

Historically nothing is less true than the idea that it is self-evident to give exclusive rights of exploitation to someone who has created a work of art. It also refreshes our cultural perspective as well to listen to the communication scholar Roland Bettig who reminds us that, traditionally, 'Asian authors and artists have viewed the copying of their works as an honour' (Bettig 1996: 213–19).

Copying – or imitation – was a necessity as well. Jean-Pierre Babylon calls it one of the grounding instruments of our civilization. Through this process many values have been transmitted which would otherwise have been lost. This has meant that the cultural heritage of former generations could serve as sources of inspiration for the cultural workers of subsequent generations who appear to be making a fresh start.[15]

On this subject it is worth listening to the Dutch painter Rob Scholte who maintains that all artistic creations derive from, and thus belong to, everyone: 'This does not mean that everything has become gratuitous. That would be an error of reasoning. People still experience something for the first time, authenticity continues to exist, and certain images keep their power of expression. As a postmodernist, however, I oppose the idea of originality, of intellectual property, of copyright.'[16] What he raises is the phenomenon of *ownership* in relation to assumed originality. There is good reason to consider the system of copyright as being based on a romantic concept of the author as someone who creates something completely original out of nothing.

In this connection, Rosemary Coombe wonders how much a star's celebrity image, for instance, and his or her value are due to the individual's own efforts and investments: 'Celebrity images must be made, and, like other cultural products, their creation occurs in social contexts and draws upon other sources, institutions and technologies. Star images are authored by studios, the mass media, public relations agencies, fan clubs, gossip columnists, photographers, hairdressers, body-building coaches, athletic trainers, teachers, screenwriters, ghostwriters, directors, lawyers and doctors' (Commbe 1998: 94–7).

The Marx Brothers, for example, took what they wanted from burlesque and vaudeville. And Madonna evokes and ironically reconfigures several twentieth-century sex goddesses (Marilyn Monroe, obviously, but also Jean Harlow, Greta Garbo, Marlene Dietrich, Gina Lollobrigida, and perhaps a touch of Grace Kelly). Let us furthermore not forget the role of the public in the creative process, about which Marilyn Monroe herself said: 'If I am a star – the people made me a star, no studio, no person, but the people did.'

The same is true in many cultures. For instance, the participation of concert party and popular theatre audiences in Ghana in the creation of the play, 'intervening to make suggestions, complete proverbs, pass comments, shout warnings', is, according to Karen Barber, 'hard to miss'. She continues: 'They supply the oxygen of public approval to new improvisations; their responses encourage the actors to expand and elaborate certain passages and to condense or eliminate others.' She concludes that 'they can thus be seen actively participating in the shaping of the show' (Barber 1997: xv).

This observation undermines the fundamentals of our present systems of copyright and authors' rights. It is not justifiable that someone should claim absolute ownership – and all the rights connected with this, through legislation that commodifies everything that has been created, invented and performed – while his or her own work clearly draws on many, many other sources of influence. It is even stranger that artistic creations, inventions and different performance interpretations can be traded, with the result that a commercial enterprise can be granted exclusive ownership of the artistic work of others, with rights that are extended for decades. The idea that the right to copy works of art can be given monopolistically to a non-creator or non-performer is doubly strange. The new owner – nowadays usually a conglomerate – is not creative at all, while in the artistic work itself countless other contributions from past and present may be represented. It is unjustifiable to forget that there is always an enormous debt to the public domain.

ARTISTS STILL CREATE

Do we need a system of intellectual property rights to promote the continuing creation of works of art? This is one of the arguments in defence of copyright that has often been used, for instance, in policy documents in the Western world. However, it is obvious that throughout history, and in cultures all over the world, marvellous creations have been made without the existence of anything like an authors' rights system. Moreover, most artists do not currently earn much money through copyright – no more than pays for a dinner a year with some friends, perhaps. Nevertheless, they continue to create.

Economists from various universities, including Ruth Towse and Wilfred Dolfsma (Erasmus University, Rotterdam), Roger Wallis (City University, London) and Martin Kretschmer (Bournemouth University), emphasize that all research indicates that the expansion of copyright in general favours investors over creators and performers. On average artists earn only a couple of hundred euros a year from copyright – often much less – while copyright worldwide remains one of the main sources of gross national product. Second, within the artistic community the distribution of incomes from copyright is highly skewed. It is not unusual for only 10 per cent of the members of a collecting society to receive 90 per cent of the revenues.

Martin Kretschmer states that the rhetoric of authors' rights 'has been largely carried by third parties: publishers and record companies, i.e. investors in creativity (rather than creators) who also turn out to be the chief beneficiaries of extended protection' (Kretschmer 1999: 2). This means that artists are mistaken if they think that it makes sense for them to be in the same coalition as the conglomerates of copyright-holders who are concerned with the defence of copyright! Aymeric Pichevin, in the context of copyright in the music industry, argues that:

> the capitalist system makes a profit from it by limiting its investment (since the work does not have to be bought) and by transferring on to the artist's shoulders part of the risk associated with the unpredictability of success in the musical field. In fact, the system favours a minority of 'stars' … but leaves the overwhelming majority of artists in a precarious situation. (Pichevin 1997: 41)

We have reason to think that most artists find themselves in the wrong coalition with cultural industries and mega-stars.

A WESTERN CONCEPT

Copyright does not benefit Third World countries either, and the individual appropriation of creations and inventions is a concept that is strange to many cultures. Artists and inventors are paid for their work, obviously depending on their fame and other circumstances, and they may be highly respected for what they have created. But in many cultures people do not expect an individual to exploit a creation or invention in a monopolistic way for many decades. After all, the artist, or inventor, proceeds with and from the work of his or her predecessors. A good example of how artistic creativity draws on both past and present can be found in Algerian rai music (this is also true of most traditional and popular music cultures such as calypso, samba, rap and many others). On the subject of the rai, Bouziane Daoudi and Hadj Miliani emphasize that 'the same theme may know as many variations as there are performers ... The basis is shared knowledge, which refers less to a repertoire of existing "texts" than a whole of social signs (*el mérioula*, *el mehna*, *el minoun*, *e ʒ'har*, etc.).' It is difficult to recognize the true author in the Western sense of copyright. In fact, the rai has no author. Until some years ago, with its entrance into the Western market system, singers 'borrowed' songs or refrains from each other and the audience spontaneously added words to a song. In the practice of the singers, the *chebs* and the *chabete*, theft, pillage and plagiarism of texts does not exist. It is a form of music that depends on the circumstances, and differs according to period, place or public. Daoudi and Miliani describe the rai as 'a continuum of a strongly perturbated social imagination' (Daoudi and Miliani 1996: 126–9 passim).

In Japan, too, the idea of payment for copyright does not belong to the common culture. Under pressure from the USA, Japan had to change its copyright law in 1996. The *International Herald Tribune* reported at the time (10–11 February 1996): 'Current Japanese copyright law does not protect foreign recordings made before 1971, meaning that Western record companies, by their estimates, are losing millions of dollars a year in royalties from copying of tunes that are still highly popular.' The article was headed 'US Takes Music-Piracy Charge Against Japan to WTO'. In other words, a difference of opinion about how far back in time rights should go – arising from a cultural difference – was interpreted as 'piracy'.

Tôru Mitsui explains that the basic concept of copyright has become familiar in Japan mainly through newspaper coverage of copyright issues concerning records, tapes and computer programs. 'But still the Japanese people do not take well to copyright, or more properly, to the idea of the individual right. Generally speaking, to claim one's right is regarded as dishonourable or undignified, especially when the right involves money' (Mitsui 1993: 141–2).

In many non-Western cultures, even when copyright is applied, it soon becomes clear that the ideology sustaining the system is not fit for the complexity of the processes of creation. In the Western world there is a sharp division – in the case of music, for instance – between the concepts of composer and performer. Not so in African music, which is usually associated with specific dances, according to John Collins. Thus, 'in the African case royalty-accruing components should, in the name of creative equity, be divided into four: the lyrics, the melody, the rhythm and the dance-step – with the melody further divided into the various contrapuntal or cross melodies and the polyrhythm into its multiple subrhythms'. However, this is not the only point since 'in African performing arts the audiences often have a creative role too, as they chant, clap and perform dance-dialogues with the musicians'. It is clear that the individual allocation of copyright cannot work. After all, 'how does one measure the degree (and value) of "originality" in a continually *reworked* piece of music?' (Collins 1993: 149–50).

Rosemary Coombe perceives a comparable impossibility in applying copyright law to the native peoples of Canada: 'The law rips asunder what First Nations people view as integrally related, freezing into categories what Native peoples find flowing in relationships that do not separate texts from ongoing creativity production, or ongoing creativity from social relationships, or social relationships from people's relationship to an ecological landscape that binds past and future generations in relations of spiritual significance' (Coombe 1998: 229). Does this mean, she wonders, that artists and authors of First Nations ancestry do not want their work valued on the market, or that they would eschew royalties for work produced as commodities for an exchange value on the market? Obviously not, she says; but she points out that 'in the debate surrounding cultural appropriation, Native peoples assert that there are other value systems than those of the market in which their images, themes, practices and stories figure and that these modes of appreciation and valuation are embedded in specific histories and relationships that should be accorded respect' (p. 381).

This observation brings us to the long-standing issue of collective rights. *Our Creative Diversity*, the Report of the World Commission on Culture and Development, published in 1996, drew attention to the fact – not for the first time in recent decades – that traditional cultural groups possess intellectual property rights *as groups*. 'This leads to the radical idea that there can be an intermediary sphere of intellectual property rights between individual rights and the (national or international) public domain.' This in turn raises the difficulty of what is to be protected. 'The simple notion provided by an imagined primeval cultural source is obviously inadequate here: the Navajo rug, for instance, contains influences which can be traced, though Mexico and Spain, to North Africa.'

The Commission suggested that the word 'folklore' should be applied to 'living creative traditions shaped by powerful ties to the past' and that the notion of 'intellectual property' was perhaps not at all the right juridical concept to use. 'A case can be made for a new concept based on ideas inherent in traditional social rules. This might be more constructive than trying to make the forms of protection fit within a framework which was never designed for them and where the existing users and developers of copyright notions resist strenuously any such development' (Pérez de Cuéllar 1996: 196).

Krister Malm relates that in 1996, the year *Our Creative Diversity* was published, the question of international copyright protection of folklore was again put on the agenda by a number of Third World governments, this time in the context of preparations for the meeting of the World Trade Organization that took place in Geneva in January 1997. 'The move to get the issue onto the agenda of the WTO meeting failed,' he reports. 'Again the failure was due to resistance from powerful industrialized countries and the culture industries to any introduction of "collective" or "cultural property" rights into the present system of intellectual and industrial property rights' (Malm 1998: 27). With the support of many countries, the decision was made that a meeting jointly organized by Unesco and Wipo (the UN's World Intellectual Property Organization) should take place in April 1997 in Phuket, Thailand.

At this meeting many Third World countries shared the view that an international legal instrument was needed. Naturally, this did not please the American and British delegates since the biggest international entertainment industries are to be found in their countries. Krister Malm reports that tensions rose

> when the US delegate said that since most of the folklore that was commercially exploited was US folklore, Third World countries would have to pay a lot of money to the US if an international convention should come about. The Indian lawyer Mr Purim answered that that was already the case with existing conventions and by the way all US folklore except the Amerindian one was imported to the US from Europe, Africa and other countries. Thus the money should go to the original owners of that folklore.

In April 1998 Krister Malm commented that nothing had thus far come out of the Phuket meeting and, in his view, it was unlikely that Western countries would take the issue of collective rights seriously in the near future (Malm 1998: 26–9 passim; see also Unesco-Wipo 1998; Wipo 2001). However, in the Ministerial Declaration of WTO's Doha meeting of 20 November 2001, the council of TRIPs was asked to examine the issue of the protection of traditional knowledge and folklore.

For Third World countries, more important still may be the fact that Western countries derive a huge revenue from intellectual property rights that Third World countries are obliged to transfer to them. James Boyle illustrates with some well-chosen examples how badly this situation works out for poor and powerless countries.

> The author concept stands as a gate through which one must pass in order to acquire intellectual property rights. At the moment, this is a gate that tends disproportionately to favour the developed countries' contributions to world science and culture. Curare, batik, myths and the dance 'lambada' pour out of

developing countries, unprotected by intellectual property rights, while Prozac, Levis, Grisham, and the movie *Lambada* flow in – protected by a suite of intellectual property laws, which in turn are backed by the threat of trade sanctions. (Boyle 1996: 124)

Transformation of ideas and raw materials and the exploitation of markets are rewarded with intellectual rights; but raw materials, including music and images as raw materials, have zero value when it comes to intellectual rights. Jutta Ströter-Bender gives an example from the field of design: 'For Western designers, too, the universe of motifs and images from "Third World" artists constitutes an inexhaustible reservoir which they use shamelessly and, of course, without correctly honouring the source of their "inspiration"' (Ströter-Bender 1995: 45). Clearly, more research is needed to gain a clearer picture of the harm being done to the cultures of Third World countries.

Noam Chomsky was probably not far off the mark when he stated in 1993: 'American companies stand to gain $61 billion a year from the Third World if US protectionist demands are satisfied at GATT (as they are in NAFTA), at a cost to the South that will dwarf the current huge flow of debt service from South to North' (Chomsky 1993: 3). Meanwhile, GATT has changed into WTO, but this makes no difference. A proportion of the sum concerns copyright on cultural 'products'. What does this amount to? It is difficult to calculate because commercial statistics differ enormously between countries. We may assume that the amount of money poor countries are required to pay for copyright is growing, partly because Southern and Eastern countries are under pressure from the West to fight piracy, which also uses up scarce police resources (see Cohen Jehoram et al. 1996: 44). At the same time, transnational cultural conglomerates are penetrating these countries ever more effectively with their entertainment and cultural products, with the result that these countries are handing over scarce hard currency to the cultural industries in the West and in Japan.

It may seem surprising that Third World countries failed to see in advance that the intellectual commons of their societies would be brought under the umbrella of the World Trade Organization and its new Treaty on Trade Related Intellectual Properties (TRIPs), through which they would be prevented from developing their own policies in this sensitive field. Friedl Weiss summarizes the struggle between North and South which took place in the years before 1993:

Although there is considerable antecedent and multilateral treaty practice on industrial and intellectual property rights (IIPRs), the subject matter, as is well known, became a matter for multilateral negotiations in the Uruguay Round only upon the insistence of industrially advanced countries (IACs), especially the United States. Developing countries (DCs) were at first extremely reluctant to enter into such negotiations as there was scarcely any common ground between them and IACs, in economic philosophy, objectives or regulatory tradition. Leading DCs, for instance, considered it inappropriate to establish within the framework of the GATT any new rules and disciplines pertaining to standards and principles concerning the availability, scope and use of intellectual property rights.

What happened? Weiss explains:

Consequently, they emphatically rejected any idea of integrating the TRIPS Agreement into the GATT itself which, they claimed, played only a peripheral role in this area precisely because substantive issues of IPRs are not germane to international trade. On the other hand, DCs were content with the integration of substantive standards of the major IPR treaties into the TRIPs Agreement. In the end the deadlock in IPR negotiations was overcome through a combination of allowing DCs and LDCs more transitional time for achieving higher standards of IPR protection and of concessions in other areas, notably textiles and parallel trade. (Cohen Jehoram et al. 1996: 8–9; see also Correa 2000)

More research is needed in order to know what the precise considerations of Third World countries were, and still are, concerning intellectual rights in the cultural field. In *The Challenge to the South*, a report written under the chairmanship of the former president of Tanzania, Julius Nyerere, bitter words were spoken about TRIPs.

The objective clearly is to install a system that would oblige developing countries to restructure their national laws so as to accommodate the needs and interests of the North. This initiative seeks to expand the scope of the system governing intellectual property rights, extend the lifetime of the granted privileges, widen the geographical area where these privileges can be exercised, and ease restrictions on the use of granted rights. (Nyerere 1990: 254–5)

The present system of copyright can be seen as a kind of Hobson's choice for artists and Third World countries; and the public domain is also losing out. Copyright seems to be treated as a sacred belief, yet the idea that it serves the well-being of all is highly questionable, as I have shown in this chapter. However, artists and Third World countries cannot act as if the system and the suing and sanctioning practices do not exist; they have no choice but to participate in the system. This presents them with an enormous strategic dilemma. At the same time we are witnessing the swallowing-up by huge conglomerates of our common public domain of knowledge and creativity.

This is not only happening in the arts. Jeremy Rifkin gives just a few examples of what could happen within the next twenty-five years, in what he calls the Biotech Century:

A handful of global corporations, research institutions, and governments could hold patents on virtually all 100,000 genes that make up the blueprints of the human race, as well as the cells, organs, and tissues that comprise the human body. They may also own similar patents on tens of thousands of micro-organisms, plants, and animals, allowing them unprecedented power to dictate the terms by which we and future generations will live our lives. (Rifkin 1998: 2)

Can we liberate ourselves from the stranglehold in which conglomerates keep us through their monopoly of copyright, patents and other intellectual property rights? In Chapter 6 I propose a number of other ways of dealing with cultural matters. I argue that artists, Third World countries and the public domain would all be better served if copyright were abolished. I will also emphasize that the cultural field and the environmental movement should join forces. The example of patents, which Jeremy Rifkin has given, makes clear that the philosophy of intellectual property rights is as harmful to our ecosystems and social systems that sustain life as it is to the cultural aspects of our existence; in both cases democratic control is being lost. But first we will see, in Chapter 4, how important it is for people to have some control over their own local artistic life, which can develop very well without the oligopolistic control of cultural conglomerates and copyright industries.

NOTES

1. Janine Jacquet, 'Cornering Creativity', *The Nation*, 17 March 1997.

2. Michel Guerrin and Emmanuel de Roux, 'Pour les photographes, la rue n'est plus libre de droits. La défense du droit d'auteur, comme celle du droit à l'image des propriétaires de bâtiments, entraîne de procès coûteux et rend difficiles les métiers de l'image et de l'édition', *Le Monde*, 27 March 1999.

3. 'Daniel Buren perd son procès contre les éditeurs de cartes postales. Deux juges donnent raison aux photographes', *Le Monde*, 8–9 April 2001.

4. Christian de Brie, 'Etats, mafias et transnationales comme larons en foire', *Le Monde Diplomatique*, April 2000.

5. 'Adieu Gorbouchka, le grand bazar de vidéos pirates de Moscou', *Le Monde*, 22 March 2001.

6. 'Success of CD Piracy Hits Music Industry', *Guardian*, 13 June 2001.

7. 'Turnabout: China's Copyright Pirates Steal the Grinch', *International Herald Tribune*, 13 December 2000.

8. 'Hackers Make Quick Work of New Music Security Code', *International Herald Tribune*, 30 October 2000.

9. 'Music Protection Faces Fresh Battle. Copying Secrets at Center of Storm', *International Herald Tribune*, 25 April 2001.

10. Ibid. See also the civil liberties-oriented website: http://cryptome.org

11. Yves Eudes, 'Un nouveau système de distribution sauvage de produits numériques', *Le Monde*, 18 April 2000.

12. 'L'industrie cinématographique menacée par le DIVX. Ce format permet de comprimer un film DVD, qui peut ensuite mis en réseau sur Internet', *Le Monde*, 24 January 2001.

13. 'Music Industry's After-Napster Blues. Alternative Sites are Harder to Police', *International Herald Tribune*, 21–22 July 2001.

14. Originally, Roland Barthes, 'La Mort de l'auteur', *Manteia*, 5 (4), 1968; also in Barthes, *Oeuvres complètes*, Vol. II: 1966–1973 (Paris: Seuil, 1994), pp. 491–5.

15. Jean-Pierre Babylon, 'La culture par la copie', *Le Monde*, 27 October 1999.

16. Interview with Rob Scholte, *De Groene Amsterdammer*, 18 December 1996.

FOUR
Local Artistic Life

DELOCALIZATION

The arts are forms of communication but, as I have said before, they are specific forms of communication. Characteristic of the arts are their aesthetic connotations. Second, they often communicate in a denser, more concentrated form than we experience in day-to-day life; and, third, the location or context in which the artistic communication takes place often indicates that something specific is going on.

Artistic creations are, moreover, often part of a something else such as, for example, a religious celebration, a fashion parade or a television show; or they may interact with a wider setting such as the architecture of a building, or an advertisement, or the design of a book. Sometimes, however, they function largely independently from other purposes. A work of art is not by definition one element in a broader context, yet it would be an exaggeration to speak about works of art as autonomous since it is difficult to imagine anything in our lives that functions *completely* independently from other things and other people.

This neutral definition of the arts as specific forms of communication makes it possible to cover and to study the broad area, in all our societies, in which people express or experience the feelings they have at a deep level: their joy, their sadness, their hidden desires, their untruthfulness, or their longing for amusement or beautiful experiences. Therefore we may also call the arts *repositories* of cultural meanings (Wolff 1989: 4). Many of these sentiments have a longer life than we ourselves have, and they are embedded in the cultural heritage we are part of. At the same time, it is appropriate to describe the arts as being 'workshops' in which cultural meanings are crafted and created. Through the work of artists and the way their work is presented, social and cultural sentiments and convictions are produced, constructed, reproduced and reconstructed. Artists refer in their creations, performances and crafts to those cultural meanings. They play with them; some deconstruct seemingly well-ordered images, sounds, words and dominant sentiments; others confirm them; they may expose dirt and ugliness, subtle tensions or cruel truths.

The definition of the arts as specific forms of communication may be a neutral one, but this does not mean that the arts are neutral phenomena. The arts leave traces in our minds; they always elicit judgements. One may like or hate a certain piece of music or a certain design, for instance; the work may be controversial or it may be considered by many people to be part of the normally accepted daily fare. However innocent it may look, it is after all a repository of cultural meaning, and the artists serve as hothouses of cultural meanings, whatever it is they are creating, from rap to opera, or from inward-looking to wildly exhibitionist.

When the stakes are so high, it is easy to understand that all artistic creations have a certain impact. In the next chapter we will come back to the issue of influence. Here, the role of the arts in social life, on a local and a global level, will be discussed. Although it has been claimed that we are all global citizens, unhindered by social convention or contextualization, we are beginning to learn again that this is only partly true, while for most people it is not true at all. We also know that it is not desirable to be completely detached from our social surroundings. After the experience of the delocalization that neoliberalism has offered us, we know even better than before that the world is too big and too complex for us to be able to orient ourselves within it and try to find something like a safe haven. This is a difficult subject, because we know for sure that many places on earth are not safe at all. There is no reason to romanticize the neighbourhood, the village or the fatherland. At the same time it is true that refugees are not fleeing to 'the world' but trying to find a refuge in a particular, more humanely organized society.

Along the same line of thinking, Anthony Smith claims:

> there are no 'world memories' that can be used to *unite* humanity; the most global experiences to date – colonialism and the World Wars – can only serve to remind us of our historic cleavages ... The central difficulty in any project to construct a global identity and hence a global culture, is that collective identity, like imagery and culture, is always historically specific because it is based on shared memories and a sense of continuity between generations. (Smith 1990: 179–80)

Focusing on the question of what current global cultural trends can offer, he gives examples of the advance of American mass culture and computerized information technology. He notes that these trends are 'in all likelihood, here to stay, at least for some decades'. He then asks: 'But what do they add up to? Can large numbers of men and women live *by* them, as well as *with* them? Do they amount to a new culture, a new lifestyle that is also a way of life, one that can inspire as well as comfort human beings for loss and grief and death? What memories, which myths and symbols, values and identities, can such a global culture offer?' (Smith 1995: 21–5). And we should make this question more specific: what memories, which myths and symbols, values and identities, can be offered by a global culture that is mainly commercially driven and, in the case of the arts, has been organized by only a handful of globally-operating cultural conglomerates?

The corporate culture they spread worldwide will be the focus of the next chapter. The subject of this chapter is the problematic position of the arts in the local context. We may agree with Anthony Smith, that the world as a whole cannot offer us the memories, myths and symbols we need as human beings; however, the reality is also that the driving force of the local context for the arts is being weakened. To what extent? Is this true for all parts of the world, and for all arts in the same way? This chapter tries to take stock of the situations where the arts in the local context are flourishing, notwithstanding globalizing tendencies, and those situations where outside forces are taking over local artistic life.

Why is this question – of whether there is still a local artistic life of any substance – an important issue? The reason is *democracy*. In any society people should have the right to communicate in their own way about what moves them, what they find exciting, what is pleasurable or what keeps them busy. This provides them with an identity, individually as well as collectively. Theatre, film, music, the visual arts, design, literature, works of mixed media, all these forms of art are essential vehicles of communication. From the democratic perspective it is desirable that major parts of the local artistic landscape of any society are related to what is going on in this particular society.

'As the world becomes more complicated,' Michael Shuman comments, 'people are increasingly solving problems at the local level.' Community empowerment, of course, is not always positive, he acknowledges, because it can serve as a cover for parochialism, tribalism and racism.

> But community is also the place we call home. It is where we work and play, where we make friends, where we raise children. It is where political institutions are most accessible and where we can find the resources, legitimacy, and machinery for collective action. A community is a trampoline on which citizens can bounce, gain momentum, and leap into international affairs with far greater force than they ever would have on their own. (Shuman 1994: 55–6)

The last thing Michael Shuman wants to do is to romanticize local communities and the artistic life taking place there. The local community is also the place where people have their quarrels, but that is part of life and part of the democratic process in any society. The symbolic battles over artistic expression, as described in Chapter 1, belong to it.

A task force of the International Forum on Globalization reported in 1999:

A high percentage of people on the earth still survive through local, community-based activities; small scale farming, local markets, local production for local consumption. This has enabled them to remain directly in control of their economic and food security, while also maintaining the viability of local communities and culture. Even in developed countries, most jobs have traditionally been connected to local economic production.[1]

The report finds that economic globalization is rapidly dismantling this local production, strongly favouring economies based on export, with global corporations in control: 'This brings destruction of local livelihoods, and community self-reliance.' The task force argues that it is 'therefore necessary to reverse directions and create new rules and structures that consciously favour the local, and follow the principles of subsidiarity, i.e., whatever activities can be undertaken locally should be.' This will be one of the themes of Chapter 6.

This emphasis on the importance of communities obviously does not mean that borders should be closed or that nostalgia should be celebrated; nor does it mean that works of art should deal only with local concerns. In the United States, more cultural openness to the rest of the world would not be a luxury. Perhaps the most interesting artists are those who go beyond daily life to express feelings related to other levels of exerience. For the sake of democracy it is important that many artists express many different things. Of course, it also enriches any society (American society not excepted) when works of art come from other parts of the world and are presented in such a way that no single culture is allowed to dominate. Just as there are no rules and regulations about the number of artists from within a particular society who should be presented so long as the cultural scene is fully democratic, so there should be no limits to the number of artists or works of art from other countries that should be tolerated.

Jan Nederveen Pieterse is right to broaden this issue when he asks: 'What is indigenous, and who decides? What are its boundaries, its circumferences? Who belongs and who does not, what is essential and what not?' (Nederveen Pieterse 1997: 134). Similarly, Irmgard Bontinck and Alfred Smudits ask, in their study on *Music and Globalization*: 'What share of domestic/local music is desirable, from the point of view that a culture should not be colonised but also from the point of view that it should not be totally isolated?' (Bontinck and Smudits 1997: 49–50). There are no absolute answers. And yet there is certainly a problem from the democratic perspective when the artistic life of any society is taken over substantially by outside forces, especially when these are mainly commercial and oligopolistic.

John Gray sums up the problem thus:

Brands for many consumer goods are no longer country-specific but global. Companies produce identical products for worldwide distribution. The popular cultures of virtually all societies are inundated by a common stock of images. The countries of the European Union share the images they all absorb from Hollywood movies more than they do any aspect of each other's cultures. The same is true of East Asia. Behind all these 'meanings' of globalization is a single underlying idea, which can be called *de-localization*: the uprooting of activities and relationships from local origins and cultures. It means the displacement of activities that until recently were local into networks whose reach is distant or worldwide ... [Globalization] means lifting social activities out of local knowledge and placing them in networks in which they are conditioned by, and condition, worldwide events. (Gray 1998: 57)

John Gray is not inclined to equate this delocalization with homogenization. 'That, again, is just what globalization is *not*. Global markets in which capital and production moves freely across frontiers work precisely because of the *differences* between localities, nations and regions.' What happens is that local, cultural markets remain, but they are becoming secondary in importance (McChesney 1998: 13). Notions of local economy concerning cultural matters and local control become anomalous and increasingly impossible (Mander 1993: 15). The product of the human, artistic work is alienated from its maker; the image of the whole or of community is disappearing (Said 1993: 270). Let's make a short *tour d'horizon* through different parts of the world to observe some examples.

Suman Naresh discusses the fact that India has opened up its market for a little over a decade, and this has made foreign audiovisual programming (television and satellite) available for the first time on a large scale.

The cultural objections being voiced in India are not simply objections to the sexual explicitness and violence in – particularly American – programming, which are offensive to Indian audiences accustomed to more circumspect representations; if they were no more than this, they could be expected to disappear after a period of adjustment, and could in the meantime be dismissed as the paternalist view of elites, undeserving of deference in an increasingly open and democratic society. Less obviously – and therefore, less tractably – the objection is that a flood of foreign programming, designed to appeal to the largest possible audience world-wide, threatens communities everywhere with a loss of cultural distinctiveness and identity; and that this loss is likely to be felt with special force by societies, such as India, that have hitherto been able to shelter themselves from the homogen-izing influences of free trade worldwide. (Naresh 1996)

Where John Gray explicitly rejects the notion of homogenization from an economic and social perspective, Suman Naresh does not hesitate to use the concept of homogenization in cultural matters. The rest of this chapter will show that this may be the case but that the concept of delocalization, in cultural matters as in economic, is the more appropriate and fits better with the diverse realities.

After all, those realities often include heterogeneous and contradictory aspects. Colin Mackerras observes, for instance, that in three theatres in Beijing strong emphasis has been placed on staging traditional operas, the more traditional the better. In all three theatres, the traditional revival was aimed mainly at tourists, especially Chinese from Hong Kong, Taiwan and the wide Chinese diaspora. 'It was a device by which Chinese from outside China could return to their native country to find their traditional culture and roots. And Peking Opera was a perfect example of this traditional culture.' Interpreting this phenomenon in the light of the tension between globalization and identity, Colin Mackerras observes that tourism has had two opposite effects at the same time. 'It has allowed more people, including Chinese, to travel to Beijing than ever before, and it has also encouraged them to seek traditional roots there, a stronger sense of identity. The tradition is both false and authentic at the same time. It is false because deliberately re-created, it is authentic because it resembles that tradition very closely and in the case of the Zhengyi Temple uses precisely the same site' (Mackerras 2000: 19–20).

A comparable situation can be found in Burma, where marionette theatre was fast disappearing. Through the development of tourism several troupes have been saved, among them the Mandalay theatre which was installed ten years ago near the royal palace. Gradually the Burmese public became interested in the form again and touring around villages has restarted. However, there is only one remaining group that presents marionette theatre in an authentic way, with a complete orchestra, singers for the main roles and six to eight actors to manipulate the puppets. The marionette players who go to the hotels and restaurants perform to music played on a cassette. From this perspective tourism has made the marionette art less rich.[2]

When speaking about local artistic life in this chapter, I am not necessarily referring to cultural life as it develops at the national level within states. First of all, there is never one, single national culture; in every society there are people from many cultures, with different artistic traditions. The extent of tolerance and inclusiveness varies from one society to another and it may be the case that one particular artistic culture is *dominant*. At the same time there are many artists who are doing things that are, for instance, less visible, less generally accepted, less economically supported – or which may even be suppressed.

The concept of 'national culture' says more about the desire of dominant groups within a national territory to consider their cultural expressions as the only relevant ones, and about their power to make it look this way, than it does about reality. In most cases there is much more going on artistically than the superficial observer perceives. Indeed, the arts are one symbolic arena of power struggles between various groups of the population, and some artistic cultures prevail over others, at least for a while. However, the particular configuration of artistic cultures – some dominant, others almost invisible in the public domain – may differ enormously between societies and countries. The artistic climate in Denmark, for instance, will be very different from that in Austria, and even more from the artistic climate in Tanzania.

Second, it is often unclear what the nation is. In 1992 the Pakistan National Institute of Historical and Cultural Research published a book entitled *Pakistani Culture: A Profile*. But even in the introduction the author, M. Yusuf Abbasi, noted: 'Pakistani culture is a new concept as the country is' (Abbasi 1992: i). At the same time it is true that in the part of the world that is now Pakistan, artists have produced work for centuries, just as people have communicated with, and responded to, these artistic creations.

In the year 2000, a debate took place in Russia about the national anthem. After the disintegration of the Soviet Union, the national hymn from the communist era had been replaced by a piece of patriotic music from the nineteenth century, a change that people soon regretted. The music had no words, and people had enjoyed singing the former Soviet hymn, so it was decided to revive the song, but with a new text. The debate was in essence a search for an understanding of what the new Russia is, a question many Russians still feel unable to answer to their own satisfaction. The enforced acts of nationalism in the USA after 11 September 2001 show that in this large country, too, the issue of what it is to 'belong' to a nation state is equally problematic. From a historical perspective, the nation state is a recent invention which has brought more problems than benefits to many former colonies

Third: 'local' artistic life means, of course, what is happening artistically at the regional, city and village level. Because many nation states are very strong, centrifugal forces are a reality to be afraid of both generally and at the cultural level – sometimes particularly at this level. Regional cultural sentiments may be used to conceal oppressive economic or social forces coming from the level of the central state. This was the case, for example, in Indonesia during the Suharto era. The regime exploited regional arts and traditional cultures, giving them some freedom to create and develop in order to increase support for its otherwise oppressive actions.

These regional traditions, according to Barbara Hatley, were cultivated, in part, as a source of the pride and sense of identity previously located in strong nationalist political aspirations, as practised during the Sukarno period.

With any separatist suggestion disallowed by strong centralized structures and an ideology of 'sameness', regional arts are promoted as a counter to excessive foreign influence – the Western-style consumerist values and media images which have flooded into Indonesia since its post-1965 opening to international capital. Local dances and rituals, shorn of elements considered discouraging to modern, development-oriented attitudes, are performed in festivals, competitions, and television broadcasts of regional performing arts. Government buildings are constructed after indigenous architectural styles, and state occasions celebrated with regional performances and pagentary. (Hooker 1993: 49)

The promotion of regional arts during the Suharto period had its limits because tolerance of local traditions also produced oppositional effects, not in a directly political sense but conceptually: it fanned an awareness about other ways to organize perceptions and experiences rather than those that the regime chose to promote (Hellman 2000).

In several European nation states, too, relations between the centre and the regions have not run smoothly. In the nineteenth century – or, in some cases, after the First World War – when nation states unified formerly loosely linked regions, people in these regions began to claim cultural and linguistic identities that separated them from the nation state. This has been followed by periods of oppression and, for the last couple of decades, by more or less enthusiastic acceptance of regional cultural differences by the national authorities. In the case of Spain, the cultural component of regional struggles for separate rights was mostly concentrated on language. In such regions it is difficult to find artistic movements that genuinely belong to the individual identity they claimed.

However, in France, for example, where no explicitly separatist regional movements exist, many very interesting films appear year after year, situated in specific regions and expressing sentiments, social situations and ambiences that, at least in part, come from these localities. This is the result of two developments, which go hand in hand. For several young film-makers it has not always been attractive to find their themes in the bourgeois environment of the metropolis. At the same time, since administrative decentralization, which has also been on the cultural level, French regions have had quite a lot of money to invest in cultural productions and events. This is an issue of cultural politics, which I will discuss in Chapter 6.

A VAST DOMAIN OF CULTURAL PRODUCTION

Before investigating several aspects of the delocalization of artistic activity I will focus on some examples from various parts of the world where there continues to be a rich, locally-based cultural life, sometimes influenced by global tendencies but not overshadowed by them. Obviously, in the context of this book, it is impossible to give an extensive overview; nor is there scope to assess how important or how widespread the artistic phenomena I refer to are. I am not concerned with making aesthetic or moral judgements; within the broad range of artistic productions and events at the local level, some things will be considered valuable by some people, and some things worthless. The force of democracy in any society is that works of art – and whether they are good, bad, ugly or whatever – will or *can* be discussed.

Karen Barber gives an impressive summing-up of the vast domain of cultural production in Africa

> which cannot be classified as either 'traditional' or 'Western' in inspiration, because it straddles and dissolves these distinctions. In recent years, Ghanaian concert parties have toured thousands of towns; Yorùbá popular theatres have broken into film, television, and video; young men and women in Nairobi have read *For Mbatha and Rabeka*; Tanzanian writers have published hundreds of detective novels in Swahili; cartoonists in Cameroon have celebrated the egregious antics of political thugs; Basotho migrant workers have sung about their experiences in the South African mines; and men and women have composed Chimurenga songs to help them to mobilize against the Rhodesian Front. These genres are not repositories of some archaic 'authenticity'; on the contrary, they make use of all available contemporary materials to speak of contemporary struggles. But they are not mere products of 'cultural contact' either, speaking about – and to – the West that has 'corrupted' them. They are the work of local cultural producers speaking to local audiences about pressing concerns, experiences and struggles they share. (Barber 1997: 2)

Similar enthusiasm is expressed by Orriana Baddeley and Valerie Fraser about Latin America, where there is 'no shortage of art produced outside the essentially bourgeois network of galleries: weavings, tapestries, embroideries and knitwear; basketry, pottery, metalwork, carpentry; figures or little scenes modelled in wax, or bread dough or sugar; items in leather, feathers, straw or wood; enamel ware, painted or engraved gourds, papier maché masks; paintings on tin, cloth, hide, wood or bark paper'. The *artesanía* of modern Latin America, the authors attest, 'constitutes a significant part of many Latin American economies as well as an important tourist attraction' (Baddeley and Fraser 1989: 119).

In Asia and in the islands of the Western Pacific Ocean, perhaps 25,000 theatre groups are performing plays from the traditional and modern repertoires. There are too many performers, too many remote regions, and there is too much daily exchange for anyone to know for certain how many groups there are exactly.

'What is known, is that theatrical arts in Asian and Pacific-island cultures are ancient, highly developed, rich almost beyond imagining in their diversity, and very much alive for large segments of the population' (Brandon 1997: 1).

In Singapore, in order to preserve Asian values, policies have been designed to help Asian art to catch up. The Festival of Asian Performing Arts includes performances that are Asian in content and produced by Asians. It was predictable that creating such a festival would trigger criticism from local artists about how one decides a performance is Asian (Tamney 1995: 167–8). How do you negotiate modern influences in the arts with tradition? Rustom Bharucha wonders. In a lecture in Utrecht (Netherlands) on 31 October 1997, he refers to India, where the many different regions are worlds in themselves, where there is an artistically and culturally rich diversity, and where people live in a whole range of different eras, from the pre-modern to the ultra-postmodern.

In the musical field, there are very many places where music-making is still related to the development of local cultures. Whereas harmony is of utmost importance in Western music, this is not the case, for instance, for Igbo drummers in Nigeria. They subvert harmony by departing from the basic rhythm (Oguibe 1995: 75). How this happens technically is of less importance here than the observation that musical structures in many parts of the world continue to be derived from the cultural heritage of those places. Obviously, this is not a static phenomenon. However, where harmony has replaced rhythm as the starting-point for a musical work, the process of delocalization is fully underway.

In Nicaragua, each region developed its particular forms of music. According to Randy Martin, this is still the case.

> The region of Masaya is renowned for its Marimba music, while the Segovias feature an almost flamenco-sounding guitar music. Bluefields has a maypole (palo de mayo) dance derived from the English court. The influence of German migration to the coffee-growing region of Matagalpa is evident in the polkas that can be found there. Each town has its annual festivals to celebrate the fruits of the harvest as well as church processionals and theatre pieces that mix Catholicism with elements from indigenous pre-Columbian forms. (Yúdice et al. 1992: 129)

In the Central Andean Highlands, music, dance, song and ritual are closely intertwined. Musical behaviour is always embedded in a particular context within the ritually and religiously-oriented cycle of the year (Baumann 1996: 19).

In Colombia completely distinctive forms of music and dance can be found in the Pacific areas, the Caribbean coasts, the Llanos western plains and the mountain highlands (Davies and Fini 1994: 18). Peter Manuel notes that the *vallenato* in Colombia traditionally accompanies folk dances but, in addition to those that deal with romantic love, its texts have often been important vehicles for social commentary, a means of speaking out against corruption or poverty. However, the *vallenato* also expresses the profound changes that have taken place in Colombian society and the economy during recent decades. A number of texts celebrate local magnates in the marijuana and cocaine trade who are known to bestow lavish gifts on those singers who praise them (Manuel 1988: 51–3).

Marta Savigliano describes the tango, as danced in the *milongas* of Buenos Aires, as 'a local cultural form in the midst of the bombardment of foreign influences, providing a non-monetary based source of leisure and even an elusive, yet very real, experience of passion' (Savigliano 1997: 32). The *gafieira* in Rio de Janeiro is the equivalent of the *milonga* in Buenos Aires: a place with a wooden floor, some tables, neon lights, offering more than a hundred and fifty rhythms of the samba, as well as the polka, lambada and mambo. Brazilians are musical gluttons, Ineke Holtwijk reports; the country swallows, reproduces and fuses sounds from different cultures. But there is a change, not so much in the broad repertoire of the music but socially. Formerly it went without saying that older women would be invited to the dance. Not so any more, unless perhaps they dress up very sexily. Since the middle classes have penetrated the *gafieira*, older women have been left out, and only young beautiful girls who dance well are acceptable (Holtwijk 1996: 40, 51).

Change is remarkable in Tanzania, too. In the communal socialist period the party watched over morality and frowned on commercial tendencies, in musical life as elsewhere. Commercialization of bands and cultural troupes was a creeping phenomenon in the 1970s and 1980s, competition for audiences grew, talent scouts searched for performers, and sexual elements gained a prominent place in the revival of some traditional dances; this, combined with the fact that commercial performers appear at beer halls, where alcohol and prostitutes are available, was condemned by the elites, who have their own more expensive places to go to, where alcohol and sexual activity are also in abundant evidence (Plastow 1996: 199–200). Nevertheless the music is still very Tanzanian.

Rien à signaler ('Nothing to report') is an Algerian rap group whose members sing in Algerian Arabic with its cracking and cutting consonants and wavering notes, and play lute, violin and drums. They sing about their raped sisters, about weariness and distress, but not about the Islamists; they fear their throats will be cut. They don't like the French hiphop of Algerian migrants, such as the group Nique ta mère ('Fuck your mother'). Such a suggestion is against Arabic culture. And what about the glorifying of the misery of the French suburbs? Misery resides in Algeria, where there is slaughter. And misery is not something to be glorified.[3] Their music is clearly a local transformation, and the content of their songs and the contradictions they speak about have unmistakably local origins.

Thai classical music and dance all but disappeared after 1932 when the courts were disbanded. In any case, this is what many Thai people felt. Nowadays, recordings of classical Thai music are very rarely heard. Nevertheless, Deborah Wong notes, Thai popular music is firmly rooted in the pantheon of contemporary Thai values (Wong 1995: 55). Failure to take this on board was also a miscalculation of Western-owned music channels such as MTV and STAR-TV operating in Asia. They were confronted with considerable economic losses as a consequence of their disregard of the different cultural values, socio-cultural settings and musical traditions in the Asian regions (Bontinck and Smudits 1997: 27).

It is difficult for an outsider to judge how far music is really grounded in local culture and local developments, and to what extent an assessment made a decade ago still holds for the present situation. Peter Manuel thinks, however, that

> in the realm of popular music, Vietnam enjoys a vitality and individuality unrivalled by contemporary musics in smaller, war-ravaged Laos and Cambodia, as well as in Thailand and Malaysia, where, with the exception of the Malay-Indonesian *dangdut* and Thai *luk-tung*, Western-style pop predominates. In spite of over a century of colonial rule and neo-colonial occupation, Vietnam succeeded in fostering a truly national, dynamic, indigenous popular music which borrows little from Western styles. (Manuel 1988: 198)

The technical innovations that started in the 1980s caused an enormous recentralization of music production and distribution, compared with the relatively cheap and decentralized production and distribution offered by cassettes and the radio. CDs and the like cannot be afforded by most people in poor countries. An interesting consequence of this is that the amount of local music on the market, obviously copied and copied over and over again on cheap cassettes, is relatively high in these countries when compared with the international repertoire (Mediacult 2000: 133–4). Peter Manuel's analysis is this:

> The backyard cassette industries are able to respond to diverse regional, ethnic, and class tastes in a manner which is not characteristic of record or film industries; the latter are mostly corporate- or state-controlled and hence tend to seek or create as broad a market as possible. Cassette technology, in other terms, offers the potential for diversified, democratic control of the means of musical production, and has engendered many new forms of music which have arisen as pop stylizations of regional folk musics. West Javanese *jaipongan* is one particularly striking example of a vital pop form which has emerged from grassroots regional expression, independent of centralized, corporate music industry manipulation and promotion. (Manuel 1988: 6)

Irmgard Bontinck and Alfred Smudits (1997) point out that in most developing countries the domestic musical repertoire represents a high proportion of sales.

In legal sales alone, Japan has a high domestic share of 72 per cent, followed by Hong Kong (54 per cent) and Taiwan (65 per cent). In the Arab region Egypt has a high domestic share (74 per cent). This is also the case for Turkey (76 per cent), Latin America overall (65 per cent), Mexico (70 per cent), Brazil (60 per cent) and Chile (60 per cent). We should remember, however, that most of this domestic repertoire has been published by one or other of the foreign-owned cultural conglomerates.

In the field of theatre in India, in almost every city, groups of committed youngsters have taken to staging street plays on topical issues.

> On any one day there are nearly 7,000 active groups in the country. All kinds of people from factory workers to college students, professors to professional theatre activists and political agitators are involved. Normally such plays are performed outside offices during lunch intervals or after office hours. In the evenings, and during holidays, festivals and fairs, the roadsides, street corners and open grounds are ideal places. The audience varies from a handful to hundreds. The performers can easily reach out to nearly 400–500 people in the open air and crowded streets without the help of amplifying systems. (Srampickal 1994: 99–100)

Jacob Srampickal mentions that each state or region in India boasts a variety of folk theatre. He observes a great difference from theatre as it is known in the West.

> While the West has tended to cast its communication in rhetorical, persuasive discourse and in more denotative written and print media, in India a much more connotative, symbolic, mythic and narrative discourse of performance has continued to be central. While Western theatre fragmented into opera, ballet and drama based on dialogue, Indian theatre maintains a composite form of singing, dancing, verse, prose dialogue, and rhetorical speech with elements of criticism. (Srampickal 1994: x–xi)

Throughout Asia there is a tradition of puppet theatre, Kees Epskamp observes: 'A ritual value is attributed to the puppets. This phenomenon occurs on a large scale from Japan to Turkey. With Islam, puppet theatre – shadow theatre, stick puppets and marionettes – spread to, for example, Greece and northern Africa' (Epskamp 1989: 123). The fact that puppets don't have an 'ego' or a 'self' could be the reason for the relative lack of embarrassment in dealing with 'delicate' issues.

Obviously, theatrical events such as these compete nowadays with films such as *Titanic*, Catherine Diamond notes in the context of her description of a *pwe*, a pagoda festival in Burma. The *pwe*, she says, is still very much the same extravagant variety show as ever but now combining religious ritual, pop songs, traditional dances, modern plays, comic skits and classical dramas – and keeping the performers on the stage from ten in the evening until seven the next morning. Despite satellite television, the public wants to see celebrities perform live, enjoy the impromptu jokes of the comedians, and participate in the communal experience of staying up all night. 'During week-long festivals, local pagoda officials hire troupes whose performance content is overseen by the Drama Association, made up of older performers who want to maintain the traditional content and contain the trend to let pop music and low comedy dominate.'

However, the drama sections of the *pwe* are steadily being eroded by those consisting of pop music. 'The Drama Association tries to stem this tide to ensure the continuation of traditional styles, to preserve the religious aspect of the performance – so that it is not given over wholly to commercial concerns – and to maintain the employment of older performers trained in traditional arts who might otherwise be sidelined.' Although attending the *pwe* in large numbers, mostly for the pop music sections, young people seem to be seeking their sentimental journey elsewhere than in the trials and tribulations of the ancient princes and princesses. 'In 1999, their attention was on *Titanic*, the quintessence of fantasy wealth and luxury – even for those who could not afford to see the film, but only stood outside gazing at the billboards. Here was their own contemporary *mintha* and *minthamee* – no longer a prince, but a poor boy who wins the love of a capitalist princess and dies saving her' (Diamond 2000: 234–6 passim).

The opposite happens as well. In Indonesia, in the late 1980s and early 1990s, theatre groups were formed with a strong Islamic commitment which attracted huge audiences to their plays, according to Barbara Hatley. These groups focus their performances on the neglect of Islamic values by the contemporary Indonesian state and society (Hooker 1993: 61).

With evident pleasure Temple Hauptfleisch presents the variety of theatrical forms to be found in the 'new' South Africa: a harvest festival in Venda, a wedding ceremony in KwaZulu, a *ntsomi*-narrative occasion in rural Transkei, a 'gumboot dance' on the Johannesburg gold-mines, a *marabi* evening in Soweto, a 'Coont carnival' in Cape Town, a 'township musical' in a Mamelodi civic hall, a satirical revue by Pieter-Dirk Uys, as well as performances of *Woza Albert* in the Market Theatre, *The Pirates of Penzance* in the Natal Playhouse and *Hamlet* in the State Theatre Pretoria. He distinguishes eight categories of forms on the theatrical menu in South Africa: indigenous, traditional, communal; indigenous, contemporary, communal; imported, Western, communal; indigenous, Western, communal; imported, Western, elite; indigenous, Western, elite; indigenous, 'alternative', Western; indigenous, hybrid.[4]

African theatre has always had a strong performative tradition that combines dance, orchestral use of drums, choral singing, mime, oral poetry, public storytelling and the elaborate use of masks (Srampickal 1994: 29). The theatre scholar

Ossie Enekwe observes that in Igbo theatre in Nigeria, which is usually performed out of doors, there is a 'dynamism of context'; almost every element is figured in a structure of constant tension and flux. The stage shifts just as the 'actors' do. 'The audience act as a counterpoint and occasionally the stage expands to incorporate it, transforming it into the centre. Focus moves from one location to another, from one section to its opposite, there is an absence of absolutes' (Oguibe 1995: 75–6).

In Nigeria, as in many other African countries, the more literary theatre is closely related to the universities. There is in Africa a long list of distinguished playwrights such as the Nobel prize-winner Wole Soyinka in Nigeria, Léopold Senghor in Senegal, Kabwe Kasoma in Zambia, Amadu Maddy in Sierra Leone, Ngugi wa Thiongo in Kenya and Efua Sutherland in Ghana (Srampickal 1994: 29). However, young authors in particular see theatre in the universities as being elitist, as having little relevance to the social realities of the country and as talking above people's heads, Adama Ulrich observes. 'Both content and language are too intellectual and are even scarcely understood by a student audience. In addition, aspects of "total theatre", which are typical of traditional African theatre forms, have been completely suppressed. The quest for "total theatre" focuses mainly on overcoming the orientation towards the written word and reinstating the multitude of forms available for theatrical expression' (Ulrich 1994: 113).

In Latin America most rural communities and urban *barrios* (neighbourhoods) continue a long tradition of observing patron-saint festivals, with processions, carnival-like fairs and forms of folk drama mixed with local civic celebration. However, in contrast to theatre in Asia and Africa, popular theatre in Latin America is less rooted in religious cults and mythic history. The popular performative tradition is related more to the high-spirited, joyful sociability of family and community fiesta, carnival and amateur community entertainment than to religious ritual. The oppressive military regimes stimulated many artists to contribute, through their creativity, to social and political popular movements (Srampickal 1994: 31).

A common denominator in popular theatre in various parts of the world is protest against modernization; it tries to maintain free speech against the total mobilization of human life towards rationalized progress and economic productivity. According to Jacob Srampickal, popular theatre 'is an attempt to restore the values of community and personal dignity in societies where technical progress and productivity threaten to become the only values'. It tries to recapture the essence of indigenous folk forms (Srampickal 1994: 37–8). This kind of theatre has been used in many parts of the world in education projects directed at the illiterate, using local knowledge and cultures and enhancing their cultural identity and ethnic and class consciousness (Epskamp 1989: 94).

Turning to film, cinematographic production in India is huge. It is noticeable that for a few years now the Indian 'dream industry' has stopped concentrating almost exclusively on fairy-tale scripts; ordinary daily life is now finding its way into the films, even if punctuated by the standard song and dance routines. Interestingly, too, the influence of female film-makers is growing. Thus, films for mass audiences and so-called art films are becoming closer to each other, as witnessed at the annual Indian International Film Festival in New Delhi. Even famous actors such as Shabana Azmi and Om Puri are performing in the more artistically-oriented 'populist' films.

However, it must be said that the distinction between 'artistic' and 'non-artistic' films is a strange one. After all, all films are artistic creations, though some find huge audiences and others only a handful of followers here and there. Whether and why the content and aesthetics of a film are of any interest depend on individual and collective judgements, not on the scale of production, distribution and audience size. However, what happens is that many films whose content or aesthetics are outside the mainstream find a less and less relevant distribution. Thus in India, those films that deal with themes outside the bounds of 'daily life' do not reach the big cinemas. However, according to Rada Sesic, Indian national television, Doordarshan, has started to buy the rights to those so-called art films and is subtitling them in twenty different languages. This is a major change, allowing these films to reach millions of people.[5]

Regionalization in broadcasting and the expansion of the number of channels and broadcast hours has increased the demand for programmes generally. More and more private producers have been creating programmes to meet this demand. Alhough the quality of programming is uneven, Nilanjana Gupta remarks that it is one of the strengths of the Indian mass media that this demand could be met by indigenous production, rather than through simply importing outdated Western, usually American, products. Doordarshan sells and markets rights to popular programming to private broadcasting companies. 'The impact of this move has been great because now these marketing agencies are in a position to influence the content of Doordarshan's programmes.' Nilanjana Gupta describes another reversal. 'The shift in Doordarshan's role from a broadcaster of enlightenment to a broadcaster of entertainment makes it difficult to justify its existence as a state-owned and state-managed network' (Gupta 1998: 54, 58).

In Africa, film-making has been always difficult and the situation has not improved. In Nigeria, several travelling theatre troupes have started to videotape their performances (Kasfir 1999: 33–4). This has changed the travelling troupes into a sort of entrepreneurs' theatre. That is, the actor-manager owns and runs the whole business. Oga S. Abah mentions that the confluence between theatre and society is brokered by commerce (Abah 1994: 81). There is also a changed

aesthetic; video and television encourage direct, naturalistic dialogue in preference to stylized, sung speech, which was one of the early features of popular
live theatre (Adeleye-Fayemi 1997: 126).

Since 1997, 1,080 video productions have been created in this way in Nigeria.
Each can be expected to sell at least 30,000 copies, and as many as 300,000 for
the really popular ones. Most of the films are in pidgin, Ibo, Yoruba or Hausa,
which are the most widely spoken of Nigeria's 250 languages. These films are a
way of telling stories, whether good or banal, and also of making money as fast
as possible. Many are shot in a week with a rented camera and using actors who
will be paid when the money comes in. The Independent Television Producers
Association of Nigeria organizes courses in which this new generation of directors and actors can learn to improve their skills.[6]

The same phenomenon can be seen in Ghana, where the production is approximately fifty films a year. Since the self-trained producers depend on the
success of their product in the local market in order to be able to make new
films, they are keen to take up themes that appeal to the audiences rather than
primarily presenting individual artistic creations, as is the case for many trained
film-makers who take up the video format only reluctantly. Birgit Meyer reports:
'the result is that the former make films that focus on urban people's struggle
against the visible and invisible forces perceived as making life so tremendously
difficult. In many popular films, problems encountered by the main protagonists
are attributed to evil forces believed to be located in the village, and salvation
is shown to come through the Christian God and turning aside from traditional
ways' (Meyer 1999: 93–5). Many films reiterate the message of Pentacostalism,
which has become increasingly popular in Ghana over the last fifteen years. 'Many
of these filmmakers are very aware, and in fact have experienced first hand, that
their products do not do very well at important African film festivals such as
Fespaco in Burkina Faso because they follow different standards with regard to
technical sophistication, aesthetics, narrative structure and message' (p. 95).

What is fascinating, Birgit Meyer reports, about the experience of watching
films with Ghanaian people, both at home and in cinemas, is the alertness and
moral engagement of the audiences. 'People would shout and encourage the
heroes and heroines, condemn the villains, cry out "Jesus!" in moments of extreme tension, and clap, shout and laugh in moments of release' (Meyer 1999:
101). People want to derive a moral message from the film. 'Watching a film thus
triggers moral engagement, and one of the satisfactions audiences get from this
is the temporary feeling of moral superiority, of being on the good side, while
at the same time being enabled to peep voyeuristically at the powers of darkness.
A good film, moreover, is supposed to provoke debate among the viewers even
after the show is finished' (Meyer forthcoming).

Asian public transport vehicles, whether Philippine jeepneys, Pakistani buses and trucks, Indian auto-trishaws or Bangladeshi bicycle rickshaws, are a reflection, as well as a manifestation, of both foreign and national popular cultures, John Lent reports. Gaudily bedecked with an assortment of emblems, motifs and slogans, they become the medium through which their owners express popular tastes. 'The paintings are very expensive – costing about US$150 to US$250 for a truck, slightly less for a bus. Additionally, the twenty days it takes for a truck to be painted (in some cases, yearly) means the driver loses about US$4,500 in business. A painting shop owner hires 12- to 13-year-old apprentices to do the backgrounds; local scenic painters are brought to do the floral designs and back of the truck' (Lent 1995: 175–7).

In France, a sudden resurrection of neighbourhood bookshops has taken place, something few people expected because of the overwhelming presence of the powerful book chain Fnac. The comeback has been caused by three factors. First, France, like many other European countries, operates the system of a 'fixed' retail price for books, which means that the chains cannot offer books at cheaper prices. Second, there is a whole new generation of extremely motivated booksellers, eager to present books that are not necessarily commercial. They organize debates with authors, advise their clients and know them personally, and make their shops welcoming meeting-points. Third, several publishers – such as Minuit, La Découverte, Seuil, Gallimard – have established a fund to support small bookshops financially in various ways.[7]

To end our journey through the vast domain of cultural production worldwide, we will observe some examples from the Arab countries. Syria has taken over the place Egypt once possessed in the field of television soap opera. The Egyptians have continued to make films in the studio while video makes it possible to go out and shoot on location. This is what Syrian directors do, shooting their stories in the cities and rural areas, thereby meeting the demands of the many satellite channels in the Gulf states. Since television programmes are expected to be politically correct, Syrian directors find many of their themes in the Ottoman period or in the time of the French mandate. In Egypt, new studios have been constructed close to Cairo, called Media City, consisting of 2 million square metres of production space. According to the French newspaper *Libération* (29 May 2002), this amounts to 'megalomaniac delirium'. *Le Monde* (29 July 1998) comments that whether or not this adventure will bring the Egyptian production of television series to the forefront again remains to be seen.

Every village in Oman participates in yearly poetry contests. People are encouraged to recite their own poems, with themes that range from romantic love to the experience of working in an office. In many other Arabic countries similar contests take place, and are immensely popular. According to an interview with Corien Hoek in Rotterdam (2000), this expresses the current vitality of Arab cultures: 'Islam has an answer to the wide gap between rich and poor and supports people in their daily struggle to survive. Apparently, this gives many people inspiration.' In general, the idea of beauty still plays an important role in the Arab world: both the beauty of nature and the religious experience that penetrates every moment of daily life. In many Gulf states, surplus oil money is available to commission artists to produce work for mosques or banks.

Fouad Ajami observes that poetry was to the Arabs what philosophy was to the Greeks, law to the Romans and art to the Persians: 'the repository and purest expression of their distinctive spirit. Easy to transport, composed to be recited in public, the classical pattern of Arabic culture had held for centuries. There were set limits on rhyme and rhythmic pattern and limits as well on subject matter. Formal and stylized, the poetry had been less a personal statement of the poet's spirit and temperament than an expression of old ideas in striking new forms, a thoroughly social medium, a creature of court life and a public possession' (Ajami 1999: 80–1).

Nico Duivesteijn suggests that visual artists in Egypt, as well as many other Arab countries, can be divided into three broad layers or categories. First, there are the people who want to separate themselves from Western influences. How do they define what is Western? It is what irritates them, what is without any feeling, without emotion. For them beauty comes from the soul. In an interview in Amsterdam (1998) he said:

> Many Arabic artists still feel themselves to be members of a collectivity, as opposed to the Western notion of individual artists asserting themselves as forcefully as possible. Arabic visual art is concerned with the surrounding world, and has parallels with poetry and storytelling, which explains in part the regular use of calligraphy. Western artists tell about the inner world of the individual. The second layer of artists is open to Western techniques but the scenes and people are unmistakably Arabic, as are the colours. The third layer consists of artists who are completely involved in the Western approach to art.

Of a completely different order is the rich diversity that the new electronic or digital media provide.[8] First, as Conrad Mewton puts it, 'the internet represents a big opportunity for musicians to claw back some of the immense power that the record companies have exercised over them for the last 50 years ... It's now commonplace for artists to finance the cost of their recordings themselves. Home studio technology is very advanced' (Newton 2001: 63–4).

Second, for many artists it has become possible, for instance, to make a high-quality film relatively cheaply, which also gives directors the freedom to experiment and to use as much or as little material as they find desirable. Digital video (DV) opens up the possibility of more intimate contact with actors or, in the case of documentaries, with interviewees, who are able to forget more easily that a recording is going on. DV means you no longer have to show up with a large crew, and this has several other consequences as well: you can work faster and it costs substantially less, which gives enormous freedom to anyone interested in making a film (provided he or she can afford a relatively small amount of money, which is certainly not always the case). With the old analogue cameras, a reel of film had to be changed every ten minutes. Digital cassettes last an hour, allowing longer, more concentrated work to be done with an actor. It is also easier to film in complicated situations where the presence of a film crew would be highly undesirable. DV has a reverse side as well: it makes it even easier to observe people, to intrude into their private lives and to control their behaviour.[9]

Third, the music business often has very little to do with music, Robert Burnett claims:

> It essentially consists of fast-moving, unit-led production, marketing, licensing and distribution functions. How much product will sell in which markets, how quickly they can ship, how fast they can restock, and so on. With the Internet as a potential high-speed digital distribution channel, phonogram companies will no longer be in a position to control the distribution chain. As a result they may be unable to shape the demand for a product. When music is distributed over the Internet, only one master copy is required. New artists who can create their own product will potentially be able to produce, market and distribute their work without the involvement of the major phonogram companies. (Burnett 1996)

However, Robert Burnett is realistic enough to recognize that key players in the multi-billion-dollar euro-music are likely to take actions so as to reposition themselves and acquire a competitive edge in the changing conditions of the new internet economy. Furthermore, 'to become known and make a profit requires promotion, and in this respect established companies with well-known names and brands are in a better position than new entrants, who need significant capital to advertise' (Mediacult 2000: 87). This may be true, unless a musician is able to set up his or her own worldwide network. If nearly all musicians, or artists in other fields, were to do this, much could change. It might then become unfashionable to deal with the conglomerates, and the public might become genuinely interested in real diversity. Or is this just a dream?

'The idea of superstars – a symptom of the mass marketing of things – is beginning to look outdated. Surely the real power wielded by a network with the ability to link music fans directly to their favourite band or label is the fantastic opportunity it gives even the smallest label or most cultish band to reach and target its fans' (Mewton 2001: 44–5). Even 'corporate mergers – in particular the Polygram/Universal and AOL/Time Warner – will mean more space for independents rather than less', Conrad Mewton remarks, perhaps surprisingly. 'More bands are being dropped and more staff are losing their jobs as a result of the corporate pruning that goes on in the wake of these deals. This in turn means that more quality people are becoming available to be snapped up by progressive indie labels' (p. 128).

Fourth, the artist gets complete control of the aesthetic presentation of his or her work. Until recently, film laboratories or music studios were inclined to moralize or to impose their aesthetic norms on the artistic outcome. The computer can do this too, ordering variations and coincidental musical structures, so using a computer becomes rather like asking the oracle for guidance! Nevertheless, what it does can be controlled; for instance, a diphthong can be reconstructed in all different varieties, as it were. None of this alters the fact that it may be extremely complex, technically, for a visual artist to get an installation working, in which, for instance, sensors, videocameras, mixers, recorders, beamers, mirrors and computers have to be linked, all with completely different variables.

Fifth, in any case, artistic practice is going to change considerably. 'As the computer becomes more widely accepted in all art forms and disciplines, these will tend to blend together more and more.' The traditional distinctions between music, dance, animation, film, video, architecture and robotics are said to have disappeared (Mulder and Post 2000: 5). This may be true, or we may wonder if image and sound can become as similar as many people seem to think. The differences are evident: the human body can't shut out sounds, but you don't have to look at an image. Furthermore, visual and auditory stimuli can result in different emotional responses.

Many visual artists work interactively. Their work may call only for a superficial involvement, but in the most interesting cases the artist makes more of a demand on the public. In a conventional museum, the public is expected to look on from a distance; not so with interactive exhibitions, which make the work of art a democratic process. The aesthetics are hidden in the software; the software controls the aesthetics. The artist offers a context, not a fixed end-point; the public interrelates with the work. This means too that the character of the artistic product is a shifting one. The work may become part of an architectural creation, for instance, as a display on the floor, in which texts, data or people elsewhere in the building can be seen. It may be a lighting device in the entrance hall of an office building, which is activated by people passing it. The work may be a broad screen in the living room at home; by using a password you get artistic creations on the screen, for which you have paid a subscription fee.

Until recently the practice of electronic music was rather static. Maybe the composer was excited when creating the work in the studio, but once the recording is complete the audience in the concert hall has to listen to a couple of sound boxes. Digital techniques make it possible to combine the practice of composing in the studio with performing. The taped sound can acquire a new life through its relation with the public, just by changing some parameters. Even the tonality of a work can be changed. The composer becomes a performer. Even more important is the fact that the physical connection between concept and performance is restored. 'Intelligence is hidden in our hands,' composer Michael Waisvisz says, and shows in practice. The computer is no longer merely a language-bound instrument.

Sixth, artistic creations are no longer necessarily intended to be for all time. What has been created by digital means and become public property on the internet can be changed at any moment. Works become continuous creations, mostly made by multidisciplinary teams. This means that the concept of copyright melts away like snow in the sun. After all, isn't copyright simply the freezing of a work of art? So, intellectual property rights on works of art become outdated as well.

These are only a few examples, taken from different places and from different artforms, showing that a cultural life still goes on here and there, not taken over by the big cultural conglomerates; and art that utilizes electronic and digital media is growing in importance.

This whole domain is, as we have seen, full of contradictions. Nevertheless, it gives us reason for hope. Culture as a people's way of life emerges and re-emerges in these moments before the transnationals appropriate it, Masao Miyoshi notes. True, cultural conglomerates are quick off the mark, and the life of independently produced cultural expressions is getting briefer. However, Masao Miyoshi is optimistic, because 'people do continue to live and try to survive, and as they manage to survive, they still produce texts and objects interpreting the meaning of social relations while giving hope and courage – without surrendering at once to mindless consumerism. In these moments of hesitation and resistance, people carve out a space from transnational corporations, and a site for further reflection and criticism' (Miyoshi 1998: 260–1).

DIVERSITY DESTROYED IN LESS THAN A DECADE

The other side of the coin is delocalization. Here too, there are many examples of the rapid economic and cultural changes that are taking place worldwide.

A film critic in the London *Times* reported in 1992 how a truly popular cinema in Turkey, which was producing between 200 and 300 films annually less than a decade before, had been destroyed by a free-trade agreement, signed in

1988, allowing the major US distributors to flood the market. David Ellwood and Rob Kroes confirm that by 1992 it had become almost impossible to find a Turkish film – or a film from any other European country – being screened in any cinema in Turkey. This, according to them, is an example of the process of conquering markets and deliberately destroying the film culture of a foreign country (Ellwood and Kroes 1994: 16–17). In 2000 and 2001 twelve Turkish films were made and five of these were a big success in their own country, attracting more than a million viewers. These films express social criticism of contemporary issues, something not in evidence until then, Nicola Monceau reports.[10]

Little is left of the Egyptian film industry, which in the 1950s and 1960s exported hundreds of films every year: about ten films, that's all. Why this huge decline? Most Arab states have their own forms of censorship; there is the competition with American products; the Lebanese civil war annihilated an important market, both in terms of financial investment and export; and for many years Arab states boycotted Egypt after its separate peace with Israel. Formerly, in Egyptian films, much attention had been paid to social questions, mostly related to the rapid changes taking place in Egyptian society and the tension between traditional and modern views on political, economic and moral life. In Raymond van den Boogaard's view, for Egyptian people the stakes had always been high; it was always a matter of life and death, happiness or disaster. In a some ways the films made a few decades ago were about showing that there were opportunities for Egyptian society and that the future could be better, despite widespread poverty. It seems this feeling has disappeared and, with it, much cinematic *élan*.[11]

By the end of the 1980s Brazilian cinema had been all but destroyed. From a hundred films a year at the beginning of the decade, production dropped to fewer than ten. Brazilian culture suffers, Aimar Labaki (1999) notes, from the results of the hegemony of the neoliberal project, 'which has transformed our citizens into consumers while public life supports only the market'. Mexico once produced more than 100 films a year, but despite a resurgence in cinema attendance in the 1990s, local production dropped to fewer than forty films in 1995, and to less than ten by 1998, according to the *Human Development Report 1999*. 'Hollywood has captured the resurgence of attendance since the mid-1990s, leaving domestic industries to struggle' (*Human Development Report* 1999: 33–4).

By 1995 the market share of Japanese films had shrunk to 37 per cent and only three of the top ten grossing films were Japanese – both postwar lows. But compared with its counterparts in Europe, which have been decimated by Hollywood, the Japanese film industry is still holding its own quite well (Schilling 1997: 11). Indeed, Hollywood enjoys 80–90 per cent of the market share in Europe while, according to Carl Bromley, national cinema in European countries – with the exception of France – is virtually dead.[12]

Vijay Menon invites us to take the case of Indonesian cinema. Indonesia, in its heyday, produced 100 films a year. Yet today the movie industry is believed to be dying. Local production is reported to have slid from 119 films in 1990, to sixty in 1991, to only twelve up to September 1992. 'One reason is the fascination that American movies hold for Indonesians, young and old alike. Despite dominating the Indonesian screens, the American movie industry wishes to sell even more.' Vijay Menon quotes *Asiaweek* (21 August 1991): 'The US Motion Picture Export Association threatened to complain to battle-ready US Trade Representative, Carla Hills, whose office has the power to include Indonesia in a "watch list" of unfair markets. Jakarta caved in. In May, it gave the US film industry greater access – in return for a 35 per cent increase in US quotas for Indonesian-textile producers' (Nostbakken and Morrow 1993: 82–3).

On the situation in Canada, the *Washington Post* reported on 2 December 1994:

> statistics reflect the cultural realities of living in Canada, which has one-tenth of the population of the United States: More than 95 percent of Canadian movie time is devoted to foreign – overwhelmingly American – films. Only 17 percent of books and magazines sold in Canada are Canadian. Drama and entertainment on English-language television here is almost entirely American-made. To hard-line free traders, such figures merely reflect the natural forces of the global market-place. To cultural nationalists, they represent a threat to Canada's already tenuous identity and 'a structural deformation' in need of immediate correction.

In 1986 there were 400 cinemas in Algeria; by the end of 2000 only ten were left; numbers of cinemagoers dropped from 40 million to 50,000 in the same five-year period, and hardly any films were produced locally. Jacques Mandelbaum notes that this spectacular fall might be imputed to the Islamic terror, had the process not already started in 1986. The sudden transition from a nationalized cinema to a film industry that had to operate on the market was a catastrophe.[13]

Some 400 publishing houses in Mexico went bankrupt from 1989 onwards; among the survivors, fewer than ten, which are nationally owned, publish more than fifty works per year. Néstor García Canclini notes:

> The global increase of the price of paper, compounded by the devaluation of the Mexican peso, is one of the reasons for this downturn. Others include the general fall-off in consumption as a result of the impoverishment of the middle and the working classes and the transformation of books into simple consumer goods, depriving them of the customs and tax incentives they previously enjoyed.

Bookshops closed and many newspapers and magazines went bankrupt or scaled down, as happened in almost all the countries of Latin America (*World Culture Report* 1998: 162–3).

In the UK there is a war between small independent publishers and Waterstone's, which owns 200 bookshops. Waterstone's belongs to HMV Media, which is one of the groups within the music conglomerate EMI.[14] What has happened? Usually in the UK, bookshops pay publishers sixty days after receiving the books, and receive a discount of 35 to 40 per cent. However, Waterstone's wrote to independent publishers, informing them that, from then on, payment would be made ninety days after receiving the books, and claiming a discount of 50 per cent. If the publishers did not accept these conditions, Waterstone's would no longer stock their books in its chain of shops – a disaster for the small publishers. So now the independent publishers have to wait longer for their money and they earn less. However, they have no means of fighting back.[15]

'The astronomical budget of one First World blockbuster may be the equivalent of decades of production for a Third World country,' Ellen Shohat and Robert Stam (1994: 186) remark. This statement neatly summarizes the nearly impossible position that poor countries and regions are in when trying to protect cultural life in their own societies.

> The difficult circumstances in which Third World filmmakers work are largely unrecognizable to their First World colleagues. Apart from low budgets, import duties on materials, and 'under the line' production costs many times higher than in the US or Europe, they also confront limited, less affluent markets than those of the First World. Furthermore, they must compete with the glossy, high-budget foreign films unceremoniously 'dumped' in their countries. (Shohat and Stam 1994: 256)

However, many of these high-budget films are actually shot in poor countries, where labour is much cheaper. For example, Mexico is frequently used by Hollywood. In Morocco, between 500 and 600 permits are granted yearly for foreign productions from feature films to commercials whose directors are attracted by the cheap labour force, the scenery and the fine weather. These countries, though, are rarely able to produce their own films, not having state support, unlike rich Western European countries. African film director Idrissa Ouedraogo wonders whether state contributions to film-making can be justified when the amounts of money involved could be used for essentials such as wells, schools and medical centres (Barlet 1996: 84). And if there is a chance, once in a while, to make a film, African directors must reckon with the fact that spare parts or replacements for broken lamps are not always available, that a storm may interrupt the supply of electricity for several days, that actors may not have a telephone, that cars may break down unexpectedly, or that an actor may have to go to the wedding of a family member who lives far away, with the result that filming has to stop for several days (pp. 240–3).

Towards the end of 1998, a third theatre festival was held in Bamako, featuring groups from Mali and neighbouring countries. The festival was highly praised for the quality of the performances and the creativity of the participants by a journalist writing for *Le Monde* who also commented on the major problems of equipment, communication, transport and finance.[16] In Tanzania, as in other countries, a constant problem for jazz bands is getting hold of instruments. Most instruments must be imported and paid for with hard currency, so musicians who do not own their own instruments become dependent on the management or the body that controls them (Malm and Wallis 1992: 116). In Nigeria, there have been instances of musicians joining one of the innumerable American churches, which are very rich and which use music to attract followers, just to acquire an electric guitar or a drumkit.

European countries produce hundreds of thousands of books a year, whereas the average for African countries is well under one thousand. European countries have on average 1,400 public libraries per country, where the public has free access to information. In Africa there are only eighteen libraries per country (Hamelink 1994a: 41). Charles Larson speaks of 'bookless societies, readerless societies, authorless societies' in Africa. What of the future, he asks, 'if the transformations of the so-called information age bypass much of the African continent?' He sees the braindrain of the continent's writers as one of the most disturbing aspects of the current situation (Larson 2001: 147–8).

There is, too, the pertinent question of what language authors from poor countries should write in. In a European language, and thus have a chance of finding a publisher who will distribute the book more widely? Or in their own language, as, for instance, the Kenyan writer Ngugi Wa Thiongo calls for? He asserts that African literature must be written in the language of the culture from which it is drawn (Chabal 1996: 9–10). Both choices have economic as well as cultural consequences. The chances of finding a publisher who will undertake global distribution of the book are small, but the market for books in African languages may be too small for publishers operating in this field to survive. Raising money for translation is in most cases out of the question.

Distribution of the work of artists from non-Western countries is deteriorating. Some decades ago it was still usual for books by Latin American writers to circulate easily in that part of the world. What was published in Buenos Aires soon came to Santiago de Chile, for instance. Now, these countries have become much more culturally isolated from each other. Spanish, German and US-based publishing companies have bought several Latin American publishing houses.

This means that in Mexico, for instance, the infrastructure of publishing has been destroyed. Nevertheless, the Western cultural conglomerates launch many extremely good South American writers on the world market. In their wake follow minor writers who otherwise would never have had a chance. This is fine for the world market; less so for cultural exchange in Latin America itself. And when the so-called Latin American boom comes to an end, there will be hardly any surviving infrastructure for the production, distribution and promotion of books for writers from the sub-continent.

The distribution of African films in Africa itself is virtually non-existent. The dominant position of foreign companies makes autonomous African distribution an anomaly (Diawara 1992: viii). The idea of getting any of the few existing African films into European cinemas is a dream which is hardly ever realized (Barlet 1996: 276–7). No product leaves Africa at a price that has been fixed by Africans themselves. Koffi Setordji, a sculptor from Ghana, remarks that the Western market also makes the decisions about the visual arts.[17] Harare, the capital of Zimbabwe, hosts an annual International Book Fair in which major British publishers are a dominant presence. Heinemann presents its glittering new educational books and of course its famous African Writers Series, all promoted with glossy catalogues. The contrast with the poor displays of African publishers' books, printed on somewhat musty paper, with pages crammed with text, and a nearly non-existent cover, is enormous.[18]

The unequal relations between rich and poor countries expresses itself also in the fact that many artists from the Third World spend most of their time in Western countries, and consequently contribute little to the development of artistic life in their country or region of origin. Their work also becomes more influenced by what they experience in the West than by the social and cultural atmosphere of their home surroundings. For the evolution of artistic creativity in the local context, this produces a deficiency. Admittedly, there have always been and still are always cultural influences going in many directions, but in this case, these artists are more or less forced to leave their country, due to unfavourable circumstances (Hannerz 1990: 243), while artists from Western countries who seek inspiration elsewhere have the choice of whether or not to do so, have the relative luxury of being able to travel when and where they like, and can return whenever they want their own country, where they find more facilities for their artistic work than an artist from a poor country can even dream of.

Some artists have to flee their own countries to avoid torture or worse, and many from the Third World go elsewhere for economic reasons. Several African visual artists have found themselves enmeshed in the Western gallery system, with unexpected consequences, usually to their dismay. According to Sidney Littlefield Kasfir: 'Commercial galleries abroad frequently hold unsold work by

African artists for years without returning it or compensating them financially'
(Kasfir 1999: 31–3).

Many African musicians, including the big stars of Algerian rai, are dependent
on Paris for their recordings, or sometimes London or Los Angeles (Daoudi and
Milani 1996: 14; Bender 1992: 94–5). It is in the Western world where they have
the chance to earn money by giving concerts, though it is exhausting being away
from home for long periods. Many contemporary composers from the former
Soviet Union stay abroad nowadays: Kondorf, for instance, lives in Canada,
Gubaidulina in the neighbourhood of Hamburg, and Smirnov and Firsovan live
in London; and there are also many who go abroad for a year, return home and
leave again after a while (Peters 1995: 122–3). Marta Savigliano, a dancer and
political scientist from Argentina, argues for the importance of extending the
meaning of 'exile' to encompass those displaced from their land and culture due
to the vagaries of the global economy (Savigliano 1995: 243).

Asian skies are likely to become crowded, John Lent predicted in 1995, adding that
many of the television channels beamed down from the skies would be American (Lent 1995: 3). And so it happened (Gupta 1998: 64–75). An all-out battle
to offer localized content, in language and subject matter, to dozens of separate
markets is being waged. With new digital technology and nine transponders on
the AsiaSat2 satellite, Rupert Murdoch's STAR-TV suddenly has the potential to
distribute between 40 and 100 new channels from its base in Hong Kong across an
area that stretches from Japan to the Middle East. Programmes are in Mandarin,
Hindi and English, but it will take much higher risk and investment to get deeper
into individual markets.[19] Nevertheless, people like to see programmes in their
own languages. This is the challenge for the Western cultural conglomerates:
winning the attention of diversified audiences with programmes in their own
languages entails making risky investments that are organizationally complex as
well. William Shawcross reminds us: 'it is hard to exaggerate the importance of
Murdoch's acquisition of STAR. The footprint of its satellites covers all Asia
and the Middle East. Altogether there are 3 billion people under that footprint
– about two thirds of the world's population' (Shawcross 1993: 10–11).

Of course, Asian leaders from Beijing to Djakarta realized very well that
this fact provides Rupert Murdoch's conglomerate NewsCorp with power and
influence, and they started to speak about the protection of Asian values and
traditions. Malaysia's prime minister Datuk Seri Mahathir Mohamad wondered
why Murdoch was paying such a high price for STAR if it was not to control
the news Asia would receive, and we may add to his question the arts and other
forms of entertainment. NewsCorp's answer came immediately, saying that it
intended to make STAR-TV 'a service that Asian families can enjoy in their

homes and a service which governments in the region will find both friendly and useful'. This answer, however, begs a lot more questions. Why should Western cultural conglomerates have the right to offer this service all over Asia on oligopolistic conditions? Can't Asians entertain themselves? Why is it better if only a few globally operating conglomerates control the production, distribution and promotion of artistic goods and services? Doesn't this dominance contradict democratic principles of diversity of conditions for the making, the selling and the reception of the arts?

'Utopia has landed on us, and we have no choice but to accept it as an unavoidable component of the liberalization of the economy being propagated by the government under the dictates of the World Bank, the IMF and the expansionist marketing strategies of Rupert Murdoch.' Rustom Bharucha argues that the most deceptive form of this utopia on television exists

> in the wide array of consumerist items that are displayed on commercials, accompanied by foreign lifestyles that are totally alien to millions of viewers. This inaccessible, yet visually immediate world of commodities, is possibly the most cruel utopia that could be inflicted on a people, whose poverty has increased in almost direct proportion to the seduction of capital engineered by the media and its corporate allies. (Bharucha 1998: 168)

There are other effects as well, Sheena Malhotra and Everett Rogers note, mentioning the influence Western television has on the notion of the 'ideal' Indian woman. Formerly, the ideal Indian woman was portrayed as a woman with large breasts, substantial thighs and an abundant stomach. In the 1990s, the Indian ideal of female beauty changed to become more aligned with the Western concept of 'thin is beautiful'. Malhotra and Rogers comment that this change

> is unhealthy because the average female Indian body type generally includes large hips. Therefore the 'Twiggy' or 'Barbie Doll' look that is idealized in Western television, especially in advertising models, is unachievable for most Indian women. Anorexia and bulimia were reported for the first time in India, eating problems that were virtually unknown in India until the recent importation of television programs from the West. A dramatic increase occurred in the number of such cosmetic surgeries as breast implants and reductions, liposuctions and nose jobs performed in India. (Malhotra and Rogers 2000: 411–12)

China has a 1.2 billion-person market, which has yet to be 'tapped'. What they need above all, according to Rupert Murdoch, is a bit of fun (Shawcross 1993: 240). His waiting game in China can be summarized as 'a lot of give, little take'. It is very difficult to win approval to broadcast, collect subscription fees and sell advertising. In March 1999 Hollywood reported having received its first signs in years that China might be willing to allow more films in. Jack Valenti, the chairman of the Motion Picture Association of America (MPAA), urged China to open its doors to American investment in studios, co-production and cinemas. After discussions with Ding Guangen, the Communist Party's chief of propaganda and with Sun Jiazhen, the culture minister, he said the MPAA would like to come in and build multiplexes, which would attract consumers to Chinese and American films (*International Herald Tribune*, 31 March 1999).

Japanese cultural industries are conquering markets in Southeast Asia on a substantial scale. However, in this process the cultural merchandise imported from Japan is gradually and increasingly discarding the traditional image of Japanese culture and ethnic character. What are perceived as Japanese cultural products could easily have American or British origins. Japan simply reassembles and packages cultural commodities from elsewhere and sells them to other countries. Leo Ching takes punk as an example. When it reached Japan, 'it lost most of its destructiveness and effectiveness, although the style has remained similar. The Japanese punk is highly uniform and its defiance is well regulated. Clothing is ripped in the same way, accessories bought and put on the same place, dance steps are performed in a very controlled and unvarying manner' (Ching 1996: 183). Ching's observation leads to the conclusion that a double process of delocalization is taking place: Western cultural influence over Japan, and after a touch of transformation in Japan, 'it is this depoliticized, domesticated, highly uniform and trendy Japanese punk style that has found its way to, for example, Taiwan' (p. 83).

Ding-Tzann Lii makes an interesting comparison between how Hollywood dominates the world and how, for instance, the Hong Kong film industry practises a 'marginal imperialism'.

> The production of Hollywood films is always global in horizon. It never targets a specific area as its potential audience; rather, it always aims at the world as a whole. Under such circumstances, a universal form which works everywhere is created, and capitalism expands globally, not locally. On the contrary, being situated in the periphery, Hong Kong is less likely to view the entire world as its potential audience or consumer. Rather, it limits itself to Chinese society, or Asia at most. (Chen 1998: 128)

This 'regionalization' enables Hong Kong to take local characteristics into account.

In America, another phenomenon – another example of delocalization – is happening. It turns out that Miami, Florida, is becoming the cultural capital of Latin America (McChesney 1999: 106). MTV Latino has its head office there, EMI

Latino moved its headquarters from Los Angeles at the beginning of 1997 and Universal opened a Latin music office in the city in the same year. They joined the other major labels' Latin divisions already located in the city. In June every year the Midem Americas, the international market of publishing rights, records and music videos, takes place in Miami. Also based in Miami are the bilingual channel CMT Latin America, HTV, the most important hispanophonic music channel in the USA, and Cisneros Television, which broadcasts from Canada to Argentina.[20] And it is also in Miami that the Festival de Cine Hispano takes place.

Keith Negus suggests some reasons for these moves on the part of cultural industries that see Latin America as a unified market which can be served more easily from one point in the USA.

> Miami is considered to be a convenient base for a number of reasons. Economically, real estate and office space are cheaper than in New York and Los Angeles. In addition, Miami is at the intersection of transportation routes to the US, Caribbean and Latin America, important for the way in which the US Latin market is connected to the musicians and consumers of Latin America. As music companies interact closely with other media operations, so Miami is significant because of the Spanish language media that are concentrated in the city (production of radio, television and printed publications). Miami boasts also a number of good-quality recording studios. (Negus 1999: 143)

Many Latin American stars are buying houses in Miami, which is becoming more and more the cultural capital of South America.

In the huge country of Brazil, an internal version of delocalization can be observed. In the 1960s, Time-Life, as a cover for the CIA, helped Robert Marinho to create his television channel Globo, which supported the military regime in Brazil. In its turn the military regime rewarded the channel with huge subsidies in the form of a taxpayer-financed telecommunications network and satellite system, a very large flow of government advertising, discrimination against rival networks, which helped sink several of them, and a failure to enforce the constitutional rule that 'the means of social communication cannot, directly or indirectly, be an object of monopoly or oligopoly (Article 220)' (Herman and McChesney 1997: 163–5). Microwave towers were built every 60 kilometres linking the major Brazilian cities so that television would be available throughout the country. Globo was able to rent half of the available links all the time.

In the case of Brazil, too, a double form of cultural delocalization can be observed. The programme formats, including for the Brazilian soaps (*telenovelas*) have been derived directly from US entertainment. What was most influential – as in other parts of Latin America – was, according to Jesús Martín-Barbero, 'the importation of the North American *model* of television. This does mean simply the privatization of the networks.' He explains: 'the heart of the model lies in the tendency to constitute, through television, a single public, and to re-absorb the sociocultural differences of a country to a point that one can confuse a higher degree of communicability with a higher degree of economic profitability' (Martín-Barbero 1993a: 180–1).

Martín-Barbero notices the tendency for television to constitute a discourse that, in order to speak to the largest number of people, has had to reduce the differences between them to a minimum. Television tends 'to absorb differences as much as possible'. He emphasizes: 'I use the word "absorb" because this best describes the way television attempts to deny differences: showing such differences with all implicit conflict stripped away.' With the construction of a national space, local and regional distinguishing features, contradictions and experiences from all over Brazil are becoming less important than the unifying national story told by Globo, which includes commercial messages in its programmes nearly every minute.

Although there are many examples of artistic diversity still flourishing, we also have to admit that in many places in the world the conditions for artistic creation, distribution and promotion have been destroyed. How to evaluate those two sides of the coin? Three observations can be made. First, while innumerable artistic initiatives happen everywhere, there is less and less infrastructural support for making diversity the dominant factor of cultural life. Instead, oligopolistic conglomerates command such a position in the market that they can decisively influence people just when they are making choices about what to visit, read or buy.

Second, cultural life thus becomes increasingly delocalized. The global market for cultural products is becoming concentrated, driving out small and local industries, the *Human Development Report 1999* observes:

> At the core of the entertainment industry – film, music and television – there is a growing dominance of US products, and many countries are seeing their local industries wither. Although India makes the most films each year, Hollywood reaches every market, getting more than 50% of its revenues from overseas, up from just 30% in 1980. It claimed 70% of the film market in Europe in 1996, up from 56% in 1987 – and 83% in Latin America and 50% in Japan. By contrast, foreign films rarely make it big in the United States, taking less than 3% of the market there. (*Human Development Report* 1999: 33–4)

Third, poor countries have been hit hard economically, many times over. For them, it is more difficult to support cultural life through public funding, and at the same time local cultural entrepreneurs cannot maintain strong market positions when faced with cultural conglomerates. At the same time we should note the enormous braindrain taking place. There is also the legacy of colonialism. Colonized Africans and Asians went to European-owned theatres to watch European and Hollywood films, for example. This 'encouraged a kind of spectatorial schizophrenia or ambivalence in the colonized subject, who might on the one hand internalize Europe as ideal ego and on the other resent (and often protest) offensive representations' (Shohat and Stam 1994: 347). Seydou Sall observes in his *Towns and Development* report on South–South relations that 'colonialism's worst crime was to undermine the self-confidence of otherwise robust and dignified people, and make them believe that somehow western culture, western religion, western values, western thought models, western technology are superior to their own' (Shuman 1994: 52).

Obviously, this is a highly controversial subject, as we saw in the example of film in Turkey, where production has decreased substantially, but where the few films made by Turkish directors have been exceptionally popular. Unfortunately, there are not many examples of this kind.

TRADITIONAL, FOLK, POPULAR, WORLD

The impression exists that, worldwide, respect is growing for so-called traditional forms of art, folk cultures, cultures with a popular base, and arts from non-Western countries that have a global common denominator, such as 'world' music. However, opposite tendencies and problematic developments can be discerned as well.

The rise of consumer capitalism, specifically the spread of cultural conglomerates, has enlarged the gap between the normal daily life and the processes of artistic creation. 'Traditional' societies hardly exist anywhere. This has consequences for traditional forms of music, dance, storytelling and visual representation. Those that do exist have nevertheless been influenced, in one way or another, by modern trends. We must also not forget, Rustom Bharucha points out, that

> if tradition lives today, it is because it has always changed in the course of history. How it changes within its own performative and cultural context is frequently undocumented and even forgotten, because the change occurs slowly, organically, in deference to the larger needs of its community. It is only in recent years through interventions like tourism, film documentation and interculturalism that the changes in 'traditional' performances have become at once more visible and swift. (Bharucha 1993: 196)

Let's take a short walk through history. The domain of traditional arts includes creations made by the community as a whole, but in many societies there were, and still are, highly professionalized forms of art as well. There were extremely sophisticated traditions in the courts, which hired musicians, puppeteers, dancers and actors, while many works of art were integrated into religious ceremonies (Barber 1997: 3; Epskamp 1989: 77). The term folk art, or folklore, has often been used to indicate traditional forms of art, but its meaning has been extended to more popular forms of art as well, encompassing the whole range of artistic creations from local communities – with the exception of arts from the higher social strata – before the cultural industry took over important segments of cultural life.

The concept of popular art includes more specifically the arts that emerged from nineteenth-century urban working-class societies. These were produced by individual, professional entertainers, but succeeded only in so far as they articulated collective values and sentiments, which the artist gave back, and confirmed, to the popular audience (Barber 1997: 3). They bore a stylistic resemblance to the more traditional arts in the local culture, but their production and consumption were associated less with special traditional life-cycle functions or rituals (Manuel 1988: 2–3). In the popular arts, thus defined, the relation between the processes of artistic creation and the community as a whole still exists. Those relations have different characteristics, distinguishable according to cultures, and changing over time.

The big change comes when the relationship between concrete existing communities, however they may be defined, and the artistic processes fades away. Jesús Martín-Barbero, taking the example of Indian crafts, says that the progressive impoverishment of peasants and semi-subsistence farming, rapid population growth and the falling prices of agricultural products push rural people into the city and encourage urban concentrations. Under these conditions, the production of crafts is so important that in some communities it has become the principal source of income. Other outside pressure comes from capitalist consumption. In this process he observes a paradox. This is that 'the tendency toward the standardization of the products and homogenization of tastes demands that production finds a way to respond to the market demand by renewing periodically the designs, innovating the aspects of textures and providing continuous differences' (Martín-Barbero 1993a: 190). Craft products contribute to this demand for continual variation of design by their rarity, their idiosyncratic patterns and even their imperfections.

All this translates into nostalgia for the natural and the rustic, a fascination with the exotic, thus opening the way for tourism, and ever stronger external pressures. Tourism converts indigenous cultures into an entertaining show, forcing the stereotyping of the ceremonies and costumes, mixing the primitive and modern in a process that always maintains the difference between the two and the subordination of the former to the latter. Finally, according to Jesús Martín-Barbero:

there is the external pressure of the state, transforming the crafts or the dances into the cultural patrimony of the nation. This exalts indigenous cultures as a common cultural capital, exploiting them ideologically in order to resolve the tendency toward the social and political fragmentation of the country ... the products of the community become separated from the local culture, dispersed fragments are reintegrated in a national-level typology of all the local cultures, a typology that becomes a patterned demand for the customs and industrial products from various cultures without which those local communities could not live. Thus, the modes of production of craft articles in indigenous communities are converted into mediating vehicles of disaggregation and individualization. There is a dislocation of the relationships between objects and uses, tempos of life and practices. (Martín-Barbero 1993a: 190–1)

In these processes different developments can be discerned. For instance, in a Zimbabwean village, Tengenenge, a community of sculptors started to make a product line from serpentine, a kind of stone found in abundance not far away. They tailored their themes to suit the market. The quality of their work was such that they became quite famous, especially among diplomats, foreign business people and development workers. The consequence is that most of their sculptures, and the best ones, now leave the country, directly from their place of production, and into the hands of foreign owners. Meanwhile their work is earning more respect in Zimbabwe too, but hardly anybody – including the National Museum in Harare – can afford to buy it. Another development is that some of the sculptors are no longer seen as members of a collective, but have become known by name, as individual artists (Rozenberg 1994).

A comparable phenomenon, where the cultural community disappears from sight, took place in the Japanese village of Sarayama, influenced by the aesthetic ideals of Yanagi Muneyoshi (1889–1961), founder of the Japanese folk craft (*mingei*) movement. He stressed that for folk crafts to be beautiful, they should be made with local natural materials in a spirit of co-operation and self-denial. The craftsman is expected to work in harmony with nature and not to be interested in financial gain. He tried to realize his ideals in Sarayama, where people lived in great poverty. By the late 1950s, Yanagi's ideas had become widely known. Because Sarayama's pottery was regarded as beautiful and truly *mingei* in character, many people wanted to buy pieces made in the community. Visitors flocked to see the potters at work; most went as tourists, but for a significant few the trip to Sarayama became a kind of pilgrimage, because the community and its pottery represented Yanagi's ideals of what 'true' folk crafts should be (Moeran 1989: 76–93).

Brian Moeran reports that it is

this growth in consumer demand that has been responsible for changes in the potters' social organization during the past twenty years. Potters have found that they can sell whatever they make. The less time they spend preparing their materials, the more pots they can throw; the more they throw, the greater their income. Farming ceases to be economically viable and co-operation breaks down; status differentials develop, based on wealth and talent; community solidarity is effectively undermined. Yet, precisely because potters adopt one or two techno-logical innovations and stop working together, precisely because they begin to make a lot of money and their individual talent is recognized, folk-craft leaders then exclaim that the quality of Sarayma's pottery is rapidly 'deteriorating'. The social and aesthetic ideals end up as mutually destructive.

Sidney Kasfir, however, doubts whether this is the case in those situations where artists from non-Western countries succeed in finding a market for their products. Speaking about Kenya, he muses on the concept of 'tourist art'; this, he says,

> seems to include all art made to be sold that does not conveniently fit into other classifications. It is easier to state what it excludes: 'international' art made by professionally trained African artists and sold within the gallery circuit, 'traditional' art made for an indigenous community, and 'popular' art that is non-traditional but is also sold to, performed for, or displayed to 'the people'. (Oguibe and Enwezor 1999: 100–1)

If the 'tourist' in 'tourist art' is not the crucial distinction that keeps West-ern authorities from admitting it to the canon, what else is to blame? 'Rather it is the belief that it is cheap, crude, and mass-produced. But all African art is cheap, in art market terms, prior to its arrival in the West.' And what about mass production? Sidney Kasfir asks.

> Even a humble curio is hand-crafted. Mass production implies the use of standard-ization techniques and assembly lines – hardly a description of what goes on in a carvers' co-operative. Even in very large co-operatives, such as that at Changamwe outside Mombasa, the hundreds of carvers are broken down into separate sheds of a dozen or fewer men who maintain close ties over many years, who train new apprentices, and who may even be relatives from the same village in Ukambani. (Oguibe and Enwezor 1999)

It is not the role of Westerners, Ticio Escobar emphasizes, to dictate which techniques should be used and which sentiments should be expressed. 'Of course it is important to support traditional techniques whenever possible, but only when the communities need it.' And further, 'what is unacceptable is to force a group to cure itself by faking emotions it no longer feels' (Mosquera 1995: 100).

Several international and national associations and initiatives support craftspeople from poor countries, finding markets for their creations. There is, for instance, the Senegalese painter Aîssa Djionne who has established an enterprise using the local talents of about a hundred weavers. She researches carefully into local techniques, motifs and materials, and produces textiles of great beauty as well as other products that are exported to Europe.

Thomas Aageson, president of Aid to Artisans, suggests that if good marketing techniques are used, public interest in handmade crafts can be raised locally and internationally. 'In any country where tourism is important, artisans hold key positions in the marketing mix, because their products visibly differentiate their country from others.' He mentions microcredit as the first step in the direction of spreading popular capitalism:

> The Grameen Bank set up a cooperative export program that employs weavers throughout Bangladesh. On the other side of the world, potters with workshops attached to their homes in Chulucanas, Peru, ship their traditional pots to Neiman-Marcus stores in the US. After a four-year investment in Peru, the US Agency for International Development (USAID) artisan program in which Aid to Artisans is involved has achieved $9.9 million in annual export sales, creating thousands of jobs among micro- and small enterprises. (Aageson 1999: 3–4)

Aageson is optimistic that if these kinds of people have a chance to make a living at home, fewer artisans will migrate to the larger cities.

Nevertheless, there remains the problem that these craftspeople and artisans can make a living only by working for foreign markets or for visiting tourists. The present economic globalization causes local products to be pushed out of the local market and replaced by cheap imports. The crafts have been broken away from the local culture, and can no longer develop in relation to the continuing stream of emotions in the society in which they are produced. Fredric Jameson comments on these cultural and economic ruptures: 'it is very easy to break up such traditional cultural systems, which extend to the way people live in their bodies and use language, as well as the way they treat each other and nature. Once destroyed, those fabrics can never be recreated' (Jameson 1998: 62–3).

Following the industrialization of cultural production and distribution, it is interesting to hear the call for 'authenticity', as if there was somewhere in history when all creativity was untouched by diverting influences. In the realm of African art, Christopher Steiner describes the kind of curious situations that the Western drive for authenticity can lead to. Academics and dealers alike consider as important an object's condition and history of use, intended audience, aesthetic merit, rarity and estimated age. It is commonly asserted that there should be no intention of economic gain on the part of the artist. It should have been used in a 'traditional' manner.

> For the Westerner, authentic African art only existed in the past, *before* European contact. For the trader, authentic African art only exists in the present, *after* European contact, when the objects were taken out of Africa and declared by the Westerners to be authentic ... Unlike the Western collector or dealer who focuses on the object itself as the source of authenticity, the trader views authenticity as something which emanates directly from the pages of a book. (Steiner 1994: 102, 103)

In 1987 representatives from eleven independent record labels met to try to find a classification in Western terms for the many different forms of music coming from non-Western countries. They decided on 'World Music'. It was agreed that this meant practically all music that didn't already have its own category, unlike, for example, reggae, jazz, blues and folk (Frith 1996: 85). However, most of these independent labels function more and more as sub-labels of the big cultural corporations (Burnett 1996: 17). Roger Wallis and Krister Malm observe that 'small countries fulfil a dual role for the music industry. They provide marginal markets for international products. They also, by virtue of their unique cultures, can provide the sort of talent that comprises invaluable raw material for international exploitation' (Wallis and Malm 1984: xiii). It is thus an illusion to believe that world music is unmediated and authentic.

According to Steven Feld :

> What world music signifies for many is, quite simply and innocently, musical diversity ... But it is as a commercial marketing label that 'world music' is now most commonly placed. In this context the term has come to refer to any commercially available music from non-Western origin and circulation, as well as to all musics of dominated ethnic minorities within the Western world. (Feld 1995: 104)

Lucy Davies and Mo Fini are also clear about this: 'The popular music of the Andes as we know it in the West has very little to do with traditional Andean music. Nevertheless, the instruments used are traditional, even if the tunes are refined for Western performance' (Davies and Fini 1994: 19).

Wolfgang Bender agrees but also thinks that the influence of world music on 'local' artistic and cultural life has not been substantial. He gives the example of the Amharic singer Aster Aweke, who for decades has been famous in her own country, Ethiopia. Iain Scott, owner of the Triple Earth label, 'discovered' her.

After her success with Triple Earth, Columbia (i.e. Sony) launched her internationally. Notwithstanding this global breakthrough, her music continues to appear in her own country on cassettes, relatively undisturbed by the deformations that are the usual consequence of global music publishing. Wolfgang Bender concludes, therefore, that in world music there are sometimes two independent economies and cultural systems operating: the global melting pot and ongoing local originality (Bender 1994: 485).

Jeremy Rifkin does not share this optimism that local cultural life is little influenced by what happens to representations of those cultures on the global markets. He reminds us that we are speaking about a world in which more than 80 per cent of the $40 billion recording industry is controlled by only a handful of companies. What has been called world music – often 'traditional' music combined with other, more contemporary music to create 'fusion' or 'hybridized music' – has grown steadily in the global marketplace over the past ten years.

> In its native guise, much of this music represents a form of cultural capital – a medium for communicating the shared values and historical legacy of a people. Indigenous music often expresses the plight and circumstances of a group or speaks to their spiritual yearnings and political aspirations. In its cultural form, music is a strong conveyer of social meaning. It mobilizes deeply held feelings. When appropriated, packaged, commodified, and sold in the form of world music, the central message of the music often is watered down or lost altogether. (Rifkin 2000: 248–50)

Of course, Rifkin is well aware that 'proponents of world music argue – with some justification – that providing a global audience for indigenous music helps foster greater understanding and tolerance among people and promotes the idea of living in a multicultural world'. However, this argument does not convince him sufficiently. He observes that 'the real impact of world music is to seriously weaken local cultures by transforming a primary channel for communicating shared meanings into a kind of packaged mass entertainment that, while it retains the form, eliminates both the substance and context that make the music a powerful expression of human sentiment'.

Without doubt, Peter Manuel observes, in most of the developing world folk music may continue to occupy a place, whether as a peripheral commercial genre, an artificially preserved museum piece, a tradition upheld by isolated groups, or a persistent yet marginal alternative to mediated musics.

> But increasingly, the entire world in which folk traditions were embedded is changing or disappearing. Television, cinema, and radio have irrevocably shattered the insularity of traditional rural life. The antenna emerging from the huddle of

sun-baked huts alters the image of the Algerian village far more than its simple appearance might suggest; for the peasant exposed to American TV, or to Indian film music, the village will never look the same, and traditional rural music will never sound the same. In a word, there is no turning back. (Manuel 1988: 22)

The issue presented here is an extremely complicated one. Later in this chapter I discuss the many different interpretations and practices that the concept of hybridity contains. After all, the discussion starts when artistic cultures have been taken out of their original context, or this original context itself changes, and hybrid forms of art start to grow, or have been pushed forward, under certain conditions.

It would be romantic, arrogant and unrealistic to say that societies and their cultures should stay as they were. Nor is this book the place to judge the quality of works of art, though from the examples I have given it can be recognized that many are of a very high quality indeed. What should be feared is that the connection between artists' creations and performances and their respective societies is in the process of being loosened irreparably.

For many Western and Westernized people this may not be a problem. For most other people there is reason for alarm; they continue to consider local societies, local economies and their related cultural life as the building blocks of civilized activities (Shuman 1998: 180).

IDENTITIES: DEMARCATIONS OF DIFFERENCES

Why is it important to reclaim a space for the development of strong cultural identities shared by people who live in a particular place, or who are connected with each in some other way? Why try to regain this space when it also includes differences of taste as well as mutual irritations? In a world in which the tendency is for everything to be in similar colours, in which texts start to duplicate each other, and music is becoming less differentiated than before, this is a question which is not easy to answer. Must we be nostalgic? Please, no! So, what then?

Even cultural magnate Rupert Murdoch thinks that a homogenized world with no room for local culture is not a bright idea. Why does he think this? Because, he answers, 'there will be fewer differences' (Shawcross 1993: 426). And differences are the products Murdoch thinks he can deliver as well. The few Murdochs of this world have more to offer than just more of the same, because difference is also what the market demands. In general terms, most people agree with Rupert Murdoch that diversity should be cherished. In general terms, too, most scholars agree that the world has not, yet, been afflicted by cultural homogeneity, and that this will probably never happen completely.

The trend that can be observed, according to Abram de Swaan, is that from the local perspective the cultural range on offer has increased but, when different local situations are compared, this diversity is becoming more and more alike. 'Globalization implies heterogenization and general homogenization' (Mediacult 2000: 205). However, this interesting statement should be put in perspective immediately. In many poor countries people lack the economic means to avail themselves of the diverse offerings from the global cultural industries. So, for instance, the 'only' available music is from the local market. We may wonder whether this 'only' is a problem, or why it is a question at all. More and more we consider cultural diversity a great asset. However, misunderstanding arises when diversity becomes equated with huge quantities of different forms of art and entertainment. Diversity, then, becomes conceptualized from the supply side. Is the cultural range on offer varied enough to satisfy different tastes, and from the commercial perspective, does it arouse plenty of enthusiasm, which stimulates buying, reading, watching or listening?

There is another possible conceptualization of diversity. In this, the aspect of cultural difference, within the framework of the concept of diversity, is emphasized. At stake is not only whether the artistic goods and values are, for instance, aesthetically varied, but whether these help individuals and groups or collectives of people construct for themselves stable cultural identities, which may differ substantially from the identities that other people feel belong to their existence (Bhabha 1994: 34).

Let's take the example of grief. The 'appropriate' sound of grief varies widely (Frith 1996: 102). The question that follows, thus, is whether it should be the undertaker who directs the family in the choice of music for the funeral, or do people have a strong conviction about what music essentially belongs to the family member they are mourning, and his or her culture? Is it *their* ritual that will be performed, or is it the ritual from the undertaker's shopping list?

In this sense a well-developed cultural identity includes the strong feeling that specific artistic expressions make us the people we want to be, and, at the same time, that other expressions disturb our lives, don't belong to who we are, or make us feel less comfortable. Of course, in these processes, people's own choices are always influenced to a degree by outside forces. We should therefore come back to the issue raised in Chapter 2: who has a decisive impact on the kind of music, theatrical imaginings, literary fantasies and visual or filmic structures that become part of someone's cultural identity? Clearly there is no romance about human beings making their own decisions; there has always been a whole gamut of influences that help construct likes and dislikes. If it wasn't the king, then it was the Church, or a passing troubadour, and these too were influenced by many other people and forces, and so on and so forth. The rise of democracy reflected the desire that people had in relation to constructing cultural – as well as political – identities, for less dependence on authorities and sources completely outside themselves. Artistic expressions should fit better, for instance, with what people themselves experience as beautiful, pleasurable or worthwhile.

The consequence of this democratic option is that there will be real differences in appreciation, which are partly personal but to a large extent connected with the social and cultural climate in which people spend their time. For a vibrant social and cultural life this is a gain. If commercial forces heavily influence the complicated processes in which people develop their cultural identity and make their artistic choices, what happens then? Of course, people are not totally manipulated. They still express their own preferences.

Nevertheless, something is disappearing: the active process of involvement in cultural matters. This is the self-construction of a cultural identity. It is also curiosity about what artists are doing. It is the rejection of what is inhuman, banal or too easy. It is the acceptance of doubt about what is really valuable. It is the recognition that these processes will not, by definition, lead to common conclusions, either between individuals or between groups of people. It is taking on the challenge to deal with those differences because, as we have seen in Chapter 1, the arts are not on the whole a peaceful affair.

In Indian film, for instance, Peter Manuel observes, the tendency of songs is to promote an amorphous, homogeneous, rootless sense of identity rather than an affirmation of local community values and regional cultures: 'One cannot but be impressed by the contrast between the limited range of topics in film songs and the breadth of subjects in folk songs, which are directly created by the masses themselves. Aside from employing local dialect, folk-song lyrics abound in references to local customs, mores, names, and sociopolitical events' (Manuel 1993: 54).

The Indian ecologist Vandana Shiva comments, in relation to the narrowing of cultural scope, in this case by the film industry, that 'intolerance of diversity is the biggest threat to peace in our times. The cultivation of diversity is, in my view, the most significant contribution to peace – peace with nature and peace between peoples.' Vandana Shiva talks of *cultivation*, 'because it has to be a conscious and creative act, intellectually and in practice' (Shiva 1995: 181). Anyone who is operating with largely commercial objectives has, almost by definition, a blind spot when it comes to complicated issues like the cultivation of diversity. Their speciality is homing in on the spending power of different publics, and their capabilities can be found on the supply side of cultural goods and values. This is not a great contribution to the ongoing development of fundamentally democratic cultural life. Of course, the idea is not that the public is the artist. However, democratic in this context means belonging to a cultural climate in which different forms of art grow, making choices which really correspond to profound needs and desires for pleasure, while discussing the impulses which artists spread around.

Marta Savigliano, political scientist and tango dancer from Argentina, describes what real popular culture is all about, using the example of the tango:

> [identity is] the demarcation of differences carried through struggles to establish for which 'people' and in the name of what 'culture' popular culture is practiced. Tango, as popular culture, is thus the battlefield/dancefloor and weapon/dance-step in and by which Argentinean identity continuously is redefined. Who the tango dancers are, where they dance, what tango style they perform in front of which tango audience: Such issues deal with gender, race, class, ethnicity, and imperialism, frequently in terms of sexuality, always in terms of power. (Savigliano 1995: 5)

Argentinian identity is thus plural, and identities are the demarcations of differences.

Rustom Bharucha is not very much in favour of the rather vague cultural hotch-potch that he sees in India. Within the boundaries of particular states, he notes that there are sharply differentiated cultures, distinguished by specific languages, gestures, types of performance and epic traditions, that are neither 'deformed' nor archaic but alive in their own context (Bharucha 1993: 240). Therefore, he claims, 'what we need in India is a stronger awareness of our intracultural affinities. It is only by respecting the specificities of our "regional" cultures that we in India can begin to understand how much we have in common' (p. 40).

The opposite has happened, according to Peter Manuel, who points out that it has often been observed that the Bombay film industry has served to promote Hindi-Urdu as a lingua franca, as well as common cinematic and musical tastes, and perhaps even a shared worldview in its vast and diverse audience. 'Indeed, it could well be argued that fondness for Hindi cinema and the music associated with it is perhaps the single most prominent consensual value among North Indians, given the weak sense of nationalism, the diversity of traditional regional and religious cultures, and the increasingly violent antagonisms between them.' He notes: 'a consensus which legitimizes an unequal social order, however, is not an unqualified good. Commercial Indian cinema (along with capitalist entertainment industries in general) has been accused of promoting consensus largely by distracting its audiences with escapist common-denominator products, while benumbing their creative and critical faculties in the process' (Manuel 1993: 12–13).

When we speak about cultural climates, such as in the cases that Marta Savigliano, Rustom Bahrucha and Peter Manuel mention, do we have in mind only local or national, in general territory-bound situations? Not necessarily. First, we should admit that a characteristic of democracy is that there will be completely different cultural climates and spheres wherever people live. Moreover, people living in different parts of the world may feel very connected with a certain artist or artistic movement, and thus share a common interest with other supporters of this artist or trend. Many people are members of several communities, including ones that are not geographically defined (Daly et al. 1994: 180).

A challenging aspect of modern society is that our cultural identity has been fed with many more artistic expressions than ever before, which might be both a richness and an overload at the same time. Is it still possible to give a multi-layered work of art the recognition it deserves? The huge quantities of cultural stimuli that, at least in the rich countries, assail our senses every day may make it quite difficult for a multilayered work to be appreciated or understood. After all, it is the reader, viewer or listener who gives the work a second birth, and this needs to be done attentively, without devouring our cultural heritage like fast food. It requires time and work on the part of the audience.

To talk about the need for cultural diversity is to talk about a subject riven with contradictions and difficulties, even though the notion of many cultures living together sounds so nice and so democratic. In Chapter 1 I indicated that the arts are often a battlefield of conflicting, and sometimes irreconcilable, values. Ellen Shohat and Robert Stam warn that a polycentric multiculturalism, which could be a beautiful dream, 'cannot simply be "nice", like a suburban barbecue to which a few token people of colour are invited. Any substantive multiculturalism has to recognize the existential realities of pain, anger, and resentment, since the multiple cultures invoked by the term "multiculturalism" have not historically coexisted in relations of equality and mutual respect.' They conclude that 'multi-culturalism has not only to recognize difference but even bitter, irreconcilable difference' (Shohat and Stam 1994: 359).

Obviously, this heartbreaking subject is not on the agenda of the cultural industries. Everything uncomfortable must be avoided; forget about it, let's entertain. However, the point under discussion here is that globalization causes growing discrepancies between rich and poor in the world, which in turn cause wars and huge waves of migration. Many people feel that the most sacred aspects of their lives are threatened, and they react accordingly. The pressure-cooker of neoliberalism makes many people selfish because they don't want to become losers. In a world tied together as never before by the exigencies of electronic communication, trade, travel, environmental and regional conflicts that can expand with tremendous speed, the assertion of *identity* is by no means a mere ceremonial matter (Said 1993: 37).

HYBRIDITY EVERYWHERE, BUT WHY?

Some scholars claim that diversity is the normal characteristic of the arts, and call it hybridity. No culture is a hermetically sealed entity and certainly not locally bound, is the claim, and thus arts from all parts of the world merge, fuse and mix. So what is new about this phenomenon? Imperialism has already consolidated the mixture of cultures and identities on a global scale (Said 1993: 336). We can go further back in history to many earlier cultural cross-overs and artistic fusions. The difference may be that the multiplicity of influences nowadays results in a qualitative change.

Thus we get assertions that our existence is explained by *mestizaje*, which is a web of times and places, memories and imaginations (Martín-Barbero 1993a: 188). All cultures are in a constant flux. Images, sounds and texts invade from all corners of the world. Even history fragments into a series of discontinuous formations. Our perception of reality has become decentred. Listening to a piece of music from beginning to end is unusual these days. We are living in overlapping polycentric circles of identity. Purity of form and content is a non-concept; every cultural form is quintessentially hybrid. In 1991, in the Centre Pompidou in Paris, an exhibition took place called *Capitales européennes du nouveau design*. At the entrance, there was a text saying that one of the characteristics of new design was 'to be the expression of a hybrid culture with "contradictory equilibriums", where all can be the opposite of all'.[21]

The blurring of genres entails a pluralistic stance towards the variability of taste, Mike Featherstone claims. 'There is less interest in constructing a coherent style than in playing with, and expanding, the range of familiar styles' (Featherstone 1991: 25–6). He observes the blurring of the boundary between art and everyday life, a stylistic promiscuity favouring eclecticism and the mixing of codes. Parody, pastiche, irony, playfulness and the celebration of the surface depthlessness of culture are top of the bill. The idea of the originality of the artistic producer is in decline, while it is assumed that art can only be repetition (pp. 7–8). Some people may call those phenomena postmodernism.

Going back even a few years in history, we see cultural cross-overs all over the place, however. Musical impulses via foreign radio stations, combined with local traditions, seem to have been the catalyst for the development of blue beat, ska and reggae (Malm 1992: 42). Indonesian popular music encompasses a range of dynamic modern forms, from acculturated Westernized rock hybrids to genres which are purely indigenous in origin and style (Manuel 1988: 205). In Thailand, the Siamese have an outstanding ability to assimilate and synthesize foreign elements, whether Indian, Chinese or Western, into Siamese ways of expression (Apinan 1992: 5).

The Greek *rebetika*, like numerous cultures worldwide, has been developed by an unassimilated, disenfranchised, impoverished, socially marginalized class, which did not tap its creativity from the circumscribed conventions of the middle class. The traditional music of the countryside was alien to them, and they were inherently predisposed to new forms of cultural expression (Manuel 1988: 18–19). The Senegalese musician Youssou N'Dour was 'discovered' by the Western musician Peter Gabriel. Some people criticize N'Dour, and say his music has become too slick and too commercial. His defence is that 'in Dakar we hear many different recordings. We are open to these sounds. When people say my music is too Western, they must remember that we, too, hear this music over here. We hear the African music with the modern' (Taylor 1997: 134–5).

Jan Nederveen Pieterse wonders how we come to terms with such a phenomenon as Thai boxing by Moroccan girls in Amsterdam (Nederveen Pieterse 1994: 169), and Leo Ching asks how to specify the source of a dress designed and labelled by a Japanese designer living in France and assembled in Hong Kong (Ching 1996: 184–5).

In Tanzania, the *makonde* artists discovered that Westerners greatly appreciated the spiritual references in their art. Some of them exaggerated this mystic side and invented extraordinary histories for the sake of their clients. The expressive style of *makonde* art also brings to mind modern classics such as the work of Picasso, Bracque, Moore and Giacometti. For the *makonde* artists this strong selling point helped opened up a market among Western buyers (Ströter-Bender 1995: 126).

At first Néstor García Canclini deplored the influence that urban consumers' and tourists' tastes had on craft. However, on a field trip to a weaving pueblo in Teolitán del Valle, he entered a shop in which a fifty-year-old man and his father were watching television and conversing in Zapotec.

> When I asked about all the wall hangings with images from the work of Picasso, Klee, and Miró, the artisan told me that he began to weave the new designs in 1968 on the suggestion of a group of tourists who worked for the Museum of Modern Art in New York. He then took out an album of clippings of newspaper reviews and analyses, in English, of his exhibitions in California. In the half hour I spoke to him I saw him move comfortably from Zapotec to Spanish and English, from art to craft, from his ethnic culture to mass culture, and from practical knowledge of his craft to cosmopolitan criticism. I had to admit that my worry over the loss of tradition was not shared by this man who easily negotiated three cultural systems. (Yúdice 1992: 38)

Perhaps this kind of thing happens a lot. And the aesthetic results of all these mixtures may be interesting, sometimes. Nevertheless, the concept and practice of hybridization are not completely unproblematic. We should distinguish the *sources* of these hybridities as they present themselves. The simplest one is that the artists travel, become inspired by what they see and hear elsewhere, and include aspects of it in their own work. In this case, we should recognize that artists from Western countries have more money, and thus more opportunity to travel. When artists from poorer countries travel it is usually to the richer countries and the trip is financed by institutes in those countries which make the choice of who will be invited.

It is rare that artists from Vietnam, for instance, have the opportunity to go to, say, Chile or Zimbabwe, whle most Western artists can choose where to find inspiration. For others, the West is the key point of reference, as in the above-mentioned case of Youssou N'Dour. We have also seen that artists from non-Western countries who are prioritized for the international market must comply with standards imposed by the cultural industries, as discussed in Chapter 2. These standards are decisions made by the managers of the conglomerates about what the buying public in the West will appreciate.

Hybridity may have more painful sources as well, such as displacement and dispersal. Many artists from Africa, Asia, Latin America, the Arab world and the former Soviet Union lack any real markets for their work in their own countries. Many of them can work only when they go to Europe or the United States, which results in a terrible braindrain for those poorer countries. What they add to the cultural life of the rich countries may be very inspiring and enhance the quality of artistic production there, but for their own societies their absence is a loss. We must think of the immigrant workers from all those countries, who bring with them a rich palette of cultures, often not recognized in the societies where they settle. We must think also of the mass of refugee artists who have had to leave behind their writing tables, their studios, their theatres, their work in progress; the communication with their audiences and their readers broken by the threats and the reality of spying, imprisonment, torture and murder. 'Hence hybridity also refers us to examining the *terms* under which blending occurs as the recoding of relations of power' (Nederveen Pieterse 1997: 135). What is the source of the intermingling of different cultures, and who are the decision-makers? What is the price that artists and their cultures pay? What pain and suffering are involved, and for whom? Fouad Ajami relates with grief that

> when the Iraqi poet Buland Haidari was buried in London in the summer of 1996, the men and women of Arabic letters who bade him farewell could not miss the poignancy of his fate. Haidari, born in Baghdad in 1926, had been twice exiled: he had fled the autocracy of Iraq to Beirut, and he had fled the anarchy of Beirut and its drawn-out troubles to London. By the time of his death a whole world

of political journalism, of Arabic letters, had put down roots in exile. (Ajami
1999: 3)

The authors of *The Empire Writes Back. Theory and Practice in Post-Colonial
Literatures* comment, in the context of racism, neocolonialism and people being
driven from their homes because of economic, cultural or political circumstances,
that 'a valid and active sense of self may have been eroded by *dislocation*, resulting from migration, the experience of enslavement, transportation, or "voluntary"
removal for indentured labour. Or it may have been destroyed by *cultural deni-
gration*, the conscious and unconscious oppression of the indigenous personality
and culture by a supposedly superior racial or cultural model' (Ashcroft et al.
1989: 9).

A danger in highlighting the concept of hybridity is failing to put it in its
historical context. To quote Elizabeth Fox-Genovese, 'the Western white male
elites proclaimed the death of the subject at precisely the moment at which it
might have had to share that status with the women and peoples from other
races and classes who were beginning to challenge its supremacy' (Shohat and
Stam 1994: 345). When nothing is sure, when everything can disappear, when
someone's deepest belief is just an accident of history, when no value has the
chance of being respected, let alone protected, and when every work of art is
just an ephemeral occasion that can be replaced by any other happening, then
the individual person as a subject is the loser. What else is left to give one a
grip on life, to contribute to the development of self-esteem, and to proclaim
one's own values as a human being? There is no longer a self present to do the
feeling (Jameson 1992: 15–16).

During the 1996 Festival d'Avignon, in France, a theatre group, Champ
d'expériences, dug a maze of underground passages through which the public
could walk being confronted here and there by different performances, images
and texts. One of the texts read as follows: 'Let's ask why the word *alienation*
has disappeared from the hit parade of current vocabulary to make place for
virtual. In this conjuring trick, it is us who disappear; it is our existence that
becomes virtual.'[22]

What is the relevance of these remarks for artistic creation, production, distribution and promotion? Works of art, whatever they may be, guide people in
their human existence. This is not an exaggeration. The music, images and texts
one likes contribute importantly to the development of personal and collective
identity. They create an emotional field in which the person can feel at home,
while at the same time opening up the possibility of communication with the
rest of the world about the issue: this is what characterizes me, but that artistic
expression, however, is not my cup of artistic tea. The arts create opportunities

for sharing, but also draw sharp dividing lines between different spheres of life. When the significance of any form of art becomes nullified and ephemeral, then human beings are losing something that is elementary: a necessary foundation for their emotional life.

Central to this chapter's discussion has been the concept of delocalization versus the democratic notion that people have the right to communicate with each other. The arts are extremely significant modes of human interaction and expression, which should not be organized only from faraway places under purely commercial conditions. It is a healthy sign that the work of many artists is still embedded, in one way or another, in their local or regional surroundings. However, in many places the infrastructure for the creation, production, distribution, promotion and reception of the arts, including all forms of entertainment and design, has been taken over by cultural conglomerates. This has far-reaching consequences for the cultural environment in which people live, raise their children, face troubles, enjoy themselves, and die.

Likewise, the many forms of traditional arts are changing considerably under a range of influences and pressures; these include the social and economic impact of the structural adjustment measures imposed on many countries, increasing poverty, tourism and other forms of modernization. Local cultures are seriously weakened by the fact that a primary channel for communicating shared meanings is being transformed into a kind of packaged mass entertainment; while this may retain the form of the traditional art medium, it loses both the substance and context that make, for instance, music a powerful expression of human feelings, as Jeremy Rifkin has put it. We have seen too that the notion of hybridity is counter-productive when it comes to the development of a varied and stimulating local artistic life.

It is with good reason that Vandana Shiva speaks about the cultivation of diversity. But even this is not enough. Intercultural competence needs to be developed between people from diverse cultural backgrounds. If people are unable to communicate, peace will remain a distant prospect.

At several points in this chapter I have touched on corporate culture, which penetrates all aspects of life, including at the local level. Now is the moment to put the production of the land of desire under the spotlight. The show must go on. But which show?

NOTES

1. *Beyond the WTO. Alternatives to Economic Globalization.* Preliminary report by a task force of the International Forum on Globalization, 26 November 1999.

2. 'La défense de la culture va bien au-delà de la politique', *Le Monde*, 22 September 2000.

3. *De Volkskrant*, 28 May 1999.

4. Temple Hauptfleisch, 'Post-colonial Criticism, Performance Theory and the Evolving Forms of South African Theatre', *SATJ*, 6, 2 September 1992: 64–83.

5. *Skrien 222*, April 1998; see also Yves Thorval, 'En Inde, un cinéma ancré dans la réalité. Terrorisme, répression, nationalisme . . .', *Le Monde Diplomatique*, June 1998.

6. Jean-Christophe Servant, 'Boom de la vidéo domestique au Nigeria', *Le Monde Diplomatique*, February 2001.

7. Maurice T. Maschino, 'Cette passion tenace des libraires de quartier', *Le Monde Diplomatique*, June 2001.

8. The following section on the electronic media draws, from among other sources, on interviews with the visual artist Anne Nigten, Rotterdam (2001) and Michel Waisvisz, Amsterdam (2001).

9. 'La caméra numérique force les cinéastes à ouvrir l'oeil', *Le Monde*, 15 August 2001.

10. Nicola Monceau, 'Pamphlets et comédies à la turque à Istanbul', *Le Monde*, 11 April 2001.

11. Raymond van den Boogaard, 'Meer dan twintig films uit Egypte te zien in zes steden', *NRC Handelsblad*, 11 February 1998.

12. Carl Bromley, 'The House That Jack Built. How Valenti Brought Hollywood to the World', *The Nation*, 3 April 2000.

13. Jacques Mandelbaum, 'Quand Alger rêve de cinéma. Trois films tournés en cinq ans, une dizaine de salles, moribondes, au lieu de quatre cents en 1986: le cinéma en Algérie n'est plus que l'ombre de lui-même. Depuis peu, pourtant, l'espoir renaît, encore fragile', *Le Monde*, 17 December 2000.

14. 'Gigantenstrijd om Britse boekenmarkt', *NRC Handelsblad*, 15 May 1999.

15. 'Guerre contre Waterstone's. La châine de librairies anglaise impose des conditions draconiennes aux maisons indépendantes, qui dénoncent des "pratiques abusives"', *Le Monde*, 19 January 2001.

16. Thérèse-Marie Deffontaines, 'A Bamako, neuf jours de théâtre et d'échange entre Mali et ses voisins', *Le Monde*, 2 January 1999.

17. 'Des artistes sous la menace constante de la précarité', *Le Monde*, 29 September 2000.

18. 'Bezoek aan de Zimbabwe International Book Fair', *NRC Handelsblad*, 11 August 2000.

19. 'Asian Network Sends Mixed Signals', *International Herald Tribune*, 11 December 1995.

20. 'L'expansion phénoménale du musique mondial du disque hispanique', *Le Monde*, 23 June 1999.

21. *Une des caractéristiques est 'd'être l'expression d'une culture hybride avec des "equilibres contradictoires" ou tout peut être le contraire de tout'.*

22. *'Demandons nous pourquoi le mot* aliénation *a disparu du hit parade du vocabulaire courant pour faire place à* virtuel? *Dans ce tour de passe-passe, c'est nous qui disparaissons, c'est notre existence qui devient virtuel.'*

FIVE
Corporate-driven Culture

AESTHETICS AND THE LAND OF DESIRE

In *Land of Desire*, William Leach describes how after 1880 American business began to create a new set of commercial enticements – a commercial aesthetic – to move and sell goods in volume. This was the core aesthetic of American capitalist culture, offering a vision of the good life and of paradise. This aesthetic was manifest in shop windows, electrical signs, fashion shows, advertisements and billboards; as free services and sumptuous consumer environments; and as the artefacts or commodities themselves. 'At the heart of the evolution of this commercial aesthetic were the visual materials of desire – colour, glass, and light' (Leach 1993: 9). But the merchandise was to be dramatized as well. Those responsible for displaying the goods therefore frequently went to the theatre to see what was going on in theatrical design. And we should not forget the music. 'It is hard to know exactly where the custom of perfoming music in restaurants, hotels, department stores and similar consumer settings came from, but a very good guess would be German immigrants with their tradition of Gemütlichkeit, a term meaning something like "pure comfort" and marked by the mixture of music, food and drink' (Leach 1993: 139).

There was also a touch of orientalism, which hinted at luxury, impulse, desire, primitivism and immediate self-gratification. In department stores, 'don't touch' gave way to 'get closer'. From Baltimore, Maryland, to Waco, Texas, the fashion show could be found in nearly every sizeable city in the country. It became a twice-yearly event. 'The way out of overproduction', wrote one fashion expert, 'must lie in finding out what the woman at the counter is going to want; *make it; then* promptly drop it and go on with something else to which fickle fashion is turning her attention' (Leach 1993: passim).

Such aesthetic interventions taught Americans to relax a little more and to take pleasure in sensual and beautiful things. This educational process, which started at the end of the nineteenth century, makes Benjamin Barber assert, 'Choosers are made, not born' (Barber 1996: 116). What America offers the world, he says, is incoherent, full of contradictions, but at the same time extremely seductive

(p. 61). One of the contradictions is that merchants 'spoke now in two voices, each at odds with the other. For work and production, business (as much as the culture at large) emphasized repression, rationality, self-denial, and discipline; but for selling and consumption, it opened the door to waste, indulgence, impulse, irresponsibility, dreaming, or qualities thought of as non-Western' (Leach 1993: 107). At the same time those paradises of freedom and consumption are full of contradictions: we are guarded as well as stimulated; we are restrained from doing what we would really like to do and from taking what we would really like to have; and encouraged at the same time to buy more than we intended to.

A controlled de-controlling of emotions is taking place, non-stop. This is also wiping out the expression of many real emotions. In the quantities of books on achieving success that are published from the end of the nineteenth century on, one of the messages is that we should learn to smile, always, in all circumstances. And in advertising, happiness is portrayed as pleasure and increased consumption (Stivers 1994: 19, 59).

A major ideological shift happened as well, in the space of decades, as William Leach's analysis makes clear:

> For many labourers and artisans, the question of the 'people's interest' was a matter of principle, not of image, a matter of their independence and freedom from exploitation; but for merchants, the question was, increasingly, one of image. It was in their interest to give the impression that they, not their employees or other workers, were the true populists and that consumption, not production, was the new domain of democracy. (Leach 1993: 117)

In former times people could see how things were produced, and bought what they needed. Consumer culture turns these processes upside down. Production becomes invisible, and people become consumers.

There is no principal constraint on *what* can be consumed: all social relations, activities and objects can in principle be exchanged as commodities. This is one of the most profound secularizations enacted by the modern world, Don Slater remarks. 'Everything can become a commodity at least during some parts of its life. While consumer culture appears universal because it is depicted as a land of freedom in which everyone *can* be a consumer, it is also felt to be universal because everyone *must* be a consumer: this particular freedom is compulsory' (Slater 1997: 27). This statement may sound categorical, but let's imagine a situation in which people consumed substantially less, only what they really needed. The economy of the whole world would collapse. Our present world economy is based on consumption, not on durability, not on sharing scarce resources, not on caring for the future. There seems, then, to be truth in what Don Slater says:

that it is 'by and large through commodities that everyday life, and the social relations and identities that we live within it, are sustained and reproduced'.

To maintain this consumption on a huge scale, a great deal of publicity is necessary. Rush Limbaugh, an American radio talk show host, is known as the 'king of conservative talk radio'.[1] He was puzzled to receive several letters from listeners wondering why he was speaking so fast all of a sudden, and subsequently discovered that a new kind of digital technology was literally snipping out the silent pockets between words, shortening the pauses and generally speeding up his speechifying. He then found out that general managers at about fifty US stations have been using this technology to speed up talk programmes so that they can wedge in more commercials. Radio stations are adding as many as four minutes of commercial time every hour, or eight 30-second commercials.[2]

Omar Souki Oliveira (1993) notes that a closer look at a Brazilian *telenovela* gives the observant viewer the impression of being in a Turkish bazaar. Everything within sight is for sale. The couch on which the characters sit, the suits they wear, the alcohol they drink, the paintings on the walls, light fixtures, carpets, lamps and so on, all are being advertised. In addition, labels in the kitchen display the brand name of pans, stoves and appliances used by the characters. When the hero goes outside, it is time to promote sunglasses, cars, shops and even banks.

Major advertisers such as Chrysler and Colgate-Palmolive require magazines to submit articles in advance for screening, to determine whether they contain any editorial content that may be considered provocative, offensive or harmful so that they can pull their advertising when they are not pleased (McChesney 1998: 19).[3] At the same time major TV networks offer their stars contracts to sell commercials; they enter into joint promotional arrangements with advertisers, each pushing the other's offerings; they show 'infomercials' produced entirely by or for advertisers and displaying their products; and they co-produce programmes with advertisers and steer others towards advertisers' demands and needs (Herman and McChesney 1997: 140).

According to Edward Herman and Robert McChesney:

> the owner and advertiser domination give the commercial media a dual bias threatening the public sphere: they tend to be politically conservative and hostile to criticism of a status quo in which they are major beneficiaries; and they are concerned to provide a congenial media environment for advertising goods. This results in a preference for entertainment over controversy, serious political debate, and discussions and documentaries that dig deeply, inform, and challenge conventional opinion – that is, the media/advertisers' complex prefers entertainment over cultivation of the public sphere. (Herman and McChesney 1997: 6–7)

Likewise, in tourism everything is for sale: people, customs, ceremonies. The community itself becomes a huge market (Schiller 1976: 15–16). The same is true of certain kinds of film-making. *Le Monde* (22 June 1992) reported that the inhabitants of Easter Island were highly indignant that their island was used for shooting the film *Rapa Nui* which was 'very Hollywood' in its content, considering it sacrilegious.

The videos on MTV, the ultimate purpose of which is to sell compact discs, cassettes, films, clothing, soft drinks or whatever, are made by musicians, actors, designers, light and sound engineers – a whole range of artists. Fredric Jameson observes that 'aesthetic production today has become integrated into commodity production generally: the frantic economic urgency of producing fresh waves of ever novel-seeming goods (from clothing to airplanes), at ever greater rates of turnover, now assigns an increasingly essential structural function and position to aesthetic innovation and experimentation' (Jameson 1992: 4–5). Again, it is the artists who are responsible for the aesthetic innovations and experimentations and what they create, perform or design for the innumerable commercials that provide the majority of them with most of their work and income is usually – and intentionally – soon discarded to be replaced by new images, new music and new sensations. They draw constantly on the culture of past and present, local and distant, but these sources of inspiration are too fragile to be exploited under any condition and for every purpose.

During the Gulf War, American president George Bush Sr referred to the 'new world order' that war with Iraq introduced. In Jerry Mander's opinion, this concept of a new world order is an accurate description of the world we live in now: 'one that permits bankers and developers to map and plan the flow of the world's resources according to an overall vision for a world economy that functions the same way everywhere, and which homogenizes lifestyle, culture, values, and the land itself' (Mander 1993: 19). Culture can become traded and its entrepreneurs promote a positive attitude without any shadow of doubt about their global interventions. Blockbuster films are designed to play as well in Bombay as they do in Brooklyn. Disney does let its characters assume local identities and speak local languages (McChesney 1998: 16), but everywhere the format of the show is the same, or at least comparable.

By the early 1980s a major cultural change had occurred in Trinidad, according to Roger Wallis and Krister Malm. Previously, calypso singers would produce new songs daily, based on the happenings of the previous twenty-four hours. It was an improvised, spontaneous culture. The calypsonians became walking dictionaries of rhymes and quaint grammatical conversations.

> Things are different now. Calypso is adapting to the terms of the music industry environment. With the introduction of large sound systems, calypsonians have had

to structure their performances more strictly. Advanced arrangements are written for ten- to fifteen-piece backing bands, and the repertoire is restricted. Instead of churning out new songs in a steady stream (albeit often with very similar melodies), the calypsonians will sing only two or three songs for the whole of the carnival/calypso season. Because of the time involved in the recording and manufacturing process (often abroad), the topics cannot be merely of current interest, referring to the events of the night or even the week before. At the start of the three-month run-up period to the carnival, a calypsonian will release a recording and proceed to market the product. Since part of the artist's income arises from sales of discs and cassettes, an effort is made to make the live performance in the calypso tent sounds as similar as possible to the recorded version (thus decreasing the value accorded to the art of improvisation and increasing the demands on the sound of the backing group). (Wallis and Malm 1984: 279)

Clearly, things are even more different now at the beginning of the twenty-first century. Are they less good or less valuable? Obviously, here, critical judgements come into play. John Tomlinson says that

cultural synchronization could in some cases increase variety in cultural experience. It must be said immediately that arguments exist that the *nature* of such experience in capitalist modernity is in some sense deficient – shallow, 'one-dimensional', 'commodified', and so on. But this is not a criticism of homogenization or synchronization as such: it is a criticism of the sort of culture that synchronization brings. (Tomlinson 1991: 113)

Fredric Jameson thinks it is evident that we are witnessing the emergence of 'a new kind of flatness or depthlessness, a new kind of superficiality' (Jameson 1992: 9).

Corporate culture is, first of all, vicarious culture, according to political scientist Saul Landau (in interview in 1998). Second, it is grammatically bound by rules of entertainment: 'Corporate culture has a grammar, and this is what should be analysed.' In this overwhelmingly corporate-driven visual culture it is, specifically, the power of words to analyse that is needed again, because 'words refer to ideas, images to sensations. Words are structured by the grammar of the language that demands a rational ordering of ideas if the words make sense. The eye is free to rove promiscuously, accepting pattern, or the absence of pattern, without the need for reason' (Hewison 1990: 63).

SOMETHING TO TELL, SOMETHING TO SELL

In the contemporary world where cultural conglomerates are able to spread their ideas of what culture should be, the crucial questions are: Whose stories are told? By whom? How are they manufactured, disseminated and received? Who controls production, distribution and exhibition? (Shohat and Stam 1994: 184). George Gerbner notes that a major shift has taken place. He points out that 'most of what we know, or think we know, comes not from the genes or personal experience but from the stories we tell. Towering structures of story-telling called art, science, religion, law, politics, statecraft, news, etc., define and direct the world in which we live' (Gerbner 1997: 13). The big question nowadays concerns who controls these processes of telling stories that challenge our fantasies, desires, dreams, imagination and memory.

George Gerbner's response on this fundamental issue is almost poetic. 'A child today is born into a home in which television is on an average of well over seven hours a day. For the first time in human history, most of the stories about people, life and values are told not by parents, schools, churches, or others in the community who have something to tell but by a group of distant conglomerates that have something to sell' (Gerbner 1997: 14). The difference between having something to *tell*, which includes stories we may not want to hear, and something to *sell*, which limits the fundamental process of human communication and exchange of ideas, is at the heart of the matter. Corporate culture has only one purpose: they sell, we buy. It creates an ambience in which consumption is more important than other human values and necessities. Later in this chapter I discuss some characteristics of corporate culture, but first let's look at what interests are getting lost in a world in which corporate culture is the driving force.

Worldwide there are no longer any mass-media businesses that could be said to represent or share basic interests with the working class, with farmers, with people of colour, with the masses of the populations in non-Western countries, with all those people who are poor, or even with the middle class. Large-circulation media owned by or representing non-business interests have largely disappeared under the impact of market forces. It has been said that everybody has the freedom to start a cultural enterprise, but even for enterprises with substantial backing, it is nearly impossible nowadays to gain entry to the decisive cultural distribution channels (Herman 1989: 206).

Gerald Sussman and John Lent state that

transnational corporate actors and their superpower state underwriters have at their disposal such transborder communication apparatuses as communication satellites; submarine cables; television programming, multimedia advertising, and public relations outlets; film, music, and book publishing, and videocassette distribution; wire service, magazine, and comic syndication; business, technical, and financial data bank access; digital and fiber-optic telephone equipment; and computer, facsimile, and telex transmission facilities; along with tourism chains and other modes of communication that channel information and impressions about the 'good things in life'. (Sussman and Lent 1991: x–xi)

The suppression of all radical progressive movements in both the Western and non-Western world in the 1970s was meant to reverse the processes of democratizing all those communication means, among other purposes. One of the first things the Pinochet regime in Chile did after the coup d'état of 11 September 1973 was to whitewash the murals produced during the Popular Unity government; it also murdered progressive people, among them many artists (Baddeley 1989: 88). Even walls were out of bounds as places for the free expression and exchange of ideas. Those same walls today are covered with publicity, designed by artists.

Video rarely tends to confront specific political or social issues, but rather to dwell on the more intimate themes of sex and romance, which makes it a purely apolitical medium, Jack Banks observes. He quotes a *Washington Post* television critic arguing that politically-oriented videos are not welcome on MTV because the broadcasting company has constructed an insular world where music is the only relevant social force. 'Rock stars adopt poses of surly rebelliousness, but what they portray themselves as rebelling against are things like table manners or having to go to school, never against the corporate or political powers that be' (Banks 1996: 202).

Folk culture loses out too when brought into the corporate arena. Nilanjana Gupta says that genuine folk culture is always intimately connected with the lives and societies of the people who created it.

Uprooting these dances or songs from the time, place and circumstances of origin and transplanting them into television studios almost inevitably creates a sense of falseness. Also, traditional cultural practices do not usually have the kind of elegance of production that television audiences have come to demand. After all, genuine folk music and dance involves many people who are participating without any particular training or practice. Placed in the decontextualized studio setting, folk dances or songs lose the vitality and purpose of the original cultural experience. (Gupta 1998: 31–2)

Respect for what belongs to the private sphere has certainly not been evident in a world where consumption of everything considered exciting seems to know no limitations. In India, women formerly sang *masala* songs in private. (*Masala* means 'spiced', meaning erotic.) Peter Manuel relates that these songs are now disseminated as public commodities to lascivious young men. 'In the process, songs in which women freely express their condition – sexual longing, or ambivalent resentment against seductive neighbours or *devars* – become vehicles for their own embarrassment and objectification when marketed as public commodities' (Manuel 1993: 175).

The German writer Heiner Müller remarks that, because of tourism and photography, even our capacity to observe has been lost. Those quick glances at what we meet along the way leave little time for reflection, memory and sensitivity towards what is really happening before our very eyes. People delegate their experiences to instruments. When we realize this phenomenon, we can better understand the Old Testamant ban on images, Müller notes. 'It is the task of the arts to prevent people from being overwhelmed by instruments and technology' (Müller 1991: 21).

SURROUNDING THE COMMERCIAL MESSAGE

Works of art are becoming more and more the settings for commercial messages and it is their task to create the ambience in which the production of desire can take place. Therefore this ambience should be attractive, exciting, self-gratifying, pleasurable and always new (Eagleton 1990: 40–1). Self-fulfilment must rank high while community or civic well-being disappear below the horizon (Leach 1993: 6). So, the cultural ambience can be anything, as long as it seduces people. It may be going back into the past, pretending that 'history is fun'; it may be a coffee concert with Mozart and cakes.

Nevertheless, there are certain ingredients that seem to work rather effectively in the promotion of desire, which is the basis of consumer culture. One, obviously, is the dramatic structure of, for instance, the soap opera, in which a broad gamut of interpersonal relations, dreams, human disasters and sexual longings are presented to ensure that the viewers' attention is never lost. This genre has discernibly different characteristics in different parts of the world. For instance, in Egypt, it is a difficult matter politically to include current events in the script. However, Usama Anwar Ukasha, the writer of *Layali Abu-Hilmiyya*, a soap with 150 episodes, managed to include moral issues such as loyalty and treason in a historical context along with unfulfilled desires, ambition and tragic loves. Individual lives become linked with political happenings such as revolutions, wars, presidents and their policies. The series sharply criticized Egypt for the road it had taken over the previous fifteen years, but discussing Muslim-inspired terrorism was going too far.[4]

Brazilian *telenovelas* show plenty of everyday situations. Most *telenovela* writers have a leftist background and use the *telenovela* to reflect the national reality. Characters indirectly defend the importance of land reform and criticize the system of health insurance, non-functioning telephones or the president's abuse of power; they are afraid of being taken hostage, they are in conflict with corrupt business people or policemen, or their enterprise is on the point of bankruptcy because of the policy of breaking down tariff barriers. However, Ineke Holtwijk notes that there is one important difference from reality:

> In the telenovela business people are taken hostage, enterprises go broke, drug dealers have their wars and slums crash down from the hills when the rain is pouring down. But the businessman comes back with his family, the drug dealer falls in love with the girl who helps him to better his life, the entrepreneur has a rich brother abroad supporting him to save his enterprise, and the inhabitants of the slum get a new piece of land from a millionaire in order to construct new houses. (Holtwijk 1996: 181)

In the *telenovela*, reality takes another turn. Omar Souki Oliveira interprets the *telenovela*'s historical purpose as adapting and dramatizing capitalistic notions to fit the Latin American taste. 'Through the portrayal of success stories, they convey the idea of social harmony and possibilities of easy upward mobility to impoverished masses' (Oliveira 1993: 128; see also Mazziotti 1996). The high quality of the Brazilian soaps is diminishing meanwhile, because the once monopolistic cultural conglomerate Globo is getting some competition from other, smaller cultural businesses, with less interest in high-quality drama. Some of them are very Christian. Also, the thematic relationship with Brazilian daily life and society is getting weaker now that Globo broadcasts its *telenovelas* to more than 120 countries. The content has become more general and at the same time more superficial.

Mary Ellen Brown notes that oppressed groups always push at the boundaries, always watch to see what is possible. 'This is one of the areas in which soap operas and their discursive networks function as a source of strength for women. They help women test the waters to see how far they can go in challenging social norms' (Brown 1994: 12). At the same time, she mentions that it is 'evident that soap operas wedge themselves into the type of feminine culture that is constructed to support dominant or hegemonic notions of femininity' (p. 59). Here, too, reality stays what it is and can be made pleasurable by the act of consuming.

Henk van Gelder judges that in the soap no interesting individuals can be seen with contradictory qualities. The characters express their sentiments directly, and this goes on endlessly, until the television boss discovers that the public is getting bored and advertisers are no longer interested. Every episode is filled with emotional situations: marriage, kidnapping, divorce, sudden paralysis, unexpected recovery, unexpected fatherhood, new loves, deceit, a car crash, miscarriage, the death of the new lover. Marijn van der Jagt compares the characters with people riding on a roller coaster, going from peaks to depths at a dizzying speed.

The existential doubt that the characters experience time and again does not last long. Philosophical discussion about recent and bizarre events in life quickly ends, because the characters do not delve deeper than to make the observation that things are just happening and are incomprehensible. The producers of television soaps do not have far-reaching intentions. Their most important task is to keep the story rolling. (*De Volkskrant*, 1 October 1997)

A recent phenomenon is the television 'reality soap'. The first in this genre is *Big Brother* (in France called *Loft Story*) in which there are no professional actors, just ten or twelve young men and women locked up together in a house for a hundred days or so. The camera registers everything, and the viewer as voyeur hopes that something 'spectacular' will happen between them: quarrels, love, fucking, whatever. For centuries, intimacy has been a prized cultural value in our Western societies, which arouses curiosity about others' intimacy.[5] *Big Brother/Loft Story* satisfies this curiosity abundantly, attracting mass audiences, as do internet sites where people have cameras in their houses and present themselves to the world. Nevertheless – or perhaps because of the hypocrisy of this 'openness' – puritanism, frenetic intimacy and anxiety about life continue to flourish.

The idea is that some of the inhabitants of the *Big Brother/Loft Story* house will develop a 'collective attractiveness' for the viewers, while others become the hate objects, encouraged by continuous popularity tests. François Jost considers the danger of this kind of programme to be less the voyeurism and exhibitionism that it promotes than the fact that it encourages the sadistic drive that exists in everybody, while the inhabitants of the *Big Brother* or *Loft Story* house pay the price for it: 'The public not only derives pleasure from the misfortune of those it watches, which is the definition of sadism, but it also adds to this the pleasure of excluding people.' We appropriate an extraordinary right over the lives of the inhabitants/participants, who are permanently handed over to the judgements of others.[6]

Besides this public celebration of sadism, the participants in the 'game' have signed a contract in which they hand over to the producer of the show all rights to their image, and which obliges them to observe behavioural rules that the producer imposes on them. French lawyers think that such a contract infringes fundamental rights to human dignity, and that it would not hold up in court.[7]

Another point of discussion is that people are now starring on television not because they are good at something, or because they have an interesting story to tell; they become famous because they are not contributing any meaning. This is a new phenomenon. Stephan Pröpper wonders whether this is terrible. Not really, if this is what it is. The problem is that those young men and women start behaving like stars and are presented in other TV shows and magazines as such. 'Self-relativization is no longer the order of the day, the more there is self-overestimation. Modesty does not have currency any more. In former times you got respect if you merited it. Nowadays, people demand it,' claimed *De Volkskrant* (9 November 1999). This can be placed in a broader social context. The claiming of respect, without any basis in reality, represents the more general feeling of people who are losers in our contemporary glittering world where success is the only acceptable norm and automatically delivers respect. If you don't behave in the way that such losers in this terrifying social game desire, they demand respect – violently if necessary.

Besides the different kinds of soap operas, there are many more aesthetic ingredients that enhance corporate-driven culture. One is that everything should go fast and that we are confronted with an abundance of images. This commercially-driven phenomenon has penetrated all areas of social existence, as well as the theatre world, as Rustom Bharucha notes:

> There is a lot of dead theatre in the world today, particularly in capitalist societies like America, whose regional theatres are like factories, where plays are manufactured in less than six weeks and performed by a group of actors who remain strangers to one another and the audience as well. Not only are these actors alienated from their means of production, they are, more sadly and irrevocably, alienated from themselves. (Bharucha 1993: 52)

Such a seemingly pluralist situation seems to offer colossal and unparalleled opportunities for every kind of artistic expression. However, the existence of the over-availability of options suggests that all forms of artistic expression can claim equal status, which is obviously not true (Gablik 1985: 75–7). Images, sounds and fragments of ideas come and go. Instead of being a richness, this huge choice leaves us with serious questions. For instance, do we have more, or less, democratic choice? Benjamin Barber comments: 'Democracy, like a good book, takes time. Patience is its least noticed but perhaps most indispensable virtue. Television and computers are fast, fast, faster, and thus by definition hostile to the ponderous pace of careful deliberation upon which all public conversation and decision making on behalf of the common good is premised' (Barber 1996: 118).

Writing in 1994, Heiner Müller, who experienced at first hand the integration of the German Democratic Republic (GDR) into the German Federal Republic, recalls that in the GDR there was plenty of time, it was a slowed-down state. And then he makes a rather unexpected comparison:

> The concept of time in socialism constitutes its real difference from fascism. For Hitler there was no world time, there was only [the present] lifetime. This un-

conditional present tense, implying that everything must happen in one's own lifetime, explains perhaps the fascination Hitler has for young people today: no future, everything now. Hitler's life was at the same time a long suicide; that was its real energy. The concept of time in socialism was fundamentally different; one always thought beyond one's own lifetime. (Müller 1994: 202)

Indeed, one of the characteristics of corporate-driven culture is the permanent tendency to annihilate the past, the memory, to be careless, to give no chance to the present experience, to destroy immediately what starts to exist, to disintegrate overall patterns of meaning, to make every choice a random phenomenon. The point here is not to praise socialism as it existed until 1989, because that had other serious shortcomings; however, consumer culture as we experience it now has many destructive aspects.

Noise! While travelling through Belgium, it occurs to me that the transport contract has come to include the obligation to listen to unsolicited background music in railway stations and elsewhere. Data from the National Health Interview Survey indicate that significantly more Americans are having difficulties with hearing. From 1971 to 1990, hearing problems among those aged forty-five to sixty-four jumped 26 per cent, while the eighteen to forty-four age group reported a 17 per cent increase; ten years later the percentages must be higher still. In the Netherlands 25,000 youngsters between the ages of fifteen and twenty-five have permanent hearing damage and will have tinnitus for the rest of their lives. What are the causes? Earsets, surround-sound stereos which can rival small recording studios, films such as *Armageddon* and *Godzilla*, discos with music of 85 decibels or more, but also the blast from leaf blowers, mowers and even vacuum cleaners.[8] Actually, by definition pleasure now seems to include making a noise, loud music, loud speaking, shouting. The volume of television and radio commercials is usually louder than that of the rest of the programming.

Obviously, quiet has always, in every century, been threatened by people who make more noise than others want to hear (Thompson 1991: 469). What is new is that technology makes it easy to produce high-decibels sounds, which, previously, even a big orchestra could not make. New, too, is the mass scale of traffic jams; and that background music has become ubiquitous; and that consumer society stimulates people to go out every weekend looking for exuberant pleasure on any and every occasion. The last thing people are expected to do is restrain themselves; the world belongs to them and should be enjoyed now. 'If the society of the spectacle is dominated by the visual image, noise is its handmaiden. The proliferation of visual images in the world is matched by an increase in the kinds and level of noise,' Richard Stivers (1994) concludes.

The continuing din is a form of pollution, which attacks not only the ears but the whole person. Noise pollution deprives people of the possibility of finding an equilibrium, physically and mentally. In the public space there are huge quantities of images that you don't want to see. With difficulty, we can try to avoid seeing them. With sound there is no escape. Jacques Attali says noise is violence. It kills. Making noise is comparable to murder (Attali 2001: 50).

Let's look at the people who enjoy playing loud music. What does it mean for them? For some, says Saul Landau in interview, it is

> a form of resistance, saying I'm not going to let you in. I'm going to play my music so loud and so offensively that you cannot enter my brain or my ear. The very forces that are trying to get hold of me, I will keep them away by making lots of noise. Watch the black kids with these huge boom boxes, blasting away, keep away from me. Or the people in their cars with the radios turned up so high: stay away from me. It is a form of resistance. Rap music, the words to rap music are aggression, aggression, aggression. Get out my way; don't touch me. I don't want to take any more shit. In its way it is an attack on commercial music. But like all other creative things the corporate culture is able to make it into a commodity and therefore transforms it from resistance into parts of its larger corporate culture. Noise itself then becomes a commodity.

Sex is another ingredient that, in one sense, is becoming more and more of a commodity; equally, the exchange of commodities is increasingly surrounded by a heavily sexualized atmosphere (Frith and Goodwin 1990: 388–9). This was not the ideal of the people who struggled in the 1960s and 1970s for sexual liberation. The ideal was to liberate eroticism, sexual pleasure and beauty from puritanical oppression. The ideal was that people themselves should be able to make their own choices about their sexuality and about what kind of images and imaginings would stimulate and delight them. The ideal was that women would no longer be seen and treated as objects to be used by men. The ideal in any case was *not* that sexual liberation would be transformed into the commercial exploitation of sex. Nevertheless, this is exactly what has happened. On the Russian television channel M1 every Saturday morning, there is a programme called *The Naked Truth*, presented by the twenty-six-year-old anchor Svetlana Pecotska. She begins the programme fully clothed, reading a news report all but indistinguishable from the headlines on other programmes. By the end, she is usually topless or nearly so.[9]

Then there is the mass production of pornography, which, at a first glance, does not seem to be such a huge problem; those who like soap operas see something hardly more subtle. What is more interesting are those aesthetically more refined erotic images which do not feature so prominently on the market. What is at stake is not only an aesthetic question, or a matter of taste; it also concerns what choices are made in life, and what kind of images and theatrical performances arouse sexual pleasure. Is sex something that should take place, straightforwardly, without too much communication between the people involved? Or are sex and the erotic playful elements in human life, in which people communicate in a way that is different from any other experience?

Obviously, we should not romanticize; sex is a daily or weekly affair as well as a fantasy. Nevertheless, the choice made in favour of more straightforward pornographic images or the more aesthetically refined erotic imagination says something about people's ideas about sexuality, individually but also collectively, in a specific society. It seems that the market for commercial sexual images and performances is a big one, or perhaps the producers of the images cannot imagine more subtle forms of sexuality.

What kind of images an individual likes to use as stimulation is a private affair. It becomes a public matter when erotic images penetrate commercial publicity. According to Margreth Hoek, this leads to unsolicited confrontations:

> Many products do not evoke desire by themselves. So, unconscious human desires become added to the product. What is decisive is that advertisers are involved in the struggle for the attention of the consumer and have no single reason to restrain themselves in this competition. The consequence is that I am confronted on the street, with unsolicited and frequent expressions of this fight. I'm getting tired of being confronted regularly with huge images that try to convey honest emotions like friendship, love, eroticism and sex through stereotypes.[10]

So, women in Paris were angry when the department store Les Galeries Lafayette showed nearly naked mannequins in six of its shop windows on the boulevard Haussmann in order to present its new collection of lingerie. Many women and members of feminist associations protested in front of the shop and on the stairs of the Opera Garnier against the merchandising of human bodies, and condemned 'the most reactionary sexist stereotypes this show presented'. Even two members of the French government, Ségolène Royal and Nicole Péry, expressed their dissatisfaction to the management of the department store.[11]

Hard-core pornography is on the increase, showing sadomasochistic scenes, rape, torture and killing of women and children. As could be expected, those kinds of scenes do not stay in the private sphere. By the end of the twentieth century corporate culture needed more shocking images to attract attention, and what could be exploited better than the combination of sex and violence? This is what we see now on huge advertisement billboards on the streets and along motorways. Of course, the big corporations don't show us all the cruel details that can be seen in hard-core pornography, but the images show enough brutal erotic domination of men over women and children that the references to the darkest aspects of human communication are easily followed. Violence is a field that corporate culture loves to exploit.

VIOLENCE TRAVELS WELL

'The rental decision that drives our video business now is a teenager/young adult decision, by and large,' Strauss Zelnick, then president and chief executive of Twentieth Century-Fox, declares. 'They are not going to rent intimate little movies, they are going to rent action adventure movies' (Ohmann 1996: 26). In the $1 trillion global film and television business companies are striving to create programmes with global reach, and without recognizable nationality. The boomlet in international co-production over the past decades has been driven by the increase both in the number of overseas television channels and networks and in programme production costs.

With global revenues now funding an increasing proportion of US film and television production, broadcasters are being forced to wrestle with a growing number of subtle and not-so-subtle conflicts with their international production partners. George Shamieh, whose PM Entertainment distributes *L.A. Heat* and other action-oriented series, is pressurized by Japanese programmers to inject more science-fiction elements into programmes, while Italian broadcasters complain of too much action, too little romance. 'One thing they all agree on is the need for the latest in gadgets and firepower,' he says. 'Audiences around the world cannot get enough of heat-seeking devices, remote pulse detectors and robots.'[12]

Indeed, George Gerbner underlines, most television and movie producers cannot break even on the domestic market. 'They are forced into video and foreign sales to make a profit. Therefore, they need a dramatic ingredient that requires no translation, "speaks action" in any language, and fits any culture. That ingredient is violence.' His analysis shows that violence dominates US exports. Through NAFTA and the WTO, even more mayhem can be dumped on the world in the name of 'free trade'. 'Far from reflecting creative freedom, the strategy wastes talent, restricts freedom and chills originality. Not the least of the consequences is the damage done to dramatic originality and integrity. Arbitrarily contrived violence is inserted into formula-driven programs according to market conditions, not dramatic need.' His conclusion is: 'violence "travels well"' (Gerner 1997: 14–15).

The statistics may differ, but all are impressive. A study commissioned by President Clinton documented that 'American children see 4,000 "play" murders and 200,000 dramatized acts of violence by the age of 18' (*International Herald*

Tribune, 3 June 1999). At the beginning of the 1990s, the American Psychological Association calculated that an average American child watches television three hours each day. By seventh grade, he or she will have seen 8,000 murders and 100,000 acts of violence. Video games make murder a more active event. An American adolescent, by the age of eighteen, will have killed 400,000 opponents or enemies merely by pressing a finger on an electronic button (Hetata 1998: 279–80).

Since 1967 George Gerbner and his staff have compiled an annual television report, Violence Profile and Violence Index. They have found that on average seven out of ten primetime programmes use violence, and the rate of violent acts runs at between five and six per hour. Half of primetime dramatic characters engage in violence, and about 10 per cent kill, as they have done since 1967. Children's weekend programming 'remains saturated with violence', with twenty-five acts of violence per hour, 'as it has done for many years' (Herman and McChesney 1997: 146). These figures are for the United States, but do not differ substantially from those in other parts of the world, because most channels show the stuff produced and distributed by the major cultural conglomerates. Even in Zimbabwe, for instance, local councils feature such films as *Kung Fu* and *Rambo* as fundraising events (Plastow 1996: 181).

Moreover, as far as violence is concerned, much local programming all over the world is not inferior to the fare served up by the transnational cultural industries. *Our Creative Diversity*, the Report of the World Commission on Culture and Development, says:

> a recent survey of programmes in India revealed that more than 70 percent of these were considered violent by the people surveyed. In another survey of nine Asian countries, all with a fairly high level of local programming, at least 60 percent were perceived to be violent. It was very much a question of local context versus foreign images. For example, concern among Thais and Koreans was focused on the 'brutal samurai and erotic dramas' of Japanese programming and the mental aggressiveness alien to their values. (Pérez de Cuéllar 1996: 123)

In China 'Hong Kong horror flicks and martial art schlock dominated movie goers' fantasies, with cops and bandits zooming across wide screens, leaving trails of carnage and destruction – buildings demolished, coprses piled high, audiences in a stupor of excitement, and local filmmakers in a daze.' Responding to an apparently insatiable appetite for such fare, Jianying Zha reports, local theatres expanded their offerings, featuring the latest releases from Hong Kong (Zha 1995: 93).

Let's look at a small sample of what the industry has to offer in the field of violence. Songs on the Beavis and Butt-head *Experience* album include 'I

Hate Myself and Want to Die' (Nirvana); 'Looking Down the Barrel of a Gun' (Anthrax); '99 Ways to Die' (Megadeth); 'Search and Destroy' (Red Hot Chili Peppers); and 'I am Hell' (White Zombie) (Barber 1996: 334). Film critic Hans Beerenkamp describes the film *Starship Troopers* by Paul Verhoeven as Darwinistic-capitalistic, in which the right of the fittest triumphs, and links the film to fascism. Many American films prepare soldiers for war. In this process they lose their individuality, which makes them better killers (*NRC Handelsblad*, 7 January 1998).

At the beginning of the 1990s there were major riots in Los Angeles after the police had beaten a man named Rodney King. This scene had by coincidence been videotaped. Lionel Tiger reports:

> Television stations showed the brutal scene repeatedly, countlessly, beyond any expectation and indeed beyond any need. It virtually reached the point that only blind people had not seen it. But the footage was evidently so gripping, and inspired such moral outrage among viewers and presenters alike, that the obvious grimness of the scene was not only unendurable but fascinating, and was exhibited, over and over. People *liked* it. (Tiger 1992: 128)

There are several television shows worldwide similar to Jerry Springer's, in which members of the invited audience accuse each other of various transgressions, mostly extramarital affairs. The show is at its best – and so it should be, otherwise it loses viewers – when those people start to beat each other, pull out each other's hair, hurl the most vile and mean insults at each other and wish each other slow and painful deaths, while the live audience yells enthusiastically, and the presenter looks innocent, pretending to be bewildered by so much aggression.

'In what used to be the dark corners of American culture, there are a prime-time cartoon with a neo-Nazi character, comics that traffic bestiality, movies that leave teenagers gutted like game, and fashion designers who peddle black-leather masks and doomsday visions. It's all open now, mass-produced and widely available,' Kevin Merida and Richard Leiby note.[13] Of the eleven major movies released on video in the United States between 6 and 23 April 1999, seven had violent themes.

As computing power has increased, computer games have become more horrifically realistic and vicious. An entire genre of games, called 'first-person shooters', encourages the player to dismember monsters and slay people. The object is to kill people; body parts fly in different directions. Eric Harris, one of the gunmen at the massacre in a school in Littleton, Colorado, was reportedly an expert player of Doom, a shooter game introduced in 1994 by Id Software of Texas. Doom's marketing strategy is hard to resist, Merida and Leiby report.

The game was given away over the internet. Players could customize their killing rooms, selecting from a cache of weapons. They could add new levels by paying for software. At least half a million copies of the game were sold or distributed.[14]

In violent films language is almost non-existent; no one wastes time explaining why the killing and shooting is happening; it's all taken for granted. Nomi Victor has developed the interesting theory that an action film is violent, less because of its 'physical' portion of violence than for this pervasive dismissal of language.[15] Jo Groebel confirms that violence as a pure entertainment product often lacks any embedding in a context that is more than a clichéd image of good and bad (Groebel 1998).

In the old days in Hollywood films, the bad guys lost in the end. There are still bad guys in today's films, but they are no longer the losers. It is the good guys who go down. Good and evil seem to be outmoded concepts and morality is a term of abuse.[16] Meanwhile, a genre called *Nouvelle Violence* has been developed, which relates to outbursts of violence in so-called more artistic films. Jon Stratton observes that the possibility of reconciliation disappears with the disappearance of the motive of the perpetrator. The lust for *pur sang*, violence without any cause and without consequence (and thus also without catharsis), presented as unexpected and inescapable, has replaced the rational and narrative forms of violence.[17] In films such as *RoboCop 3*, *Cyborg*, *Universal Soldier*, *Terminator* and *Eve of Destruction*, pain is an important ingredient, Samantha Holland notes. 'Whatever the individual cyborg's inability to feel pain in these movies, it *always* has the ability to *inflict* pain through physical violence. The cyborg film constantly foregrounds physical violence – and especially physical violence directed towards *bodies*' (Featherstone and Burrows 1995).

This kind of violence becomes even stronger when it is related to sex, which is increasingly happening. Hong Kong gangster films are a form of buddy movie. They teach that homosexual tenderness leads to violent death. In Japanese pornography and 'eroduction' films, torture is seen by some Japanese critics as a kind of 'purification ceremony', Brian Moeran explains.

> Usually the victims in these films are women and, according to Shinto and Buddhist beliefs, women are basically impure because of the association of menstrual blood with pollution. Their sexuality, however, can be purified through rape and, in the eroduction films, we find that victims are such innocent symbols as uniformed schoolgirls, nurses, or newly married housewives, who almost invariably become attracted to their rapists. (Ryan 1989: 162–76)

Some rappers whose lyrics decry racism routinely denigrate women and gays.[18] Gangsta rap celebrates the world of the material, the dog-eat-dog world in which black male sexism is the order of the day. If the purpose is to arouse controversy, it works (hooks 1994: 118).

'In times of backlash, images of restrained women line the walls of the popular culture's gallery,' Susan Faludi observes. 'We see her silenced, infantilized, immobilized or, the ultimate restraining, killed' (Faludi 1991: 70). Marilyn French is happy with the taboos that exist on the expression of anti-Semitism or racism. 'Yet popular works dwell lovingly on the rape, mutilation, and murder of women. People disagree about morality, but certain acts are so blatantly cruel and evil that almost every human being finds them repugnant. Is not hatred and violent abuse of women such an evil? Why is it permitted to be portrayed?' (French 1993: 178–9). It is not the eroticization of the female image that disturbs, Marilyn French notes, but the fact that it is eroticized in order to be appropriated. In the last chapter I will come back to the question of freedom of expression, censorship and self-restraint.

There is nothing new under the sun. A couple of thousand years ago Romans took pleasure in watching prisoners or slaves being eaten by animals in the Colosseum. Some people do enjoy seeing blood and the suffering of victims. Why otherwise are people officially given the opportunity to witness executions in America's state prisons? (Tiger 1992: 129–31).

I would like to ask you to imagine yourself at a bullfight, a *corrida de toros*, in Spain. The atmosphere is one of exaltation even as you arrive. The game between the *torero* and the *toros* is about to begin. All the prescribed rituals are carried out. The bullfighter is fired up by passionate music, while the applause and cheers of the audience increase his courage. He provokes and elegantly evades the attacks of the bull. The play becomes more and more dangerous; the question of which of the two will be claimed by death becomes more real. The spectacle approaches its crisis. I wonder: Is this pleasure?

I ask myself the same question when a week of watching television shows me hundreds of people being killed, women raped or attacked, nature and natural resources wasted and misused – a carnival of mayhem and rapine. Is this pleasure? The destruction of life and nature wounds me, and should not be presented as entertainment. Although it is necessary to inform people about the cruelties of human life – in news, theatre, film, dance, literature, the visual arts – I would not present them as entertainment, fun or spectacular diversion. Compassion and the longing for understanding would be my only motive for presenting scenes of horror or cruelty. Many cultures in the past as well as in the present provide cruel and brutal spectacles as mainstays of public entertainment. Perhaps in certain cultures these performances were embedded in a set of formal rituals or liturgies that made the depicted pain acceptable according to the dominant way of thinking. Such conventions could have established boundaries around these eruptions of brutality.

The bullfight, for example, might constitute a solemn moment in the cycle of the seasons. Perhaps the difference with our present Western culture is that the performance of cruelties is now more show than ritual, lacking the structure of a coherent cultural framework to give it meaning and resonance. Despite these differences, the fundamental similarity is that these violent spectacles enshrine cruelty and death, and that enjoyment is found in depictions of injury and horror.

There have always been those who seriously questioned the performance of cruelties, mayhem and destruction as a way of making life exciting and bearable. The nature of pleasure depends on a variety of underlying cultural premises and on the (temporary) outcome of the social and cultural struggle in this important dimension of human life. In the present discussion, in which the arts are considered to be factories and repositories of cultural meaning, we must examine the subject of pleasure as it is fabricated on a massive scale by cultural industries. Pleasure is their stock-in-trade, their raison d'être, their point of creative departure and their main source of income. The cultural industries are largely responsible for setting contemporary standards of what is considered acceptable and desirable pleasure. The fact that they do so on an unprecedentedly massive scale means that we must take their formative influence on this aspect of life seriously.

It would be a misunderstanding to think that this kind of extreme violence is something that can only be found in commercial cultural products. Nothing is less true. The early Expressionists yearned for war, as did the Futurists. Even after the First World War the celebration of violence did not become less, but greater. Hans Magnus Enzensberger remembers that the writings of De Sade acquired a cult readership characterized by worship of violence, which still goes on. Ernst Jünger propagated the purifying violence of the steel thunderstorm. Céline flirted with the anti-Semitic mob, and André Breton declared that the 'most simple surrealistic deed is to go onto the street with a gun in the hand and to shoot as long as possible into the crowd' (Enzensberger 1993: 67). Ariel Dorfman analyses Latin American literature and finds that the characters created by writers such as Asturias, Carpentier, Fuentes, Vargas Llosa, García Márquez and Sábato are searching, through violence, for a sign of their own essence or of the order of the universe.

> That violent situation has one primordial characteristic, present in all contemporary Hispanic American narrative: the fact that the violence is not chosen, but rather is assumed and accepted in order to find the characters' own identity. It never occurs to Borges' characters, for instance, to reject aggression or to intel-

lectualize it: They live it; they may have chosen the form of their violence, but not the fact of violence itself. (Dorfman 1991: 37–8)

The Italian-Danish theatre director Eugenio Barba is, according to Rustom Bharucha,

> not unwilling to use a 'violent' vocabulary to express the 'laws' of acting. Taking his cue from masters of traditional performance in Asia, he speaks frequently of the 'killing' of the 'natural' rhythms of the body, without which the 'fictional body' of the actor can never be shaped. He also speaks of the 'second colonization' of the body, which emerges through resistances that enable the actors to discover new, more 'immediate' and 'spontaneous' energies.

Rustom Bharucha wonders whether we really have to 'kill' something before creating something new. 'Can one not work within the existing ("natural") resources, and allow something to emerge from them?' (Bharucha 1993: 56). The Belgian theatre maker Jan Fabre also declares that aggression can be found in all his performances. 'Art must be aggressive, always. For me, this is the only way to show something. It concerns evidently sublimated aggression because most of the artists are cowards. Aggression is a form of communication' (*De Volkskrant*, 16 June 1984).

However, another approach to violence is possible; it considers aggression as the failure of human communication. It is up to artists and their producers to decide what they will show, what they will give an insight into, or flirt with: the suffering caused by the failure to establish respectful communication between human beings, or the violent 'solutions' to failed human communication and the idolization of pain, torture, rape and killings?

INFLUENCE

What is going on in my mind, I wonder, when I see advertisements in the street, in newspapers or magazines, or on television? The films and the images I watch, the music I listen to, and the books and magazines I read, how do they affect my sensibility? How do they influence the choice I always have to make between allowing myself to listen to morality and staying comfortably on the surface? How do they frame my desire for pleasure, and for what kind of pleasure? Do they evoke a desire for calmness in my mental setup, or for unrest? In short, how do the many traces of corporate culture, which is presently the dominant form of culture in many corners of the world, influence my private life?

Honestly speaking, I must confess that I don't know the answer to all these questions, although I can make guesses. So, when my knowledge about the influences of corporate culture on my own life is incomplete, what can I know about their effect on others? Especially about their effect on others who do not share the cultural ambience in which I am living in my own country, and who live a long way away, in cultures I understand only partially, if at all?

The question of the influence caused by such heterogeneous and multilayered matters as organized images, sounds, dramatizations, groups of words, colours and movements of the body, is not easy to answer. Quantitative methods are only partially helpful. For instance, we may find out that hardly anybody will go out and start shooting after having watched a violent film. When we have discovered this, it would be easy to say that people don't imitate the behaviour they have seen, so there is no influence. However, everybody knows that influence in the social and individual context does not work that way. Everything we hear, see, read or experience leaves traces. It may confirm what we have felt already, it may give an uncomfortable feeling, it may enhance the good mood one is in, it may irritate or make one aggressive. Partly this is an individual matter, but it also concerns collectively shared feelings and judgements.

Mostly, we are not greatly aware of all that penetrates mind and body. This is because we try to move in circles that correspond more or less to the cultural spheres we judge to be pleasant and satisfying. Mentally, we also build up a filter to exclude artistic sensations that do not fit with our preferences. The consequence can be that we live on two levels: knowing what is going on around us, while having an explicit negative reaction to it, and at the same time not fighting actively the sounds, images, texts and so on, which we more or less reject. When we can't change the surrounding cultural ambience, we may at least try to survive.

Despite the complexity of the question of influence, I will nevertheless put forward some arguments about how the many aspects of corporate culture work. First, though, I want to raise the question of whether there is an influence at all. Over the last couple of decades, the impulses governing the organization of cultural life in many countries have changed radically. So now is the time to get to grips with how this influences people's lives and cultures, especially because we can expect that over the coming decades the corporate approach will more and more govern the ways in which people entertain themselves, which images they should see, what they should listen to and what they should avoid or ignore.

The world of consumer goods and cultural ambiences that the big conglomerates peddle has an attractive side, and so it should; otherwise there would be no reason for the public to be open to the cultural messages being communicated. There is no doubt that many people enjoy going shopping, enjoy the cultural spheres the companies create, enjoy the aesthetics of commercials, and get genuine pleasure and increased self-esteem from all that is available to them (Webster 1995: 99).

Of course, people deal differently with all the artistic phenomena that come at them from all sides. There are many individuals in the world, many cultures, many different ways of interpreting cultural codes, and many changes in taste and fashion. It would be strange if everyone received and responded to such a multitude of cultural messages in exactly the same way. As postmodernist scholars put it, there are multiple readings of these cultural texts, and text in this postmodernist discourse is a metaphor for every type of expression, which may be music, images, movements of the body, theatrical dramatizations, colours and indeed words (Ching 1996: 181–2). John Fiske notes that audiences have 'a great deal of power' in negotiating the texts that the various media produce (Fiske 1987: 309). In the next few pages we will examine whether or not that power really does amount to 'a great deal'. He argues that people are not 'cultural dupes', not a passive mass and not at the political mercy of the barons of the industry. I would suggest, for a start, that it may be more complicated than that.

Stephan Oaks is president of Curious Pictures Corporation in New York, a company that produces commercials. He reports that 'our thirty-second commercials take anywhere from six to twelve weeks to do. The average budget for such a little film is $120,000 to $300,000' (Ohmann 1996: 73–4). He and his team have discussions with their clients on just about every frame. 'The process is intense from beginning to end with meetings about things that, of course, are quite absurd, but are all the pieces that make up the thirty-second commercial that goes on the air, influences people, and then gets imitated.' As he says, he is sure that commercials influence people, and the businesses that commission the production company are even more sure, otherwise they would not spend such huge amounts of money on advertising.

Together advertisers spend $8–10 billion yearly on the production of TV spots in the United States alone. They would only spend that amount of money if it made sense for them to do so. Commercials influence not just randomly and haphazardly, but in quite specific ways. Enterprises look at the results of their publicity campaigns from day to day, and when these do not satisfy them they change their advertising strategies accordingly. No precise results can be predicted, but not having their commercial messages, in whatever form, widely distributed would be terminal for the company and the capital behind it.

Every day, according to the Association of American Advertising Agencies, the average person is exposed to 1,600 advertisements (Coombe 1998: 316). The average American adult sees approximately 21,000 commercials a year. The 100 largest corporations in America pay for roughly 75 per cent of commercial television time and 50 per cent of public television time (Korten 1995: 153). Television networks in the USA now broadcast 6,000 commercials a week (McChesney 1998: 20). Brazil occupies eightieth position in the world ranking of educational investment, and seventh in advertising expenditure (Oliveira 1993: 126). Obviously, the figures may differ, and in different parts of the world the spread of corporate culture may be more or less intensive. However, altogether the onslaught of commercially influenced images, music, dance, theatre pieces, films and texts is immense and is growing everywhere in the world.

Observing the fact that commercials as well as programmes have a substantial influence on people's behaviour and emotional life, we should recognize as well that it is artists who make both the advertisements and the entertainment. William Leach mentions that in the United States at the end of the nineteenth century, 'mass market corporations and retailers were able to choose among an ever-swelling group of commercial artists to design billboards, posters, catalogues, and display advertising in newspapers and magazines' (Leach 1993: 52). Artists make the music, perform the plays, create the sound effects, the sculptures and the multimedia events, and paint, design, dance and write.

When we think about the enormous amount of advertising that goes on, one point immediately comes to mind: commercials influence people in quite specific ways. How could it be possible for the cultural programming and the ambience surrounding these commercials *not* to influence people, in specific as well as general ways? If a medium has influence by sending out a commercial, it is unlikely that one minute later, in the same medium, there would be no influence at all when the show, soap, film, concert or whatever, continues. It is even probable that the influence of the cultural programming is nearly as great as that of the commercials. It may be a little more diffuse because in a cultural programme there is no direct commercial message. However, many commercials no longer have clear messages either.

Like advertising, all art and entertainment conveys an atmosphere or mood, reflects a way of life, suggests, for instance, an idea of pleasure. Its impact can be as powerful as that of direct commercial messages. It may be even stronger if the video, poster, image, photo, play, show, film, soap, book or song has enormous aesthetic appeal.

People respond in a variety of ways to works of art, partly depending on their cultural background, just as they do to commercials. However, the range of responses is not limitless, first, because it is not that easy to stray outside the margins of interpretation and meaning suggested by a good artist, as if these do not exist. A good work of art has a seductive power, and the listener, reader or spectator has to work hard to undermine its power and interpret it or respond to it completely differently from the way(s) intended by its creator. Not everybody is able to do this, or wants to make the effort.

Second, every channel of communication and every other broadcaster presents a cultural programme in a certain atmosphere, attaches a certain mood to it, places it within a context, and thus increases the likelihood of particular interpretations while reducing other possible interpretations. Media that depend on commercials have to make sure the surrounding programming provides a consumer-friendly context. Their survival and success depends on being able to arouse positive feelings about the whole ambience they create, including the programmes. Through the contextualization they offer at the same time a restricted range of possible interpretations, which are in their interest. Their programmes should not lead to too much serious controversy. The intention is that people enjoy the whole package – the advertising and the artistic programming – which are becoming more and more closely interrelated, and that they buy accordingly.

It would be a mistake to think that the real problem is that people are dupes. Audiences do, in fact, interpret messages in various ways. They transform them to correspond with their individual experiences and tastes. On the other hand it is out of the question that they themselves can be active in influencing programming and interpretation to meet their wishes and needs.

For Herbert Schiller, the key point is just this: people are not dupes but they do not control the corporate means of communication. Nevertheless, audiences do count in the huge publicity battles for their hearts and purses, but not in the way that many communication scholars suggest. 'The managers of cultural industries are acutely sensitive to the moods and feelings of the nation's many publics. It is their job, for which they are paid handsomely, to make day-by-day, if not hour-by-hour, assessments of these feelings. When they are mistaken, as they frequently are, they lose their jobs.' He concludes that the audience, active or not, is on the receiving end of these commercial forces and the changes they are producing. 'Its perspectives cannot avoid being influenced by them' (Schiller 1989a: 153–6; see also Tomlinson 1991: 36).

The prime objective of this massive battle for the public is to deliver affluent audiences to advertisers; audience service is a means, not an end (Herman 1997: 7). In other words, the media 'produce' the audience, which can then be sold as a commodity to the advertisers (Lury 1993: 50).

Worldwide advertising in 1995 was estimated at $261 billion. This is likely to increase sevenfold in the quarter of a century that follows. By 2020 commercials will add about $2,300 to the amount spent on shopping by Americans, $1,100 in Western Europe and $600 in Eastern Europe, which is more than the average income of most people in the world presently (Ginneken 1996: 56). Obviously, in the price of a product we are paying for the advertisement, the sponsorship and the creation of the involvement with the brand. It is a form of involuntary taxation – because, after all, we can't avoid paying for it – but one over which there is no parliamentary control. So, we may call this taxation without representation. And this is against all the rules of democracy.

Jaap van Ginneken remarks that most of these amounts spent on advertising are spent on media, but are not generally spread across all the media. Specific kinds of media and formats will be favoured and others not. The consequence is that certain types of media and formats are strengthened, and others are not. The huge sums destined for publicity determine thus, for a major part, which media can exist at all, and which ones will disappear or will have difficulty surviving (Ginneken 1996: 56).

The influence that corporate culture has is thus not only on behaviour and people's ways of thinking, but also on whether or not specific types of media exist. From a democratic perspective this is risky.

AROUSING DESIRE, AWAKENING MEMORY, CREATING FANTASY

How does corporate culture affect people's lives? Broadly speaking, we can say that it works in two ways: on the one hand by promoting certain values and ways of behaviour, such as, for example, individual consumption or competition; on the other by being silent about a whole complex of more socially directed values, such as, for instance, solidarity or care. Perhaps the latter type of influence is even more important than the former, although it is largely forgotten. Since corporate culture has a formative effect, what is significant is what it does not speak about, namely how to construct collectively a more humane, just and ecologically sustainable society. At the end of this chapter I come back to this issue.

One of the eye-catching effects of corporate culture is the engineering of demand for consumer goods. Luis Augusto Milanesi suggests that television influences consumption not only by advertising, but even more through its entire programming. The textile and fashion industry could not have developed in Brazil without television, he asserts. The engineering of demand is crucial to monopoly capitalism and in this respect fashion is indispensable. Television became a symbol of modernity in itself by propagating a modern consumption pattern (Vink 1988 39).

Post-Fordist marketing desegregates markets and consumption into 'lifestyles', 'niche markets', 'target consumer groups', 'market segments'. These are not defined by broad social demographic structures, and do not correlate with them easily, if at all, but rather by cultural meanings which link a range of goods and images to a coherent image. The broader claim is, Don Slater notes, 'that lifestyle marketing not only identifies and targets existing lifestyles but rather *produces* them by organizing consumers according to meaningful patterns, constructed and distributed through design, advertising and the media (which are themselves increasingly segmented and "narrowcast" rather than mass)' (Slater 1997: 191)

He observes that we no longer consume things, but signs. Indeed, non-material goods play an ever-greater role in the economy and consumption. However, the concept of 'service' is ambiguous. Many services can include considerable material components. So, McDonalds sells billions of (very material!) hamburgers, tourism involves major infrastructural development; 'Nonetheless, much consumption comprises such things as information, advice and expertise, leisure events and activities, entertainment.' But even material commodities appear to have a greater non-material component.

> This includes the extension of 'commodity aesthetics', so that much of a product seems to comprise design, packaging and advertising imagery. Mars does not sell chocolate bars but rather a 'taste experience'. Part of this increasingly non-material composition is attributed to the *mediation* of goods. That is to say, we encounter objects (and services, experiences and activities that have become objectified as commodities) increasingly in the form of representations: in advertising, in portrayals of lifestyle in films, TV, magazines, in mediated encounters with celebrities and stars and so on. (Slater 1997: 193–4)

The media not only set agendas and frame debates but also inflect desire, memory and fantasy (Shohat and Stam 1994: 356). They suggest what reality looks like, a world where memory is no longer needed. 'Visual images become a substitute for memory,' Richard Stivers regrets. 'Television requires us to live in an unstable present where memory only gets in the way of the pleasurable loss of self that comes from vicariously living through images.' But television also leaves us imprisoned in the order of reality. 'Without the infusion of the order of truth, of the attribution of meaning, reality becomes even more terrible, even more unbearable than it would be otherwise.' Television and visual spectacle in general empty existence of meaning, he judges. 'This is in itself a major cause of the sense of apocalyptic doom, for hope derives solely from the order of truth. The opposite of hope, of course, is despair' (Stivers 1994: 143).

Another area in which corporate culture has an influence is in the broad field of educating people, showing what values are important in life, and what kind of lifestyle is desirable. The integrated cultural colossi have become the educators and guardians of the social realm, Herbert Schiller notes. 'They select, or exclude, the stories and songs, the images and words that create individual and group consciousness and identity' (Schiller 1993: 466). He describes the American model, epitomized by, for instance, the Disney creations, which relies heavily on explicitly extolling the benefits of technology – there are no costs – and an orderly social environment, preferably one without workers, and the pleasure of middle-class consumption. 'In these "family entertainments" the existence of social inequality is minimized or denied, and whatever historical efforts have been made to overcome such inequities are ignored' (Schiller 1989a: 41). Disney, both the boss and the company, consider themselves as schoolmaster, family consultant, civic guardian, spiritual guide and protector of the great prescripts of social life (Eudes 1989: 262).

An important aspect of Hollywood is that it presents an image of how old ways of life are broken up and new ones set in place (Jameson 1998: 63). The media interfere in the psychological processes of adolescence, in the crisis of identity that many experience at this age, while creating new fashions and new styles. In the analysis of Stuart Hall and Paddy Whannel, these media

> provide one set of answers to the search for more meaningful and satisfying adult roles. And the danger is that they will short-circuit this difficult process by offering too limited a range of social models for young people to conform to, a kind of consumer identity, which could be dangerous even when ultimately rejected by them. There seems to be a clear conflict between commercial and cultural considerations here, for which commercial providers take no responsibility. (Frith and Goodwin 1990: 30)

Rachel Dwyer notes that one of the most striking features of Hindi cinema in India is the operation of a star system, where the star emerges as a text, the focus of discourses on sexuality, desire and the body, love and the family.

> These discourses come together in the 1990s in a new genre of films that shows the rising cultural confidence of the new middle classes, as they depict their cultural aspirations in the huge-budget romantic films, which have been the super-hits of the last decade. These films depict the nature of sex, romance and the family in the context of the super-rich and set the pace for India's upwardly mobile. (Dwyer 2000: 96)

Hindi cinema represents the ambitions of a growing middle class in a more or less coherent manner, which is becoming more relevant in India since the country opened its markets to foreign products; so the cinema becomes teacher, guide and challenging example.

This becomes explicit as well in an increasing cult of the body, where youth and health represent economic and cultural capital.

> This explains the rise of a dieting and fitness culture, and the fashion and beauty industries. This has led to a perceived decline in the traditionally high status of the elderly, many of whom fear that they will spend their old age in old people's homes rather than with their families. This valuing of the young body has been

accompanied by the increasing visibility of the erotic couple, notably in advertising, film and television. (Dwyer 2000: 50)

Earlier in this chapter I focused on the issue of violence and the way it presents itself more and more as an acceptable part of corporate culture. Here I will raise the issue of whether such representations of violence in all the many different forms of art and entertainment have any influence on the behaviour of people.

In 1987 an English boy re-enacted *First Blood*, in which Sylvester Stallone played Rambo. The result was sixteen people dead. In 1995 a girl and a boy attacked a shopkeeper. The attack paralysed her. The girl and boy claimed to have been inspired by *Natural Born Killers*, a film by Oliver Stone, in which two serial killers in love murder fifty-two people. In both cases a demonstrable link exists between the examples and the shootings; the killers more or less reconstructed the scripts. However, such direct imitations of violence do not happen often – hardly ever, considering the huge quantity of violence presented in our contemporary artistic cultures.

It has happened more than once – especially in the United States – that someone has opened fire at random, killing a substantial number of people. In most cases such massacres are not a direct imitation of something seen in a film or one of the other media. It often happens that the killer is discovered to have spent a great deal of time in culturally violent ambiences such as neo-Nazi organizations, where killing is regarded as fun. But mass killings do not happen daily. They are spectacular, but negligible compared to what the media have to offer in the field of violence.

If there is no direct relationship between such violent acts and the violent films people have seen, the cruel songs listened to or the bloodthirsty comics read, then it is difficult to prove that the one has been influenced by the other. This may be true, but is not reason enough to say that the matter ends there, Marilyn French insists. She posits as an example the way that opponents of anti-pornography feminists demand proof that pornographic works foster or inspire male violence against women.

> But the intersection of culture and life is not quantifiable or provable. One cannot *prove* that violence against women in pornography leads to violence against women in life any more than one can *prove* that the disparagement of blacks and Jews pervasive in nineteenth-century culture *caused* the horror of African colonialism or the Holocaust. The mere suspicion of a connection is considered sufficient reason to refuse to legitimize hatred of groups. Only when it comes to women does our culture suspend this restraint. (French 1993: 178–9)

Marilyn French considers that there is reason enough to worry. 'Most films and television shows are produced by men for men. Their main purposes are to show white males triumphant, to teach gender roles, and to cater to men's delight in male predation and victimization of women.' This is not surprising when we realize that nearly all studies around the world show that men are much more attracted to violence than women. Jo Groebel (1998) notes that one can assume that 'in a mixture of biological predispositions and gender role socializations, men often experience aggression as rewarding'. He asserts: the 'media play a major role in the development of cultural orientations, world views and beliefs, as well as in the global distribution of values and (often stereotyped) images. They are not only mirrors of cultural trends but also channel them, and are themselves major constituents of society.'

Concerning violence, he remarks that the quantity of aggressive content daily consumed by children and adolescents has dramatically increased.

> As real violence, especially among the youth at the same time is still growing, it seems plausible to correlate the two, media violence and aggressive behaviour. With more recent developments, video recorders, computer games and the internet one can see a further increase of extremely violent images which obviously find much attention. Videos present realistic torture scenes and even real murder, computer games enable the user to actively simulate the mutilation of 'enemies', the internet has – apart from its prosocial possibilities – become a platform for child pornography, violent cults, and terrorist guidelines. (Groebel 1998)

The least one can say is that all these images contribute to the 'moral makeup' of the people who enjoy this stuff (Hetata 1998: 279–80). Morality does not come out of the blue; configuration of moral principles is formed in a continuous process. A relevant question therefore concerns what stimuli and experiences are prominent in these formative processes. Theatrical presentations, images, sound landscapes and dramatic storylines can have a strong impact; they are the ingredients of media violence. This is the power of the arts.

In many shows there is a combination of violence, crude behaviour and humour. The humour legitimates the violence, as do the cheering and laughter of the audience. Children tend to think that something can't be that terrible if it makes people laugh. So, they think that violence is not terrible, or at least has nothing to do with reality.[19] However, even children who play violent computer games believe that these are making them less nice people. Dutch research indicates that one out of three children believes that playing computer games makes children less kind and agreeable.[20] Of course, only a very few people will feel the temptation to cut a dead body into pieces after having surfed the net and looked at particularly violent material. But Jo Groebel concludes that such images blunt sensitivity; people get used to them. 'Therefore you consider lighter forms of violence rather normal. Slapping someone or kicking him or her in the stomach, as long as there is no bloodshed, this is not really what you would call violence, is it?' What happens meanwhile is that the norm shifts and blurs.

Media violence 'compensates' for one's own frustrations and weaknesses in problem areas, Jo Groebel continues. 'It offers "thrills" for children in a less problematic environment. For boys, it creates a frame of reference for "attractive role models".' Media violence also has another effect, George Gerbner notes. He observes that 'heavy' television viewers, who necessarily see a lot of violence day after day, are more likely than comparable groups of 'light' viewers to overestimate the likelihood of becoming involved in violence. They come to believe easily, for instance, that their neighbourhood is unsafe. 'Insecure, angry, mistrustful people may be prone to violence but are even more likely to be dependent on authority and susceptible to deceptively simple, strong, hard-line postures and appeals. This unequal sense of danger, vulnerability and general unease, combined with reduced sensitivity, invites not only aggression but also exploitation and repression' (Gerbner 1997: 16).

Living daily in culturally aggressive contexts stimulates many more people than ever before to think they have a 'right' to whatever they want, that nobody can deny them 'their' right, and they should get it straight away. Some people have signs in the rear windows of their cars, that say 'I don't speak, I handle'. Others shout loudly in the street without any clear purpose, but just to impress passers-by, showing that they think consideration for others is a foolish idea, making the public space unsafe, not yet really threatening – but it may happen any moment. Causing tension in this way is satisfying, creates a sense of power. This may be enough in itself, or it may happen that the 'right', whatever this might be, will be enforced, while destroying streetlamps or something else en-countered along the way, or that an old person is attacked, or that a fight with police creates heros. Consequently, the public space or the workplace becomes less safe, which makes more people feel unsafe, and they in turn are more likely to be attracted to authoritarian policies, and so on.

From the local public space to the global level may be too big a step to make when speaking about the influence of media violence. Nevertheless, Denise Caruso notes that ultraviolent media systematically employ the same psycho-logical techniques of desensitization, conditioning and vicarious learning as were used during the Vietnam war to teach soldiers to kill automatically in battle encounters, yet respect authority and make split-second distinctions between friends and enemies.[21]

Ellen Goodman wonders whether it is possible to understand a culture of vio-lence without talking about war. She emphasizes: 'I don't mean war movies or war video games. I mean the real thing. The news has been full of the massacre at

Littleton, Colorado, and the bombing in Yugoslavia – reports that are simultaneous but stunningly disconnected.' She continues: 'Have we forgotten the history of
war, that it is the socially acceptable, socially heroic culture of mayhem ... How
many of us accept as "normal" boy stuff the video games that we are now told are
virtually training sessions for military desensitization? Do we abandon our sons
to the culture of violence out of a subconscious agreement that boys may have to
be our warriors?' Her conclusion is: 'To have a discussion about violence without
talking about war is like talking about war without talking about death.'[22]

Several philosophers, including Pierre Baudrillard, celebrate what they call the
techno-body which can be harmed as much as it may give satisfaction. Vivian
Sobchak reproaches him with the comment that such a concept of the body 'is
thought always as an object and never *lived* as a subject. And thought rather than
lived, it can bear all sorts of symbolic abuse with indiscriminate and undifferentiated pleasure. This techno-body, however, is a porno-*graphic* fiction, objectified
and written beyond belief and beyond the real' (Featherstone and Burrows 1995:
205–9). Vivian Sobchak first read Baudrillard while she was recuperating from
major cancer surgery on her left thigh. 'Indeed, there is nothing like a little
pain to bring us back to our senses, nothing like a real (not imagined) mark or
wound to counter the romanticism and fantasies of techno-sexual transcendence
that characterize so much of the current discourse on the techno-body that is
thought to occupy the cyberspaces of postmodernity.'

Many scholars, supporting the arguments of the leaders of cultural industries,
assume that people can distinguish between what they see or hear on one side
and reality on the other. It doesn't mean a thing when people watch *Beavis and
Butt-head* scenes featuring a poke in the eye with a pencil, with blood spurting
out, or a dog thrown into a washing machine followed by an insane giggle of
approval. Indeed, kids have always tuned into cartoons and movies in which
characters are splattered or blown away. Only things are a bit wilder now, with
far more blood and gorier and nastier images.[23]

Does it really not mean a thing to them? Let's remember the fairy-tales we
were told as bedtime stories when we were children, some of which were cruel.
Parents have to reassure their children that there is a difference between fiction
– all the frightening adventures in the fairy-tale – and reality, what happens in
daily life. In many cultures a theatrical representation of something is as strong
as that something could have been or is in reality. Fiction expresses reality.

It is probably a rationalistic Western notion to split fiction from reality. Just
as swallows are the heralds of the spring and vultures indicate decay and rotting, strong artistic expressions are the sensors of realities such as pain, danger,
threat, abundance, passion or eroticism. You may not notice the swallows or the

vultures any more. You may not observe the signs, but the decay and rotting are happening; and it's better to notice the signs. When you read a comic you may erase from your mind the fact that behind the comical or entertaining fictional shooting and killing is the reality that real people are shot and killed. By giving attention to the fictional killing and not reacting, you detach yourself from the pain and the suffering that is shown there. Silently you become co-responsible for a generally shared feeling that pain is pleasure, that violence is a satisfactory solution. At the very least, your imagination is not challenged to find more peaceful alternatives. Acceptance of a brutal form of artistic expression as normality reveals a desensitized mentality. It shows that the sensor is not reacting; there is no revolt. And what you regularly choose to read is, in a sense, what you are. The kind of film you like to watch is you. Abstract atonal music or conventional sound-pictures, crude rhythms or polished sound structures, whatever you prefer to listen to, this is the expression of your sensibility, or desensitization.

Of course, this is not the only determinant of what kind of person you are. However, your concept of fiction is an indicator of your spiritual housekeeping, When you laugh while watching the heads of the 'enemies' roll, and think of it all as just fiction, it may be that you are no longer registering the signs and signals, no longer responding to reality. The signs indicate that cruel acts are taking place and murders are filling our mental space. The reality is what we see, hear or read has happened throughout history, still happens and will happen again. The reality is that we are not even mourning that we are unable or unprepared to keep alive everybody who can be kept alive.

THE STORY CORPORATE CULTURE DOESN'T TELL

Expressions of corporate culture surround us every day, in the arts, in entertainment, in advertisements, in aesthetically packaged blandishments to consume, and in lifestyles. These stimuli are mostly very well made, aesthetically polished, leave no room for doubt, promote the belief that private interests are more important than the common good, and they are generally coherent in the promotion of the basic conviction that the interests of all are safe in the hands of entrepreneurs.

Since these leaders of commerce, industry and entertainment direct so much of the social and cultural life of so many people, the ideas about the world they are presenting are of concern. As we have seen, there are many types of influence coming from the institutions that produce corporate culture. These can be described as demonstrable causes, which generate effects. Another way in which corporate culture exerts influence is through the broad range of issues that it does *not* raise, that it *neglects* systematically or *refuses* to include in its presentations.

What are the values that are absent from the dominant discourse within consumer culture? We must think of values such as respect, equality, sobriety, wisdom, conviviality, morality, human solidarity, community, sustainability or the conviction that inflicting pain or celebrating violence should be avoided. Not everything in the world is exciting, nor should it be. Tensions between people should be diminished and competition brought back to a minimum. People should not be urged to desire material things they never can acquire and should not be prevented from thinking about what is really necessary in their lives. What is socially detrimental should not be part of programming and publicity; the argument that something should be presented just because it sells lacks moral substance. All these questions are actually non-issues for the world of corporate culture.

Twenty years ago a value system still existed among poor black people in the USA that emphasized the sharing of resources. That value system has long been eroded in most communities by an ethic of liberal individualism, which affirms that it is morally acceptable not to share, bell hooks notes. 'The mass media has [sic] been the primary teacher bringing into our lives and our homes the logic of liberal individualism, the idea that you make it by privatized hoarding of resources, not by sharing them' (hooks 1994: 170). Through the strengthening of materialistic values, sympathetic feelings towards others are weakening, tending to diminish the spirit of community and the strength of communal ties (Herman and McChesney 1997: 153).

This is also what Jacob Srampickal finds in Indian film: 'to the majority of filmmakers film is a medium to entertain the masses and thus make huge profits. Hence there can be hardly any social education through this medium' (Srampickal 1994: 16). Consumer capitalism promotes an individualistic way of life, as opposed to a collective one. It entails a lifestyle that is home-centred to the detriment of civic relations. People are supposed to be predominantly passive *consumers* of what capitalism has provided, instead of active citizens, workers or creators. Hedonism and self-absorption predominate and find encouragement. Frank Webster observes that 'consumer capitalism is thus an intensely private way of life, with public virtues such as neighbourliness, responsibility and social concern increasingly displaced by a concern for one's individual needs which should be met by purchases in the store and shopping mall' (Webster 1995: 94–5).

For sure, corporate culture does not encourage people to join a union, or to organize themselves otherwise in defence of their interests (Chomsky 1998: 53). As private citizens we are supposed to be able to stand up for our own interests. Assertiveness is a much-praised value. You should claim your 'rights' loudly, whatever these may be. But the fact that most people are running risks that exceed their capacity to defend themselves on their own is not the regular message spread about by corporate culture. It does not empower people for the things that are really important in life. The last thing corporate culture is interested in is addressing the serious concerns of life such as coping with grief, fear, risk or uncertainty; or work, responsibility, creativity, being a parent, or being an adolescent; or enjoying life without using up all one's energy; or thinking about how the entrepreneurial spirit might co-exist with a far smaller disparity in incomes; or speaking openly about sexuality and showing eroticism without reducing it to banality, just to name a few issues that are remarkably absent from the corporate agenda. In a society organized around mass media, the existence of messages that are outside the media is restricted to interpersonal networks, thus disappearing from the collective mind, according to Manuel Castells (1996: 336).

When people live daily *in* the ambience of corporate culture and are obviously to some extent moulded by it, when they are hardly ever confronted in a serious way with such complicated questions, how can they know that other issues exist than those they see, read or hear daily in the showcases of corporate culture, and that alternatives are imaginable? The problem, Don Slater notes, is that 'we do not consume in order to build a better society, to be a good person and live the true life, but to increase private pleasures and comforts' (Slater 1997: 28). In the world of corporate culture education is a personal investment in a well-paying career, instead of being the occasion for learning how to grow to wisdom and to develop as an independent, responsible and creative person.

Corporate culture cuts human beings off from the roots that anchor them to the past, to a specific culture. A channel such as MTV places the viewer in a schizophrenic state, isolated in the present and unable to escape the dominant culture or develop a coherent alternative worldview, says Jack Banks (1996: 7). Corporate advertising tends to forge a connection in people's minds between private interests, which are the interests of the transnational conglomerates, and the public interest. As a result, says Tony Clark, 'a global "mono culture", prompted by increasing corporate control of the world's media, is emerging which not only disregards local tastes and cultural differences, but threatens to serve as a form of social control over the attitudes, expectations, and behaviour of people all over the world' (Clark 1995: 9).

From the land of desire, in which there is no principal constraint on *what* can be consumed, to the story corporate culture doesn't tell, we have come a long way. There is a difference, indeed, between having something to tell in varied social contexts, and telling stories in order to sell something. Worldwide there are no longer any mass-media firms that could be said to represent or share basic interests with people who are without power. We live surrounded by commercially-oriented messages – mostly artistically coloured and set to music – which often contain violence.

Do these influence people? It would be strange if the programmes that are juxtaposed or interwoven with the publicity did not leave traces in people's minds. The least we can say is that the different media suggest what reality looks like and play a major role in the development of cultural orientations, worldviews and beliefs. As Herbert Schiller puts it, the media select, or exclude, the stories and songs, the images and words that create individual and group consciousness and identity. We may also wonder as well how it would be possible to understand cultures of violence without talking about war.

I have already made several references to Chapter 6. The idea behind my research has not only been to investigate the consequences of economic globalization on artistic cultures worldwide; it has also been to formulate possible solutions as to how to combine freedom, which artistic processes desperately need, with sufficient protection, by which diversity can flourish on the local level where people live. To combine freedom *and* protection may look like trying to square the circle, but let's try.

NOTES

1. 'The New CNN Courts the Conservatives', *International Herald Tribune*, 16 August 2001.

2. 'High-tech Radio Squeezes in Ads', *International Herald Tribune*, 7 January 2000.

3. Milton Glaser, 'Censorious Advertising', *The Nation*, 22 September 1997.

4. Lila Abu-Lughod, 'Wie zijn wij, waar gaan wij naar toe? Egyptische soaps geven antwoord', *Soera*, September 1997.

5. Interview with Boris Cyrulnik, *Le Monde*, 6–7 May 2001.

6. Interview with François Jost, *Le Monde*, 6–7 May 2001.

7. 'L'envers du décor de "Loft Story"', *Le Monde*, 6–7 May 2001.

8. Susan Levine, 'In a Loud and Noisy World, Baby Boomers Pay the Consequences', *International Herald Tribune*, 1 February 1999; see also *NRC Handelsblad*, 28 October 2000.

9. 'On Russian TV, the "Truth" and Nothing But', *International Herald Tribune*, 10 October 2000.

10. Margreth Hoek, 'Liever geen seks en geweld', *De Volkskrant*, 16 September 1996.

11. Pascale Krémer, 'Les Galeries Lafayette retirent leurs modèles vivants des vitrines', *Le Monde*, 23 April 1999.

12. 'Tailoring Film and TV for the World', *International Herald Tribune*, 2 October 1997.

13. Kevin Merida and Richard Leiby, 'Out of the Dark, into the Mainstream: America's Cult of Violence', *International Herald Tribune*, 24–25 April 1999.

14. Ibid.; 'Family Guidance Can Blunt Effect of Video Games', *International Herald Tribune*, 26 September 2000; see also Herz (1997: 83–90).

15. Frank Moretti, 'Markets of the Mind', *New Left Review*, September–October 2000: 111–15.

16. Jurriën Rood, 'De verloren wedstrijd', *De Groene Amsterdammer*, 14 June 1995.

17. Jos de Putter, 'Nouvelle Violence', *Skrien*, 191, August–September 1993: 4–7.

18. 'Corporate Rock Sucks', Editorial, *The Nation*, 25 August–1 September 1997.

19. 'Is Jerry Springer schadelijk voor kinderen?', interview with P. Valkenberg, *De Volkskrant*, 31 March 2000.

20. 'Lekker ziek', *De Volkskrant*, 25 June 1999.

21. Denise Caruso, 'Reality vs. Fantasy: How Video Games Put Killing into Play', *International Herald Tribune*, 29 April 1999.

22. Ellen Goodman, 'Kosovo and Littleton Make Curious Bedfellows', *International Herald Tribune*, 21 May 1999.

23. Robert Scheer, 'Violence is Us', *The Nation*, 15 November 1993.

SIX
Freedom *and* Protection

SQUARING THE CIRCLE

Hundreds of thousands of writers, actors, dancers, musicians, visual artists, designers, film-makers and multimedia artists worldwide create and perform daily, in their own surroundings, crossing frontiers, and more and more penetrating the digital and electronic domains. Some find their sources of inspiration explicitly in their cultural heritage; others are more inclined to lean over the fence into the future. The organizational and economic context for most of them is small or medium-sized.

This huge quantity is exactly what we should have: great varieties of artists working independently of the oligopolistic industries; serving different tastes; using diverse techniques and materials; walking in the ways of completely different aesthetics and contents; some focusing on creations that demand a serious effort to get a grip on, others' work being more of an open book; some serve huge audiences, others mainly find recognition with small groups of people.

Nevertheless, as we have seen in the previous chapters, the cultural situation worldwide is less encouraging than it may look at first glance. Cultural conglomerates have too much power over the production, distribution and promotion of substantial parts of our artistic landscapes. They control the copyright of more and more works of art. Most artists don't do well economically. Local artistic life is becoming delocalized. Cultural initiatives at the local level count less than the moods, influences and concrete artistic products created by a limited number of centres of production, which fill the world with a corporate culture in which increasing consumption is the ultimate aim. To repeat: as George Gerbner has said, in former times the stories we know came from the family and various social institutions which had something to tell, whereas now the stories come from the corporations, which have something to sell.

From a democratic perspective, this oligopolization and delocalization of the production, distribution, promotion and intellectual ownership of the arts, in the broad sense that I have defined them, needs to be undone. The artistic manifestations that surround us every day should no longer be controlled by a limited number of forces. The local levels where people live, raise their children, and share their pleasure and sadness, should again become the focal points of artistic movements, and this includes 'local levels' that are digital communities. The corporations, which have something to sell, should no longer be the main controllers of cultural life. This chapter formulates some ideas and concrete proposals towards achieving the purposes described here.

Of course, we should not live in a fool's paradise, trying to square the circle. First, we have to realize that, worldwide, the tendency is towards *more* monopolization and more corporate culture. However, at the same time counter-movements are starting to express themselves loudly – think of Seattle or Porto Alegre – although admittedly not coherently enough yet. Second, the most difficult issue seems to be raising awareness that *economic freedom* and *freedom of expression* are two completely different compartments of social and cultural life, although they are commonly and erroneously equated. Next, we should be conscious that a multiplicity of artistic expressions do not flourish in every society. To give a chance to real differences, and to arts that are not necessarily immediately popular, demands a conscious effort.

We may be happy that in many places very many artists are working, albeit on a very modest scale. The question, however, is: can their creations and performances, their entertainment and their seriousness, play a relevant role in social and cultural life? Do they add something to the mental, visual, auditive and textual atmospheres that surround diverse groups of people every day? Can substantial differences of artistic and cultural contents, aesthetics and tastes live together, more or less peacefully? Can there be public discussions and under-standing about types of artistic expression that hurt people, about what some people consider banal, or about differing or conflicting tastes? Can morality play a role in the consideration of works of art? How does this fit with freedom of expression, which is a vital human and social value? Can many more artists than is now the case make a decent living from their activities?

Market forces, which actually have oligopolistic claims, do not provide the appropriate setting for the development of democratic artistic rights – crucially, one in which very many different artists can make their voices heard, through their work. People are different, so the sources that develop their sensibilities towards colours, compositions, contours and artistic codifications should be dif-ferent as well. The arts – however entertaining they may be – educate us and present registers in which our feelings develop. These communication processes should not be disturbed by commercial messages.

Of course, every artist tries to sell his or her work. This is a commercial act. And the organizers and promoters of their work do the same. Of course, everybody should make a living. The problem starts, however, when commerce becomes the hub of their activities, and when their work is reduced to being the raw material and ideas that the cultural industries and commercial corporations transform or distort to meet their own tastes and economic needs, presenting the work only in surroundings designed to increase their own profits. The artistic aspects of human communication, which can be found in musical structures, in the many resonances of words and in the spell cast by images, become troubled when corporate intentions come first.

Obviously, many people love what the cultural conglomerates offer them, so the seductions of corporate culture are not to be dismissed. One part of the attempt to square the circle is thus to respect those feelings, yet to analyse what is lost – from a democratic perspective – when the creation, production, distribution, promotion and reception of works of art, as broadly defined, is corporate-driven. Other structures for cultural production and distribution need to be created, in which a diversity of artists and small and medium-sized cultural enterprises can flourish. *Why shouldn't such structures generate artistic work that appeals to a sizeable number of people?* There is no hard and fast rule that only what comes out of the cultural industries can be enjoyable on a wide scale.

This chapter tries to formulate other perspectives and conditions for artistic creation, production, distribution, promotion and reception. However, when all dominant forces are going in one direction it is not easy to get a clear picture about what the future could look like. So this is not a blueprint for a new society. My proposals are building blocks that may help to orient our way of thinking and proceding. In any case, it is worth contributing an artistic, cultural perspective to the project of larger movements worldwide that are trying to push economic globalization in another direction. So my proposals should be read in the context of discussions about the unequal division of wealth in the world, and about ecological issues, in the knowledge that digitalization is turning on their heads many individual human, social, economic, cultural and political relations.

TRADE: ANOTHER WORLD WAR

The 1948 Universal Declaration of Human Rights states in Article 19: 'Everyone has the freedom of opinion and expression.' Two aspects are interesting here. 'Everyone' implies a shift away from an elite concept of culture (Hamelink 1994b: 187–8) and from other kinds of monopolistic sources producing culture, but this first part of the Article also has also an active tenor: self-expression is an entitlement for anyone who wishes to exercise it. This conceptualization becomes even more active in the rest of the Article: 'this right includes freedom to hold opinions without interference and to seek, receive and impart information and ideas through any media and regardless of frontiers'. The arts, including all forms of entertainment, are specific forms of communication, as defined earlier in this book, and thus fall within the remit of this Article. What the Universal Declaration of Human Rights implies is nothing less than that everyone has the right to be active in the realm of artistic expression.

This becomes even more explicit in Article 27, which states: 'Everyone has the right freely to participate in the cultural life of the community.' Participation includes not only dancing, writing, painting, or making music or films; it also comprises active involvement in the artistic life of a community. As we have seen, many kinds of communities exist, one of which is the locally demarcated area where people live. There are also communities comprised of, explicitly, or more vaguely, people who share comparable economic positions, religious convictions, social and cultural attitudes, or specific kinds of humour, for instance. They may live near to each other, or not. In any case, people who belong, or feel they belong, to one or more communities have an active right to participate in the cultural life of those communities. My point in Chapter 4 about the importance of a thriving local artistic life fits well with the value that the Universal Declaration of Human Rights gives to communities.

One element from Article 19 should still be stressed. This is that everybody has the right 'to seek, receive and impart information and ideas through any media and regardless of frontiers'. Specifically, the concepts of 'seeking' and 'receiving' cover what we would call nowadays the right of access. Important, too, is the fact that the Article says this should be 'through any media and regardless of frontiers'. This has far-reaching consequences. People should have the right of access to all media, not only the most obvious ones. From the democratic perspective this is indisputable. All voices should be heard and everyone should be able to play an active role in the public domain of any society. Otherwise, only the loudest or most powerful voices will be heard, only the most visible images insist on being seen. Democracy thrives when minority points of view play an active role in the social and cultural field of experience, and this includes the whole gamut of artistic expressions, none of which should remain hidden.

Even before the Universal Declaration of Human Rights came into existence in 1948 the first General Assembly of the United Nations, October/November 1946, passed a resolution in which it declared that freedom of information was a fundamental human right. *The Economist* commented that most delegations gained the impression that the Americans favoured the notion of freedom of information so as to ensure a free market for their news agencies. This impression was intensified by American opposition to the attempts of the Chinese and Indian governments to protect their national news agencies (Hamelink 1978: 16).

This American attitude became known as the doctrine of the free flow of information, including entertainment and the arts generally. Freedom of expression as a human right became confused with the economic freedom of news and cultural enterprises, possibly dominating the news and cultural flows all over the world. Herbert Schiller comments: 'Unexceptional and even highly desirable as an abstract standard, in practice the free-flow idea gave a green light for the global penetration of the products of US media-cultural conglomerates like CBS, Time, Inc., J.Walter Thompson, 20th Century-Fox and others. Any nation's effort to regulate that flow was sternly rejected as tantamount to totalitarianism' (Schiller 1989a: 142). The 1950s and early 1960s saw the free-flow doctrine implemented globally, with massive media flows from a few Western centres – mostly New York, Hollywood, London – to peoples and nations around the world (Schiller 1989b: 294).

Why did some nations seek to regulate the flows of information and cultural products? In some cases, it was indeed for totalitarian reasons – the state controlling what people read, watched or heard. In others it was in order to ensure that local artistic life and the provision of news were not dominated by outside forces or oligopolies. This became a particular problem for former colonies that gained their independence in the early 1960s. After a decade they found that their means and possibilities of communication were negligible compared to the communicative force the Western powers were spreading worldwide. The free flow of information had become a one-way flow from the West to the rest of the world.

In many non-Western countries the free-flow philosophy, and even the idea behind the Universal Declaration of Human Rights, was contested for other reasons. Ziauddin Sardar points out that the Universal Declaration of Human Rights assumes a universal human nature common to all peoples: 'The Declaration presupposes a social order based on liberal democracy where the society is simply a collection of "free" individuals. Again, the individual is seen as absolute, irreducible, separate and ontologically prior to society' (Sardar 1998: 68–9). The basic philosophy of many social and cultural systems in many parts of the world is different from this, however. This is the reality Western countries do not want to know about. 'Since an autonomous, isolated individual does not exist in non-Western cultures and traditions, it does not make sense to talk of his or her rights; and where there are no rights, it is quite absurd to speak of their denial or annulment.' Ziauddin Sardar gives the example of Hinduism, in which the notion of dharma, one of the fundamental concepts of Indian tradition, leads us to symbolic correspondence with the Western idea of human rights.

> Dharma is a multilayered concept and incorporates the terms, elements, data, quality and origination as well as law, norm of conduct, character of things, rights, truth, ritual, morality, justice, righteousness, religion and destiny. In Sikhism, the

prime duty of a human being is sewa: there is no salvation without sewa, the disinterested service of the community. The rights of the individual are thus earned by participating in the community's endeavour and thereby seeking sakti. (Sardar 1998: 70)

This does not mean that individual rights do not have any value, but they should be seen in a broader context, which Ziauddin Sardar again elucidates with an example: 'The notion of an individual person's rights is not unknown to Islam. Thus, individual rights in Islam do not stop at personal freedoms but include economic, social, cultural, civil and personal rights as well' (Sardar 1998: 72–3). Ziauddin Sardar's observations make clear that a lot of work needs to be done, first, to understand the different concepts of human rights and give them due respect, and, second, to learn to live with such varied concepts.

Perhaps a first step is a short text by the Council of Canadians, which, at least, broadens the concept of human rights from one concerned with the individual to one that also has collective implications, which are largely kept out of the mental framework in Western countries.

As citizens in a democratic society, we all have rights. The Universal Declaration of Human Rights and other international covenants and charters enshrine a number of these, including the right to adequate food, clothing and shelter; the right to employment, education and health care; the right to a clear environment, our own culture and quality of public services; the right to physical security and justice before the law. Central to all of these is the right to participate in decisions that affect our lives. (Hines 2000: 28)

Going back to the beginning of the 1970s we see that within the framework of the United Nations and of Unesco, Third World nations started to discuss three issues: they demanded greater variety in sources of information, less monopolization of the forms of cultural expression, and preservation of some national cultural space from the pervasive commercialization of Western cultural outpourings. 'There was no doubt in the minds of Third World cultural figures that the products of Western cultural industries had an effect on the peoples to whom they were targeted' (Schiller 1989a: 142). Important topics were the need to reverse US and Western European domination, and introduce new international norms regarding media content, balanced coverage, reciprocal exchanges and technological equality. Kaarle Nordenstreng summarizes the demands thus:

Focusing on the right to seek and impart information as well as the right to receive it, these proposals fostered the democratization of access to mass communications and its social accountability to the people it addressed and served. The reform movement also demanded an equitable share of the spectrum as a global resource held in trust for all nations, not simply for those who had got there first. (Preston et al. 1989: 124)

The international, mostly Third World, effort to change the global cultural pattern reached a peak in the autumn of 1976, at the 19th General Conference of Unesco in Nairobi, Kenya. At that meeting the US delegation was obliged to take note of the opposition it faced and to acknowledge what up to that time Washington had denied routinely, that there were indeed international 'information imbalances' (Schiller 1989a: 143). This was when the idea of creating a New World Information and Communication Order was developed. What would this look like? To get a grip on this question Unesco established a commission, presided over by the Irish scholar Sean McBride, which presented its report *Many Voices, One World* in 1980 (Unesco 1980). The West immediately attacked this report as being communist and seeking to curtail democracy, the free flow of ideas, the market forces that shape telecommunications, the press and the computer industries.

Even the most cursory glance at the McBride Report, Edward Said comments, 'will reveal that far from recommending simpleminded solutions like censorship, there was considerable doubt among most of the commission members that anything very much could be done to bring balance and equity in the anarchic world information order' (Said 1993: 291–2). Nevertheless, in 1984 the United States left Unesco. William Harley, a State Department consultant on communications, gave as an explanation for this action that Unesco 'has taken on an anti-Western tone'. The organization had 'become a comfortable home for statist, collectivist solutions to world problems and for ideological polemics' (Herman 1989: 245–6; see also Preston et al. 1989).

Edward Herman observes that the US position implies that 'statist' solutions are unnatural, illicit and 'political', whereas private-enterprise initiatives are natural and apolitical. He comments that this is

completely arbitrary and an expression of a *political* preference, a preference that is not even consistently maintained by US officials. They do not insist that 'statist' illiteracy programmes are illicit, and even in the communications field they do not maintain that government underwriting of satellite technology for the private sector produced an unfair, 'statist' basis for the technological edge of the private US communications industry. 'Statist' means government intervention in those selected areas where the government does not intrude in the United States, and/or where it is US policy to support private sector initiatives. (Herman 1989: 245)

Koichiro Matsuura, Unesco's director-general, managed in autumn 2002 to persuade Washington to rejoin the organization. We must fear that the USA is returning to Unesco in order to obstruct the agenda described below.

The question of the unequal balance between the rich and the poor countries in the communications field has, until now, not been on Unesco's agenda. Yet it is an urgent issue. Too many questions raised in the debate on the New World Information and Communication Order have still not been answered, *Our Creative Diversity*, the Report of the World Commission on Culture and Development, declares. 'What is to be done when information flows from and within the least developed countries are so meagre and the means so highly concentrated?' The report states that 'in the industrialized and information-saturated nations, concentrations of ownership are leading to a demand for a better balance between market freedom and the public interest, making it necessary for governments to attain social goals the market fails to achieve' (Pérez de Cuéllar 1996: 106). To broaden the discussion, the Universal Declaration of Human Rights can surely not have meant that only some commercial groups should effectively have the power to communicate, while the majority of the world's population is the passive audience that must wait and see what the corporations present them with.

Meanwhile, we have entered a situation which Jack Valenti, the president of the Motion Picture Association of America, described in May 1992 thus: 'Whether we like it or not, we are now in a World War of Trade.' This is the phenomenon I described in Chapters 1 and 2 of this book. At the global level, responsibility for culture has been shifted from Unesco to the World Trade Organization (WTO). This means that even the most modest efforts to achieve some balance between freedom of communication and providing some protection so that everyone in the world can enjoy this freedom have been suppressed. Until 1984, there was some recognition in Unesco that the exchange and development of artistic cultural values would suffer if market forces alone decided what was to be created, produced, distributed and promoted. This platform was not very effective, but at least there was one place in the world where the unequal communications balance could be discussed.

In 1985 responsibility for culture was apparently transferred from the world's cultural organization, Unesco, to the body where free trade is the only guiding principle – initially the GATT, which became the WTO in 1995. This organization considers works of art and entertainment and cultural values only as products, as it does education, health, ecology and so on. The idea that there are certain values that should be protected and not depend solely on market forces does not exist in the context of the WTO. It is true that GATS – the General Agreement on Trade in Services, one of the WTO treaties – still has a blank page concerning culture, called cultural exemption in France, that says that culture is also included in the free trade agreement. However, states are not obliged to open their markets completely to foreign cultural products. This means that culture is exempted from the rulings of the free trade regime. This was a demand from the European Union led by France and against the wishes of the USA. The concept of 'services' includes the arts. States still theoretically have the right to make regulations concerning culture that protect their internal market. However, the example of Canada, as already indicated in Chapter 4, shows that the effects are minimal. Let's look at a few more statistics: the US share of Canadian cultural markets stands at 95 per cent for movies screened, 84 per cent for musical recordings sold, 83 per cent for magazines sold at newsstands, 70 per cent for music played on radio stations, 70 per cent for books sold, and 60 per cent for English-language TV programming (Schiller 1999: 79–80).

In many places all over the world comparable figures can be found. Such developments, where cultural delocalization is the order of the day, are the logical consequences of the present free trade agreements. Crucial concepts in recent negotiations on traded services were 'market access', the 'right of permanent establishment', and 'national treatment'. Cees Hamelink argues that the 'combined effect of such norms rules out any local protection of domestic service industries, inhibits the development of indigenous service industries, and diminishes local control over key service industries'. He reminds us that among such industries are the mass media, telecommunication services, advertising, marketing and tourism; therefore 'it becomes clear that the application of these norms reduces local cultural autonomy. Local cultural markets are monopolized by transnational corporations that leave little space for local cultural providers.' He continues: 'liberalizing world trade to the extent that smaller and less-resource-rich countries open their services markets to outsiders, stimulates the development of consumerist lifestyles and erodes the competitive capacity of people's own cultural industries' (Hamelink 1994a: 100). The issue of consumerist lifestyles has already been discussed in Chapter 5.

In this part of the chapter I have moved from the Universal Declaration of Human Rights to the unsuccessful attempts of Third World countries to get the question of equal communication rights for all countries and groups of people worldwide on to Unesco's agenda. The idea of establishing a New World Information and Communication Order has been destroyed. In the late 1980s, considering culture and communication mainly, or only, as tradable products became the dominant vision and practice. It turns out that the Universal Declaration of Human Rights can be interpreted in multiple ways. Does it imply that care should be taken that, among other rights, communication rights can be exercised by 'everyone', or do we have to wait and see what the outcome of the free flow of economic information is? Should freedom of expression be complemented by certain forms of protection to guarantee that everyone in the world can 'seek, receive and impart information and ideas through any media and regardless of frontiers', in the cultural field as in other domains? My intention in this chapter is to try to find a balance between freedom and protection.

Meanwhile, it has become clear that the concept 'universal' in the Universal Declaration of Human Rights is disputable for many countries in Asia and the Arab world. In 1993 the United Nations organized a conference in Vienna, the purpose of which was to reconfirm the principles of human rights. Cees Hamelink relates that, in the conference's preparatory process, the concept of universality was challenged by several parties.

> In the Cairo Declaration on Human Rights in Islam (9 June 1993) the member states of the Organization of the Islamic Conference made human rights subordinate to Islamic religious standards. The declaration provided that the rights and freedoms it stipulated are subject to the Islamic Shari'a. The Bangkok Declaraton of the Asian preparatory conference stated that, in the protection of the human rights, differences in national, cultural and religious backgrounds had to be taken into account. (Hamelink 1994b: 64–5)

In fact, the Vienna Declaration recognized that universality does not equal uniformity, and said that 'the significance of national and regional particularities and various historical, cultural and religious backgrounds must be borne in mind'. Despite all the turmoil, the Vienna World Conference on Human Rights managed to reinforce that human rights were universal. Let's see the implications of this hard-won decision for artistic cultures worldwide.

RETHINKING ECONOMIC GLOBALIZATION

Wendell Berry notes:

> There can be no such a thing as a 'global village'. No matter how much one may love the world as a whole, one can live fully in it only by living responsibly in some small part of it. Where we live and who we live there with define the terms of our relationship to the world and to humanity ... A culture is not a collection of relics or ornaments, but a practical necessity, and its corruption invokes calamity. A healthy culture is a communal order of memory, insight, value, work, conviviality, reverence, aspiration. It reveals the human necessities and the human limits. It clarifies our inescapable bonds to the earth and to each other. It assures that the necessary restraints are observed, that the necessary work is done, and that it is done well. (Berry 1986: 123–43)

What we need to have, indeed, is 'a sense of community and a notion that an individual's well-being is determined to no small extent by the community's well-being' (McChesney 1997: 5). It is a misguided belief that commercially directed relationships and electronically mediated networks can substitute for traditional relationships and communities. Jeremy Rifkin emphasizes: 'Traditional relationships are born of such things as kinship, ethnicity, geography, and shared spiritual visions. They are glued together by notions of reciprocal obligations and visions of common destinies. They are sustained by communities whose mission it is to reproduce and continually secure the shared meanings that make up the common culture.' He argues that commodified relationships, on the other hand, are instrumental in nature. 'The only glue that holds them together is the agreed-upon transaction price. The relationships are contractual rather than reciprocal in nature. They are sustained by networks of shared interests for as long as the parties involved continue to honour their contractual obligations' (Rifkin 2000: 241–3).

In the last few decades, in some parts of the world, some aspects of our well-being have been guaranteed by the common project called the welfare state. This welfare state is 'slowly but surely [being] dismantled, and ideologists of free trade sacrifice national traditions of care, shared responsibility, and social commitment for the uncertain benefits of foreign investment and competitive standing in a global economy', Rosemary Coombe notes (1998: 4). And in many parts of the world, cultures – including their artistic aspects – have become delocalized, as we have seen in Chapter 4.

The almost unimaginable question is how can we rebuild communities and cultures that are related to the life of people, their daily pleasures, sorrows, material needs, moral doubts, animosities, and concerns about the quality of their surrounding environment? How can we make a decisive change so that the arts people enjoy do not come almost exclusively from oligopolistic sources far away from their own artistic and cultural impulses? How can we counter the commercially-driven activity that currently dominates artistic creation, production, distribution, promotion and reception? How can we ensure that the revival of communities is not a nostalgic, romantic or narrow-minded affair? How can we link communities – whether 'local' or based on other uniting factors – with organisms such as the state, regional authorities and the United Nations, whose task should be to ensure the observance of social, human and cultural rights, and to determine the contexts in which people can claim their rights?

Needless to say, this programme is too large to deal with exhaustively in one book, especially when everything is going in the direction of more economic globalization and corporate concentration. What I propose here are some conditions that may open the way for a cultural turn-around worldwide, in favour of the artistic life that belongs to the places and communities where people live, raise their children, eat and drink, and unavoidably die.

Obviously, the first thing is to rethink completely the concept of unhampered free trade. The politics of laissez-faire may look like the obvious, most natural and normal way of doing things. Nothing is less true, John Gray argues. 'Encumbered markets are the norm in every society, whereas free markets are a product of artifice, design and political coercion. *Laissez-faire* must be centrally planned; regulated markets just happen. The free market is not, as New Right thinkers have imagined or claimed, a gift of social evolution. It is an end-product of social engineering and unyielding political will' (Gray 1998: 17). He argues that the implications of these truths for the project of constructing a worldwide free market in an age of democratic government are profound. 'They are that the rules of the game of the market must be insulated from democratic deliberation and political amendment. Democracy and free market are rivals, not allies' (p. 17). Looking at what is happening generally in the world, he finds that the natural counterpart of a free market economy is a politics of insecurity.

The ideology of the free market also supports the idea that the political space in any society should remain empty. This is harmful. After all, what is the role that politics should play in any society, specifically in a democracy? It should be to achieve coherence in the context of many different social, economic, cultural, normative and ideological interests, to take care that the will of the people on all these matters emerges, and that this is respected and becomes the guiding principle in the deliberations and moments of decision-making on all issues that concern the life of individual people and society as a whole (Went 1996: 59). The free market ideology considers these processes less important and less enriching for individual citizens than whatever the free hand of the market can bring them.

A telling contemporary example may contradict this belief. The internet was a brilliant technical achievement that could never have happened in the free enterprise marketplace. Nicholas Baran argues that 'the Internet has been a model of what can be achieved through the combination of public funding and innovative technology' (Baran 1998: 132). The concept of community, and the idea of adding something valuable to communal life, becomes superfluous in the value system of neoliberalism. The consequence, for instance, is that the internet today 'is being transformed into an electronic shopping mall and sales catalog. And it is only a matter of time before the Internet's most useful attributes disappear in the wake of commercialization' (p. 132). Let's see what counter-movements are developing nowadays; the struggle is not yet over.

While right-wing political movements have since the 1970s been very much in favour of pushing back the role of the state, the left has dealt with the state in a very careless way, becoming rather undecided about its role. The state meanwhile was functioning as the locus of moral oppression, and the welfare state was accepted as being there for ever, so why care about the state as an institution that should play a vital role? Internationally, the left was also inclined to show more solidarity with comrades all over the world than with those at home. For many recently decolonized states the concept and practice of a national state were new; difficult to establish the state as an entity and as the 'place' where conflicting interests are solved peacefully, when formerly the main centres of decision-making had been local communities.

A Dutch writer, Herman Franke, looking back at the 1960s and 1970s, concludes that he had an over-optimistic notion of human nature. 'However, people are not by nature nice to each other, as I once thought and hoped. Yet I am convinced that most people are greedy predators that need to be protected against each other. Otherwise the strongest devour those who are weak, unscrupulously.' He concludes that for this very reason state interventions are needed, as are public authorities that make laws to prevent people killing each other and turning the world into a garbage dump out of the desire for profit. Reacting against the postmodernist tendency to preach the end of all ideologies, he exclaims: 'Forget it. This is exactly what those greedy grabbers would like.'[1] The ideology that is needed more than ever is that what is fragile and different should be protected.

Another active role for the state to play – in the case of some states, for the first time – concerns what we may continue to call the welfare system, as Will Hutton does. 'What is in reality required from the welfare system is that it provides boundaries to the operation of markets, underwrites social cohesion and helps produce the values that sustain the co-operation without which successful economies cannot flourish. Instead of privatization, the welfare state needs more democracy and more sensitivity to real needs' (Hutton 1996: 307). John Gray specifies that 'effective state institutions are needed to monitor the impact of humans on the natural environment, and to limit the exploitation of natural resources by unaccountable interests' (Gray 1998: 200–1). Benjamin Barber wonders: 'If theme parks are now talking about "privatizing government," and taking over many functions of the state, is there a way for citizens to do the opposite and "publicize private markets," compelling them to be accountable, and demanding from them at least some degree of public-interestedness?' (Barber 1996: 148).

Obviously, the role of cultural conglomerates and other transglobal corporations within specific states and communities should be redefined and should be brought within the framework of regimes that combine entrepreneurial freedom and a whole set of obligations. Tony Clark, writing for the International Forum on Globalization, introduces in this context the concept of a corporate charter. By formulating such charters, 'social movements can then identify potential areas of corporate vulnerability and strategic points for citizen action, not only for challenging corporate power in relation to public policy making, but also for redefining the nature, role, and rights of corporations' (Clark 1995: 19).

However, there are also some fundamental questions that cannot be regulated by a charter alone. There is more at stake, and this is the size and the exclusively profit-making purpose of cultural conglomerates that threaten the existence and the vitality of civic cultures, Benjamin Barber notes. He gives the example of book production.

> When books become a niche category for media octopi like Murdoch or Viacom with commercial entertainment tentacles and political information (news) tentacles and television tentacles and publishing tentacles, but no civic or literary torso, the future of the word and the civic and literary cultures it supports becomes extremely uncertain. When words are subordinated to pictures (film, television, or videocassette) whose producers are indentured to profit, democracy is unlikely to be a beneficiary. (Barber 1996: 127)

Later in this chapter I discuss some proposals for how to bring back cultural enterprises to more normal sizes and proportions, so that there can once again be a huge diversity of them on the market.

Ibn Khaldun says in *The Mugaddimah*: 'Only tribes held together by group feeling can live in the desert' (Mowlana 1997: 1). This wisdom confronts us with a huge dilemma. In the present world we need the state as a rule-making and rule-maintaining entity. In order to regulate the big corporations, including in the artistic or cultural field, we can't do without a system that has the legitimacy to make regulations, having at the same time law-enforcing power. But we also know that many people feel they belong to smaller entities than the state. In many parts of the world this was always the norm, Ngugi Wa Thiong'o points out.

> One of the functions of the state is to ensure that the various forces in society keep their place in the social fabric by policing rules that are often codified into laws. In societies that did not have a state, the function of holding together was carried out by culture. The domain of culture embodied the desirable and the undesirable in the realm of values. The values were contained in stories, songs, and other cultural practices of the community. Thus stories, dances, festivals, rituals, and even sports reinforced each other in the production, reproduction, and dissemination of ethical and moral ideals. (Ngugi Wa Thiong'o 1998: 8)

The challenge is thus both to reinforce the state again as an entity that protects the variety of interests of people – interests that are not corporate driven – and to ensure that this entity creates as much space as possible for people to make locally the decisions that touch their daily life. Herman Daly and John Cobb observe that 'in many instances the nation-state is already too large and too remote from ordinary people for effective participation to be possible. Decentralization of the economy within the nation-state should accompany nationalization in relation to the global economy' (Daly and Cobb 1994: 174). They also argue that many regions within the United States should become relatively self-sufficient.

Consistently and systematically, traditional communities have been destroyed in many parts of the world, especially in the rural areas where most people in the Third World still live, Daly and Cobb note. And then they make a statement that gives pause for thought: 'If India had adopted Gandhian economics, there would be far less heavy industry there, but there would also be far fewer urban slums and far healthier rural life. The prosperous middle class would be smaller, but the desperately poor would also be far less numerous' (Daly and Cobb 1994: 166). Their analysis does not result from romantic or nostalgic feelings. It is a hard fact that the lives of many people all over the world have worsened substantially during the last few decades. A ruthless delocalization has taken place that affects their agricultural methods, their economies, their social care, their cultures, their artistic representations, all of which could have served as sound foundations for their further development. In 1998 Sherif Hetata wrote: 'The countries that form the Group of Seven, with their 800 million inhabitants, control more technological, economic, informatics, and military power than the rest of the approximately 430 billion who live in Asia, Africa, Eastern Europe, and Latin America. Five hundred multinational corporations account for 80 percent of world trade and 75 percent of investments' (Hetata 1998: 274).

Herman Daly and John Cobb remark that 'the dominant patterns of economic development throughout the world have been quite the reverse of community development'. The solution will not be to cut states into many smaller states. The example of former Yugoslavia and its decade-long wars is not encouraging. The result is many people killed, social and economic infrastructures destroyed, and the formation of several small states that don't have the ability to protect their citizens' economic, social, cultural and ecological interests, not to speak of locally grown arts which don't play any significant role at present. There are only losses.

So, we need strong states, while realizing at the same time that as the world has become more complicated more and more people are wanting to solve problems at the local level. How might things look? Colin Hines imagines the alternative, arguing that 'everything that could be produced within a nation or region should be. Long-distance trade is then reduced to supplying what could not come from within one country or geographical grouping of countries. This would allow an increase in local control of the economy and the potential for it being shared out more fairly, locally' (Hines 2000: viii).

Walden Bello sums up some of the priorities for what we might call a model of limited deglobalization of the domestic economy. First, 'while foreign investment of the right kind is important, growth must be financed principally from

domestic savings and investment. This means progressive taxation systems.'
Second, he recognizes that export markets are important. However, 'they are too
volatile to serve as reliable engines of growth. Development must be reoriented
around the domestic market as the principal locomotive of growth.' The third
priority is making the domestic market the engine of development. The link-
age between sustained growth and equity should be repaired again. 'Achieving
economic sustainability based on a dynamic domestic market can no longer be
divorced from issues of equity.' Fourth, of course, regionalism can become an
invaluable adjunct to such a process of domestic market-driven growth, if it has
not been guided 'by a perspective of neoliberal market integration'. Fifth, he
observes that 'the centrality of ecological sustainability is said to be one of the
hard lessons of the crisis' (Bello et al. 2000: 21–2).

One of the core issues is redirecting financial flows and the way tax money is
spent. 'The amounts of money spent by all countries to lure in foreign companies,
or keep existing ones, inevitably means that tax money won't be spent on local
needs' (Hines 2000: 163–4). Structurally the situation in the world should be
changed in such a way that countries and regions do not feel tempted to compete
with each other to have foreign enterprises operating within their borders. There
should be control on capital which 'prevents further liberalization, severely limits
speculation, ensures money stays predominantly local and that what money does
leave countries for foreign investment or aid has a *Protect the Local, Globally*
approach' (p. 79). Export subsidies and insurances should be abolished and
changed into subsidies for local investments. The present incentive systems in
the rich countries, which encourage enterprises operating abroad, should be
abolished. Instead, incentive structures should be created that reward socially
and environmentally responsible practices.

Colin Hines asserts that 'democratic control over capital is the key to providing money for governments and communities to rebuild local economies and
improve environmental and social conditions for job opportunities'. He suggests
that a Tobin-type tax on international capital transactions can curb currency
speculators. Taxing all stock market transactions would thus be a means of re-
regulating finance capital. Other measures would be 'controls on capital flows,
taxes on short-term speculative transactions, [and] tightening of easy credit
that allow speculators to multiply the size of their "bets" way beyond the cash
required to cover them'. Colin Hines also suggests that a wide and coordinated
attack on corporate tax evasion is required, including offshore banking centres
(Hines 2000: 91).

What would this mean for the arts? In many countries one of the most important forms of support for the arts has been public funding. One of the greatest
threats of globalization is the erosion of the whole financial underpinning of

governments. Corporations find it possible to get away with paying hardly any taxes, in rich and poor countries alike. Erosion of public financing, the government revenue base, is an important aspect of what is threatening the arts. In that sense any activity that helps to keep business and economic activities more local is helpful for the arts, because it creates a tax base again, by which cultural activities too can be financed. At the same time, if enterprises are to cease being volatile transients all over the world, they must change from being exploiters of human and material resources into participating and responsible organizations. Perhaps, the most important point is that with the localizing of economic life there would be a community again in which artists can play interesting roles (plural!).

However, this should not be romanticized. There is also the danger that stressing the need for more local cultural life means creating 'a false dichotomy between the global and the local, assuming that the global entails homogenization and undifferentiated identity whereas the local preserves heterogeneity and difference' (Hardt and Negri 2000: 44). In recent decades corporate-driven globalization has taken over the construction of local cultural and artistic ambiences. This hegemony therefore has to be addressed in the local as well as the global context.

Actually, we should go back to the Universal Declaration of Human Rights, which gives all people the right to communicate, individually and collectively, through artistic as well as other means. This, however, has been threatened by unhampered free trade. There is thus a need for a powerful institution that can defend public interests; in the contemporary world this can only be the state. We need to make private markets public again. Cultural conglomerates and other mega-enterprises should be subjected to a corporate charter which limits their size. The economy should be controlled locally again, while reducing long-distance trade, taxing progressively, controlling capital movements, abolishing export subsidies, and deglobalizing economies. Strong local economies will again generate the public funding for, among other things, cultural initiatives, specifically the arts.

In order to realize these drastic changes a new world order is necessary. We should invent the almost unthinkable.

A NEW INTERNATIONAL TREATY ON CULTURAL DIVERSITY

Peter Fuchs, director-general of the International Committee of the Red Cross, says it would be enlightened self-interest if captains of industry contributed to the creation of stable societies, because a market is only as stable as the society in which it is based. By the same token, organized crime arguably poses the most acute threat to private business. 'Therefore, enlightened self-interest should be sufficient incentive for entrepreneurs and shareholders to look beyond short-term growth and profits, and to invest some of those profits in long-term measures aimed at stabilizing society in order to avert tensions and armed conflict.'[2]

This would be a modest beginning to what could become a new world order. However, there is reason to fear that competition between huge corporations, including cultural conglomerates, is so fierce that there is no strong incentive to look to the future – even their own, let alone the future of humankind. Nevertheless, these enterprises should be counterbalanced. This can't be done by individual states alone because the corporations are operating globally, and certainly not by any kind of regulation by local or regional political authorities. This means that there needs to be a global political entity that can set a framework of regulations, directives and codes of behaviour, with the authority to bind enterprises and national governments alike. Jan Pronk, chairman of the 2000 Climate Conference, said in September 1997 that 'the present trend of weakening the United Nations should be stopped'.[3] Three and a half years later, George W. Bush Jr, in the first months of his presidency of the United States did the opposite and sped up the process of weakening this organization. That the USA paid its dues to the UN for the first time for years after the attacks of 11 September 2001 does not change this fact.

It must be clear to all other states that the citizens of the world can't wait on the government of the USA to construct a new international legal order. The situation we live in is urgent. In the words of the Mexican writer Carlos Fuentes: 'Uncontrolled, globalized markets can become a synonym for robbery.' According to him the situation is dangerous because societies are at the mercy of a minority of multinational corporations and of a fleeting abundance of investments 'that like the swallows are here today and gone tomorrow'.[4] It is intolerable that the most important issues about human livelihood are decided solely on the basis of profit for transnational corporations. The economy *must* come under some supervision (Daly and Cobb 1994: 178).

To make this more concrete, John Gray proposes among other measures 'a regime of global governance … in which world markets are managed so as to promote the cohesion of societies and the integrity of states. Only a framework of global regulation – of currencies, capital movements, trade and environmental conservation – can enable the creativity of the world economy to be harnessed in the service of human needs' (Gray 1998: 199). The possibility of something like a world government is still light years away. Therefore the concept of *global governance* seems to be an attractive one. The condition is that 'there must be sufficient power at the world level to deal with urgent problems that can be dealt with nowhere else' (Daly and Cobb 1994: 178).

But where this power can be found, concretely, remains the question. Marie-Claude Smouts is sceptical about the concept of global governance and the practice it promises. She calls it an ideological tool for a politics of minimal state involvement.[5] Bernard Cassen refers to a draft white paper on European governance, from the European Commission, which would have as a consequence that all regulations and procedures concerning the exercise of power at the European level would be revised. 'This will put all actual – and constitutional – forms at risk of representative democracy and would privatize public decision making.'[6] What is true for Europe is also true at the level of the whole world. Also the idea of global governance is too weak a concept for restructuring the world away from global neoliberalism into a place where local economic and cultural life has priority again, coordinated by something like a global government.

One condition for achieving this is the creation of a completely new form of World Trade Organization as one of the institutions of the United Nations. At present the WTO operates quite outside the UN framework. Colin Hines would like to call this new body (replacing WTO) the WLO, the World Localization Organization, based on his proposal, the General Agreement on Sustainable Trade (GAST) (Hines 2000: 130). Of course, the body that sets the rules for trade worldwide, including cultural commerce, should be answerable to the General Assembly of the United Nations. Commerce concerns all countries in the world. So all countries should collectively decide on the terms of the commercial exchange of goods and services. This new WTO (or WLO) would establish the conditions for access to the use of the major natural resources and would also set the prices of raw materials, as Samir Amin proposes. This body 'should also take responsibility for planning targets for inter-regional trade in industrial products, reconciling general competitiveness, with distributional criteria favouring the disadvantaged regions, and the creation of conditions which permit the improvement of incomes of disadvantaged workers' (Amin 1997: 104–5).

Realism obliges us to be aware that a new WTO of this kind will not be created today or tomorrow. Consequently, something else should happen to give nations the full right to protect cultural diversity in their own societies, regions and local communities. As Saul Landau states in an interview: 'There is a need for a Global New Deal, which means that the responsible global entity – Unesco, the United Nations? – would consider culture as a right. That is the right to preserve your culture as a way of preserving your identity.'

How can we organize this right? And in what global context could it acquire a legally recognized base? These are complicated matters which need urgently to be solved but which are not easy at all. At the present moment, the United Nations is not the strong body that might be hoped for. To be realistic, the United States is not at all in favour of dealing with cultural affairs within the framework of the General Assembly of the United Nations. We have seen that Unesco has been seriously weakened and that making regulations about culture has been transferred from the cultural agenda to the business of trade. Trying to speak in the context of the current WTO about the right to protect the development of cultural diversity in one's own society, in one's own country, will not receive a hearing. From top to bottom the WTO has a neoliberal agenda, in which the use of the word 'protection' is taboo. Moreover, a trade organization should not be the place where cultural policies are made at the global level. The last thing WTO should pretend to be is a substitute for the United Nations, covering all matters on earth. Besides, too, the popular legitimacy of the WTO is weak.

So there is a need for a new international legally binding instrument that gives states the right to take the measures they deem appropriate or necessary to protect the development of cultural diversity in their own societies, without being afraid of WTO-sanctioned retaliation for not having opened up their cultural 'markets' sufficiently to outside forces. Obviously, we should recognize that states are weak compared with the power of the big corporations and, in the context of this book, of the cultural conglomerates. Most states have contributed, willingly or unwillingly, to giving the WTO the powerful position it has now. All of this may be true; nevertheless, states are the only instruments we have at present which can protect some essential human values against the forces of commerce, if their populations so desire.

The idea of a new international legally binding instrument – an international convention on cultural diversity[7] – has been formulated by an informal network of around forty ministers of culture from many parts of the world who meet annually in the assembly of the International Network of Cultural Policies, presided over by the Canadian minister of culture and heritage, Sheila Copps. In September 2001, a new non-governmental organization, the International Network for Cultural Diversity, was founded in Lucerne, Switzerland, one of its aims being to contribute to the establishment of a new international legally binding instrument on cultural diversity. This would be an international treaty like the Landmine Treaty or the Convention on Biological Diversity. A treaty signed by many countries would give those countries an instrument to withstand WTO pressure to forget about all forms of protection for cultures and the arts and to deal with those essential expressions of human values as if they were trade products (which, by the way, should in many cases be protected, too, as discussed above). Philippe Douste-Blazy, the former French (conservative) minister of culture, is right to make the observation that the play is global, so 'the political solutions can only be negotiated at this level'.[8] Why is a new international instrument of this kind – an international convention on cultural diversity – the only way to give culture the full protection it needs? Ivan Bernier, a law professor from Quebec, states that there are already an impressive number of multilateral, bilateral and regional instruments dealing with culture. 'However, the vast majority of them totally ignore the problem of preserving the diversity of cultural expression in the face of the mounting globalization of the economy.' I quote here at length some of the deficiencies Ivan Bernier points out in this regard.

> The most serious and obvious deficiency lies in the fact that the existing instruments take a fragmented approach to the problem of preserving cultural diversity, coming at it from various distinct standpoints such as human rights, intellectual property rights, heritage protection, cultural policies, language rights, cultural pluralism, cultural development, international cultural cooperation, etc. What is lacking is an instrument like that on bio-diversity, which would clearly identify the nature of the threat that globalization poses to cultural diversity and would establish principles and rules for ensuring that this diversity is preserved. Even though globalization has some potential in this regard, it also clearly poses some serious dangers that need to be considered.
>
> Most of the instruments pertaining to this issue (and there are not very many) confine themselves to stating that cultural products are not products like any other. One could reply that if this situation exists, it is because of the lack of consensus on this issue, and the actual challenge is to bring about a rapprochement between the cultural perspective and the commercial perspective. There is some truth to this, but in order to achieve such a rapprochement, the cultural perspective must first be openly expressed. It is still as if everyone is afraid to say that each state is entitled to determine from a cultural standpoint and on the basis of its own conditions and circumstances the policies needed to ensure the preservation and promotion of cultural diversity because of concern that the liberalization of trade in the world would be hampered. Though, cultural expression is a key factor in the ability of various cultures to adapt to the changes imposed on them by globalization. To address the question of the relationship between culture and commerce exclusively from the standpoint of commerce is to subject culture to commercial imperatives and thereby prevent it from playing its own role. The ultimate outcome of this approach will likely be the impairment of both cultural diversity and international trade.
>
> This imbalance, which is especially pronounced in the audio-visual field, appears in the cultural exchanges of both developing and developed countries. Developing countries, for their part, generally have domestic markets with quite limited resources and are usually dependent for most of the cultural products they consume on imports from a few developed countries, where the dominance that one or a few countries have in their domestic markets is generally achieved at the expense of foreign productions. Imports from developing countries are virtually

non-existent in these cases. In both instances, cultural diversity suffers, not only in regard to the expression of national cultures but also in regard to openness to other foreign cultures. (Bernier 2001)

In Ivan Bernier's analysis, if the new instrument on cultural diversity is to be limited from a formal point of view to a simple declaration it could end up in the same position as a large number of other instruments that do not really respond to the challenge of globalization. 'What is needed, at a bare mimimum, is an instrument that reflects the positive commitment of the signatory states to take action in favour of cultural diversity and that contains a mechanism for monitoring this commitment.'

If states can gain the full right to protect the development of cultural diversity in their own societies, creative thinking can start about what kinds of measures should be taken. For sure, not every country will come up with the same kind of policies. What is needed depends on circumstances and on what have traditionally been considered appropriate ways of dealing with culture, balancing freedom for arts and cultures with the protection required in order to allow a rich bouquet of cultural diversity. Many states also need to find new ways of proceeding, of setting up new regulations and cultural policies, because under the conditions that prevail at the beginning of the twenty-first century there are new hurdles to surmount.

What are the kind of regulations and policies that could be established in order to protect and promote cultural diversity in specific countries? Without being exhaustive, I suggest several approaches in the pages that follow.

THE ROAD AWAY FROM CULTURAL CONGLOMERATION

In March 1998 the *New York Times*'s comment on Bertelsmann's purchase of Random House was that it was business as usual in the publishing world:

the trouble is simply how familiar this sale feels. It provokes only a sigh, which suggests how much we have come to take for granted the steady convergence of all media under ever widening corporate umbrellas. But in that convergence . . . something is lost – call it the broadly dispersed ownership of media outlets, call it even a productive democratic inefficiency in the marketing of information. The road away from conglomeration will be a hard one to find.

Our Creative Diversity, the 1996 report of Unesco's and the UN's World Commission on Culture and Development, wonders: 'Can the media professionals sit down together with policy-makers and consumers to work out mechanisms that promote access and a diversity of expression despite the acutely competitive environment that drives the media moguls apart?' (Pérez de Cuéllar 1996: 117). In Chapter 2 we saw that the cultural conglomerates have oligopolistic control over the channels of production, distribution and promotion. The big questions, therefore, are about how to recapture the open space in which many more artists of every kind can create works of art, how to distribute them effectively, and how to communicate information about them with diverse levels of society. The relevant issues are whether enough independent locations for artistic workers exist, along with adequate public access to artists' work, adequate protection against price controls in oligopolistic markets and enough opportunities for new-comers in media markets. Cees Hamelink states that 'even if the oligopolist could demonstrate duality, fairness, diversity, critical debate, objectivity, investigative reporting, and resistance to external pressures in his offerings to the marketplace, there would still be reason to provide regulatory correction as the marketplace would effectively be closed for newcomers and thus not constitute a free market' (Hamelink 1994: 174–5). Accordingly, the great challenge is to restore democracy in a cultural perspective. This is all the concept of *access* is about.

Certainly in the rich parts of the world the infrastructure for the creation and diffusion of works of art is almost unlimited, but only a very small number of decision-makers decide what is in or out. The right of access means the right not to be excluded. This right 'becomes more and more important in a world increasingly made up of electronic mediated commercial and social networks' (Rifkin 2000: 237–9). Jeremy Rifkin asserts that *governments* should play an active role in assuring and guaranteeing people's fundamental right to communicate with each other. 'Can basic freedoms and real democracy continue to exist?' he asks.[9] Yes. And there is a role to play for governments representing states that are strong *and* convinced enough to intervene in the free play of the market.

Countries and regions all over the world should have the full right to exempt cultural communication from the present policies of free trade as formulated in the treaty of the World Trade Organization, as stated earlier. The arts are not commercial products like any others. Commercial freedom in general should be matched with the right to protect, for instance, domestic economies and the local ecology. From the cultural perspective, it should be a basic right that countries and regions can take measures to promote the growth of real diversity in the production, distribution and promotion of all forms of the arts. This means that governments should be entitled to have their own support systems and to set rules (quota systems) about what quantity of foreign cultural products may go through the various domestic cultural outlets. GATS, WTO's general agreement on trade and services, presently has a blank page concerning culture. This means that culture is exempted from the rulings of this treaty. What kinds of regulations might be useful?

In South Korea the Coalition for Cultural Diversity in Moving Images has been active for several years and has broad popular support. One of the main results of this coalition – and its predecessor, the Screen Quota Watchers – is that the screening of foreign films has been limited to a maximum of 149 days per year for each venue. Korean films' share of their home market grew from 16 per cent in 1993 to 36 per cent in 2000. The coalition has been acting as the watchdog for the Korean movie industry and is working to protect the sovereignty of Korean media culture as well as cultural diversity.

The trend we examined in Chapter 4 is what the Korean Coalition for Cultural Diversity in Moving Images observes as well: 'many national motion picture industries have gone bankrupt or are on the road to decline due to the strong offense by Hollywood equipped with strong capital, technology, and distribution networks. However, Hollywood, which is in effect a monopoly that controls 80–90% of the global picture market, is not satisfied yet.' South Korea has managed to avoid disaster. The coalition thinks that all countries should adopt a quota system, 'a policy to keep the market share of audiovisual contents from a certain country to under 50% of the total domestic market'.

In a supporters' declaration, the Korean Coalition for Cultural Diversity in Moving Images asserts that 'countries around the world should maintain the right to provide various measures (subsidies, tax benefits, broadcasting quotas, screen quotas, etc.) to protect their own media culture. Without such a right, cultural diversity may not be guaranteed and this can have a detrimental impact on mankind.' The declaration also urges that 'bilateral and multilateral negotiations such as the WTO agreement recognize cultural exceptions in the audio-video service sector, which include motion pictures'. There is a real desire to see the co-existence of domestic media and greater cultural exchanges among countries.[10]

Moving on from South Korea's positive experience with quotas, the next issue is to consider what constitutes a menace to democracy: how few owners, controlling what percentage of a nation's mass communications and other channels of cultural exchange? (Bogart 1994). In other words, how many buyers and sellers are required for a market to be competitive? 'Enough so that no one alone can appreciably influence price,' Herman Daly and John Cobb remark. 'Competition is what keeps profit at the normal level and resources properly allocated.' Obviously this has a tendency to go in the wrong direction. 'To the extent that competition is self-eliminating we must constantly reestablish it by trustbusting.' They call this a practically forgotten word in the current age of mergers and takeovers. Nevertheless, trustbusting is a necessity, because 'monopoly is by definition anticompetitive, but even bigness that falls short of monopoly presents a problem' (Daly and Cobb 1994: 49–50).

At the end of 2000 Bertelsmann and EMI tried to merge. The consequence would have been four rather than five music conglomerates globally. The European Commission thought this would create an oligopolistic market and, in the end, put so many conditions on both 'partners' that the deal became unattractive to both of them. However, four rather than five, five rather than four – what's the difference? After all, with five there is still an oligopolistic market, which continues to make it easy for controlling interests to refuse, in this case, the distribution of certain kinds of music. In order to regain communication freedom drastic measures should be taken, which should lead to the existence of 'a large variety of autonomous media, a diversity of owners, and many channels accessible to the public' (Hamelink 1994a: 90–1).

How can this be achieved? For a start, a fundamental principle should be that cultural products coming from one foreign country may not have a market share bigger than 25 per cent, and a media owner should be permitted to possess only one media outlet, as Ben Bagdikian proposes (McChesney 1997: 67–8). Robert McChesney comments that this 'may be inefficient from a market perspective, but it is a small price to pay from a social perspective'. A historical example may help us understand that there is nothing strange about such a policy in itself. 'It is worth noting that when the United States reorganized the Japanese media during its occupation following the Second World War, it placed limits on media ownership because it saw that concentrated media control could be a barrier to the formation of a political democracy. It is time for the United States to take some of its own medicine.'

Another, additional, anti-monopoly rule, sustaining a plurality of voices, would be setting maximum levels of market share for sectoral cultural markets and for each geographic market. Clive Hollick thinks that 10 per cent of the total share of national media is the maximum that any single privately owned organization should be allowed to control. Otherwise, 'in the absence of such a transparent set of rules the media industry will continue to muddle along with the current incoherent and illogical regulations which are prey to political and commercial manipulation and offer scant protection for the overriding public interest of plurality of ownership' (Hollick 1994: 56–7).

In Italy this is an urgent question, predating the 2001 electoral victory of media magnate Silvio Berlusconi. In 1995 Italy held a referendum on the conglomeration of the media, which the left lost. Daniel Singer comments in *The Nation* (3 July 1995) that the fact that Berlusconi could keep control of his monopolistic media imperium was 'the outcome of some fifteen years of intellectual retreat by the left, during which the Italians were taught that private was beautiful, profit virtuous and money the only criterion of achievement'. He warns: 'Unless the left learns how to tackle the unlimited power of money and the commercialization of culture, even if it gains office it will merely make its contribution to our

Orwellian future. Although it takes a specific form in Italy because of Berlusconi's control of the media, the problem is not limited to that country, or indeed to that side of the Atlantic.'

Most governments in the rich part of the world provide financial support to companies involved in exports or foreign investment, as mentioned above. Sarah Anderson and John Cavanagh mention, for instance, that 'in the United States the Export-Import Bank provides loans and loan guarantees to exporting firms, while the Overseas Private Investment Corporation provides insurance to US companies investing overseas'. They calculate that, worldwide, such agencies support exports totalling $432.2 billion, about 10.4 per cent of total world markets. 'In addition, governments also commonly fund programs to market products abroad and sometimes subsidize export industries' (Anderson and Cavanagh 2000: 15). However, the principle of the freedom of expression does not mean that cultural exports should be facilitated on such a scale, meanwhile suppressing local artistic life in many places in the world. Herman Daly made a plea, in his farewell lecture when leaving the World Bank, for the Bank and all of us to move away 'from the ideology of global economic integration by free trade and export-led growth and towards a more nationalist orientation that seeks to develop national production for internal markets as the first option, having recourse to international trade only when clearly much more efficient' (George 1994: 205). This principle would give ample space to cultural exchange, but not at the price of harming the development of local artistic life.

In the further range of regulations it can be imagined that limits would be put on the quantity of foreign capital that cultural industries might have, in relation to the number of cultural enterprises deemed desirable in the particular country or part of the world. It is obvious that strict controls should be implemented to prevent tax evasion by cultural enterprises, which themselves should be organizationally transparent too, both matters that might, for instance, cause the multimedia corporation of Rupert Murdoch great problems. Tony Clark argues that 'measures could also be taken to seize corporate assets on behalf of communities as well as expel corporations from jurisdictions by denying access to resources, markets, and labour' (Clark 1995: 27–8). Even the existing anti-trust regulations in various countries, which can easily be applied rigorously to the present megalomaniac concentrated situations in the cultural field, are not applied, Benjamin Barber notes. 'The courts step in not to preserve a public good nor to impede a developing monopoly but only to assure that stockholders' profitability will be the only criterion of a deal' (Barber 1996: 85).

Robert McChesney regrets that the analysis of the commercialization of the internet is predicated upon the thorough absence of any political debate concerning how best to employ cyberspace. 'Were communication issues to become political issues, there is no reason why the Internet could not be redirected from its current main emphasis of serving business' (McChesney 1997: 34–5). It might indeed seem a difficult field to regulate. However, the big enterprises operating in the digital world are known or can be known. In the past the internet seemed a great mystery in which messages and activities could not be traced. For libertarian purposes this was fine. Less fine was that anybody who wanted could evade all the regulations that exist in 'normal' society. This problem is nearly over. It is becoming ever easier to trace all signals, even obscure ones, back to their senders. For the bulk of communication this was already the case. 'The claim that technology makes regulation more difficult, even impossible, is a fallacy. On the contrary, it makes it easier. At the heart of satellite and cable technology is a highly sophisticated subscription payment system. Any interruption to the flow of funds to the broadcasters would quickly lead to blank screens' (Hollick 1994: 58). Thus if the internet is nothing special compared to the 'normal' world, all the measures mentioned above, and those that will follow, could be applied to cultural conglomerates and other cultural enterprises operating in the digital world.

If the ideal is that many artistic initiatives flourish in every society, it is still unavoidable that some of them won't be successful on the market, not yet, or perhaps not at all. Nevertheless, the maintenance of such a diversity is important for reasons of democracy, as we have seen already. It is a public responsibility to take care that a substantial number of artists – individually or in groups or other kinds of associations – can work and thus make available many different cultural creations. At the same time the state, representing the public interest, should not intervene in the artistic processes and their contents. Its role is to ensure that diversity in the cultural field can exist, and for the rest to wait and see what happens, and leave judgement on aesthetic quality and importance of the works to the public debate and the critics.

One misunderstanding should be avoided, and this is that the state is withdrawing completely from economic life, which is the current neoliberal philosophy. However, reality is different. For instance, 500 American-based corporations were official advisers to the US team involved in the negotiations leading to the establishment of the WTO in the early 1990s, among them Jack Valenti, chairman of the Motion Picture Association of America, and his team (Starr 2000: 13). Noam Chomsky, too, is sceptical about the philosophy of minimizing the state, and reminds us that the Pentagon has a more than considerable budget, 'because it's the major pipeline for public subsidy to high-tech industries' (Chomsky 1998: 18). The relevant questions are: about which areas the state should intervene in, and for which interests, and where it should refrain from intervening.

The purpose of state intervention, for the task we have in mind, is to reconquer enough space in the broad field of communications for the cultural public domain to flourish. One option, Nilanjana Gupta suggests, is that 'new cable and satellite systems, and new teletext and cable-signal systems, could be wholly developed within public ownership, not for some old or new kind of monopoly provider, but as common-carrier systems which would be available by lease and contract, to a wide range of producing and providing bodies' (Gupta 1998: 63). This would mean that the privatization of the carriers of culture would be stopped, and systems developed that are open on lease to everyone, not only to oligopolists. Thus, the capital flows that went in the direction of private initiatives would be diverted towards the public domain.

An alternative could be a form of public–private partnership. Competition, we are told, brings prices down, which may be doubted. In any case, in oligopolistic or even monopolistic situations we can no longer speak of competition. From the cultural perspective it is important, for all different kinds of arts and entertainment initiatives, that there are multiple possibilities to access the various means of communication, and this goes for the owners of cultural enterprises as well. In the public interest, governments should encourage the larger and more effective civic uses of cable, satellites, fibre optics and computers (Barber 1996: 113).

At present giant companies such as AT&T are planning the creation of a fibre-optic ring around Africa. According to *Our Creative Diversity*, the report of the World Commission on Culture and Development, 'they are serving their long-term strategic interests. The major international operators and suppliers of telecommunications seek to establish themselves in such markets with the intention of replacing existing unreliable networks by new ones to be used by a specialized, mostly international, corporate clientele.' Such projects raise many questions, says the Report. 'It cannot be assumed that new services, when they appear, will be automatically responsive to the needs of the people' (Pérez de Cuéllar 1996: 116). All the more since a ring around Africa does not serve the people living *inside* the continent. A publicly supported system would have other priorities.

Since the means of communication – cable, satellite, cinemas, whatever – are often monopolized in one way or another, and since the measures mentioned above cannot be immediately effective, other measures need to be taken too. Clearly, the information and communication networks that are currently in private hands should be open to all artistic and cultural initiatives. So the owners of those networks should be obliged to let different artists involved in different cultural programmes and initiatives use their networks, for a substantial part of the time and for modest prices, in some cases even for free. We should not forget that all these private operators are using the public space and the public domain for their operations. In return they should open their systems to the public interest.

The same might be the case, for instance, for the few oligopolistic electronic bookshops. There is Amazon.com and there is Barnesandnoble.com, and perhaps a few smaller ones. They too should have obligations in relation to the cultural public interest and offer a service to those who would otherwise stay outside the system of book distribution.

In France, Jean-Marie Messier, the former president-director of Vivendi-Universal, published a long article in the French daily *Le Monde* (10 April 2001), in which he explained that his enterprise would contribute to a 'more diverse, more open and more tolerant world'. He claimed that he believed in local cultures, and called on artists and cultural enterprises to work together and to give every chance to diversity.

Some days later a small French publisher, Jean-Pierre Turberque, director of Editions Italiques, challenged Messier by saying that he assumed Vivendi-Universal would now distribute his books and give support to the cultural diversity to which Italiques contributes![11] Jean-Pierre Turberque points very precisely to one of the problems caused by cultural conglomerates which, after all, decide what will be available, for example, in the bookshops. Therefore he demands that Vivendi-Universal should also play a *public* role *vis-à-vis* book distribution, and act as a common carrier. Its channels should be open to the broad field of cultural communication, including products that are not the choice or the source of profit of the cultural conglomerate itself.

The challenge for any society is to provide opportunities, outside the control of the market-driven conglomerates, for the production, distribution and presentation of music, the visual arts, mixed-media works, theatre, film, literature, dance, opera, musicals and other kinds of entertainment, which might unlock the potential of all these artistic creations and enhance rather than diminish a robust cultural democracy (Banks 1996: 206).

Compared to the situation where, for instance, many galleries present a variety of forms of art that exist in a specific society, things are completely different when there is only a limited number of cultural enterprises, producing, distributing and operating on a mass scale. Enterprises operating on a mass scale are by definition behaving in an oligopolistic way on the cultural market, and this needs to be corrected for the sake of democracy. Public authorities should therefore take responsibility and reinforce the broad diversity of artistic production, including on the supply side. For example, they could ensure that it includes a substantial quantity of domestic cultural product, whether film, shows, music, theatre, books, design, visual arts or mixed media. The same could be applied to thematic coverage.

Clive Hollick refers to the situation in the United Kingdom where all terrestrial broadcasters 'are subject to public service and programme obligations and complex ownership rules which have together created a structure for the industry in which quality and diversity flourished free from political partiality and beholden to no particular interest group'. He concludes that to protect the public good governments should ensure that all media organizations, whether terrestrial, satellite or new telecommunications technologies, are subject to the same rules and compete on a level playing field (Hollick 1994: 55–6).

One of the tricky issues is the question of accountability. We will come back to this issue later in this chapter when we look at censorship, freedom of expression and people exercising self-restraint on moral grounds. Concerning regulatory obligations one question should be dealt with here, and this is the broad field of advertising. We need to restore, or even introduce, the practice of distinguishing very clearly between programmes and advertisements. Unless we want a full-blown consumer society, where the only concern is to focus all attention on the need to consume, there should be many moments in daily life that are publicity-free. I would say, most moments. Public authorities have a responsibility to set standards and equal rules for all, in relation to time and space for publicity.

Much work needs to be done to make clear again that freedom of artistic expression cannot be compared, or put on an equal footing, with advertising freedom. Freedom of artistic expression is about debate, about the exchange of arguments and feelings; the freedom of communication is about parody, about continuously questioning what has been presented as truth; freedom of artistic expression allows contradictions and confrontations, and it is the context in which democracy can come about. This should be cared for and should not be disturbed by communication that has no democratic intentions at all. The language of advertising is not related to any of those democratic values. It tries to prevent debate. It states authoritatively what is valuable. Morality is not its cup of tea. Its messages are often obtrusive, and it tries to be as little accountable as possible.

Indeed, much work is to be done in a world in which democratic freedom of artistic expression and advertising freedom have become hopelessly confused. Robert McChesney notes, for instance, in relation to the United States: 'So it has been that much of the "expansion" of the US First Amendment in the past generation has been to protect commercial speech (e.g. advertising) and profitmaking activities from government regulation, effectively making such "speech" part of the constitution and therefore off-limits to political consideration' (McChesney 1997: 48).

Until recently, in many countries one of the greatest forms of support for artistic diversity was public funding. One of the greatest threats coming with globalization is the erosion of the financial underpinning of governments. More and more corporations are able to avoid paying taxes in the countries where they

KING ALFRED'S COLLEGE
LIBRARY

have activities, as indicated above. Many Third World countries do not benefit financially and economically from the operations of the big Western corporations. These phenomena are just as much threats to the diversity of artistic production, distribution and promotion. Any measure that helps to keep more business local means that more resources stay at the local level, and that a tax base remains for the maintenance of the public domain, including the broad field of the arts.

The idea of the taxation of the artistic commons has been underlined by Lawrence K. Grossman, who claims that the US government should take a chunk of the proceeds from the current communications gold rush and use it to subsidize public interest programmes, which are being pushed aside by the sports-and-entertainment prospectors. 'The nation is entitled to a decent return on public property – the airwaves that it gave away free to communication companies.'[12] Robert McChesney proposes a tax on advertising too. 'Some $212 billion will be spent to advertise in the United States in 1999. A very small sales tax on this or even only that portion that goes on radio and television could generate several billion dollars' (McChesney 1999: 309).

The basic principle should be that the more an enterprise holds a monopolistic or oligopolistic position, in one country or worldwide, the more it will be wrapped up with regulations making sure that the public domain concerning the artistic creation and communication can flourish. This does not hamper the freedom of communication, because those enterprises can continue to exist, only not with the monopolistic or oligopolistic power as before. The freedom of communication becomes threatened when the diversity of artistic production, and the distribution of all those works of art, will be overruled by the operations of only a limited number of cultural conglomerates. When no market dominating positions exist, fewer regulations are necessary.

CULTURAL POLICIES

Until now the emphasis has been mainly on substantially limiting the power and the bandwidth of the cultural conglomerates operating in the different fields of the arts and entertainment. Now we will see that governments have also a perfect right, and duty, actively to create the conditions in which a large number of suppliers can offer a broad variety of works of art from every genre, and for all tastes and preferences, for 'high', 'low' or whatever. Governments have a perfect right to intervene and to support those artistic and cultural activities – those public goods – in which the market has no interest, or which market forces are pushing away from public attention (Barber 1996: 29).

Public authorities should protect what comes into being and what cannot count immediately on the approval of huge crowds. The protection of what only some people want to see, hear, read or experience belongs to the process of guaranteeing the continuity of cultures.[13] Communication freedom is an essential value for society, so governments should not only refrain from interventions in cultural and artistic processes, they also have the duty to create the conditions in which citizens can communicate with each other freely, including through the arts.

A Dutch choreographer, Rudy van Dantzig, was invited to stage a ballet for the Cleveland/San José Ballet on the occasion of their twenty-fifth anniversary. The jubilee became a disaster for the company. The expected sponsorship money did not materialize. Even directors of highly respected groups like this know from experience that there is always a big question mark against sponsorship money. Sometimes it comes in, sometimes it doesn't. With dismay Rudy van Dantzig watched the company dwindle from one day to the next. One morning he reported: 'Most of the dancers have left already – some of them after fifteen years dancing with the troupe. Things are going very fast in America.' His summary of what cultural policy or the lack of cultural policy in Cleveland seems to be: pack your things and take off.[14]

Coming from Europe he observes that sponsorship in the United States sometimes has frightening, and humiliating, aspects. At the start of the performance a speaker thanks the wealthiest donors – often they stand up; in the foyer sponsors show their glitzy wares; and after the performance the exhausted dancers are expected to participate in receptions, while being admired. Patricia Aufderheide remarks that things were different in the USA a couple of centuries ago; at the time public authorities still knew they had a role to play in building up a civic culture. She gives the example that in 1792 Congress brought down the cost of distributing newspapers by mail. 'That made news a cheap, widely available commodity in the new nation. Congress knew what it was doing. The point was to foster civic knowledge about other parts of a widely dispersed nation, and a sense of participation in nationhood. This was a costly decision' (Aufderheide 1997: 167–8).

This is just one example out of many, which makes clear that a civic culture needs to be fostered; it never comes out of the blue. This is particularly true for the arts. There is much misunderstanding about how artistic creation develops, certainly in a world in which the fame of 'stars' is so hyped. It is easy to forget how much time it takes for an artist to produce something valuable; how much urgency and fragile conviction is needed to reach the point where something comes into being that is so richly layered that it continues to express something worthwhile, whether through music, theatre, dance, film, painting or design, or written words. In all cultures the development of artistic talent takes time, energy, care and money.

We should not forget that all those artists we respect have made substantial creative investments, often over a long period. We should not forget that a satisfying and rich cultural life in any society does not consist only of a handful of celebrities. The richness derives from the huge quantity of artists and groups and initiatives that are, perhaps, less famous, but that contribute something special to our feelings, consciousness, enjoyment; maybe only for small groups of people, sometimes for huge numbers of people, and later again for a circle of aficionados. This mélange should be cherished. When the market does not provide this diversity, it is a public duty to sustain what is new, fragile or an important contribution to diversity. The truth is that certain artistic creations and presentations have always needed some financial underpinning, from the king, from a church, from a rich person, and now from the state. After all, much artistic work is labour-intensive. This often makes the price higher than can be paid on the market, for the time being, or even for a long time to come.

Obviously, support mechanisms for the arts will differ according to the states, regions and local communities that devise them. Nevertheless, some indications can be given about the directions that active cultural policies could take. In what I describe below, many suggestions for cultural policies are derived from the recommendations found in the National Cultural Policy Reviews that the Council of Europe organized in Eastern European countries at the end of the 1990s.[15] The purpose of these reviews is to raise awareness about how to combine freedom of expression, initiatives developing in the cultural market, and the role that public authorities should play in protecting artistic diversity, which makes cultural life richer and more democratic than it would otherwise be. I have deliberately chosen the suggestions expressed in the National Cultural Policy Reviews of the Eastern European countries, because most of these countries are not in good shape economically, and because they are developing new democratic rules for cultural policy.

To start with, it is important that political parties articulate cultural policy programmes. They must be aware that leaving cultures to market forces only will result in cultural life becoming arid. There are so many types of artistic expression that cannot survive on the market, at least at the moment, or maybe never will. They should be protected. This must be followed by national, regional and local debates on what kind of cultural life is desired, from the democratic perspective, with one eye on the fact that the cultural future must be nurtured by new and unexpected forms of artistic expression. Such transparent debates act as learning grounds for the development of civil society. Conclusions reached are far more likely to be 'owned' by those directly affected. In any case it is true that 'culture needs enthusiasts, people who feel motivated to work hard, often for unimpressive salaries. For the sake of creativity they feel this is important to themselves and to those with whom they associate. Culture needs not only the people who retain and develop traditions through their own artistic activity but also the enthusiasts who provide a necessary infrastructure' (Wallis and Malm 1984: 120).

In the whole process, one guiding idea should be central, and this is the so-called 'arm's-length principle'. Governments and ministries of culture should not define what culture is and how it must operate. Their role is being enabler, facilitator and gate-opener. What the market does not offer should be financed and facilitated by the state and the regions and the local public authorities, but they should stay at an arm's-length distance from the practice of cultural life. Artists should not be the servants of the state, even when the state, which in a democratic society is the whole of the population, pays for their work or makes it easier to do. Decisions about subventions for artistic projects and initiatives should be taken as much as possible in arts councils, or the like, in which the members are independent, not involved in the issues concerned, and they should rotate every two or three years, so as to avoid becoming too tied up with specific projects.

It is desirable to formulate new and revised legislation for the support of the arts, which serves as a framework, but which should not be too rigid at the same time. After all, artistic life is always fluid, which necessitates short-, medium- and long-term planning. The most interesting policies create solid infrastructures for the arts while giving enough space at the same time to many different initiatives, which may need to be acted on immediately. A good mechanism to keep cultural policies on the right track – which means serving the development of a democratic and inspiring cultural life – is the installing of an independent Observatory of cultural life which monitors the implementation of cultural policies, and analyses any changes and initiatives taking place.

One of the major sources of tension is always that some initiatives may be supported by public financial means which do not attract huge crowds of visitors or readers or listeners but which are none the less important for the development of cultural life for one reason or an other. Such initiatives should be encouraged; efforts should be made get a substantially larger audience than is presently the case, while keeping the right not to compromise in the artistic sense. After all, the arts come into existence through communication with audiences, even when these are small – but attentive and critical. Challenging methods of cultural education in and outside school are needed, introducing young people to a broad variety of cultural expression in their own society and abroad. The arts are not an open book for everybody and there is more that is worthwhile than what happens to be popular at a certain moment, often because of market forces. This means that cultural and educational ministries and regional and local public authorities should work closely together.

We should realize that many countries are extremely poor. Diomansi Bombote remarks that formerly, in the traditional societies of Africa, artists were looked up to and regarded as important protagonists in the process of economic and social development. Meanwhile they became artists by profession, for which the state and the regions as the new authorities should take responsibility. However, 'the exceptionally severe economic crisis affecting Africa has become the main alibi of political decision-makers. The proportion of national budgets earmarked for culture is shrinking from year to year' (Bombote 1994: 25). Such national, regional and local processes of formulating what kind of cultural life we want to have and what kind of cultural policy should be implemented, keep the social importance of the arts and the protection of a diversity of artistic expression on the political agenda. The first target would be that at least the budgets for culture stay as they are and don't diminish further: something like a moratorium, waiting on better times.

Such cultural policies can also be clear focal points for governments and NGOs from the rich parts of the world, which should contribute to well-defined cultural activities, certainly when this concerns the installing of stable infrastructures for the production, distribution and promotion of the different forms of the arts. In this chapter I have also described methods to reduce the dominance of cultural conglomerates and have proposed taxing them in different ways, which together may reinforce domestic cultural life, economically too. The search for new sources of funding for cultural life can certainly be intensified, provided that it does not result in simultaneous disengagement by public authorities. Substantial support for many artistic initiatives can be provided through granting tax exemptions, as well as tax reductions on donations for cultural purposes. However, diversity will not be promoted if these regulations stimulate the growth of cultural industries that are already big and dominate the cultural market.

A sensitive issue concerns the management of cultural initiatives and institutions, whether they are small, medium-sized or large. In an extremely competitive world the task of cultural leaders has become more complicated. The challenge is that they learn to combine adequate management tools with the capacity to listen to the artists, to their rhythm of creation, to their necessities, while respecting the cultural impact of their work. Board members of cultural institutions, whose task is to keep the institution on the right track, should be trained to combine managerial firmness with a fine-tuned understanding about the place of their specific group, museum, festival, or whatever else, in the broader cultural context of their societies. It would be a good sign of cultural policy if specific arts management training was supported as well.

In many cases the distribution of cultural funds, in particular at the national level, can be seen to be uneven. The National Cultural Policy Review on the Russian Federation, for example, stipulates three topics that need close attention.

First, preservation currently takes precedence over creation. Second, support for the big cultural institutions is favoured at the expense of aid for innovation. Third, the country's two main cities, Moscow and St Petersburg, are relatively privileged in comparison with the schemes the federal government can carry out in the provinces. The report recommends that a progressive but resolute refocusing of financial efforts should be initiated in order to remedy these disparities. Geographical inequalities should be compensated. The circulation and exchange of regional and local productions should be stimulated and supported. In any case, support for cultural life cannot be reduced to preserving existing cultural institutions and ways of doing things. It is important to avoid the situation where too much finance goes to a few prestigious cultural institutions and nothing is left over for the broad field of artistic cultures.

For the sake of democracy, and maintaining peace in society, it is crucial to support the artistic practices, cultural events and infrastructures of minorities of many different kinds. Specifically, governments should ensure respect for the right to equality of treatment for all languages and cultures of the minority ethnic groups spread over their countries. A clear-cut aspect of cultural policies should be an explicit philosophy of decentralization and equal treatment for minorities, otherwise it will never happen.

It makes absolute sense to place cultural institutions at a certain distance from the cultural ministry or from cultural departments of regional or local public authorities. Why should these govern the daily affairs of such institutions? It is wise to make such institutions more independent from the interventions of bureaucrats, which should not mean full-scale privatization. It is possible and desirable to create legal structures that make the cultural institutions less attached to government without throwing them, and for instance their collections, into private hands. The public commons should be safeguarded.

A very important aspect of cultural policy is that information should be free and not a commodity. It belongs to the domain of universal human rights that opportunities should be created for self-improvement. Therefore it is extremely important to build up a broad network of public libraries, which in some parts of the world are not only powerful symbols of the past, but also potential beacons or landmarks for the future (Greenhalgh and Worpole 1995: 8–9). Liza Greenhalgh and Ken Worpole stipulate that 'the role of the library in providing information services is in large part to empower citizens, and by this means to help bridge the gap between the "information rich" and the "information poor"' (p. 15). A tremendously important service that public libraries can offer is to provide their users with access to information and artistic expression of all kinds that the digital domain is beginning to provide, but which is not that easy for everybody to find. There is a need to carry out comprehensive surveys of the economic position and the social security of artists. For most of them it is difficult to make a living from their work. What support mechanisms can be installed, now or in the future? How can they be trained to sell their work or performances, and on what kinds of markets? What can be done with taxes in order to ease their financial position? It is absolutely true that in poor countries huge subsidies are not available, but it is more than possible that other facilities could be granted to them. It is extremely important to support them in gaining access to the new digital communication worlds.

In this context it should be said again that the intellectual and creative commons in the world of the internet must not be turned into private property. Owned by nobody, the web could become the common property of all. Free speech is both free trade and free gifts. For Third World countries this is an even more urgent question than for artists in other parts of the world. Many artists start their own worldwide digital distribution networks. They should be supported in developing the tools so that they can become known by large enough publics here and there (provided the communication channels have not been dominated by a handful of conglomerates).

In the present globalized world it is astonishing that neighbouring countries have less cultural exchange than they had some decades ago. This is a big loss. On the most elementary level it would be useful for states to learn from each other about what may be the best practices in the area of cultural policies. Countries in the same region tend to have certain experiences, possibilities and problems in common. Sharing their experiences would make it possible to find common solutions. For instance, how to deal with cultural conglomerates that dominate the whole region and and suppress cultural variety. Even more challenging is to develop informal and formal common cultural infrastructures for collaboration and cultural exchange. This would provide artists with more work, but more importantly it would help people to learn from each other, to be inspired by the work of artists from nearby countries.

Some Western European countries have their institutions that operate overseas, like the German Goethe Institute, the British Council, the Alliance Française and the Spanish Instituto Cervantes. These institutions tell the rest of the world what is going on culturally in their countries of origin. Groups of countries from the Arabic world, parts of Africa, Asia or Latin America could join forces and have their cultural representatives in other parts of the world, allowing artists from their regions to make their work known elsewhere.

Coming from a rich part of the world I feel very shy about advising other countries how to develop their cultural policies. I am not offering any blueprints. I'm aware that not all can be achieved immediately, because of the precarious economic situation in many parts of the world, but if issues of cultural policy are not raised, studied and discussed, they will never appear on the political agenda.

One of the arguments of this book is that unhampered free trade is not a sound condition for economic development in general and certainly not for the development of a diverse cultural life, which is connected in one way or another to the places where people live. Equally, diversity in the arts and the celebration of a rich domestic cultural life are a strong force against neoliberal economics, raising awareness that there is something to defend which is more valuable than what consumer culture has to offer. One of the defence mechanisms is to develop a wide range of cultural policies.

One such cultural policy could address the fact that in most parts of the world films from neighbouring countries no longer cross the border. In this case, we should think about how countries might work together in their own region to reverse this cultural deficiency. This is just one example of many, many kinds of cultural polices that can be developed, in all artistic fields, within countries and between neighbouring countries. I hope it may act as a stimulus for starting the creative processes of discovering completely new and appropriate cultural policies that can sustain cultural diversity; at the same time I am aware that this specific example needs a lot of discussion, calculation and strategy-building.

REGIONAL INFRASTRUCTURES FOR THE DISTRIBUTION OF FILMS

In this section I focus on one artform where a specific, regional policy change might enhance diversity enormously; this is film. Films made in many parts of the world rarely travel within their own continent, scarely reach other parts of the world and are unlikely to achieve even adequate distribution within their own countries. The best-known films are those made in Hollywood, with the notable exceptions of India and Hong Kong. From a democratic, cultural and economic perspective, the failing distribution of domestic films causes a problem, which is, however, reversible.

It is an enriching contribution to the cultural and social life of any society for its various publics to have access to a wide diversity of films, including films that have their roots in the local surroundings, in one way or another. This diversity is needed because the last thing we should want, especially in a democracy, is a homogenized population. People have different sentiments, different feelings of pleasure and sadness. What is entertaining for one is boring for another. The codes that some films are wrapped in work perfectly for certain groups of the population, while for others the aesthetic texture is wrong.

From the cultural perspective, the strength of any democracy lies in the fact that different sentiments, different types of content and different aesthetic realms can be expressed, communicated and enjoyed. The whole gamut of artistic experiences that people breathe in daily provides them, above all, with an identity. Identities should not be created only by outside forces that have no relation at all to specific societies, and certainly not when these forces also have an oligopolistic market position.

Thus the artistic life of any society, whether within a particular country or a region, should not be taken over by forces that are not genuinely connected with what is happening in that society. Obviously, this does not mean that borders should be closed. There should be a balance between what comes from outside and what is bred in the local environment where people fall in love, quarrel, raise children, work, are unemployed, steal, fight bitterly over social rights, have their festivities, drink too much, smoke hash, make legal decisions with far-reaching consequences, and die. This is an important reason why the overall presence of films that come from Hollywood should be diminished considerably.

During the failed Millennium Round of the World Trade Organization in Seattle it became clear that free trade should be balanced by protection in the different fields of social, economic, ecological and cultural life. Abstract neo-liberalism and free trade should no longer be the only principles guiding, for example, the distribution of films throughout the different regions of the world. Even GATS, WTO's general agreement on trade and services, gives all countries and regions in the world space to develop their own audiovisual policies, because culture has remained a blank page in this treaty, as mentioned earlier. This implies that any policy measures to protect culture are allowed. It is the task of public authorities to change their passive attitudes towards, for instance, film distribution and to develop radical new policies that genuinely and efficiently deal with the distribution of films in their own parts of the world.

In most cases it is currently almost impossible to find distribution outlets for films in the local region. A quarter of a century ago many distributors still thought that films from neighbouring countries could find a sufficiently broad public to make the buying of rights not particularly risky. This situation has changed. Nowadays it is rare that a distributor takes the risk of buying a film from a nearby country. There is the cost of the rights; translation, dubbing or subtitling will be involved; and a promotion campaign must be undertaken to give the film a place in the minds of people. Experience teaches us that most distributors do not see any market value in films that originate from their own part of the world. The risks are too high, and financially it is safer to deal with films from Hollywood.

This practice, and this too cautious attitude, can be changed. What kind of policies are needed? The proposal is this. Groups of countries establish together a Regional Film Service. In Europe this would be done through the European Union, which would extend its programme to Eastern Europe. In Latin America it would be through Mercusor. And so on. In the first years of its existence a Regional Film Service would get investment finance from the regional authorities and several not-for-profit associations. With this money the rights to a couple of hundred films from all parts of the region will be bought, they will be subtitled or dubbed, copies will be made and region-wide marketing mechanisms will be organized. Distributors in all the countries of the region will get the films for free. Then they will do what they always do: rent out the films through various outlets at prices that are competitive, lower than for Hollywood products. The distributors keep a percentage of the money earned; the rest goes to the Regional Film Service, which after some years will no longer need further financial contributions; and even most of the film producers will be making enough money from their films for national or regional film subsidies to be less necessary.

Such a system, which obviously needs to be carefully elaborated and costed, provides both cultural and economic benefits. The cultural gain is clear: the cinematographic diversity that exists in the region will be re-established and may become a living reality and provide enjoyment for many people. It is interesting that most films to date have been produced not by cultural conglomerates but by middle-sized or even small producers. In the proposed system this diversity of producers can stay alive, which is extremely important for the survival of cultural democracy. The economic gain is this: a substantial part of the money earned from these films will stay in the region.

This proposal is, as I have said, a first step towards a new approach to the regional distribution of films made in that region. Initially, it will cost the regional authorities some money, but this should no longer be necessary after a couple of years, when these films find a big enough audience in their own region. Some general observations must be made. There is the need to consider whether for a relatively short period a quota system should protect the regional audiovisual market, until films made in a particular region once again do well in their own region. It is clear that any quota system has disadvantages and can be bypassed. It can work only if it helps to build a sustainable market.

THE MELTDOWN AND ABOLITION OF COPYRIGHT

In this chapter I am trying to formulate suggestions and proposals for bringing artistic life back into the public domain. In Chapter 3 we saw that copyright is no longer an undisputed concept and also that the practice is not beneficial to most artists, to Third World countries and to the public domain. What should be done about copyright, which has grown into one of the most important commercial products of the last several decades? Should we even carry on with the concept and practice of copyright? I will suggest that there are better means of serving artists and cultural life in general, in all parts of the world.

It has become more and more obvious that the system of copyright takes too much creative and intellectual material out of the public domain; it can hamper future artistic creation; it does not really support artists and Third World countries; and not much more than a few cultural conglomerates between them hold the rights to an enormous amount of intellectual and creative output, and profit from copyright. Martin Kretschmer provides a lucid summary: 'It is perhaps the cardinal weakness of Western style copyright that it tries to balance the interests of creators, investors and consumers and regulate the industry all in one conceptual and legislative effort' (Kretschmer 1999: 21). Considering the unfeasibility of the present copyright system, it makes sense to look at whether a system can be developed that is more advantageous for the diversity of artistic creation and for the protection of the public domain.

First, though, there has to be a clear idea of what we are aiming for. Rosemary Coombe describes the contradiction that needs to be resolved:

> culture is not embedded in abstract concepts that we internalize, but in the materiality of signs and texts over which we struggle and the imprint of those struggles in consciousness. This ongoing negotiation and struggle over meaning is the essence of dialogic practice. Many interpretations of intellectual property laws quash dialogue by affirming the power of corporate actors to monologically control meaning by appealing to an abstract concept of property. Laws of intellectual property privilege mono-logic forms against dialogic practice and create significant power differentials between social actors engaged in hegemonic struggle. (Coombe 1998: 86).

The central concept, then, is *dialogic practice*. This should be given a chance again, through the range of cultural expression that is produced and used in our societies. The essence of our artistic communication as human beings – the whole gamut of words, signs, tones, images, colours and movements of the body – should be liberated from the control of the corporate holders of the property rights on these forms of artistic expression. Our cultural heritage from the past and also from the present should once again be part of the public domain, so that it can be used collectively and serve as a source of inspiration for future creativity. Intellectual property issues should be subordinated to the protection of human rights, specifically freedom of expression and the right to information. If this were to happen, we might witness the emergence of completely new dynamics in all artistic and cultural fields.

Equally important is that the majority of artists, in rich and poor countries alike, receive a decent income from their creative work. It is also important that their creations and performances should be treated with respect.

To retain the copyright system as it now exists, is, for the many reasons given earlier, neither a desirable nor a feasible option. It is not realistic to think that by amending the present system it is possible to break the power of the cultural conglomerates, which finds its base in the possession of as many intellectual property rights as possible. It should also not be forgotten that the copyright system is rooted in a romantic concept of originality, which is disadvantageous for the public domain.

What is striking is that in the present system the notion of the individual artist's rights, originally considered fundamental to the the concept of copyright, no longer exists in many situations. Many artists can get their work distributed and promoted only when they hand over most or all of the rights to a producer or other rightholder. What we observe is that the individualistically-oriented philosophy of the European copyright system has been diluted considerably. We can see too that more and more people are coming to the conclusion that the present system of authors and copyright is no longer the best way to deal with the public domain and the interests of the mass of cultural workers. Good examples are Linux and the Free Software Society, which create free places in the digital domain, not because they like free places in an otherwise benign system of authors and copyright; not at all. However, at present the only possibility of replacing copyright by better approaches is to create free domains. Their aim is to supersede the whole system of copyright and authors' rights by approaches that respect the public domain more and that give better remuneration to those who are really doing the work.[16]

Why shouldn't we take the next step and abolish the whole system of authors' rights and copyright and replace it with a system that provides better payment to artists in Western and Third World countries alike, gives due respect to their work and brings the public domain back to a central place in our lives?

THE NEED FOR RESPECT AND NEW CREATIVE DYNAMICS

An important issue connected with copyright is *moral rights*, which still have a stronger base in the European authors' rights system than in the Anglo-Saxon copyright approach. Moral rights protect the integrity of a work of art and science against infringement. However, if we recognize that the copyright concept is full of romanticism, and if we are aware that the moral rights aspect freezes works of art in quite unnatural ways, then a logical conclusion is getting rid of moral rights as they have been defined in our legal contexts.

Of course, we can admire the work of a certain artist enormously, as Roland

Barthes has indicated (see Chapter 3), and we can agree that we should deal with a certain work of art carefully. This observation does not lead necessarily to the conclusion that the artist, or a 'rightholder' may be the absolute ruler of 'his' or 'her' creation or performance or interpretation, and for decades. Of course, too, everybody should have the freedom to use the work of another artist and make creative changes and adaptations, from substantial to very subtle. As I said earlier, this is what has always happened in most cultures throughout history, and clearly it is what most artists working in the digital domain are doing. They sample and do not consider that they are stealing. When works of art, including all foms of entertainment and design, are no longer frozen by the monopolistic control of the owners of intellectual property rights, we will see completely new cultural dynamics emerge.

In Western society we have created a bizarre situation whereby we automatically end up in court when we think the ownership of an artistic creation, the copyright, has been violated. Thus, we criminalize creative interventions to earlier made work, in short the dialogic practice. However, if we conclude that there is no ownership in the absolute sense, then there is nothing to be violated or to be brought before the court. Nevertheless, as things now stand, we have given the judicial authorities the role of cultural arbiters: they are guardians of 'originality'; they rule that digital sampling without permission is liable to penalty; they seem to know that cultural adaptations, or the 'dialogic practice' to quote Coombe again, are the wrong way of doing things; they evaluate the continuation of cultural life according to the law of tort; they freeze ongoing cultural creation for decades and decades, making cultural life more boring than it needs to be.

There is no escaping the fact that we, the people, who create the public domain, need to discuss once again the value of ongoing artistic creativity. There is no reason to pass the responsibility for cultural judgements, which we should make ourselves, to the judicial system. Central to our cultural debates should be the question of whether the use of (parts of) works by other artists happens with *respect* and gives rise to an abundance of new creativity. Or should we conclude that it is often casual or lazy, resulting in work that is boring or even objectionable? Does it make our culture a poorer or a richer part of human existence? What happens is that an artist who borrows too easily from a predecessor or a contemporary will be stigmatized.

Let us imagine, however, an artist who copies the work of another artist and pretends that it is his or hers; there is no adaptation, no cultural comment on another work of art, no parody, no trace of original creativity by the copying artist. What should we think of such a situation? Obviously, this is outright stealing and should be brought under the jurisdiction of criminal law. It is possible to imagine a new article in criminal law, which says that anyone who deliberately copies the work of another artist, in any medium, without the intent to adapt, enrich or parody it, while maintaining all the external characteristics of the original work, will be punished with ... !

To summarize: at present the artist or entertainer or designer is the owner of what he or she has made, according to civil law. So he or she may sell this creation, for instance the design of a chair, to someone else, who wishes to produce it for a market. What is the producer buying? A model; and the right to be the first to use it. This does not prevent another artist from making an adaptation of the design and selling it to anyone who wants to produce it for a market, too, even if the adaptation is minimal. The new product may be nicer, less attractive, cheaper, more expensive, or whatever. We may conclude, therefore, that everyone should have the right to adapt, revise or process what has been made by another artist, designer or entertainer. Clearly this is a very broad right.

The consequence is that in the field of the performing arts, for example, the concept of performing rights is anachronistic. An actual performance is by definition an interpretation or an adaptation. Everybody is free to make a performance of a created work. Through this actual performance a new work comes into being. The performer has the ownership, according to the rules of civil law, of this new work, and may sell this, as said before. But everyone else is, again, free to adapt this interpretation and make their own interpretation, and so on and so forth. To give another example, a painter who makes a painting that looks very much like Van Gogh's sunflowers is by definition making an adaptation. You can never make the work exactly the same as another painter has done. The consequence of this way of reasoning, and the practice that flows from it, is that completely new cultural dynamics will come into being, or rather there will be a return to the processes of cultural development of former times, which did not freeze artistic evolution.

This is the legal part of the story. Another question is whether someone would be praised for painting the sunflowers a second time. This depends on the work's quality, and on whether the artist has shown enough respect for the work that is the apparent source of inspiration. The public debate and struggle on critical judgements and interpretations is open to all!

Let us now think about outright piracy for commercial purposes, which happens not infrequently, as we have seen in Chapter 3 – and about the exchange of music, films and so on, which started with Napster. All these situations may also seem to be theft. However, as Jessica Litman points out, most individual end-users do not observe copyright rules in their daily behaviour. People do not feel guilty when they buy a pirated copy, or exchange music on the internet. 'People don't obey laws that they don't believe in.' This is indeed the case. 'If 137 million members of the general public copy, save, transmit, and distribute content without paying attention to the written copyright rules, those rules are in danger of becoming irrelevant.' Huge amounts of energy, time and money spent on the task of educating people about copyright law are wasted (Litman 2001: 112–14).

The notion of ownership seems to disappear from our consciousness when people are confronted with things produced on a mass scale. The smaller the scale of the production and distribution, the more likely people are to consider that the artistic creation or performance belongs to someone, and to pay the artist accordingly.

Jessica Litman gives several reasons for why copyright does not work nowadays. 'Copyright is now seen as a tool for copyright owners to use to extract all the potential commercial value from works of authorship, even if it means that uses that have long been deemed legal are now brought within the copyright owner's control' (Litman 2001: 14). She goes on to raise other serious issues: 'If copyright is a bargain between authors and the public, then we might ask what the public is getting from the bargain. If copyright law is about a balance between owners' control of the exploitation of their works and the robust health of the public domain, one might ask whether the system strikes the right balance' (p. 79). What has happened is that copyright has become less about incentives or compensation than about control, and so it has been converted into a trade issue, which might be good for the balance of trade of the United States and to a lesser degree for some other Western countries, but it is at the expense of cultural democracy and diversity (p. 80).

Most tragic, maybe, is that Western copyright policy is becoming our information policy, by which all democratic control on the exchange of ideas is being replaced by the monopolistic control of a handful of owners of copyrights. All these arguments lead Jessica Litman to conclude that the kind of balance that existed in the copyright system formerly has now gone. Copyright law never gave copyright owners rights as extensive as those that they have recently argued are their due. Under the present conditions she does not see any chance of re-establing the old system in which there was a better balance between the public domain and the interests of creators, performers and their producers. 'Whatever approach we choose, we will need to find a different balance. The new players whom we are trying to account for – hundreds of millions of consumers of networked digital technology who dwarf the current stakeholders on the basis of numbers alone – are too big an elephant to travel the length of a boa constrictor without permanently distorting its shape' (Litman 2001: 115).

The copyright system, then, is beyond reform. It is too much corrupted by monopolistic industrial interests. So, let's abolish it. Or, perhaps it's truer to say that a spontaneous meltdown of copyright is taking place.

However, someone who has composed, for instance, a song, is the owner of this specific song. This is an ownership title like all forms of ownership, which have been regulated according to civil law. Therefore, a system of copyright is superfluous. It must be understood that this is a new notion of ownership as non-material, unlike the usual form of ownership, which concerns material goods.

The new form of ownership of artistic creations includes the idea that ownership may not be of unlimited duration. It is possible that this right becomes diluted, when, for instance, so many imitations are going around that the point at which the creative cycle started is no longer recognizable, or when the artistic creation has been distributed on such a scale that the relation between artist and end-user has been lost. Apparently there is a volume limit and when this has been crossed the ownership title disintegrates. We may compare this situation with the claim of landless farmers in Brasilia against large landowners. When ownership in the cultural field is too dominant, it loses its self-evident right. Freedom of communication and freedom of expression then demand their legitimate place.

As has always happened in all cultures in the past, everybody should feel free to adapt an artistic work, or a part of it, to change it and use it creatively. In our present Western copyright system this is forbidden: the 'owner' of the work may go to court and seek punishment for the infringer of copyright. The opposite should happen: creative adaptations should be encouraged, which will result in completely new creative dynamics.

SUBSTANTIAL REMUNERATION FOR ARTISTS

At first glance it may seem unconvincing to claim that the average artist, in Western and Third World countries alike, would be in a better position without the system of authors' rights. However, there is reason to take this as a serious option. Why is this so? Probably the most radical aspect of the proposal is that the attention that the cultural industries now organize for their super-stars would fade away. It would no longer make sense for them to invest heavily in such eye- and ear-catching phenomena if they could not merchandise them exclusively. If anyone was allowed to change any work of art creatively, or even a small part of it, this would have far-reaching consequences. Quite apart from adaptations of films or musical compositions, people could also create new creative worlds out of the gadgetry that presently surrounds every industrially-constructed cultural product. The motivation to do this might be that it could be done more creatively and interestingly, or more cheaply, or both. In any case, this change would give us more vivid cultures.

It is not difficult to imagine that business people and corporations, who now invest tens or even hundreds of millions of dollars in one cultural product, would soon realize that the desired profits from their investment would never be harvested in markets where completely new forms of cultural dynamics exist. Of course, they would continue to produce, distribute and promote, but probably on a more modest scale. Moreover, all kinds of regulations, which we proposed earlier in this chapter, would limit the scope of their activities considerably. This means that something extremely important would be happening. What would be removed is the over-investment in cultural products, which currently constrains democratic processes in the arts, including all forms of entertainment and design. Making an interesting film would not require hundreds of millions of dollars or returns on this investment from all corners of the world market, which makes democratic access to the cultural field for a diversity of creators, cultural producers and distributors almost impossible. Likewise, investing tens of millions of dollars in a record is disproportionate.

This change in the market structure would have interesting consequences for the average artist. The 'normal' situation would be restored and artists – no longer having to contend in a market dominated by 'stars' – would once again find many markets and different publics for their work, in their own surroundings and on a global scale through the internet. Thousands upon thousands of artists could make a reasonable income through their performances or through sales of their work, which is presently not the case. Not only would this mean a major improvement in the position of artists themselves; the creative activity of so many artists would also result in substantial cultural diversity.

In the new system, there would be a second source of income for artists as well. With the abolition of copyright, enterprises and other users of artistic work will be freed from having to pay copyright dues and from the bureaucratic paperwork that is bound up with it. Collecting societies would have no reason for existence, which would mean substantial savings. This does not mean that there should be no payment for the use of artistic work; of course there should be substantial remuneration for artists. After all, enterprises and other commercial users of artistic creations and performances make use of music, images, designs, texts, film clips, dance, paintings, multimedia performances and so on in order to create a particular ambience and through this increase their turnover and profits. For most enterprises this is the main reason for their use of artistic material and ideas; for some, actually dealing in the arts is their principal activity. One may think, for instance, of an enterprise that sells postcards of works of art.

There should therefore be a tax on a certain percentage of the turnover of those enterprises that use or sell artistic material in one way or another. One may reasonably guess that this means nearly all enterprises. The tax should be related more or less to the intensity of the use of the artistic material by a specific enterprise, and the economic importance it has for such an enterprise. One can imagine that, for instance, a record shop woud pay a higher tax than a barber's shop that has the radio on.

The money collected through this tax would be put in special funds whose procedures have been regulated by law. Three kinds of recipients, with drawing rights, are proposed. One part of the money would be destined for the further development of the artistic life of the particular society. This, together with subsidies and other financial support, would be an important source for financing artistic institutions, festivals and various initiatives in the fields of film, video, the visual arts, design, music, dance, theatre, literature, photography, multimedia and so on. Obviously the money should go to all kinds of different artistic purposes as they present themselves in the given society, and not only to those traditionally considered 'high art'. The basic idea should be a democratic one. This means that all different voices and imaginations should have the chance to present themselves and to be financially supported in case profit-making is not (yet) possible.

The second part of the money collected will go to individual artists in all the different artistic fields. It will give them the chance to receive a salary for the period of creation or production of a work of art; let's say for six months, a year or two years. This will make it possible for artistic work to be developed outside the framework of cultural institutions, festivals and so on. Here too the basic principle is to ensure the development of a broad range of artistic work in all cultural fields.

The third part of the money raised should be used to support artistic life in non-Western countries. The reasons for this should not be difficult to understand. It should be clear that most of the profits derived through the use of artistic materials are made in Western countries, but many of the sources of these artistic creations have a non-Western origin. This should be recognized. Another reason is that these countries are presently suffering an enormous braindrain. It is important that artists have the chance to stay at home, to make a living in their own surroundings and contribute to the artistic life of their own societies without being dependent on Western producers, agents and others.

With this tax on the use of artistic material, there would no longer be a direct connection between the actual use of the work of a certain artist – measured in volume, time or other measurements – and the remuneration he or she receives. This is reasonable. After all, there are many sources that have contributed to the creation and production of a particular work of art, including the cultural wealth that the public domain provides for free! Our present concept of copyright involves too much romanticism about originality for it to be the starting-point for the distribution of levies for the use of artistic material. Nevertheless, the money raised could be divided according to certain categories of artists, depending on the range or importance of their work.

It will be apparent that the case I have made for the abolition of copyright is just a start. There is a lot of intellectual work to be done in order to refine the basic philosophy and think through the practical consequences of the proposal for the various arts fields. The purpose should be to work out a new system in which artists and their intermediaries have full confidence, which provides many cultural workers in the Western and Third World countries alike with better remuneration, opens up the public debate on the value of artistic creations and performances, helps support and maintain the public cultural domain, ensures that there are enough sources of artistic inspiration available for future artistic creations, and breaks the monopoly of the cultural conglomerates that the present system of copyright gives them.

We face this challenge because it is becoming increasingly clear that a paradigm shift is taking place. Until quite recently, in the modern Western world, the assumption was that we could pinpoint the real, existing author. Nor was there any doubt about the concept of what a 'work' consists of. So the copyright system could function. We had solid concepts – the author and the work – that provided a philosophical argument and a justification for the system. Now that it is becoming less clear who the author is, the question of originality resurfaces; and at the same time the idea that a work is something fixed – for now and for ever – is evaporating. Digitization is speeding up the process whereby the present copyright system falls apart.

PROTECTING CULTURAL HERITAGE

Cultures are continuously being transformed. People have always travelled, bringing with them and receiving different artistic influences. In Chapter 4 we discussed the concept and practices of hybridization. The changes and conflicts happening over time within any society have also left their traces in the content of the different artforms and on the ways they are created, produced, distributed and received. We should not forget either that wars, invasions, processes of colonization and brutal forms of external or internal domination have influenced and even exterminated important elements of material cultures and artistic practices.

If this is the 'natural' course of history, why should cultural expression be protected nevertheless? Here again, in this chapter on freedom *and* protection, the concept and practice of protection becomes extremely relevant. First, a basic principle should be that external elements should not have the right to force changes on other cultures. People should be entitled to shape their own cultural life. Of course, in these processes foreign cultural influences will play a role as well, but this should be secondary to the developments and cultural struggles going on within the 'local' society. We have already stressed the importance of preventing the cultural life of any society from being taken over by a handful of cultural conglomerates. Here the question is about the destruction of cultures, which continues to happen as a result of wars and worldwide unequal economic development.

During the 1991 Gulf War the bomb attacks on Iraq not only killed people and ruined the economy of the country, they also destroyed much of the rich cultural heritage, a heritage which, according to the dominant Western ideology, suddenly did not exist. *Foreign Affairs* told us in its Winter 1990–91 issue that Saddam Hussein came from 'a brittle land, a frontier country between Persia and Arabia, with little claim to culture and books and grand ideas' (Said 1993: 297). However, Iraqi civilization is one of the oldest in the world, and virtually the whole country is an archaeological site. Why did this cultural heritage vanish from memory? Obviously, so that there was no call for this wealth to be spared during the bombing, which would have made the attacks almost impossible.

Second, within any country democracy requires a wide variety of cultural activities. This means allowing space for all sorts of new developments. But it also means taking care to conserve what has been handed down from the past. Why? There are various reasons. People may feel such work has a beauty that continues to inspire them. Or what has been passed down may still contribute to shaping individual and collective identities in the present. The effect of modernization and globalization may be that traditional cultures no longer have a chance to develop slowly but are swept away overnight.

These reasons may at the same time be sources of conflicts within the society. Which cultural creations fall into which categories, and for whom? Which groups within society are not bothered about these arguments and sentiments? What are the tensions that preserving the cultural heritage provokes? How much tourism, for example, can a fragile historic monument bear? Does conservation and preservation mean turning material cultures and artistic expression, which were once dynamic, into static phenomena that no longer have any live relationship with developments in our own society? Who will pay for protection, and who will organize it?

In 2001 the ruling Taleban in Afghanistan demolished two huge statues of Buddha standing near the town of Bamian. Created centuries before the birth of Islam – one of them was believed to be the tallest in the world – they were destroyed because they were deemed to be 'un-Islamic idols'. The Taleban's religious leaders hold that Islamic prohibitions against depicting the human form require that all statues be destroyed. In any case, this is the dominating viewpoint resulting from much internal struggle in the country itself.[17] Molly Moore and Pamela Constable remind us that

> history is replete with examples of the destruction of culturally significant sites in the name of religion. In the 16th century, Spanish conquistadors in the New World attempted to wipe out the indigenous Mayas' religion by tearing down temples and using the stones to build churches. The Chinese government demolished more than 6,000 Tibetan Buddhist monasteries before and during the 1966 to 1976 Cultural Revolution. Hindu extremists demolished a 16th-century mosque in the northern Indian town of Ayodhya in 1992.[18]

The destruction of the Buddhas in Bamian brings into discussion a third dimension of the protection of cultural heritage. This is the international one. What might justify the international community interfering in matters that seemingly belong to the jurisdiction of national states, and which basically should be resolved through the internal struggle in any particular society, as argued above? Let's look first at the international Muslim world. On 11 March 2001 the Islamic Conference Organization, uniting fifty-five countries, sent a high-level delegation to Kabul, the capital of Afghanistan, to try to prevent the destruction of the statues. Among them was the mufti of Egypt, Sheikh Nasr Farid Wassel. Clearly this organization did not think that this was an internal affair for Afghanistan only. The act of destruction concerned the whole Muslim world, where there are differing opinions about whether images may exist.[19] It is also important to note that minority cultures and religions in Muslim countries should be respected.

There is also a more widespread point of view that the international community has both the right and the duty to defend what is beginning to be considered as 'universal cultural heritage'. Several arguments come together in this wish to preserve exceptional expressions of specific cultures or of the meeting of different cultures, as is the case with the Buddhas in Muslim surroundings. Many claim that the diversity of cultures worldwide should be respected, as should their material expressions.

In order to avoid the world becoming one that looks the same everywhere, we should cherish differences, notably the most beautiful and impressive signs of the broad variety that belongs to the world's history. Some of these exceptional works of art are fragile, and may be harmed by wind, water, pollution or being visited by too many tourists. Their symbolic value may have been contested in the past, inside the country or externally, and may still be. We should learn to understand how painful some parts of a cultural heritage may be for some people; and we should acquire the capacity to deal with the sorrow and the joy in a human and respectful way.

The Hague Convention on armed conflicts says that cultural goods should be protected during war. We have seen that, for instance, during the Gulf War this treaty was not respected. The International Court of Justice for Former Yugoslavia has listed as a crime the destruction of historic monuments during the attack on the harbour of Dubrovnik. Since 1972 Unesco has promoted the idea of a universal cultural heritage, listing significant sites and buildings. Unesco's director-general, Koïchiro Matsuura, has challenged the international community not to remain passive; it should not tolerate criminal destruction of this heritage.

In the context of the destruction of the Buddhas in Afghanistan he asserts that 'crimes against culture should not stay unpunished'.[20] It is clear that the world community, and Unesco specifically, does not always have the practical means of saving important cultural symbols. Nor does Unesco have sufficient financial resources to assist poor countries in preserving their extraordinary cultural symbols.[21] However, with the modest means it had available, it helped, for example, transform the popular quarter Pelourinho, in the Brasilian city Salvador de Bahia, from an open sewer into a place that draws the black population from far and wide.

Dominant forces in the world, including colonial powers and settlers, have stolen many superb works of art from first-nation people; these can now be seen in the museums of rich countries. The UN Draft Declaration on the Rights of Indigenous Peoples provides that human remains must be disposed of in a culturally appropriate manner, as determined by the indigenous people, and that movable cultural property is to be returned wherever possible (Redmond-Cooper 1998). What should be done?

In general it is true that works of art should be returned to where they came from, but then there is one huge dilemma: these works were stolen in the first place because the countries were poor and could not defend themselves against intruders. In the globalized world, the same countries are unable to sustain themselves economically; the one is probably related to the other. As a consequence the conditions for conserving fragile works of art are usually poorly developed, and the possibility that these will be stolen from museums and depots is not negligible, considering the pervasive and widespread corruption that exists. Should these works be given back if it means they will almost certainly disintegrate or be stolen again?

From the importance of having substantial parts of your cultural heritage physically within your own society (see also Chapter 4 on the value of having a flourishing cultural life locally) to getting rid of economic inequality worldwide, seems to be only one step. The precondition for cultural objects going back to the places they came from is that those societies are rich enough to create safe havens for the maintenance of important collections of their own cultural heritage. The state of law should also prevail, guaranteeing that what belongs to the public domain will stay within the public domain. However, this is becoming more and more of a problem in rich countries too, where plunder of the common cultural good is the order of the day, just as in the Third World. This raid on the arts will be discussed below.

Cultural heritage obviously covers much more than the built heritage. Attention should also be paid to the protection of languages and of the performing arts. On the subject of traditional music, Gilbert Roux considers that this music survived the shocks of cross-fertilization for such long periods because the mixing did not take place on the massive scale and at the speed that it does today and because people were very attached to their musical identity, to their differences – quite the reverse of what is going on in so-called world music. He fears that traditional musics, which have been profoundly integrated into people's daily lives, will disappear. Of course, they should be archived, but this is not enough. The further development of such kinds of music should be sustained.[22] The policies I have proposed earlier in this chapter may forge the infrastructure for the protection of varieties of music, including those that belong to centuries-old cultural heritages.

There are several thousand languages spoken in the world and some five hundred written ones; however, according to Unesco's estimates, more than two-thirds of printed materials are produced in English, Russian, German and French. One may wonder who has the right to speak (Tomlinson 1991: 11). Bill Ashcroft, Gareth Griffiths and Helen Tiffin remind us that one of the main features of imperial oppression was control over language. 'The imperial education system installs a "standard" version of the metropolitan language as the norm, and marginalizes all "variants" as impurities' (Ashcroft et al. 1989: 7). Ashis Nandy comments that the West's centrality in any cultural dialogue in our times has been ensured by its dominance over the language in which dialogue among the non-Western cultures takes place.

> Even when we talk to our neighbours, it is mediated by Western assumptions and Western frameworks. These inner demons have subverted most forms of attempted dialogue among the non-Western cultures. All such dialogues today are mediated by the West as the unrecognized third participant ... For, whether we recognize it or not, there is a major, powerful, ongoing, official dialogue of cultures in the world. The format of that dialogue has been standardized, incorporated within the dominant global structure of awareness, and institutionalized through powerful international organizations. In this dialogue, the key player naturally is the modern West. (Chen 1998: 144–5)

In relation to the economic globalization that is affecting and changing all cultures, Hamid Mowlana fears the disappearance of oral or traditional cultures that have been 'major resistance forces in the face of cultural domination' (Mowlana 1993: 396). *Our Creative Diversity*, the Report of the World Commission on Culture and Development, notes that one of the most sensitive issues is that of language, for a people's language is perhaps its most fundamental cultural attitude. 'Indeed the very nature of language is emblematic of the whole pluralist premise – every single language spoken in the world represents a unique way of viewing human experience and the world itself.' The report concludes that language policy, however, like other policies, is still used as an instrument of domination, fragmentation and assimilation. 'It is hardly surprising that claims for language are among the first rights that minorities have asserted; such claims continue to pose problems ranging from the official and legal status of minority languages, language teaching and use in schools and other institutions, as well as in the mass medias' (Pérez de Cuéllar 1996: 59).

In his report of the June 1996 Conference on Language Rights held in Barcelona, Walter Mignolo makes the point that the weakening of the state from the 1970s on was counterbalanced by the strengthening of communities that had been repressed during the previous decades of nation-building and state consolidation. Asia and Africa were the locations of decolonization movements. Latin Americans experienced a revival of indigenous movements for their rights, their lands, their languages, from which emerged a new Indian consciousness. Indians who had been employed by the state, either as community development workers or as schoolteachers, were looking 'not only for a new Indian identity but also for a chance to put pressure on those in positions of power and in government in order to influence the future of Indian polity' (Mignolo 1998: 43–4).

On the other hand, he notes that technological globalization contributed to the process of raising awareness about the protection of local languages among other claims, because indigenous activists and their international supporters could be linked through the web of transnational information networks. Walter Mignolo says that one of the paradoxes of globalization is 'that it allows subaltern communities within the nation-state to create transnational alliances beyond the state to fight for their own social and human rights' (Mignolo 1998: 44).

In the Spanish region of Catalonia, film distributors are obliged to offer copies in Catalan of successful films that have been dubbed into Spanish, as are cinema owners for a quarter of their programming. On television a substantial number of programmes should be in Catalan, as must half the songs on radio.[23] Even in a rich country such measures protecting local languages are a costly affair; try to imagine how difficult this is in poorer parts of the world. South of the Sahara there exist a myriad different languages and dialects; try to imagine what it would cost to make films in local languages and how unreachable this ideal is, unless through video, as takes place on a massive scale in Nigeria (see Chapter 4).

In any case, it should be clear that an important contribution to the protection and active use of many languages is to invest heavily in translation, taking care that people can communicate orally and in writing in their own languages, but can be heard as well in other parts of the world. This does not mean only translations from the original language into one of the Western languages, usually English; it also means translations from, for instance, an African language into an Asian language. In the case of literature, Bill Ashcroft, Gareth Griffiths and Helen Tiffin argue that 'one of the most persistent prejudices underlying the production of the texts of the metropolitan canon is that only certain categories of experience are capable of being rendered as "literature"' (Ashcroft et al. 1989: 88). The opposite should happen: all experiences should have the chance of being expressed in the original language of the people who have those experiences, and then being translated into many different languages. This would certainly cost money, but for the sake of peace and mutual respect this expense would be more than worthwhile.

Even so, it seems that the language issue is fraught with contradictions. Abram de Swaan refers to the case of people succeeding in their fight for language rights. Alas, what is decisive 'is not the right of human beings to speak whatever language they wish, but the freedom of everyone else to ignore what they say in the language of their choice' (Swaan 2001: 52). Another bitter reality is that 'in fact, the more languages are formally assigned equal status, the less chance they stand of holding their own against the one dominant language, usually English, sometimes French' (p. 187).

THE RAID ON ART

In 1999 Emmanuel de Roux and Roland-Pierre Paringaux published an impressive book entitled *Razzia sur l'art. Vols, pillages, recels à travers le monde* (*The Raid on Art: Worldwide Theft, Plunder and Receiving*). When the belief in and practice of unhampered free trade rules the world, when cultural values are being undermined and the public domain is shrinking in the face of the competition for individual personal enrichment, it should not be surprising that works of art, too, which can fetch high prices on the world market, are being massively plundered. They are attractive 'products' which are easy to steal, unless the storage place has been guarded like a bunker, and even then they are not necessarily secure.

The authors describe how everything is sought for its monetary value, from

African idols to Eskimo masks to Russian icons. Dozens of temples in Angkor, deep in the bush, are easy prey for Cambodian soldiers and their Thai clients. The civil war in Afghanistan created the conditions for the plunder of the museum of Kabul. And if Hong Kong has become one of the global art capitals it is thanks to the bleeding of the archaeological heritage of China to whom it belongs. In the Middle East, Assyrian *bas-relief* sculptures have been appearing on the international market since the 1991 Gulf War.

In Africa, from where much art has been 'exported' over the last hundred years, the museums are the first target. Then there is the underground treasure. From Nigeria in particular, but also from Mali, Niger and Ghana, clandestine archaeological excavations feed the markets worldwide. For one piece sold, often a whole site is destroyed irreparably. Every armed conflict, from Biafra to former Zaïre and from Liberia to Mozambique, has brought quantities of art objects on to the Western market, at least those that have not already been destroyed. The decline of animism in favour of Islam, Christianity or syncretic religions has the same result.

In Latin America, Emmanuel de Roux and Roland-Pierre Paringaux continue, sites of great cultural importance have regularly been pillaged by organized gangs; this is the case in Peru, Columbia, Mexico, Guatemala, Ecuador and elsewhere. In Bolivia, ancient communities are seeing their heritage threatened. In Eastern Europe, post-communist mafias have discovered in the arts a gold mine that permits them to launder money and make tidy profits. Gangs empty churches in the Czech Republic, Slovakia, France and Italy, and in Cyprus the rich Greek-Byzantine past offers the chance of a lifetime. French castles have not been spared, despite more and more sophisticated alarm systems. In Italy, in 1998 alone, more than 31,000 art objects were stolen. In the European Union, Belgium and the Netherlands have been identified as being lax in dealing with receivers (Roux and Paringaux 1999: 16–8).

Honestly speaking, it would be a miracle if this raid on art could be stopped under the present conditions of free trade, minimal custom controls, safe havens for money-laundering, unequal economic conditions between North and South, and mass-scale transport of goods. In more and more countries politics has been infected by mafia influences, payoffs have become normal, and black money coming from drugs, piracy, illegal arms deals, the breaking of economic boycotts and raids on art has become more intertwined and 'united' than workers' movements ever dreamt possible! Control mechanisms worldwide are weakly developed and many states, such as the Netherlands, prefer to make life for art dealers in their countries relatively easy. Under the present neoliberal economic conditions worldwide, all states compete with each other to attract investment and commercial activities. This pernicious condition hinders the setting-up of effective international regulations and even the maintenance of the few existing international treaties.

The plundering of the arts everywhere in the world obliges countries to set up extensive registration systems of works of art. Otherwise, it cannot be proved that a certain work belongs to this or that owner or comes from a particular church or museum. This is a costly affair, even for the rich countries. Some registration systems have been developed. The Art Loss Register is a London-based initiative by big art traders and insurance companies. Its competitor is the Active Crime Tracking System, which has an enormous database with at least 4 million entries. The Getty Museum in Los Angeles has developed an Object Identification System, in collaboration with, among others, Unesco and the International Council of Museums (Roux and Paringaux 1999: 300–8).

Tracking down the illegal art trade is extremely complicated because most countries have completely different forms of legislation. The Unidroit Treaty, which is about to be made operative, requires traders to prove that they have acquired a work of art after taking all the necessary action to satisfy themselves about the origin of the object and the legal character of the transaction. If this cannot be proved, the work of art can be sent back to the country of origin (Roux and Paringaux 1999: 314–15; Schipperhof 1997).

ALL THAT'S FRAGILE NEEDS PROTECTION

Over the last couple of decades more and more people have concluded that the earth's ecology is deteriorating; with this theme we bring cultural developments into a broader, perhaps unexpected context. Those people have come together in organizations such as Greenpeace and Friends of the Earth. Obviously, the aim of these movements is to become superfluous as quickly as possible. Ecological movements seek to realize something very concrete: a radical change in the way we deal with our natural environment. To achieve this we need another way of thinking about nature, another sensibility about what kinds of balance are needed in order to realize sustainable development.

It is interesting that more and more people are making direct connections between this urgent need and the issues discussed in this book concerning artistic cultures worldwide. We tend to think that the broad field of the arts is separate from the agenda of the ecological movements. To some extent this is true, but as long as human beings exist, so too do the arts. People will continue to make music, tell or write stories, carve or paint or draw images, and express themselves through theatre or dance. However, there is another question that interests us here, namely who controls the creation, production, distribution, promotion and reception of the arts, worldwide and locally, and, linked to this, what kinds of content are resulting from these processes? From this point on, the comparison between ecology and culture starts to take shape. We may acknowledge that ecological environments, like the arts, will not disappear. However, in relation to our natural environment the relevant question is, as in the artistic domain, who is in control and thus what the qualitative outcome is.

Jeremy Rifkin, linking culture and ecology, observes:

> culture, like nature, can be mined to exhaustion. If culture is overexploited and wasted, the market risks losing the proverbial hen that lays the golden eggs. Cultural diversity, then, is like biodiversity. If all the rich cultural diversity of human experiences around the world is exploited for short-term gain in the commercial sphere and not allowed to recycle and replenish, the economy loses the broad pool of human experiences that are the stuff of cultural production. (Rifkin 2000: 247–8)

He calls preserving biodiversity and cultural diversity the two great social movements of the twenty-first century (pp. 257–8).

This is also true for the protection of languages, between 50 and 90 per cent of which will be extinct in 100 years' time. The threat to biodiversity could be 20 per cent for all biological animal species and 17 per cent for plants. Tove Skutnabb-Kangas and Robert Phillipson claim that 'linguistic and cultural diversity seem to be *mediating* variables in sustaining bio-diversity itself, and vice versa, for as long as human beings inhabit the earth' (Skutnabb-Kangas and Phillipson 2001: 41).

The damage being caused by economic globalization challenges us to consider forging a coalition between movements concerned with protecting the environment and the seemingly more diffuse field of culture and the arts. Movements like those concerned with the environment do not exist for the arts. There are creators, performers, intermediaries and publics, who have many completely different motives and interests. The arts is a never-ending story, at first glance not driven by one clear purpose.

What is the rationale for linking these two areas of social concern? Despite the differences between them, both face serious problems with common characteristics. For example: the processes shaping the environmental conditions of our lives and those shaping our artistic cultures are, more and more, coming into the hands of only a few huge corporations. This means that democratic control and public interests are slipping below the horizon and being replaced by profit-making considerations. Does this mean that diversity will disappear? Yes and no. We can buy many different yoghurts or pharmaceutical products, and in the record shops there is music from all corners of the planet on sale. However, the centres of decision-making are under oligopolistic control, which, first, is undemocratic and, second, promotes increasing uniformity, for instance of production methods and taste. What people consider as pleasurable or worthwhile is being steered in more or less the same direction.

From the ecological perspective, diversity is a matter of life and death, as many people are beginning to realize. From the cultural perspective diversity has also become an important subject for discussion. The issue here is democracy. Our natural environment is a fragile edifice; it requires care to ensure that the necessary checks and balances are respected and our natural resources are not exhausted. For Wendell Berry ecological and cultural questions are one and the same.

> A culture is not a collection of relics or ornaments, but a practical necessity, and its corruption invokes calamity. A healthy culture is a communal order of memory, insight, value, work, conviviality, reverence, aspiration. It reveals the human necessities and the human limits. It clarifies our inescapable bonds to the earth and to each other. It assures that the necessary restraints are observed, that the necessary work is done, and that it is done well. (Berry 1986: 43)

The maintenance of cultural diversity also demands work. It is not self-evident that the freedom of artistic communication can flourish indefinitely. Opportunities for artistic expression that goes against the grain, is rebellious, unpopular, or is in the process of germinating, must be defended again and again. Certainly this is the case when profit-making motives and consumerist attitudes dominate the cultural and economic processes that influence artistic creation, production, distribution and reception.

Perhaps surprisingly, it becomes clear that ecological and cultural concerns have a great deal in common. This is particularly the case for the intellectual property regime, which for decades has allowed individuals or corporations exclusive rights to the use of inventions and creations. This subject has already been discussed in Chapter 3 and revisited earlier in this chapter. The argument for the legitimacy of this monopoly is the assumed originality of the creation or invention. However, there is no poem without the existence of former poems, and every invention draws on the enormous public stock of knowledge from past to present. Originality is a romantic concept. Thus, the claim to monopolistic intellectual property rights is not justifiable. What links cultural and ecological movements is that intellectual property rights which, within these fields, mainly concern patents and copyright, are becoming big business. Most inventions and artistic creations, past and present, are now in the hands of a very few conglomerates – whether in the area of pharmaceuticals, food or culture, to take just three broad examples. This gives them the power to select or create ambiences that favour their profit-making aims. Vandana Shiva concludes that the 'dominant interpretation of Intellectual Property Rights leads to a dramatic distortion in the understanding of creativity, and as a result, in the understanding of the history of inequality' (Shiva 1995: 12).

There are other, perhaps less obvious, phenomena that link artistic and ecological concerns. Corporate conglomerates hire, on a massive scale, designers, actors, dancers, writers, musicians and film-makers whose work stimulates the buying and consuming that increases the profit margins of these enterprises. From an ecological perspective this drive to consume, for which many artists create the necessary seductive ambience, is harmful.

Digitalization has not yet prevented book production from growing ever bigger. In the hope of achieving a bestseller publishers produce many titles in huge quantities and wait and see which ones become a success. The hundreds of thousands of books that don't sell are destroyed soon after publication. This massive production is not only a cultural waste but also has devastating ecological effects.[24]

Pollution and acid rain are not only bad for the health of human beings, they are also a catastrophe for our material cultural heritage. It is not possible, for instance, to go on cleaning old churches indefinitely; eventually, nothing of their fine architectural detail is left to clean. Let's jump, next, from the past to the present. More and more entertainment reaches us by computers. The digital world is less virtual than many people would like to think. One of the its material aspects is the enormous consumption of energy needed to keep the whole digitalized world working. When computers become outmoded, which happens all the time, they are thrown away, placing further strain on the environment (Hamelink 1999: 101–2).

Culture and ecology are linked in so many ways. Considering the origin and character of the environmental movement and of the cultural domain, it is understandable that the two are not in contact with each other. However, the need to protect what is fragile, and the threat to diversity in nature as in the arts, makes it necessary for environmental and cultural movements to join forces. Such a coalition should not be based on trying to establish a uniformity of taste; instead, ensuring the necessary conditions for cultural as well as ecological diversity should be the focus. Moreover, the mistaken notion that the arts should be the adornment of the ecological struggle should be avoided. The purpose should be to reverse the detrimental trends in both areas. And it is easier to explain to people that there are serious common problems and concerns than to convince them that a particular, isolated field of activity is in a dreadful mess, especially if this is what gives them great pleasure.

Equally, it is a mistake to expect artists on their own to forge a cultural movement against the harmful developments of globalization in its current form. First, most artists are not very good organizers. Second, and more important, everyone needs to have the conviction that a democratic society requires a rich variety of artistic expression. It is clear that the ecological movement needs a counterpart in the cultural field. The coalition of ecological and cultural movements should operate globally, as well as at the local and regional level. What should its agenda be? To protect and revive diversity, and to protect and increase respect for what is fragile, ecological and cultural. As Steven Feld says, 'every instance of thinout of planetary diversity is currently connected to the real thinout of cultural, linguistic, and artistic diversity' (Feld 1995: 120).

THE PRODUCTION OF DISCOURSE IS ALWAYS CONTROLLED

In the first chapter I described the arts as an area of human life full of conflict and struggle. The stakes are high, as we have seen throughout this book. Unsurprisingly, therefore, in all societies the question of constraints on artistic expression is always a thorny one. The ways in which some people communicate may cross the boundaries of what others deem acceptable. To complicate matters further, the world can't be divided into the good guys, who defend freedom of expression in all circumstances, and the bad guys, who feel that certain restrictions on human communication are desirable in the light of, for instance, social, cultural or religious sensibilities. Let's try to balance on a tightrope between freedom and protection by giving some examples.

The reality is that every individual human being believes that certain things should not be said, painted, expressed through dance. At the same time every human being feels that certain types of cultural expression are more worthwhile than others and should have every possible chance of being communicated. In general, these beliefs and feelings are not just individual affairs but shared by specific groups of people. It is important to emphasize that the extent to which freedom or control prevails depends on who at any particular time has the power to allow openness or to censure or ban certain artistic messages.

Michel Foucault observes that in every society, the production of discourse is controlled, selected, organized and redistributed through various procedures (Tomlinson 1991: 9). John Tomlinson comments that the point Foucault wants to make is that 'discourse is in principle boundless – it "proliferates to infinity". Anything can be said, but societies regulate this anarchic proliferation with various practices of containment. One of the most obvious practices is that of "prohibition"' (p. 9). But perhaps the more interesting of the practices Michel Foucault describes are those that 'regulate discourses, as if it were, *from within* – not prohibiting discourse, but keeping it in check by tying it to certain regulative principles'.

Prohibition and the more subtle forms of containment are the subject of the next few pages. Freedom of expression is obviously an extremely important principle, but other values may exist that make it desirable to restrain oneself in some respects when painting a canvas, writing a text, or shooting a film. In this sense I disagree with Salman Rushdie when he refers to freedom of expression and argues that without the freedom to offend, 'without the freedom to challenge, even to satirize all orthodoxies, including religious orthodoxies, it ceases to exist. Language and the imagination cannot be imprisoned, or art will die, and with it, a little of what makes us human' (Rushdie 1992: 396). Nevertheless, I would say, it also makes us human when we *respect* others' opinions. And it makes us extremely humane when we do not agitate, through artistic or other means, for people to be killed, for instance.

However, I do agree with Salman Rushdie that the controversy about his work and the Iranian fatwa calling for his death should not be seen as a struggle between Western freedoms and Eastern unfreedom. 'The freedoms of the West are rightly vaunted, but many minorities – racial, sexual, political – just as rightly feel excluded from full possession of these liberties; while, in my lifelong experience of the East, from Turkey and Iran to India and Pakistan, I have found people to be every bit as passionate for freedom as any Czech, Romanian, German, Hungarian or Pole' (Rushdie 1992: 396). Altogether, it may be clear that we are discussing an extremely complicated issue to which simple answers and solutions do not exist. A number of examples may show the contradictions that are part of real life.

Moraeus Hanssen leads the Municipal Cinema Co. in Oslo, Norway, a branch of the city government that owns all thirty-one cinemas in Oslo. She must approve every commercial film before it is shown. At stake, in her view, is the mental health of Norwegian young people. 'I care much more about my public than I do about the movies. This industry can be very, very gruesome. You live just once on earth, and I don't want people wasting their time watching stupid movies filled with violence and raw sex.' Norwegian officials describe their position on films as progressive rather than backward. They hope that American law-makers, shaken by a series of high school shootings, will take steps to dam the global flow of disturbing images in film and other media. Moraeus Hanssen concedes that a relationship between violent films and violent behaviour is hard to prove and that youngsters are savvy about film technology, but she also believes that they need help to identify the good, the true and the beautiful. 'I am against censorship,' she insists. 'What I am is an editor.'[25] We will come back to the question of curbing violence later in this chapter.

Let's move to another part of the world, Indonesia, where one of the traditional forms of theatre is Longser, and one of the groups that is prominent in updating this kind of theatre is the LAP group, or LAP project. In 1997 a contract for performances for Indosiar, a commercial Indonesian TV company, was cancelled. Why? The group was obliged to purge their scripts of all so-called SARA issues, which is an acronym indicating questions of ethnicity, religion, race and class. The shows had to be more populist with stories empty of political references. This was in the last days of the Suharto regime.

After the fall of Suharto something remarkable took place with the LAP group. What they actually did was 'recycle' old stories with minor alterations. Instead of using the new freedom of speech and absence of explicit censorship to become 'truly' political (which might have been expected, considering that the whole project was a commitment to relate their performances to political and social conditions of contemporary Indonesia), they themselves saw their plays as becoming more populist. Jörgen Hellman comments that 'this cannot be explained with commercial reasons since they do not earn any substantial amount of money on their performances'. One explanation frequently given is that the group may have 'a kind of writer's cramp, a sort of performance anxiety'. For Jörgen Hellman this is not a satisfactory explanation of the loss of energy in the group. 'As it turned out, one word recurred in all conversations with artists (inside LAP and outside) and that is *Bingung*', which means that they are confused by the new post-dictatorship situation. What happened is that the artists 'perceived SARA issues to be even more sensitive to put on stage today than before. Especially, of course, ethnic and religious issues.' Conflicts in these areas are indeed greatly disturbing the normalization of Indonesia. The consequence is that LAP has become reluctant to touch upon these kinds of issue 'and their confusion made them turn into populism' (Hellman 2000).

At the beginning of the 1990s, when he was setting up his Asian operations, cultural mogul Rupert Murdoch claimed that satellite technology posed an unambiguous threat to totalitarian regimes everywhere, and to their capacity to censor. Murdoch's satellite was beaming BBC broadcasts highly critical of China's thuggish leaders. Robert Sherrill reports that 'the thugs – with whom Murdoch was eager to do business – complained. So he did what came naturally: He kicked the BBC off the air.'[26] Why are satellite operators dependent on governments, which are no more virtual than satellite technology is? Christopher Hird analyses that, first, 'there is real difficulty in measuring audiences – which they eventually need to do to entice advertisers onto their services. But second, and more important, for their paid-for services planned for the future they need one of two things: a well regulated cable network or direct broadcasting to people's homes. To achieve either of these they need the co-operation of governments' (Hird 1994: 34–5). Here the interests of the satellite companies and the politicians converge. The Chinese, for instance, are opposed to dishes because of the difficulty of having control over them; and the cultural conglomerates fear that dishes make it easier to decode the signals, depriving them of important revenues. So, both favour cable. Meanwhile, the dream of unhampered communication that bypasses censorship has disappeared from view.

There are other strange contradictions. Marilyn French, for instance, is astonished that the Indian government censors films for political content and also forbids scenes of lovemaking or kissing, whereas showing rape on screen has been allowed (French 1993: 178–9). It is interesting that in 1996, when the Miss World contest was due to take place in India, there was widespread public disapproval and protest as people considered it shameful for women to be presented in this way.

From all these cases, which could be multiplied endlessly, it becomes clear that the outcome of what is or isn't shown or published emerges from a process where there are many different and conflicting interests, moral positions and power structures. Todd Gitlin talks about the process as a chain of a thousand microdecisions made by a thousand personnel about a thousand stories (Gitlin 1997: 8). This has two consequences. First, accountability in relation to questions of freedom of expression, restraint and censorship is diffused. It is not only top-down censorship that should concern us. As Todd Gitlin observes, for most cultural conglomerates 'accountability is not their game' (p. 12). Therefore the second consequence is that we should consider the question of freedom of expression in broader contexts. It can never be an absolute. Why, for instance, should commercial speech, such as advertising, have the same freedom as we cherish for journalism, which is the case in the United States? (McChesney 1997: 48). We should demand from commercial messages a higher degree of accountability, because advertisements have by definition the tendency to tell only (tiny) parts of the truth. It is also in the public interest not to be confronted everywhere and every moment of the day with commercial publicity.

The need to respect other people's opinions and feelings may require that artists restrain themselves. Not everything that can be said should be said. The Latin American writer Eduardo Galeano considers that the writer who thinks that he can say anything he likes with impunity is contemptible: 'We are all responsible for what we say and what we do' (Steenhuis 1990: 159).

Using the example of hate speech, Ursula Owen of Index on Censorship describes the kind of dilemma that needs constantly to be thought about. 'Words can turn into bullets, hate speech can kill and maim, just as censorship can. So, as dedicated opponents of censorship and proponents of free speech, we are forced to ask: is there a moment where the *quantitative* consequences of hate speech change *qualitatively* the arguments about how we must deal with it.' She wonders whether there is 'a point of necessary intervention somewhere on the continuum between the ugly, offensive but more localized public expression of hatred and the successful establishment in a community or society of a culture of hatred in which the instigators of hatred become its authorisers, become authority itself?' (Owen 1998).

The question to be debated is what kind of intervention should be taken, and who has the power to do so? Let's continue with the example of hate speech. Can it be censored, and would it be wise to do so? Or, would it be more effective to raise public awareness that hate speech destroys democracy and is the first step in the direction of the physical elimination of individuals or groups of people who are seen by some as the enemy? If this awareness is widespread, the breeding ground for such hate speech diminishes considerably. The answer to these complicated dilemmas is not that easy, and depends on the actual (historical) situation in any given society. Many types of speech may seem to be less offensive than, for instance, outspoken hate speech. But what to think, for example, about entertainers who have made it fashionable to insult people and who make boorishness and crudeness popular? In general it can be said that these kinds of issues can be resolved only when large numbers of people are prepared to discuss them seriously and at length, and to build up a broadly developed public opinion that opposes these kinds of humiliating forms of communication.

In the autumn of 1997 at the Royal Academy in London, the exhibition *Sensation: Young Artists from the Saatchi Collection* created a controversy centred on one of the paintings. Entitled *Myra*, it was by Marcus Harvey and depicted Myra Hindley, a woman who in the 1960s had brutally murdered a number of children. Shocked spectators threw paint at the image of this serial killer (see Stallabras 1999: 201–10) and the exhibition attracted huge crowds. Was this because the artist was deliberately being provocative? Philosopher Ger Groot argues that contemporary art has made the intermingling of horror and beauty an important theme. For critics and public alike, the measuring rod for the progress of modern art is more and more its destructive powers. This is not a new phenomenon, Groot claims. It started with Romanticism, and it expressed, for instance during the First World War, the cruel reality that lay behind the orderly and optimistic veneer of the Enlightenment. Later, in the disenchanted twentieth century, we learned all about chaos, violence and irrationality. So, the artist who pretends to tell us about terror and the frightening aspects of life shows us what we already know. Art no longer unveils pain, but repeats it. It becomes an anachronism of depiction of aggression and destruction, and this makes no sense according to Ger Groot.

He argues that this is not the last word about art. On the contrary, it has the capacity to create a truth of its own. Therefore we should build up public awareness that the idea that art should shock is outdated. Let artists stop showing cruelty and violence. Surrounded by despair, there is a new and unheard-of theme that artists can offer the world, Ger Groot says. This is how we can be reconciled. Artists have the unique chance to confirm, 'that life is good to live, despite all it appears to be'.[27]

THE DIGITAL DOMAIN IS NOT WHAT IT SEEMED TO BE

How can freedom be guaranteed on the digital highway, while at the same time keeping out undesirable artistic material that would be forbidden in 'normal' societies? How can freedom *and* protection be reconciled in this new terrain?

We have already noted that the new means of communication provides excellent opportunities for getting round the dominant powers who control the production and distribution of the arts. Artists can trace people potentially interested in their work, and they can develop their own markets fit for their kinds of artistic creations and performances. The expansion of freedom of expression is not an unmixed blessing, however, because the internet is also a haven for paedophiles, terrorists, political extremists and illegal arms traders, for obscenity and for racist hate speech.

Every society censures certain forms of communication and approves others. The arts are in the centre of our symbolic battlefields. The big question is obviously how this struggle will be worked out in the digital domain. Meanwhile it has become clear that the idea of the internet as a perpetual feast of freedom is an illusion. Nothing about the digital world is virtual. It is not dreamland, it is a hard material world in which financial, economic and cultural interests play big roles, just as in the 'normal' world. There are things taking place and forms of communication happening on the internet that are not allowed at all in some societies. Why should this be so? If we accept that both freedom *and* control should exist in the digital domain too – and I do, with some pain in my heart! – then the next question is how this combination can be effected.

Adam Newey, who has worked for Index on Censorship, suggests that the responsibility for moral choices about what to read and what to avoid should be in the hands of individuals. 'Relying on individuals rather than the government to make choices about the content of what they and their families receive optimises the free speech rights of adults' (Newey 1999: 35). This sounds appealing, but not in its absolute form. In the 'normal' world, we love to have free choice but, whether or not we like the specific legislation within this field, every society has its laws that say certain types of expression are not tolerated. This problem cannot be solved by Adam Newey's suggestion that people may try to find help to control what enters the house through the internet. He comes up with filters, as did US president Bill Clinton, or with what he calls 'walled gardens'. 'The user knows that there is no danger of accidentally stumbling on a pornographic newsgroup, for example' (p. 33). If someone doesn't enter a porn shop, he or she may know the same! But in many societies, for good reasons, producing, distributing and buying hardcore pornography is not allowed. Obviously, this kind of legislation should apply in the digital domain as well. Why not? If certain things are not tolerated in a particular society, it is not enough to say that individuals may filter them out. As Isabelle Falque-Pierrotin says, 'self-regulation does not replace the law or the judge'. The task is, therefore, to make more explicit the principles of the law in all environments.[28]

This has happened in France, or at least a start has been made. At the end of 2000, the French courts ruled that Yahoo! Inc., operator of the popular internet search engine, must do what it could to block French users from visiting auction sites selling Nazi memorabilia. The *International Herald Tribune* commented that, to cyber-libertarians, this was an outrage: 'The French are presuming to regulate speech on an American Web site used primarily by American surfers. But the French argue that disseminating this stuff is illegal under French law, so French citizens ought to be prevented from viewing it in cyberspace.'[29] Yahoo! was told to clear its site, implying that it could divide the Net into geographic chunks and regulate each one separately. If the Net could be zoned in this way, regulation and national sovereignty suddenly seemed possible. The *International Herald Tribune* noted: 'the French cannot put pressure on obscure collectors of Nazi memorabilia, who don't care if they break French law. But they can pressure international players like Yahoo! and so get at their real enemies.'[30]

Suddenly, the seemingly borderless internet is running up against real borders. In recent cases, judges in Germany and Italy have come to similar conclusions to those of the French court, declaring that national boundaries do indeed apply to the 'virtual' world.

> The legal battles are being fostered by new technology that appears to make those online checkpoints possible. In the past year, software programs have reached the market that are supposed to figure out where people are at the instant they gain access to a Web site. By conducting real-time analyses of Internet traffic, a technique sometimes called geolocation, those software programs can try to determine the country, the state and, in limited cases, even the city from which a person is surfing the Internet.[31]

Obviously, the next step in technology will bring an individual internet user right into focus.

This has enormous consequences. It means from the democratic perspective that it is necessary to have precise laws that say who has the jurisdiction to penetrate people's private spheres, and also that the courts have to play a decisive role in relation to these sensitive questions. Actually, there are two battles to fight at the present moment. One is safeguarding privacy and protecting freedom of communication, the other is about how to apply to the internet the normal rulings of every society about which forms of communication are not tolerated.

It has become clear that providers cannot pretend to be carriers only; they control the gates though which messages enter. At the same time, it would be wise for nation-states to set up an Independent Council for the Digital Domain, which would supervise the application of the law and the rulings of the courts concerning the internet. Now that it seems that providers, who by definition operate on national territories, can be made responsible for what passes through their gates, this does not mean that regulation at the global level will be unnecessary. However, the United Nations, which would be the appropriate institution to deal with these matters, is no longer politically equipped even to discuss, let alone regulate, the worldwide imbalance in the production and distribution of artistic goods and values, and news and information. A step forward would be an open debate in the General Assembly on freedom and control in the field of the new digital media and communication channels.

I am aware that what I have tried to do in this chapter – introducing the concept of protection and accordingly proposing quite a lot of concrete measures that can be implemented – is swimming against the tide. The tide is neoliberal, despite the fact that more and more people are beginning to say in Seattle, in Genoa, for instance, that a different future is possible. The world is not for sale, it is often said. The many protests that led up to the G8 conference in Genoa, July 2001, were, according to Michael Hardt and Antonio Negri,

> based on the recognition that no national power is in control of the present global order. Consequently, protests must be directed at international and supranational organizations like the Group of Eight, the World Trade Organization, the World Bank and the International Monetary Fund ... If it is not national but supranational powers that rule today's globalization, we must recognize that this new order has no democratic institutional mechanisms for representation, as nation-states do: no elections, no public forum for debate.[32]

In the movements that oppose the present neoliberal globalization, the cultural and artistic sectors of our societies are not overwhelmingly present. In this book I have argued that this is a serious mistake. Economic globalization has an enormous impact on artistic life everywhere in the world. Therefore, in this chapter, I have made some proposals that may contribute to the flourishing of artistic diversity, including at the local level.

We should be attentive and assist the creation and distribution of the arts, in the way that a midwife attends a birth. A work of art that is worthwhile is something fragile and needs protection.

NOTES

1. Herman Franke, 'Links!', *De Groene Amsterdammer*, 21 January 1998.

2. Peter Fuchs, 'The Private Sector Needs to Look More to the Common Good', *International Herald Tribune*, 10 January 1996.

3. Jan Pronk, 'Against Transnational Greed', *De Groene Amsterdammer*, 9 October 1997.

4. Carlos Fuentes, 'Another French Chance to Make Idealism Work', *International Herald Tribune*, 18 June 1997.

5. Bernard Cassen, 'La piège de la gouvernance', *Le Monde Diplomatique*, June 2001.

6. Ibid.

7. For the draft of this text and further developments, see: www.incd.net

8. Philippe Douste-Blazy, 'Ne perdons la bataille mondial de l'audiovisuel', *Le Monde*, 30 May 1999.

9. Jeremy Rifkin, 'La vente du siècle', *Le Monde*, 3 May 2001.

10. See: www.screenquota.org

11. Jean-Pierre Turberque, 'Survivre pour la diversité culturelle', *Le Monde*, 19 April 2001.

12. Lawrence K. Grossman, 'These Airwaves are Public Property', *International Herald Tribune*, 24 August 1995; see also Pérez de Cuéllar (1996: 121–2) which launches a comparable proposal.

13. H. J. A. Hofland, 'De buigende elite', *NRC Handelsblad*, 30 June 1999.

14. Rudy van Dantzig, 'Geen salaris, maar don't worry. Cultuurbeleid in Cleveland: impakken en wegwezen', *De Volkskrant*, 21 September 2000.

15. See also Cliche et al. (2001). This report identifies four categories of cultural policies: (1) Individual Support schemes for creative artists ranging from awards to grants (project, work, travel), scholarships or compensation packages; (2) Market Support for artistic work such as public purchasing programmes for books or artworks; (3) Dissemination Support for artistic work including target groups; (4) Legal and Social Frameworks. A comparable report on performing artists is underway.

16. See also Bernard Lang, 'Des logiciels libres à la disposition de tous. Contre la mainmise sur la propriété intellectuel', *Le Monde Diplomatique*, January 1998.

17. Pamela Constable, 'Obliteration of Buddhas Signals Preeminence of Taleban Hardliners', *International Herald Tribune*, 21 March 2001; Françoise Chipaux, 'La destruction des bouddhas ne fait pas l'unanimité chez les talibans', *Le Monde* 13 March 2001; see also Flandrin 2001.

18. Molly Moore and Pamela Constable, 'Muslims Cry Out Over Taleban Destruction of Buddhas', *International Herald Tribune*, 12 March 2001.

19. Henri Thincq, 'L'image dans l'Islam, un statut controversé. Le Coran prescrit la lutte contre les idoles, mais les icônes et autres représentations peuvent servir de support à la parole divine', *Le Monde*, 13 March 2001.

20. Koïchiro Matsuura, 'Les crimes contre la culture ne doivent pas rester impunis', *Le Monde*, 16 March 2001.

21. Interview with Saïd Zulficar, secretary-general of Patrimonie sans Frontières, 'Trop d'intérêts politiques et financiers parasitent les efforts de l'Unesco', *Le Monde*, 13 March 2001.

22. Gilbert Roux, 'Je préconise l'ethnomusicologie d'urgence pour ces musiques de tradition orale', *Le Monde*, 30 September 1997.

23. 'Catalaanse taalstrijd veroorzaakt woede bij bioscopen en publiek', *De Volkskrant*, 4 July 1998.

24. Marc Crispin Miller, 'The Crushing Power of Big Publishing', *The Nation*, 17 March 1997; see also Crispin Miller (1997: 119).

25. Moraeus Hanssen, 'Not Coming Soon in Oslo: Movie Violence', *International Herald Tribune*, 9 July 1999.

26. Robert Sherrill, 'Citizen Murdoch. Buying His Way to a Media Empire', *The Nation*, 29 May 1995.

27. Ger Groot, 'Kunst in tijden van Dutroux', *De Groene Amsterdammer*, 22 October 1997.

28. Isabelle Falque-Pierrotin, 'Quelle régulation pour Internet et les réseaux?', *Le Monde*, 2 December 1999.

29. 'National Sovereignty Wins One Against the Worldwide Net', *International Herald Tribune*, 28 November 2000.

30. Ibid. In November 2001 a federal judge in the USA ruled that Yahoo! Inc. did not have to comply with the French order because the First Amendment of the US Constitution protected content generated in the United States by American companies from being regulated by authorities in countries that have far more restrictive laws on freedom of expression (*International Herald Tribune*, 9 November 2001).

31. Lisa Guernsey, 'Law's Long Arm Reaching onto the Net. As Tracking Gets Easier, More Judges Decide National Rules Apply Online', *International Herald Tribune*, 16 March 2001.

32. Michael Hardt and Antonio Negri, 'The New Faces in Genoa Want a Different Future', *International Herald Tribune*, 25 July 2001.

SEVEN
Everything of Value is Defenceless

The Dutch poet Lucebert says: 'Everything of value is defenceless.' This is a serious warning. With the words of the poet in mind, we must, nevertheless, do everything possible to defend what is valuable in the arts. What I have tried to do in this book is to identify where the defence lines are weak and to make some proposals for protecting and promoting cultural diversity for the sake of artists and the public generally. Looking back, I can identify several major issues that motivated my research.

The arts are an arena of struggle. I defined the arts as 'specific forms of communication' but they are neutral in terms of their content or the aesthetic value that might be attributed to them. They include all forms of graphic design, architecture, fashion, the audiovisual facets of advertisements, ritual music, Japanese animations, Indian ragas and computer games that may be full of violence. And, of course, poetry. Having said this, we can observe that in most contemporary societies artistic expressions give rise to different responses. This may be very mild: what you like is not my cup of tea. At the other extreme is the killing of artists because of what they express. So, this neutral, inclusive concept can give rise to social unease and even great conflict.

The reality is that artists, the public and critics never operate in a neutral, innocent environment. No work of art or entertainment is just fun, or just beautiful. Every artist takes sides within a broad range of choices. Why is one musical work with a certain tonality considered better or more acceptable than another? Once the work of art has been created or performed it places itself within a certain historical, social or cultural context, or the people affected by it situate it in this way. The work is always imbued with a particular ideology, which is mostly not explicit. It belongs to a stream of feeling, thinking and doing; and this is due to its artistic kernel, or to the ambience in which it functions, or both.

This has consequences for artists. They may think that what they are creating or performing simply emerges from within themselves, as if divinely inspired: in other words that creativity is an uncontrolled and uncontrollable process. But this is only partly true. At the end of the day what they make public is their choice. They choose the kind of influences they admit into their thinking. They choose the surroundings they live in, the activities they engage in and their vision of human beings and society. Many of these choices are not made entirely consciously, it is true, but they could make other choices. Artists and their work should not be a mystery.

No work of art is neutral in its effects. This means that artists have a responsibility for what they produce. So, too, do intermediaries who 'transmit' the works of artists to audiences or readers. What effects or atmosphere are they aiming for? Do they want to contribute something beautiful or deliberately ugly? How do they name what they present to the public? Are there ethical boundaries that they decline to cross? Although the public may forget that these kinds of questions are relevant to them, they are undeniably real. When the world is fuller than ever before of music, images and texts, the moral question is neither easy nor popular.

Therefore we desperately need critics who have both the courage and the capacity to analyse works of art. What is behind the seductive power that certain cultural products exert? However fascinating or seductive, a work of art is not an open book; it should be subject to critical and public debate. Or will this task be left to the marketing departments of cultural enterprises?

The present neoliberal world order favours the concentration of cultural industries in huge conglomerates. These have enormous production capacities, but even more important is their oligopolistic control over most of the channels of distribution and promotion of artistic creations, or what they call entertainment. It is not mass culture that they put on the market, but cultural products that are produced, distributed and promoted on a mass scale. For their operations to be as profitable as possible, mass audiences throughout the world have to buy the book, watch the programme and buy the spin-offs.

The product is no longer just a film or a book or a CD, but all of this, plus games and additional merchandising. Because of the systematic efforts to seduce clients, which sometimes fail, it becomes more and more difficult for other artistic creations and performances, produced, distributed and promoted on a smaller scale, to reach audiences. The cultural conglomerates swallow up public attention. This clearly militates against the cultural diversity that is so greatly needed.

At the same time, the conglomerates buy as many intellectual property rights as possible in the cultural field. It is important for them to control the pipelines of distribution but equally important to own the huge stocks of 'content', without which the pipelines have little monetary value. Content is king, and this kingdom is what the conglomerates get by owning copyright on millions of melodies, texts and images from all over the world.

For several reasons this is deplorable. It privatizes the public domain of creativity and knowledge, which should be the common stock for the development of future creations. Private owners are the ones to decide what is created and performed, and at what price. At any moment they can claim that a new work has been based on a fragment of a work they own. Intellectual property rights freeze our cultures. The octopus-like character of copyright denies artists the right to adapt other artists' work freely, which in the past happened in all cultures. It is not true that artists will no longer create if copyright, which did not exist until a couple of centuries ago, ceases to exist. Most artists today do not expect to earn anything from copyright. The copyright system, like the system of patents, is disadvantageous to Third World countries. It places substantial parts of their collective heritage of creativity and knowledge in the hands of Western enterprises, without even giving the artists fair remuneration. In the digital domain artists are doing what Bach, Shakespeare and thousands of artists in all cultures have always done: they draw on parts of the work of other artists for their new creations, which in our present copyright system is strictly forbidden. Originality   which is the philosophical justification given for the system of copyright – is a doubtful concept. Most of what artists use originates from the public domain. This fact will remain unrecognized as long as rights holders continue to have monopolistic control over artistic material for decades.

It would therefore be best to abolish the present copyright system. It might just disappear of its own accord as a result of the increasingly sophisticated communication and exchange going on digitally between users of the more sophisticated peer-to-peer (P2P) follow-ups of Napster. How then would artists, in rich and poor countries alike, make an income? If the copyright system no longer existed, everybody could feel free to adapt – to a greater or lesser extent – any artistic creations, even those in the possession of the cultural industries. This would have two consequences. It would make it less attractive to conglomerates to invest heavily in blockbuster products and the associated gadgetry. The extent of their control would diminish substantially, which would give many more artists the space and opportunity to reach a diverse public again and earn reasonable money, instead of being pushed out of the cultural market. And it would result in completely new creative dynamics. Artists could adapt or improvise on any work of art or entertainment without being summonsed to appear in court. It then becomes important to reintroduce the concept of respect: what use made of works of art is respectful, and what is disrespectful?

From the democratic perspective it is axiomatic that cultural diversity must be allowed to develop. Many voices should have the right to be heard, and people should have the chance to be confronted with different kinds of images, theatrical imaginations, literary texts and musical landscapes. Not only is this diversity crucial; it is also important to ensure that it is generally accepted and that people will develop intercultural competence.

Cultural diversity and intercultural competence are values that do not exist automatically. Some protection is needed. In a world where the mass scale dominates, effort and care are needed so that very many different producers, distributors and promoters of artistic creations and performances can survive economically. What can be done? For a start, within any one country, cultural products from abroad should not have a market share greater than 25 per cent. The situation allowing one conglomerate to 'own' several different cultural media must be ended. If necessary, and for the time being, quota systems could help the undisturbed development of cultural diversity in local areas. The stronger the market position of a cultural industry, the more public obligations it should have; for instance, to ensure that existing cultural diversity has enough outlets. In the context of the WTO's current policies, individual countries have less and less right to protect their culture from the devastating effect of market forces. Therefore, all countries should actively contribute to creating and bringing into effect an International Convention on Cultural Diversity, which would give them the right to take those measures they think necessary for the development of cultural diversity in their part of the world.

This means that national governments should be encouraged to take seriously the task of formulating and implementing cultural policies. The examples I have mentioned make clear that cultural policy entails forging the conditions in which cultural diversity can flourish, including making regulations to dismantle all forms of market domination; and these should be stricter than bodies such as the British Office of Fair Trading would apply to other economic sectors. In such a vulnerable area as artistic creation, production and distribution, a market position of 15–20 per cent by one conglomerate already spells danger to the project of ensuring that many voices are heard. Moreover, for as long as the cultural environment remains precarious, national, regional and local authorities should support diverse artistic initiatives by providing finance (through subsidies, for example) and addressing logistical and infrastructural problems so that artists can communicate their work to as wide a public as possible.

Public authorities should avoid the temptation to intervene in artistic choices and processes. Measures to protect artists and their work from dominant market forces in the cultural field should not result in new forms of restriction. Cultural policy should find a balance between protection and allowing the arts to develop in complete freedom. The authorities need to wait and see what artists create, and celebrate any exceptional work that emerges (something that will not happen every day).

We are witnessing a battle over the digitizing of cultural processes. This may be happening a little more slowly than it seemed to be in the late 1990s, but it will continue, and it is a fascinating struggle. For artists, the internet represents a great opportunity to claw back some of the immense power that, for instance, the record companies have exercised over the last fifty years. Independent film-makers, too, can make high-quality films relatively cheaply. Directors have more flexibility, are less afflicted by the heavy burden of technological conditions and are more able to concentrate on interaction with actors. Artists can organize the distribution of their own work on the internet without being dependent on intermediaries like record companies. This trend may mean that the idea of the 'superstars' becomes outdated. Some artists, liberated from the pressure of studios or laboratories, may gain control over the further treatment or 'elaboration' of their work. The character of many works of art may change, depending on the way interactivity develops. Artists might conceivably offer landscapes of images, sounds and texts to private individuals in their homes via internet subscriptions. A concert of electronic music is often dull to watch. This changes radically when musicians are able to intervene on stage in the tape they have prepared; the composer becomes a performer who can use sensors to manipulate his or her composition. Artificial distinctions between so-called 'high' and 'low' culture may become less important or disappear altogether.

In his article 'Napster Gives Musicians a Chance to be Heard' (*International Herald Tribune*, 1 August 2000), Philip Kennicott makes the point that a century ago music that was shared by millions of listeners was an inseparable part of daily life and could immediately establish a bond between strangers. This would have been called folk music. 'The very notion of possessing it, of controlling who could hear it and exchange it, of making profit from it, would have been ridiculous.' He argues that with Napster, Freenet, Gnutella, Morpheus and other comparable systems that allow exchange of music, this fundamentally collective idea of folk music may have come back. 'This gives musicians the chance to be heard, promote their concerts and make a living from their work. Because, after all, the vast majority of working musicians belong not to the world of celebrity but to the world of unions, work shifts and the struggle for decent health benefits.' They stand to gain more from the publicity power of the internet than they would lose from programs like Napster. And, 'people don't, by nature, enjoy ripping off artists. Most of us are happy to pay to see a play or a live performance.'

This affects artists, whose interests are no longer served by remaining in a coalition with the cultural industries in order to defend the concept of copy-right. There is another sense in which we should revise our ideas about the benefits that cultural conglomerates purport to give us, Philip Kennicott claims (and although he refers to Americans, his argument can be applied to people throughout the world):

Americans make the mistake of equating a particular kind of popular culture – the big-splash stuff promoted by corporate America – with 'American' culture, as if blockbuster movies and million-selling albums present a whole and coherent account of creative life in America. It's tempting to believe that widely shared entertainment products are the cultural glue that holds people together. But that kind of popular culture is very different from what was once known as folk culture. The difference is simple: Corporate America owns popular culture. Nobody owns folk culture. Napster threatened to erase the distinction.

With Napster, there was the possibility of short-circuiting the entire commercial process, he observes. 'Napster didn't threaten music, music making or musicians. It merely threatened one very specific kind of cultural production: the mass musical object. We have placed far too much emphasis on these objects, allowing them to stand in for culture itself.'

Isn't it absurd that there are enormous numbers of people all over the world who write, make music, make movies, perform, paint, dance – as professional artists or amateurs or somewhere in between – but that all their creativity and craftsmanship are denied a role of any significance in public life?

Isn't it absurd that oligopolistic corporations pretend that they and they alone can satisfy people's every need in the artistic domain, whether through dance, theatre, music, film, literature, the visual arts or mixed media?

Isn't it absurd that we allow huge cultural conglomerates to take over the shaping of our cultures, and the formation of our individual and collective identities; that we subject ourselves to all the conflicts and awkward and painful situations belonging to those cultural processes? Digitization and the internet can help change this, reduce the power of cultural enterprises and give ample space to hundreds of thousands of artists all over the world and their publics.

Freedom – which is as important as protection – is a more complicated concept than many people would like to believe it is. In the Western world freedom tends to be regarded as an absolute, even more in the United States than in Europe. The First Amendment of the American Constitution places hardly any restrictions on the right to free expression.

There are good reasons for not considering freedom of expression an absolute good that supersedes all other values. It is equally important to respect the feelings and beliefs of other people, not to threaten them with words and not to incite them to hatred or murder. Of course, in the arts, things can be said that otherwise would remain unspoken. For the development of democracy and a vibrant society this is an important stimulant, and it is desirable that artists exercise this freedom. They should feel not over-responsible or afraid to break social, cultural and economic taboos. On the other hand, they should be extremely responsible, because their expressions are more penetrating than many other forms of communication, certainly when the artistic work has aesthetic force. To play with violence is not an innocent affair. To make loud music in public places may harm or offend many people. To use images that are extremely important to some people in disrespectful ways may cause pain and suffering. The question should always be posed: is it necessary? Before arguments are brought to court, with consequent bitter fighting, it would be wise if certain people in society could mediate, to try to heal the wounds and lessen despair, hatred and misunderstanding. One thing is sure: in modern societies there will sometimes be conflicts about the right of free expression versus the perceived need to exercise restraint. Another thing is sure too: that no society in the contemporary world is without serious problems. So there is reason enough to learn how to deal with both aspects of the argument so that freedom of expression is complemented by respect for other values.

Clearly, the debate about freedom of expression in relation to the internet has only just begun. There has been a great deal of mystification about this 'virtual' place which purportedly allows democracy to flourish through free and unhampered debate. We know now that things are more complex than this. The internet is not a virtual place. It is a hard material world, where a lot of money goes around, where the gadgetry is extremely material and where very real interests are at stake. It is another space for communication, but it has new characteristics. There is no reason, however, to think that the rules and laws valued in the 'outside' world should not be applicable to this new digital territory. They should be applied in appropriate ways; and what is appropriate and effective should be the core of the discussion. Otherwise, it will be the secret services that develop the rules governing this territory.

In many non-Western parts of the world, freedom of expression, as formulated in the Universal Declaration of Human Rights, is less self-evident than people would like to believe. In the Arab world, Asia and Africa, many different views exist about human rights, and it is the concept of individual human rights that is most contentious. It is also the lack of social and collective rights that many people miss in the Western approach. With a certain arrogance, most leading forces in the Western hemisphere disregard or reject the observations made by others concerning human rights and – important in the context of our discussion – concerning freedom of expression and communication. This is a missed opportunity.

The right to communicate freely also has far-reaching economic consequences. According to the Universal Declaration on Human Rights, everybody has the right to express their feelings and ideas freely and to communicate them. The logical consequence of this would be that the conditions must exist to enable everybody to exercise this right. However, by equating this cultural right with the economic freedom nearly to monopolize the channels of communication worldwide, a strange situation has been created. This economic freedom gives a limited number of cultural conglomerates decisive power over what can be expressed, heard, read or watched. Such a dominant economic position is against the intentions of the Universal Declaration on Human Rights. Thus, freedom of expression for everybody is an additional reason to restrict substantially the size and power of the cultural industries worldwide.

I began by saying that this was a book about the arts. Now the work has been done, I discover that something has remained undone during the years of research and writing. So now it is time to play the flute again because this is what I have forgotten to do for a long time!

Bibliography

Aageson, Thomas H. (1999) 'Indigenous Artisans and Sustainable Development in Latin America and the Caribbean', Keynote Address, Second OAS/World Bank Working Meeting on Cultural Heritage Partnership, 16 February 1999.

Abah, Oga S. (1994) 'Perspectives in Popular Theatre: Orality as a Definition of New Realitics', in Breitinger 1994: 79–100.

Abbasi, M. Yusuf (1992) *Pakistani Culture. A Profile* (Islamabad: National Institute of Historical and Cultural Research).

Adeleye-Fayemi, Bisi (1997) 'Either One or the Other. Images of Women in Nigerian Television', in Barber 1997: 125–31.

Ajami, Fouad (1999) *The Dream Palace of the Arabs. A Generation's Odyssey* (New York: Vintage Books).

Amaral, Roberto and Cesar Guimarães (1994) 'Media Monopoly in Brazil', *Journal of Communication*, 44 (4), Autumn: 26–38.

Amin, Samir (1997) *Capitalism in the Age of Globalization* (London and New Jersey: Zed Books).

Andersen, Robin (1995) *Consumer Culture & TV Programming* (Boulder, CO: Westview Press).

Anderson, Sarah and John Cavanagh, with Thea Lee (2000) *Field Guide to the Global Economy* (New York: New Press).

Ariès, Paul (2002) *Disneyland. Le Royaume Désenchanté* (Villeurbanne: Editions Golias).

Armbrust, Walter (ed.) (2000) *Mass Mediations. New Approaches to Popular Culture in the Middle East and Beyond* (Berkeley: University of California Press).

Ashcroft, Bill, Gareth Griffiths and Helen Tiffin (1989) *The Empire Writes Back. Theory and Practice in Post-Colonial Literatures* (London: Routledge).

Attali, Jacques (2001) *Bruits. Essai sur l'économie politique de la musique* (Paris: Fayard/PUF).

Aufderheide, Patricia (1997) 'Telecommunications and the Public Interest', in Barnouw et al. 1997: 157–72.

Baddeley, Oriana and Valerie Fraser (1989) *Drawing the Line. Art and Cultural Identity in Contemporary Latin America* (London and New York: Verso).

Balanyá, Belén, Ann Doherty, Olivier Hoedeman, Adam Ma'anit and Erik Wesselius (2000) *Europe Inc. Regional & Global Restructuring and the Rise of Corporate Power* (London: Pluto Press).

Banks, Jack (1996) *Monopoly Television. MTV's Quest to Control the Music* (Boulder, CO: Westview Press).

Baran, Nicholas (1998) *The Privatization of Telecommunication*, in McChesney et al. 1998: 123–33.

Barber, Benjamin R. (1996) *Jihad vs. McWorld* (New York: Ballantine Books).

Barber, Karen (ed.) (1997) *Readings in African Popular Culture* (Bloomington and Indianapolis and Oxford: Indiana University Press and James Currey).

Barber, Karen, John Collins and Alain Ricard (1997) *West African Popular Culture* (Bloomington and Indianapolis and Oxford: Indiana University Press and James Currey).

Barlet, Olivier (1996) *Les cinémas d'Afrique noire. Le regard en question* (Paris: l'Harmattan).

Barnet, Richard J. and John Cavanagh (1994) *Global Dreams. Imperial Corporations and the New World Order* (New York: Simon and Schuster).

Barnouw, Erik et al. (1997) *Conglomerates and the Media* (New York: New Press).

Barrett, James (1996) 'World Music, Nation and Postcolonialism', *Cultural Studies*, 10 (2): 237–47.

Barthes, Roland (1968) 'La mort de l'auteur', *Manteia*, 5 (4); see also Barthes, *Oeuvres complètes*, *Vol. II, 1966–1973* (Paris: Editions du Seuil, 1994): 491–5.

Baud, Pierre-Alain (1995) *La danse au Mexique. Art et pouvoir* (Paris: l'Harmattan).

Baumann, Max Peter (ed.) (1996) *Cosmología y Música en los Andes* (Frankfurt am Main and Madrid: International Institute for Traditional Music and Iberoamericana).

Behrens-Abouseif, Doris (1999) *Beauty in Arabic Culture* (Princeton, NJ: Markus Wiener).

Bello, Walden (1994) *Dark Victory. The United States, Structural Adjustment and Global Poverty* (Penang: Third World Network).

— (2002) *Deglobalization. Ideas for a New World Economy* (London: Zed Books).

Bello, Walden, Nicola Bullard and Kamal Malhotra (2000) *Global Finance. New Thinking on Regulating Speculative Capital Markets* (Dhaka, London and New York: New York University Press and Zed Books).

Bender, Wolfgang (1992) *La musique africaine contemporaine. Sweet mother* (Paris: l'Harmattan).

— (1994) 'Das Nigerphone Lanel – Afrikanische Musik braucht keine Hilfe', in Anna-Maria Brandstetter (ed.), *Afrika hilft sich selbst* (Münster-Hamburg: LIT Verlag).

Benghozi, Pierre-Jean (1989) *Le cinéma: entre l'art et l'argent* (Paris: l'Harmattan).

Benjamin, Walter (1963) *Das Kunstwerk im Zeitalter seiner technischen Reproduzierbarkeit* (1936) (Frankfurt am Main: Suhrkamp).

Bernier, Ivan (2001) 'A New International Instrument on Cultural Diversity', Paper presented at the second conference of the International Network for Cultural Diversity, Lucerne, Switzerland, 21–23 September.

Berry, Wendell (1986) *The Unsettling of America. Culture & Agriculture* (San Francisco, CA: Sierra Club Books).

Bettig, Ronald V. (1996) *Copyrighting Culture. The Political Economy of Intellectual Property* (Boulder, CO: Westview Press).

Bhabha, Homi K. (1994) *The Location of Culture* (London and New York: Routledge).

Bharucha, Rustom (1993) *Theatre and the World. Performance and the Politics of Culture* (London and New York: Routledge).

— (1998) *In the Name of the Secular. Contemporary Cultural Activism in India* (Delhi: Oxford University Press).

— (2000) *The Politics of Cultural Practice. Thinking Through Theatre in an Age of Globalization* (London: Athlone Press).

Bogart, Leo (1994) 'Consumer Games', *Index on Censorship*, 23, September–October: 17.

Bolton, Richard (1998) 'Enlightened Self-Interest: The Avant-Garde in the 1980s', in Kester 1998: 23–50.

Bombote, Diomansi (1994) 'Hard Times for African Artists', *Copyright Bulletin*, XXVIII (4): 24–8.

Bontinck, Irmgard and Alfred Smudits (1997) *Music and Globalization*, Final Report prepared for the Annual Report of World Culture and Development of Unesco, Vienna, July.

Bové, José and François Dufour (2000) *Le monde n'est pas une marchandise. Des paysans contre le malbouffe. Entretiens avec Gilles Luneau* (Paris: La Découverte).

Boyle, James (1996) *Shamans, Software, and Spleens. Law and the Construction of the Information Society* (Cambridge, MA and London: Harvard University Press).

Brabec, Jeffrey and Todd (1994) *Music, Money and Success. The Insider's Guide to the Music Industry* (New York: Schirmer Books).

Brandon, James R. (ed.) (1997) *The Cambridge Guide to Asian Theatre* (Cambridge: Cambridge University Press).

Brecher, Jeremy and Tim Costello (1994) *Global Village or Global Pillage. Economic Reconstruction from the Bottom Up* (Boston, MA: South End Press).

Breitinger, Echhard (1994) *Theatre and Performance in Africa: Intercultural Perspectives* (Bayreuth: Bayreuth African Studies Series).

— (ed.) (1999) *Uganda: The Cultural Landscape* (Bayreuth and Kampala: Bayreuth African Studies 39 and Fountain Publishers).

Brown, Mary Ellen (1994) *Soap Opera and Women's Talk. The Pleasure of Resistance* (Thousand Oaks, CA, London and New Delhi: Sage Publications).

Brünner, José Joaquin (1998) *Globalización cultural y postmodernidad* (Santiago: Fondo de Cultura Económica).

Brünner, José Joaquin and Carlos Catalan (1995) *Televisión. Libertad, mercado y moral* (Santiago: Editorial Los Andes).

Burnett, Robert (1996) *The Global Jukebox. The International Music Industry* (London and New York: Routledge).

Castells, Manuel (1996) *The Information Age: Economy, Society and Culture. Volume I: The Rise of the Network Society* (Malden: Blackwell).

— (1997) *The Information Age: Economy, Society and Culture. Volume II: The Power of Identity* (Malden: Blackwell).

— (1998) *The Information Age: Economy, Society and Culture. Volume III: End of Millennium* (Malden: Blackwell).

— (2001) *The Internet Galaxy. Reflections on the Internet, Business, and Society* (Oxford: Oxford University Press).

Caughie, John (ed.) (1996) *Theories of Authorship* (London: Routledge).

Cavanagh, John, Daphne Wysham and Marcus Arruda (eds) (1994) *Beyond Bretton Woods. Alternatives to the Global Economic Order* (London and Boulder, CO: Pluto Press).

Chabal, Patrick (ed.) (1996) *The Postcolonial Literature of Lisophone Africa* (London: Hurst & Co.).

Chen, Kuan-Hsing (ed.) (1998) *Trajectories. Inter-Asian Cultural Studies* (London: Routledge).

Ching, Leo (1996) 'Imaginings in the Empire of the Sun. Japanese Mass Culture in Asia', in Whittier Treat 1996: 169–94.

Chin-tao Wu (2002) *Privatising Culture. Corporate Intervention since the 1980s* (London: Verso).

Chomsky, Noam (1993a) 'Notes on Nafta', in Dawkins 1993: 1–6.

— (1998) *Common Good. Interviews by David Barsamian* (Chicago, IL: Odonian Press).

Clark, Tony (1995) 'Dismantling Corporate Rule. Towards a New Forum of Politics in an Age of Globalization', San Francisco (a set of working Instruments for Social Movements, prepared on behalf of the International Forum of Globalization; working draft).

Clarke, Tony, and Maude Barlow (1997) *MAI. The Multilateral Agreement on Investment and the Threat to Canadian Sovereignty* (Toronto: Stoddart).

Cliche, Danielle, Ritva Mitchell and Andreas Wiesand, 'Creative Artists, Market Developments and State Policies', Background Paper for EU Presidency conference, Conditions for Creative Artists in Europe, Visvy, Sweden, 30 March–1 April 2001 (Bonn: ERICArts).

Cohen Jehoram, Herman, Petra Keuchenius and Lisa M. Brownlee (eds) (1996) *Trade-Related Aspects of Copyright* (Deventer: Kluwer).

Collins, John (1993) 'The Problem of Oral Copyright – the Case of Ghana', in Frith 1993: 146–58.

Coombe, Rosemary J. (1998) *The Cultural Life of Intellectual Properties. Authorship, Appropriation, and the Law* (Durham, NC and London: Duke University Press).

Correa, Carlos M. (2000) *Intellectual Property Rights, the WTO and Developing Countries. The TRIPS Agreement and Policy Options* (London and Penang: Zed Books and Third World Network).

Crispin Miller, Marc (1997) *The Publishing Industry*, in Barnouw et al. 1997: 107–33.

Daly, Herman (1994a) 'Farewell Lecture to the World Bank', in Cavanagh 1994: 109–17.

Daly, Herman E. and John B. Cobb Jr (1994) *For the Common Good. Redirecting the Economy Toward Community, the Environment, and a Sustainable Future* (Boston, MA: Beacon Press).

Daoudi, Bouziane and Hadj Miliani (1996) *L'aventure du raï. Musique et société* (Paris: Éditions du Seuil).

Davies, Lucy and Mo Fini (1994) *Arts and Crafts of South America* (London: Thames and Hudson).

Dawkins, Kristin (1993) *Nafta. The New Rules of Corporate Conquest* (Westfield, NJ: Open Magazine, Pamphlet Series).

Delmas, Benoît and Eric Mahé (2002) *Bal tragique chez Vivendi. La chute de la maison Messier* (Paris: Editions Denoël).

Derrida, Jacques (1993) *Spectres de Marx. L'État de la dette, le travail du deuil et la nouvelle Internationale* (Paris: Galilée).

Diamond, Catherine (2000) 'Burmese Nights: the Pagoda Festival Pwe in the Age of Hollywood's "Titanic"', Paper presented at the conference Audiences, Patrons and Performers in the Performing Arts of Asia, Leiden University, 23–27 August.

Diawara, Manthia (1992) *African Cinema. Politics & Culture* (Bloomington and Indianapolis: Indiana University Press).

Dolfsma, Wilfred (1999) 'How Will Music Industry Weather the Globalization Storm', Paper presented at the AFEE/AEA meetings, New York, January.

Dorfman, Ariel (1991) *Some Write to the Future. Essays on Contemporary Latin American Fiction* (Durham, NC and London: Duke University Press).

Douzinas, Costas (2000) *The End of Human Rights* (Oxford: Hart Publishing).

Doy, Gen (2000) *Black Visual Culture. Modernity and Postmodernity* (London: I.B. Tauris).

Doyle, Gillian (2002) *Media Ownership* (London: Sage Publications).

Duvignaud, Jean and Chérif Khaznadar (1995) *La musique et le monde* (Paris: Babel and Maison des cultures du monde).

Dwyer, Rachel (2000) *All You Want is Money, All You Need is Love. Sex and Romance in Modern India* (London and New York: Cassell).

Eagleton, Terry (1990) *The Ideology of the Aesthetic* (Oxford: Blackwell).

— (1997) *The Illusions of Postmodernism* (Oxford: Blackwell).

Edelman, Murray (1995) *From Art to Politics. How Artistic Creations Shape Political Conceptions* (Chicago, IL and London: University of Chicago Press).

Eliot, Marc (1993) *Rockonomics. The Money Behind the Music* (New York: Citadel Press).

Ellwood, David W. (1994) 'Introduction. Historical Methods and Approaches', in Ellwood and Kroes 1994: 2–18.

Ellwood, David W. and Rob Kroes (eds) (1994) *Hollywood in Europe. Experiences of a Cultural Hegemony* (Amsterdam: VU University Press).

Enzensberger, H. M. (1993) *Aussichten auf den Bürgerkrieg* (Frankfurt am Main: Suhrkamp).

Epskamp, Kees (1989) *Theatre in Search of Social Change. The Relative Significance of Different Theatrical Approaches* (The Hague: CESO).

Eudes, Yves (1982) *La conquête des esprits: L'appareil d'exportation culturelle américain* (Paris: François Maspero).

— (1989) 'La société Disney, un modèle de "communication totale"', in *La communication victime des marchands. Affairisme, information et culture des masse*, Preface by Claude Julien (Paris: La Découverte and Le Monde): 252–72.

Faludi, Susan (1991) *Backlash: The Undeclared War Against American Women* (New York: Doubleday).

Farchy, Joëlle (1999) *La fin de l'exception culturelle?* (Paris: CNRS Editions).

Featherstone, Mike (1991) *Consumer Culture & Postmodernism* (London, Newbury Park, NJ and New Delhi: Sage Publications).

Featherstone, Mike and Roger Burrows (eds) (1995) *Cyberspace/Cyberbodies/Cyberpunk. Cultures of Technological Embodiment* (London: Routledge).

Feld, Steven (1995) 'From Schizophonia to Schismogenesis. The Discourses and Practices of World Music and World Beat', in Marcus and Myers 1995: 96–126.

Fiske, John (1987) *Television Culture* (London: Methuen)

Fjellman, Stephen M. (1992) *Vinyl Leaves: Walt Disney and America* (Boulder, CO: Westview Press).

Flandrin, Philippe (2001) *Le trésor perdu des rois d'Afghanistan* (Monaco: Ed. du Rocher).

Fox, Elizabeth (1994) 'Communication Media in Latin America', *Journal of Communication*, 44 (4), Autumn.

French, Marilyn (1993) *The War Against Women* (London: Penguin Books).

Frith, Simon (1989) (ed.) *World Music, Politics and Social Change* (Manchester: Manchester University Press).

— (ed.) (1993) *Music and Copyright* (Edinburgh: Edinburgh University Press).

— (1996) *Performing Rites. On the Value of Popular Music* (Oxford: Oxford University Press).

Frith, Simon and Andrew Goodwin (eds) (1990) *On Record. Rock, Pop, and the Written Word* (New York: Pantheon Books).

Frow, John (1996) 'Information as Gift and Commodity', *New Left Review*, 219: 89–108.

Fuller, Peter (1988) 'The Search for a Postmodern Aesthetic', in Thackara 1988: 117–34.

Gablik, Suzi (1985) *Has Modernism Failed?* (London and New York: Thames and Hudson).

García Canclini, Néstor (1995) *Culturas híbridas. Estrategias para entrar y salir de la modernidad* (Buenos Aires: Editorial Sudamericana).

— (ed.) (1996) *Culturas en Globalización. América Latina – Europa – Estados Unidos: libro comercio e integración* (Caracas: Editorial Sociedad and Clacso).

Garretón, Manuel Antonio (ed.) (1993) *Cultura, autoritarismo y redemocratización en Chile*, México (Fondo de Cultura Económica).

George, Susan (1994) *Faith and Credit. The World Bank's Secular Empire* (London: Penguin Books).

Gerbner, George (1997) 'Marketing Mayhem Globally', in Servaes and Lie 1997: 13–17.

Gerbner, George, Hamid Mowlana and Kaarle Nordenstreng (1993) *The Global Media Debate: Its Rise, Fall, and Renewal* (Norwood, NJ: Ablex Publishing).

Ginneken, Jaap (1996) *De schepping van de wereld in het nieuws. De 101 vertekeningen die elk 1 procent verschil maken* (Houten: Bohn Stafleu Van Loghum).

— (1998) *Understanding Global News* (London: Sage Publications).

Gitlin, Todd (1997) 'Introduction', in Barnouw et al. 1997: 7–13.

Gray, John (1998) *False Dawn. The Delusions of Global Capitalism* (London: Granta Books).

Greenberg, Reesa (ed.) (1996) *Thinking About Exhibitions* (London and New York: Routledge).

Greenhalgh, Liz and Ken Worpole (with Charles Landry) (1995) *Libraries in a World of Cultural Change* (London: Comedia).

Groebel, Jo (1998) *The Unesco Global Study on Media Violence* (Paris: Unesco).

Gründ, Françoise (1995) 'La musique et le monde', in Duvignaud and Khaznadar 1995: 9–11.

Gupta, Nilanjana (1998) *Switching Channels. Ideologies of Television in India* (Delhi: Oxford University Press).

Gürsel, Nedim (1993) *Paysage littéraire de la Turquie contemporaine* (Paris: l'Harmattan).

Hamelink, Cees (1978) *De mythe van de vrije informatie* (Baarn: Anthos).

— (1994a) *Trends in World Communication. On Disempowerment and Self-empowerment* (Penang: Southbound and Third World Network).

— (1994b) *The Politics of World Communication* (London: Sage Publications).

— (1999) *Digitaal fatsoen. Mensenrechten in cyberspace* (Amsterdam: Boom).

Hannerz, Ulf (1990) 'Cosmopolitans and Locals in World Culture', *Theory, Culture & Society* (on Global Culture), 7 (2–3): 237–51.

Hardt, Michael and Antonio Negri (2000) *Empire* (Cambridge, MA and London: Harvard University Press).

Hellman, Jörgen (2000) 'Revitalisation of Traditional Longser: Blurring the Genres', Paper presented at the conference Audiences, Patrons and Performers in the Performing Arts of Asia, Leiden University, 23–27 August.

Herman, Edward S. (1989) 'U.S. Mass Media Coverage of the U.S. Withdrawal from Unesco', in Preston et al. 1989: 203–84.

Herman, Edward S. and Robert W. McChesney (1997) *The Global Media. The New Missionaries of Global Capitalism* (London and Washington, DC: Cassell).

Herz, J. C. (1997) *Joystick Nation. How Videogames Ate Our Quarters, Won Our Hearts, and Rewired Our Minds* (Boston, MA: Little, Brown and Company).

Hetata, Sherif (1998) 'Dollarization, Fragmentation, and God', in Jameson and Miyoshi 1998: 273–90.

Hewison, Robert (1990) *Future Tense. A New Art for the Nineties* (London: Methuen).

Hines, Colin (2000) *Localization. A Global Manifesto* (London: Earthscan).

Hird, Christopher (1994) 'Media: Murdoch', *Index on Censorship*, 23, September–October: 27–35.

Hoffmann, Hilmar (ed.) (1999) *Das Guggenheim Prinzip* (Cologne: Dumont)

Hollick, Clive (1994) 'Media: Regulation', *Index on Censorship*, 23, September–October: 54–8.

Holt, John (1996) '"Trampled Surface": Six Artists from Pakistan', *Third Text*, 36, autumn: 87–90.

Holtwijk, Ineke (1996) *Kannibalen in Rio. Impressies uit Brazilië* (Amsterdam: Prometheus).

Hooker, Virginia Matheson (ed.) (1993) *Culture and Society in Indonesia* (Kuala Lumpur: Oxford University Press).

hooks, bell (1994) *Outlaw Culture. Resisting Representations* (New York and London: Routledge).

Human Development Report (1999) (New York and Oxford: Oxford University Press).

Huot, Claire (2000) *China's New Cultural Scene. A Handbook of Changes* (Durham, NC and London: Duke University Press).

Hutton, Will (1996) *The State We're in* (London: Vintage).

— (2002) *The World We're in* (London: Little, Brown).

Jacobsen, Michael and Ole Bruun (2000) *Human Rights and Asian Values. Contesting National Identities and Cultural Representations in Asia* (Richmond, Surrey: Curzon).

Jameson, Fredric (1992) *Postmodernism, or the Cultural Logic of Late Capitalism* (Durham, NC: Duke University Press).

— (1998) 'Notes on Globalization as a Philosophical Issue', in Jameson and Miyoshi 1998: 54–77.

Jameson, Fredric, and Masao Miyoshi (eds) (1998) *The Cultures of Globalization* (Durham, NC and London: Duke University Press).

Kasfir, Sidney Littlefield (1999) *Contemporary African Art* (London: Thames & Hudson).

Kester, Grant H. (ed.) (1998) *Art, Activism & Oppositionality. Essays from Afterimage* (Durham, NC and London: Duke University Press).

Khayati, Khémais (1996) *Cinémas arabes. Topographie d'une image éclatée* (Paris: l'Harmattan).

Klein, Naomi (2000) *No Logo. No Space, No Choice, No Jobs* (London: Flamingo).

Klein, Ulrike (1993) *Der Kunstmarkt* (Frankfurt am Main: Peter Lang).

Korten, David (1995) *When Corporations Rule the World* (San Francisco, CA: Kumarian Press and Berrett-Koehler Publishers).

Kretschmer, Martin (1992) *Intellectual Property in Music. A Historical Analysis of Rhetoric and Institutional Practices*, unpublished paper, City University Business School, London.

— (1999) 'Intellectual Property in Music: A Historical Analysis of Rhetoric and Institutional

Practices', special issue Cultural Industry (ed. P. Jeffcutt), *Studies in Cultures, Organizations and Societies*, 6: 197–223.

Kroes, Rob (1992) *De leegte van Amerika. Massacultuur in de wereld* (Amsterdam: Prometheus).

Labaki, Aimar (1999) 'Cinco Instantâneos de la Cultura Brasileira/La culture brésilienne: cinq instantanées', *Teatro del Sur/Revista Latinoamericana*, 10, May.

Lamy, Pascal (2002) *L'Europe en premier ligne* (Paris: Seuil).

Lang, Tim and Colin Hines (1994) *The New Protectionism. Protecting the Future Against Free Trade* (London: Earthscan).

Larson, Charles R. (2001) *The Ordeal of the African Writer* (London and New York: Zed Books).

Leach, William (1993) *Land of Desire. Merchants, Power, and the Rise of a New American Culture* (New York: Vintage House).

Lent, John A. (ed.) (1995) *Asian Popular Culture* (Boulder, CO: Westview Press).

Liberty (1999) *Liberating Cyberspace. Civil Liberties, Human Rights and the Internet* (London: Pluto Press).

Lieberman, David (1997) 'Conglomerates, News, and Children', in Barnouw et al. 1997: 135–55.

Litman, Jessica (2001) *Digital Copyright* (Amherst, NY: Prometheus Books).

Louvel, Roland (1996) *L'Afrique noire et la différence culturelle* (Paris: l'Harmattan).

Lury, Celia (1993) *Cultural Rights. Technology, Legality and Personality* (London: Routledge).

Mackerras, Colin (2000) 'Power, Identity, Modernity and the Performing Arts Among Diasporas: Background Ideas from the Chinese Case', Paper presented at the conference Audiences, Patrons and Performers in the Performing Arts of Asia, Leiden University, 23–27 August.

McChesney, Robert W. (1997) *Corporate Media and the Threat to Democracy* (New York: Seven Stories Press).

—— (1998) *The Political Economy of Global Communication*, in McChesney et al. 1998: 1–26.

—— (1999) *Rich Media, Poor Democracy. Communication Politics in Dubious Times* (Urbana and Chicago: University of Illinois Press).

McChesney, Robert W., Ellen Meiksins and John Bellamy Foster (eds) (1998) *Capitalism and the Information Age. The Political Economy of the Global Communication Revolution* (New York: Monthly Review Press).

McPhail, Thomas L. (1981) *Electronic Colonialism: The Future of International Broadcasting and Communication* (Beverly Hills, CA and London: Sage Publications).

Malhotra, Sheena and Everett M. Rogers (2000) 'Satellite Television and the New India', *Gazette*, 62 (5), October: 407–29.

Malm, Krister (1998) 'Copyright and the Protection of Intellectual Property in Traditional Music', *Music, Media, Multiculture* (Stockholm: Musikaliska akademien).

Malm, Krister and Roger Wallis (1992) *Media Policy and Music Activity* (London and New York: Routledge).

Mander, Jerry (1992) *In the Absence of the Sacred. The Failure of Technology and the Survival of the Indian Nations* (San Francisco, CA: Sierra Club Books).

—— (1993) 'Metatechnology, Trade, and the New World Order', in Nader 1993: 13–22.

Manuel, Peter (1988) *Popular Musics of the Non-Western World. An Introductory Survey* (New York and Oxford: Oxford University Press).

— (1993) *Cassette Culture. Popular Music and Technology in North India* (Chicago, IL and London: University of Chicago Press).

Marcus, George E. and Fred R. Myers (eds) (1995) *The Traffic Culture. Refiguring Art and Anthropology* (Berkeley, CA: University of California Press).

Marsden, Christopher T. (ed.) (2000) *Regulating the Global Information Society* (London: Routledge).

Martín-Barbero, Jesús (1993a) *Communication, Culture and Hegemony. From the Media to Mediations* (London: Sage Publications).

— (1993b) 'Modernity, Nationalism, and Communication in Latin America', in Nordenstreng and Schiller 1993: 132–47.

Mazziotti, Nora (1996) *La industria de la telenovela. La producción de ficción en America latina* (Buenos Aires, Barcelona and México: Paidós).

Mediacult (2000) *Musik und Globalisierung* (Vienna: Mediacult).

Mewton, Conrad (2001) *Music & the Internet Revolution* (London: Sanctuary).

Meyer, Birgit (1999) 'Popular Ghanaian Cinema and "African Heritage"', *Africa Today*: 93–5.

— (2001) 'Money, Power and Morality: Popular Ghanaian Cinema in the Fourth Republic', *Ghana Studies*.

Mignolo, Walter D. (1998) 'Globalization, Civilization Processes, and the Relocation of Languages and Cultures', in Jameson and Miyoshi 1998: 32–53.

Mitsui, Tôru (1993) 'Copyright and Music in Japan. A Forced Grafting and Its Consequences', in Frith 1993: 125–45.

Miyoshi, Masao (1998) '"Globalization", Culture, and the University', in Jameson and Miyoshi 1998: 247–70.

Moeran, Brian (1989) *Language and Popular Culture in Japan* (Manchester and New York: Manchester University Press).

Morley, David and Kuan-Hsing Chen (1996) *Stuart Hall. Critical Dialogues in Cultural Studies* (London and New York: Routledge).

Morris, Nancy and Silvio Waisbord (eds) (2001) *Media and Globalization. Why the State Matters* (Oxford: Rowman and Littlefield).

Mosquera, Gerardo (ed.) (1995) *Beyond the Fantastic. Contemporary Art Criticism from Latin America* (London: Iniva, International Institute of Visual Arts).

Mostyn, Trevor (2002) *Censorship in Islamic Societies* (London: Saqi Books).

Moulin, Raymonde (1992) *L'artiste, l'institution et le marché* (Paris: Flammarion).

— (2000) *Le marché de l'art. Mondialisation et nouvelles technologies* (Paris: Flammarion).

Mowlana, Hamid (1993) 'New Global Order and Cultural Ecology', in Nordenstreng and Schiller 1993: 394–417.

— (1996) *Global Communication in Transition. The End of Diversity* (London: Sage Publications).

— (1997) *Global Information and World Communication* (London: Sage Publications).

Msiska, Mpalive-Hangson and Paul Hyland (eds) (1997) *Writing and Africa* (London and New York: Longman).

Mulder, Arjan and Maaike Post (2000) *Book for the Electronic Arts* (Amsterdam and Rotterdam: De Balie/V2).

Müller, Heiner (1991) *Jenseits der Nation. Heinrich Müller im interview mit Frank M. Raddatz* (Berlin: Rotbuch Verlag).

— (1994) *Gesammelte Irrtümer 3. Texte und Gespräche* (Frankfurt am Main: Verlag der Autoren).

Myers, Fred R. (1995) *Representing Culture. The Production of Discourse(s) for Aboriginal Acrylic Paintings*, in Marcus and Myers 1995: 55–95.

Nader, Ralph (ed.) (1993) *The Case Against Free Trade. GATT, NAFTA, and the Globalization of Corporate Power* (San Francisco and Berkeley, CA: Earth Island Press and North Atlantic Books).

Naresh, Suman (1996) 'How the idea of cultural exception is viewed around the world. The view from India', Paper presented at the conference Cultural Aspects in International Trade of Goods and Services: is There an Exception?, XVIIIe Réunion annuelle de l'Institut du droit et des practiques des affaires internationales, Paris, 6 December.

Neale, Steve and Murray Smith (1998) *Contemporary Hollywood Cinema* (London: Routledge).

Nederveen Pieterse, Jan (1994) 'Globalisation as Hybridisation', *International Sociology*, 9 (2), June: 161–84.

— (1995) 'Globalization and Culture: Three Paradigms', *Perspectives on International Studies*, Institute for International Studies, Meiji Gakuin University.

— (1997) 'Multiculturalism and Museums: Discourse About the Other in the Age of Globalization', *Theory, Culture & Society*, 14 (4): 123–46.

— (ed.) (2000) *Global Futures. Shaping Globalization* (London: Zed Books).

Negus, Keith (1992) *Producing Pop. Culture and Conflict in the Popular Music* (London: Arnold).

— (1999) *Music Genres and Corporate Cultures* (London and New York: Routledge).

Newey, Adam (1999) 'Freedom of Expression: Censorship in Private Hands', in Liberty 1999: 13–43.

Newton, K. M. (1988) *Twentieth-Century Literary Theory. A Reader* (London: Macmillan).

Ngugi Wa Thiong'o (1998) *Penpoints, Gunpoints and Dreams. Towards a Critical Theory of the Arts and the State in Africa* (Oxford: Clarendon Press).

Nordenstreng, Kaarle and Herbert I. Schiller (1993) *Beyond National Sovereignty. International Communication in the 1990s* (Norwood, NJ: Ablex).

Nostbakken, David and Charles Morrow (1993) *Cultural Expression in the Global Village* (Penang: Southbound).

Nyerere, Julius K. (chairman) (1990) *The Challenge to the South. The Report of the South Commission* (Oxford: Oxford University Press).

Oguibe, Olu (1995) *Uzo Egonu. An African Artist in the West* (London: Kala Press).

Oguibe, Olu and Okwui Enwezor (eds) (1999) *Reading the Contemporary. African Art from Theory to the Marketplace* (London: Iniva, Institute of International Visual Arts).

Ohmann, Richard (1996) *Making & Selling Culture* (Hanover and London: Weslyan University Press).

Oliveira, Omar Souki (1991) 'Mass Media, Culture and Communication in Brazil: The Heritage of Dependency', in Sussman and Lent 1991: 200–13.

— (1993) 'Brazilian Soaps Outshine Hollywood: Is Cultural Imperialism Fading Out?', in Nordenstreng and Schiller 1993: 116–31.

Ortiz, Renato (1997) *Mundialización y cultura* (Buenos Aires and Madrid: Alianza Editorial).

Owen, Ursula (1998) 'Hate Speech', *Index on Censorship*, 19 (1), January–February: 37–9.

Paglia, Camille (1992) *Sex, Art, and American Culture* (New York: Vintage Books).

Passet, René (2000) *L'illusion néo-libérale* (Paris: Fayard).

Pavis, Patrice (1995) *Theatre at Crossroads of Culture* (London and New York: Routledge).

Pearce, Susan M. (1998) *Collecting in Contemporary Practice* (London: Sage Publications).

Pérez de Cuéllar, Javier (1996) *Our Creative Diversity. Report of the World Commission on Culture and Development* (Paris: Unesco).

Peters, Peter (ed.) (1995) *Zoeken naar het ongehoorde. 20 Jaar Schönberg Ensemble* (Amsterdam: International Film and Theatre Books).

Petrella, Riccardo (1994) *Limits to Competition. The Group of Lisbon* (Cambridge, MA: MIT Press).

Pichevin, Aymeric (1997) *Le disque à l'heure d'Internet. L'industrie de la musique et les nouvelles technologies de diffusion* (Paris: l'Harmattan).

Plastow, Jane (1996) *African Theatre and Politics. The Evolution of Theatre in Ethiopia, Tanzania and Zimbabwe. A Comparative Study* (Amsterdam and Atlanta, GA: Rodopi).

Plattner, Stuart (1996) *High Art, Down Home. An Economic Ethnography of a Local Art Market* (Chicago, IL and London: University of Chicago Press).

Poshyananda, Apinan (1992) *Modern Art in Thailand* (Singapore: Oxford University Press).

Postman, Neil (1987) *Amusing Ourselves to Death* (London: Methuen).

— (1993) *Technopoly. The Surrender of Culture to Technology* (New York: Vintage Books).

Prasad, M. Madhava (2000) *Ideology of Hindi Film. A Historical Construction* (New Delhi: Oxford University Press).

Preston, William Jr, Edward S. Herman and Herbert I. Schiller (1989) *Hope & Folly. The United States and Unesco 1945–1985* (Minneapolis: University of Minnesota Press).

Primo Braga, C. A. (1990) 'The Economics of Intellectual Property Rights and the GATT: A View from the South', in Lonnie T. Brown and Eric A. Szweda (eds), *Trade-related Aspects of Intellectual Property* (Buffalo, NY, reprinted for Transnational Legal Studies Program, Vanderbildt University School of Law, Nashville).

Pronk, Jan (2000) 'Globalization. A Developmental Approach', in Nederveen Pieterse 2000: 40–52.

Raboy, Marc (ed.) (2002) *Global Media Policy in the New Millennium* (Luton: University of Luton Press).

Raghavan, Chakravarthi (1990) *Recolonization. GATT, the Uruguay Round & the Third World* (London and Penang: Zed Books and Third World Network).

Ramonet, Ignacio (1997) *Géopolitique du chaos* (Paris: Galilée).

— (1999) *Tyrannie de la comunication* (Paris: Galilée).

Redmond-Cooper, Ruth (1998) 'Museums in the Global Enterprise Society – International Opportunities and Challenges', *Art, Antiquity and Law*, 3 (2), June.

Rifkin, Jeremy (1998) *The Biotech Century. Harnessing the Gene and Remaking the World* (New York: Putnam).

— (2000) *The Age of Access. The New Culture of Hypercapitalism, Where All of Life is a Paid-for Experience* (New York: Putnam).

Rouet, François (1992) *Le Livre. Mutations d'une industrie culturelle* (Paris: La documentation Française).

Roux, Emmanuel de and Roland-Pierre Paringaux (1999) *Razzia sur l'art. Vols, pillages, recels à travers le monde* (Paris: Fayard).

Rozenberg, Rob (1994) *Zimbabwe. Huis van steen* (Amsterdam: Menno van de Koppel).

Rushdie, Salman (1992) *Imaginary Homelands. Essays and Criticism 1981–1991* (London: Penguin Books).

Ryan, Michael and Douglas Kellner (1988) *Camera Politica. The Politics and Ideology of Contemporary Hollywood Film* (Bloomington and Indianapolis: Indiana University Press).

Said, Edward W. (1991) *Orientalism: Western Conceptions of the Orient* (London: Penguin Books).

— (1993) *Culture and Imperialism* (New York: Alfred A. Knopf).

Sakai, Cécile (1987) *Histoire de la littérature populaire japonaise. Faits et perspectives (1900–1980)* (Paris: l'Harmattan).

Sakr, Naomi (2001) *Satellite Realms. Transnational Television, Globalization and the Middle East* (London and New York: I.B. Tauris).

Sardar, Ziauddin (1998) *Postmodernism and the Other. The New Imperialism of Western Culture* (London: Pluto Press).

Sassen, Saskia (1991) *The Global City. New York, London, Tokyo* (Princeton, NJ: Princeton University Press).

— (1998) *Globalization and Its Discontents. Essays on the New Mobility of People and Money* (New York: New Press).

Savigliano, Marta E. (1995) *Tango and the Political Economy of Passion* (Boulder, CO: Westview Press).

Schatz, Thomas (1997) 'The Return of the Hollywood Studio System', in Barnouw et al. 1997: 73–106.

Schechner, Richard (1995) *The Future of Ritual. Writings on Culture and Performance* (London and New York: Routledge).

Scheps, Marc, Yilmaz Dziewior and Baraba M. Thiemann (eds) (2000) *Kunstwelten im Dialog. Von Gauguin zur globalen Gegenwart* (Dumont: Global Art Reinland).

Scheuer, Jeffrey (2001) *The Sound Bite Society. How Television Helps the Right and Hurts the Left* (New York and London: Routledge).

Schiffrin, André (1999) *L'édition sans éditeurs* (Paris: La fabrique).

Schiller, Dan (1999) *Digital Capitalism. Networking the Global Market System* (Cambridge, MA and London: MIT Press).

Schiller, Herbert I. (1976) *Communication and Cultural Domination* (White Plains, NY: International Arts and Sciences Press).

— (1989a) *Culture Inc. The Corporate Takeover of Public Expression* (New York and Oxford: Oxford University Press).

— (1989b) *Is There a United States Information Policy?* in Preston 1989: 285–311.

— (1992) *Mass Communications and American Empire* (Boulder, CO: Westview Press).

— (1993) *The Context of Our Work*, in Nordenstreng 1993: 464–70.

— (1996) *Information Inequality. The Deepening Social Crisis in America* (New York and London: Routledge).

Schilling, Mark (1997) *The Encyclopedia of Japanese Pop Culture* (New York: Weatherhill).

Schipper, Mineke (1989) *Beyond the Boundaries. African Literature and Literary Theory* (London: Allison & Busby).

Schipperhof, Tjeerd (1997) 'Legale verzamelaar nog lang geen antiquiteit', *Boekmancahier*, 33 (9), September: 336–8.

Schneier-Madanes, Graciela (ed.) (1995) *L'Amérique latine et ses télévisions. Du local au mondial* (Paris: Anthropos).

Sen, Krishna and David T. Hill (2000) *Media, Culture and Politics in Indonesia* (Melbourne: Oxford University Press).

Servaes, Jan and Rico Lie (eds) (1997) *Media and Politics in Transition. Cultural Identity in the Age of Globalization* (Leuven and Amersfoort: Acco).

Shawcross, William (1993) *Murdoch* (New York: Touchstone).

Shiva, Vandana (1995) *Captive Minds, Captive Lives. Ethics, Ecology and Patents on Life* (Dehra Dun, India: Research Foundation for Science, Technology and Natural Resources).

— (1997) *Biopiracy. The Plunder of Nature and Knowledge* (Boston, MA: South End Press).

— (2001) *Protect or Plunder? Understanding Intellectual Property Rights* (London: Zed Books).

Shohat, Ella and Robert Stam (1994) *Unthinking Eurocentrism. Multiculturalism and the Media* (London and New York: Routledge).

Shulman, Seth (1999) *Owning the Future* (New York: Houghton Mifflin).

Shuman, Michael (1994) *Towards a Global Village. International Community Development Initiatives* (London and Boulder, CO: Pluto Press).

— (1998) *Going Local. Creating Self-Reliant Communities in a Global Age* (New York: Free Press).

Skutnabb-Kangas, Tove and Robert Phillipson (2001) 'Dominance, Minorisation, Linguistic Genocide and Language Rights', in *Images of the World. Globalisation and Cultural Diversity* (Copenhagen: Danish Centre for Culture and Development), pp. 32–47.

Slater, Don (1997) *Consumer Culture & Modernity* (Cambridge: Polity Press).

Sloterdijk, Peter (1983) *Kritik der zynischen Vernunft*, Vols 1 and 2 (Frankfurt am Main: Suhrkamp).

Smiers, Joost (1998) *État des lieux de la création en Europe. Le tissu culturel déchiré* (Paris: l'Harmattan).

— (2001a) 'La propriété intellectuelle, c'est le vol! Pladoyer pour l'abolition des droits d'auteur', *Le Monde Diplomatique*, September.

— (2001b) 'L'abolition des droits d'auteur au profit des créateurs', in *Réseaux* 19 (110): 61–71.

— (2002a) 'The Abolition of Copyrights: Better for Artists, Third World Countries and the Public Domain', in Towse 2002: 119–39.

— (2002b) 'The Role of the European Community Concerning the Cultural Article 151 in the Treaty of Amsterdam', Research Paper (Utrecht: Utrecht School of the Arts).

Smith, Anthony D. (1990) 'Towards a Global Culture?', *Theory, Culture & Society* (on Global Culture), 7 (2–3): 171–91.

— (1991) *National Identity* (London: Penguin Books).

— (1995) *Nations and Nationalism in a Global Era* (Cambridge: Polity Press).

Smyth, Gareth (2000) 'Yusuf in the Dark', *Index on Censorship*, 1: 169–73.

Soulillou, Jacques (1999) *L'auteur, mode d'emploi* (Paris: l'Harmattan).

Soupizet, Jean-François and Laurent Gille (ed.) (2001) *Nord et Sud numérique* (Paris: Hermes).

Srampickal, Jacob (1994) *Voice to the Voiceless. The Power of People's Theatre in India* (London and New York: Hurst and Co. and St Martin's Press).

Stallabrass, Julian (1999) *High Art Lite. British Art in the 1990s* (London and New York: Verso).

Starr, Amory (2000) *Naming the Enemy. Anti-Corporate Movements Confront Globalization* (London: Zed Books and Pluto Press).

Steenhuis, Aafke (1990) *In de cakewalk. Schrijvers over de 20ste eeuw* (Amsterdam: Van Gennep).

Steiner, Christopher B. (1994) *African Art in Transit* (Cambridge: Cambridge University Press).

Sterling, Bruce (1992) *The Hacker Crackdown. Law and Disorder on the Electronic Frontier* (London: Penguin Books).

Stivers, Richard (1994) *The Culture of Cynicism. American Morality in Decline* (Oxford and Cambridge, MA: Blackwell).

Ströter-Bender, Jutta (1995) *L'art contemporain dans les pays du 'Tiers-monde'* (Paris: l'Harmattan).

Sussman, Gerald and John A. Lent (1991) *Transnational Communications. Wiring the Third World* (London: Sage Publications).

Swaan, Abram de (1985) *Kwaliteit is klasse* (Amsterdam: Bert Bakker).

— (2001) *Words of the World* (Cambridge: Polity Press).

Swann, Paul (1994) 'The Little State Department: Washington and Hollywood's Rhetoric of the Postwar Audience', in Ellwood and Kroes 1994: 176–95.

Tamney, Joseph B. (1995) *The Struggle Over Singapore's Soul. Western Modernization and Asian Culture* (Berlin and New York: Walter de Gruyter).

Taylor, Diana (1991) *Theatre of Crisis. Drama and Politics in Latin America* (Lexington: Kentucky University Press).

Taylor, Timothy D. (1997) *Global Pop. World Music, World Markets* (New York and London: Routledge).

Tenbruck, Friedrich H. (1990) 'The Dreamer of a Secular Ecumene: The Meaning and Limits of Policies of Development', *Theory, Culture & Society*, 7 (2–3), June: 193–206.

Thackara, John (ed.) (1988) *Design After Modernism. Beyond the Object* (London: Thames & Hudson).

Thompson, E. P. (1991) *Customs in Common. Studies in Traditional Popular Cultures* (New York: New York Press).

Thompson, Kenneth (ed.) (1997) *Media and Cultural Regulation* (London: Sage Publications and Open University).

Thornton, Sarah (1995) *Club Cultures. Music, Media and Subcultural Capital* (Hannover and London: Wesleyan University Press).

Throsby, David (1998) 'Music, International Trade and Economic Development', *World Culture Report*: 193–209.

Tiger, Lionel (1992) *The Pursuit of Pleasure* (Boston, MA: Little, Brown).

Titon, Jeff Tod (ed.) (1992) *Worlds of Music. An Introduction to the Music of the World's Peoples* (New York: Schirmer Books).

Tomlinson, John (1991) *Cultural Imperialism. A Critical Introduction* (London: Pinter).

— (1999) *Globalization and Culture* (Cambridge: Polity Press).

Towse, Ruth (2002) *Copyright in the Cultural Industries* (Cheltenham: Edward Elgar).

Twitchell, James B. (1992) *Carnival Culture: The Trashing of Taste in America* (New York: Columbia University Press).

Ulrich, Adama (1994) 'Theatre at Nigerian Universities. Development, Aporias and Possibilities', in Breitinger 1994: 113–20.

Unesco (1980) *Many Voices, One World. Towards a New More Just and More Efficient World Information and Communication Order*, Report of the International Commission for the Study of Communication Problems (New York: Unesco).

Unesco-Wipo (1998) 'Unesco-Wipo World Forum on the Protection of Folklore', Phuket, Thailand, 8–10 April 1997 (Paris: Unesco).

Veer, Peter van der (1997) '"The Enigma of Arrival": Hybridity and Authenticity in the Global Space', in Werbner and Modood 1997: 90–105.

Vink, Nico (1988) *The Telenovela and Emancipation. A Study on TV and Social Change in Brazil* (Amsterdam: Royal Tropical Institute).

Virolle, Marie (1995) *La chanson raï. De l'Algérie profonde à la scène internationale* (Paris: Karthala).

Wagnleitner, Reinhold (1994) 'American Cultural Diplomacy, the Cinema, and the Cold War in Central Europe', in Ellwood and Kroes 1994: 196–210.

Wallis, Roger and Krister Malm (1984) *Big Sounds from Small Peoples. The Music Industry in Small Countries* (London: Constable).

Wallis, Roger, Charles Baden-Fuller, Martin Kretschmer and George Michael Klimis (1999) 'Contested Collective Administration of Intellectual Property Rights in Music: The Challenge to the Principles', in *European Journal of Communication*, 14 (1) March.

Waterman, Christopher Alan (1990) *Jùjú. A Social History and Ethnography of an African Popular Music* (Chicago, IL: University of Chicago Press).

Webster, Frank (1995) *Theories of the Information Society* (London and New York: Routledge).

Went, Robert (1996) *Grenzen aan de globalisering?* (Amsterdam: Het Spinhuis).

Werbner, Pnina and Tariq Modood (eds) (1997) *Debating Cultural Hybridity. Multi-Cultural Identities and the Politics of Anti-Racism* (London: Zed Books).

Westenbrink, B. N. (1996) *Juridische aspecten van het Internet* (Amsterdam: Otto Cramwinckel).

Whiteley, Nigel (1993) *Design for Society* (London: Reaktion Books).

Whittier Treat, John (ed.) (1996) *Contemporary Japan and Popular Culture* (Richmond, Surrey: Curzon).

Wipo (2001) *Intellectual Property Needs and Expectations of Traditional Knowledge Holders* (Geneva: Wipo).

Wolff, Janet (1983) *Aesthetics and the Sociology of Art* (London: Allen and Unwin).

— (1989) *The Social Production of Art* (New York: New York University Press).

Wolveren, K. G. van (1991) *Japan. De onzichtbare drijfveren van een wereldmacht* (Amsterdam: Rainbow).

Wong, Deborah (1995) 'Thai Cassettes and Their Covers: Two Case Histories', in Lent 1995: 43–59.

World Culture Report (1998) *Culture, Creativity and Markets* (Paris: Unesco).

Yúdice, George, Jean Franco and Juan Flores (eds) (1992) *On Edge. The Crisis of Contemporary Latin American Culture* (Minneapolis and London: University of Minnesota Press).

Zha, Jianying (1995) *China Pop. How Soap Operas, Tabloids, and Bestsellers are Transforming a Culture* (New York: New Press).

Index

20th Century-Fox, 6, 172

Aageson, Thomas, 117
Abah, Oga S., 96
access: concept of, 190; right of, 171, 173,
190
accountability, 197, 231
acid rain, effects on buildings, 227
acting, violence in, 151
Active Crime Tracking System, 224
actors, alienation of, 141
adapt, revise and process, right to, 211
Advance Publications, 36
advertising, ix, 1, 10, 11, 23, 27, 53, 54,
131, 132, 133, 137, 151, 153–6, 157,
163, 165, 176, 197, 231; higher volume
of, 142; in US, 154; proposed tax on,
198; strategies of, 153; use of art in, 46
aesthetic innovation, structural function
of, 134
aestheticization of everyday life, 11
Afghanistan: destruction of Buddhas by
Taliban in, 219; war in, 217–18
Africa: cultural production in, 89; film
production in, 96, 107
African art, 117, 118
Ahua, Atsen, 65
Aid to Artisans, 117
Ajami, Fouad, 99, 127
Algeria, film production in, 104
alienation, 128
Allen, Paul, 56
Alliance Française, 204
Amazon.com, 55, 196
America Online, 53
American Business Committee for the Arts
(BCA), 46

American culture *see* United States of
America
American Digital Millennium Copyright
Act, 61
American Psychological Association, 146
American way of life, seductive nature of,
131
Amin, Samir, 186
Andean music, 118
Anderson, Sarah, 193
anthrax, 146
anti-trust legislation, in cultural field, 193
AOL–Time Warner merger, 22, 59, 101
Arabic literature, 128
Arabic visual artists, 99
arm's-length principle, 201
Arnault, Bernard, 43–4
art: necessity for aggressiveness in, 151;
power of, 160
Art Loss Register, 224
art works: as continuous creations, 102;
definition of, 216; non-neutrality of,
239; power of, 154; prices of, 42
artistic production, not for all time, 102
artists: ambiguous role in society, 154; as
cowards, 151; as independent workers,
41; creative investment of, 200; income
of, 209, 213–16; killing of, 238; lack of
travel options of, 127; murder of, in
Chile, 137; not very good organizers,
227; relevance of, 169; rights of, 209
arts: as arena of struggle, 1–9, 238; as field
of communication, 10, 81, 82; as guide
in human existence, 128; as modes of
human interaction, 129; as producers of
ideology, 11; as symbolic
battlegrounds, 2; as workshops of